A HISTORY OF SOUTH AFRICA

A History of South Africa

ROBERT LACOUR-GAYET

Translated by Stephen Hardman

Hastings House, Publishers
New York 10016

First published in the United States of America
by Hastings House, Publishers 1978

First published as *Histoire de l'Afrique du Sud*, 1970
First published in Great Britain, April 1977
First edition, second impression December 1977

Library of Congress Cataloging in Publication Data
Lacour-Gayet, Robert.
  A history of South Africa.

  Translation of Histoire de l'Afrique du Sud.
  Bibliography: p.
  Includes index.
  1. South Africa—History. I. Title.
DT766.L3313 1978   968   77-20025
ISBN 0-8038-3052-1

Printed in Great Britain by
The Camelot Press Ltd, Southampton

To South African historians and librarians

Contents

PART THREE

An Attempt at Separate Development 1834–75

PART FOUR

Economic Revolution and Political Tension 1867–99

PART FIVE

Towards Unification 1899–1910

PART SIX

Towards Independence and the Republic 1910–61

PART SEVEN

South Africa in Recent Years 1961–76

Maps

Maps by Cartographic Enterprises

Foreword

I first visited South Africa nine years ago, when my publisher asked me to write a history of the country. I had just written a history of Canada, and immediately I was struck by the similarities and, even more, by the differences between the two subjects. At the time I knew little about South Africa. Yet I was not unaware of the conflict of opinion this country has provoked, and I found myself fascinated by the intensity of the controversy.

At first I felt as if I were entering a virgin forest, so thickly wooded and so mysterious that I sometimes feared I would never find my way out. But the farther I advanced, the more clearly I perceived, beyond the dark regions in which I was floundering, landscapes whose lines and hues captivated me. I began to realize that here a long and tragic drama had been enacted in the course of which the accidents of history had brought together ethnic groups who had no common ground for mutual understanding and who had been forced by circumstances to live side by side.

I was brought up in the liberal tradition of open-mindedness, to which I remain strongly attached. In other words, I respect the opinions of others and I try to give my judgements the character of objectivity and impartiality indispensable to a historian. In this book, as in my others, I have attempted to remain faithful to that principle. I hope that my English-speaking readers will appreciate this, and I thank them in advance for their understanding and goodwill.

A return visit to South Africa in the autumn of 1976 has enabled me to bring the last two chapters of my book up to date. It has not altered the basic conclusions at which I had arrived in 1967. It has, on the other hand, increased my confidence in the future of a country which is at the present time displaying an extraordinary capacity for adaptation.

During these two visits, each lasting several weeks, I have had the opportunity of talking to persons of all shades of opinion, of all races and from all walks of life. In this way I have been able to ascertain the point of view of each ethnic group. The arguments of the Opposition parties have been put to me with the same frankness and conviction as those of the government majority. The persons with whom I have discussed these things are too numerous for me to mention individually, but I should at least like them to know how grateful I am to them for receiving me with such courtesy and explaining their most interesting views.

Prologue

Southern Africa is usually described by geographers in broad, simple terms. 'For long a remote and closed universe linked with the rest of the old world only by the wide, solid, dry and denuded isthmus of the high plateaux of East Africa . . .'; 'A majestic simplicity: a vast interior plateau, depressed in the centre and descending abruptly on to a belt of marginal regions . . .'; 'an upturned saucer', observe those fond of comparisons. Indeed, in this country six times the area of Great Britain, it is hardly possible to distinguish more than three types of region: a coastal belt bordered by high mountains; a series of tablelands rising from south to north in gentle slopes or across precipitous mountain barriers and then running down again towards Rhodesia; and, to the west, a desert which isolates the more favoured territories from the Atlantic.

The tip of the continent forms a world apart, a unique place where in winter the rains brought by the monsoon fall from May to August. Seawards the horizon seems boundless, but inland it is limited. To the north the view is blocked by a series of mountain ranges lying parallel to the coast. As one looks out over the Atlantic or the Indian Ocean, however, the imagination is free to roam. Colouring and vegetation are different to east and west. To the west, a rough sea and its waves of ever-changing hues, sometimes green, sometimes azure, dashing themselves against the rocks; and clouds which, low enough to cling to Table Mountain[1] overlooking Table Bay, produce violent downpours. The east is reminiscent of the Mediterranean. Here the hills are covered with silver-leaf trees, yellow-wood trees, eucalyptus, umbrella pines, and proteas; below lie long sandy beaches and a blue sea whose calm is suddenly shattered by fierce storms.

Far away to the north-east, beyond the appropriately named Garden Route which passes amid masses of wild flowers, a botanist's paradise, lies Natal, another oasis. The Drakensberg range,[2] whose summits rise to 11,000 feet, separates Natal from the interior, sloping down to the coast in foothills. On the lower slopes the vegetation is luxuriant, but the tropical climate does not produce in this region the wonderful softness that pervades the Cape and its environs.

---

[1] The mountain was thus named by a Portuguese in 1503, because of its flat summit; it is about 3,800 feet high.
[2] See Chapter 8. One of the highest peaks is named Mont-aux-Sources, a name invented by French Protestant missionaries in 1836.

It is in the *veld* that one must look for the South Africa of legend, the country of the trekkers, gold and diamonds, the Zulu and the Prince Imperial of France, and the Boer War. The mysterious and evocative word *veld* is defined by geographers as 'a region whose natural vegetation is more or less suitable for pasturage'. Although this description does differentiate the *veld* from both forests and cultivated land, it gives little idea of the variety of countryside to which the word is applied. In fact, twenty-two different types of *veld* have been distinguished. They begin to the north of the Cape, beyond the reddish plains of the Great Karoo, where cacti and acacias grow round the water sources. They then extend for some six hundred miles across the Orange Free State and the Transvaal, their apparent uniformity revealing subtle differences. The Low Veld, a region of shrub, barely rises above 3,000 feet. The Middle Veld stretches in an arc from the confluence of the Vaal and Orange rivers to the sources of the Olifants; here the only eye-catching features are the *kopjes*, cone-shaped and flat-topped hillocks produced by a long period of erosion, which played such an important part in the Boer War; this is a landscape of yellowish tints where, in the springtime, life suddenly explodes in greenery and blossom. Finally, the High Veld rises from south-west to north-east, from 4,000 to over 6,000 feet, a savannah of thick grass with the trees concentrated round the rivers and pure air that gives the purple outline of the mountains a perfect clarity.

To the west, in striking contrast, is the Kalahari desert, more than 300,000 square miles in area, where lie 'enormous heaps of red sand which are piled up by the winds in great longitudinal dunes'; here and there the presence of an oasis is indicated by a thin covering of grass over its approaches. After a tropical storm the soil can for a time support cattle; but such occasions are rare, since rainfall is minute (a little over four inches annually, sometimes less).

Drought is, indeed, the scourge of South Africa. Though abundant in Natal and in the Cape Peninsula, rainfall becomes less from east to west. Consequently the country is almost totally deprived of forests. The land is barren for two-thirds of its area, its rivers providing little irrigation: to the west they run sluggishly down valleys and to the east rush into gorges interrupted by waterfalls. Only two are navigable: to the north of the Cape, the Berg, up which boats of low tonnage can navigate for about thirty miles; and, emptying into the Indian Ocean at East London, the Buffalo, whose mouth has been sufficiently dredged to give access to transatlantic liners. Everywhere else the estuaries are blocked by sand-banks. The coasts are no more hospitable. There are a few natural harbours—Walvis Bay on the Atlantic coast, in South-west Africa; Cape Town, near the tip of the continent; and, farther east, Port Elizabeth, East London and Durban. But the coastline as a whole offers only reefs, a sky often blanketed by fog and a sea capable of generating storms, to which innumerable shipwrecks bear witness.

In this land so old that it is said to have formed part of the continent which, until the Jurassic period, extended from Australia to South America, it is possible that man emerged for the first time.

Man was preceded by the Australopithecines. In 1924, at Taung to the north of Kimberley, in a fissure containing fossil-bearing deposits, a South African anthropologist, Dr Dart, discovered a skull whose anatomical features seemed sufficiently pronounced for him to have no hesitation in describing it as 'hominoid'. Twelve years later he and a colleague, Dr Broom, began systematic excavations around Johannesburg and Pretoria. The two anthropologists were not disappointed, for they unearthed numerous types of Australopithecine at Sterkfontein, Makapan, Kroomdrai and Swarthrans.

It is thought that these creatures of the late Tertiary period had not advanced beyond the subhuman stage. Their brain capacity is too small and their faces jut forwards, suggesting a slight similarity to a monkey's physiognomy. They resemble man in the curve of the jaw, the diminution in the size of the front teeth, the shape of the thigh-bone and, in particular, the broadening of the pelvis, which is astonishingly like that of a Bushman.

Having more or less acquired the vertical position, the Australopithecines moved about on two feet. Were they capable of cultivating the land? It is quite possible that they had learnt to make crude stone tools. What part did they play in the ascent of man? Should they be seen as representing man in his ancestral form, or merely as a marginal offshoot? The first hypothesis is the more widely accepted today. However, 'whatever the final interpretation, it can be said,' writes Professor Piveteau, 'that in South Africa human palaeontology has achieved one of its finest successes.'

Even if man and Australopithecine are mutually exclusive, the former was the immediate successor of the latter. Southern Africa is extraordinarily rich in archaeological evidence testifying to the complexity of its prehistory, for the oldest and the least developed peoples had been driven back into the lands to the south of the Zambezi, where they remained over a long period. The frequent invasions which followed left behind them the accumulated evidence of successive cultures that are difficult both to identify and to date.

Palaeontologists are, however, agreed on certain points. In the first place, it seems that in this part of the world the art of stone-working followed an evolution parallel to, but not simultaneous with, that of Europe. On the other hand, many characteristics have been observed to be peculiar to southern Africa. First—and this is a remarkable fact—southern Africa served as a land of refuge where peoples who have disappeared from all other parts of the world have often survived even to the present day. Another, no less important, feature is that there was no neolithic age in southern Africa. There the palaeolithic age was prolonged by the Bushman civilization. Three periods can be distinguished: the early period which, by its duration and its vitality, proves that this region was one of the principal centres of 'hominization'; the middle period, when more advanced tools were fashioned; and the late period, when rock-faces were decorated with engravings and paintings which the Bushmen proceeded to imitate.

Bones found at Broken Hill, in Rhodesia, and at Saldhana, to the north of Cape Town, have pointed to the existence of creatures who may have derived from the same stock as the Neanderthal man of Europe. Two other discoveries, at Boskop in the Transvaal and at Florisbad in the Orange Free State, have revealed human types which also show indisputable similarities to the *homo sapiens* of the modern era. Finally, it is important to emphasize that 'among all these ancient types there is no trace of the Negro proper. A study of the prehistoric populations of northern and eastern Africa would lead to the same conclusion.'

And so, perhaps, the human adventure began in southern Africa. . . .

PART ONE

The Dutch East India Company
1652–1806

List of Dates

I

The Beginnings of the Cape Colony

On 8 July 1497, in the reign of Manuel the Fortunate, the inhabitants of the little town of Restello[1] on the Tagus, two miles south-west of Lisbon, witnessed a spectacle whose historical significance they doubtless did not appreciate. A procession was making its way towards the harbour. In front were priests and monks surrounded by a large crowd. Then followed Vasco da Gama, commissioned by the king to seek a route to the Indies, and described by his historians as 'cold, harsh ... severe'—not much imagination is needed to realize how proud of his destiny and how confident of success he must have felt on that day. Behind him came the hundred and fifty or so men who formed the crews of the four caravels placed under his command. Captain, officers and seamen walked barefoot, holding candles and chanting litanies; before going on board, they knelt and received absolution.

Four months and ten days later, the explorers sighted the most westerly point of the African coast. As far as the islands of Cape Verde, which the Portuguese had reached forty years earlier, they had followed the classic route which several of their fellow-countrymen had taken previously. But then Vasco da Gama made a bold decision: he ignored the Gulf of Guinea and struck out into the open sea. For the next ninety-three days the only land sighted was St Helena. At last, on Saturday 18 November, the magnificent scenery of the Cape was sighted.

The ship's trumpets rang out in exaltation. On 20 November, a historic day, the Portuguese entered the Indian Ocean: '... they sailed so near the coast that besides its fresh verdure they saw many animals and men ...' They made a few contacts with these mysterious people, but this was not the real purpose of their voyage. They continued sailing north-east and, six months later, reached the west coast of India.

Nine years earlier Bartholomew Diaz, sailing up the east coast of Africa, had arrived at the Great Fish river, some sixty miles beyond the site of what is now Port Elizabeth. But a mutiny among his crew forced him to turn back. As he made his way into the Atlantic again, he observed a narrowing promontory; impressed by the violence of the waves, he

[1] Today the suburb of Belem.

called it the Cape of Storms. Whether it was he or John II, king of Portugal, who finally baptized it the Cape of Good Hope is of little importance: one should simply be grateful to whoever invented this poetic name.

The limited achievement of Bartholomew Diaz inspired no immediate successors. It was the discovery of the Indies that had fired imaginations. In the years that followed, a succession of flotillas set sail regularly from Lisbon. Only the French tried to compete with the Portuguese. In 1527 the shipping merchant Jean Ango, an enterprising man who was at the same time financing expeditions to the North Atlantic, chartered three vessels which eventually reached the Cape. But this venture led to nothing. Jacques Cartier's expedition seven years later proved that His Most Christian Majesty's ambitions lay in the west and not in the south. Neither was there much to be feared from the Spaniards, whose expansionist aims were also being concentrated on the Americas. England, still more concerned with European affairs than with colonial enterprises, seemed no more than a minor power, and few people could have expected the prodigious blossoming which she was soon to enjoy. Thus, to the south of the Equator, in both West and East Africa, the Portuguese were alone. During the sixty years or so of their monopoly, however, they paid little attention to the Cape of Good Hope. A scholar who has examined the log-books of more than a hundred and fifty ships which called there between 1488 and 1649 found, for the sixteenth century, only ten Portuguese ships.

When, in 1502, repeating his exploit of 1497, Vasco da Gama set out again on the route to the Indies, he cast anchor on the east coast of the continent, to the north-west of Madagascar, as he had done on his first voyage. He was surprised by what he found there: a seaborne trade with India of such magnitude that at first he thought the ground coveted by his fellow-countrymen had already been occupied. The Arabs had, in fact, established themselves in this region as early as the tenth or eleventh century. Their merging with what appears to have been a fairly advanced local civilization had produced a flowering of a kind to be found in no other part of Africa. The Portuguese watched in amazement as iron, copper, cotton goods, pearls, ivory and, above all, gold passed before their eyes. It seemed scandalous that the benefits of such wealth should remain in the hands of infidels.

Events followed the usual pattern. Their firearms gave the conquerors an overwhelming superiority. Destruction and pillage began, and soon the Whites had asserted their pre-eminence, building three fortresses, at Sofala, Mozambique and Mombasa, to protect their possessions. It was a fascinating country. The ruins of edifices built by the Queen of Sheba could be seen from the neighbouring hills. Even more important, by following the Zambezi it was possible to reach the fabulous empire of the Monomotapa where, it was said, one had only to bend down to gather gold from the ground. The 'Lord of the mines of gold and silver', as the Monomotapa had been styled, was in no position to resist the ambitions of the Portuguese, who reduced him to bondage and, for good measure, baptized him.

Why, in these circumstances, should the Portuguese have been interested in southern Africa? Their route had been decided: to put in at St Helena and at Mozambique, then, with the monsoon behind them, India. To call anywhere else was to risk a clash with unfriendly natives or shipwreck on dangerous coasts. Precedents were hardly encouraging. Neither side trusted the other, and soon the duel between arrows and bullets began. When in 1510 the Viceroy of India, Francisco d'Almeida, was himself killed in an ambush, his successors were even more determined not to set foot in this inhospitable country.

Unfortunately, the shipwrecks which occurred so frequently on the coast of what is now Natal often left them no choice. The wreck of the *São João*, in 1552, is understandably famous. As was often the custom amongst the Portuguese and Dutch, the ship's commander, Manuel da Souza da Sepulveda, had taken with him his wife, Doña Lenora, a young and attractive lady of noble blood. When the ship ran aground on a reef, the crew of two hundred and twenty men, with some four hundred slaves, set off boldly into the bush, leaving behind those of their companions who were too weak to follow. Eventually they encountered a small tribe which did not appear hostile. Don Manuel must have been very naïve, for he distributed his weapons to the natives in the hope of making friends. As usual, all was well at first. Gradually, however, the Whites found themselves scattered in small groups and defenceless. The natives stripped them of their clothes. Doña Lenora fought like a tigress, but in vain. Finding herself naked, she 'cast herself upon the ground, shaking down her hair to cover her, for it was very long'. Her husband tried to calm her, telling her that she was, after all, in the state in which God had created her. Doña Lenora would not listen. 'Then she made a pit in the sand and buried herself thus to the waist.' Her bosom was covered with an old mantilla, her only remaining garment. Then Don Manuel vanished into the brush, never to be seen again.[1]

Towards the latter part of the sixteenth century new navigators appeared on the route to the Indies.

First among them were the subjects of Queen Elizabeth I. England was embarking on her great adventure. In 1580, during his voyage across the world, Drake rounded the Cape of Good Hope. He thought the scenery magnificent and the Cape the most beautiful he had seen anywhere in the world, but his enthusiasm bore no fruit. Eight years later, Cavendish did not linger in this region any longer than his predecessor. Not until 1620 was an attempt made to take possession. In that year two naval officers,

[1] Only a few slaves escaped, and it is from them that this oral tradition originates.

Shillinge and Fitzherbert, believed they could immortalize themselves by hoisting the English flag at the extremity of Africa. Far from congratulating them, however, the Admiralty disowned them. Obviously, on the banks of the Thames as on the banks of the Seine, America was the only magnet that attracted explorers.

Amsterdam thought differently. The achievement of Holland, this small nation which had started from nothing and whose determination succeeded in overcoming apparently insurmountable obstacles, was indeed astounding: to anyone who forgets its origins the South Africa of today is incomprehensible. Admittedly, the Dutch did benefit from the blunders of their master. Spanish subjects for the past half a century, so they might have remained if Philip II had not acceded to the throne in 1556. This son of Charles V had a sense of greatness, but he was afflicted with the worst fault that can befall a statesman: the inability to trim his ambitions according to his resources. Moreover, he loved uniformity. His empire was Catholic, except for the Netherlands, to the north of the Meuse. A man of the sixteenth century, unable to accept that subjects should have a religion other than that of their prince, he resolved to remove what to him seemed a blemish on his empire. He had underestimated Protestant tenacity. After fifteen years of conflict, during which his tactics of terror and enticement proved equally futile, the country that was to become Holland detached itself from the future Belgium, declaring its independence. Perhaps Philip II thought that a success in the south would compensate for his failure in the north, for in 1580, on the pretext of a dispute over the royal succession, he abolished the dynasty of Braganza and annexed Portugal, proclaiming himself its king.

In the strength of Madrid and the weakness of Amsterdam lay, paradoxically, the origins of the Dutch Empire, an enterprise which Philip II almost forced on his former subjects. As long as Portugal had remained sovereign, the Dutch had been the sole distributors for Europe of the merchandise brought back from the Far East by Portuguese ships. As soon as he was master of Lisbon, the king of Spain decided it would be a shrewd move to refuse access to it to a people whom he persisted in regarding as rebels. By putting an end to their activities as middlemen, however, he merely made them his rivals. In the prosperous Netherlands there was no shortage of money, nor of seamen proficient in seamanship, and a readiness to take risks was certainly not lacking. The merchants of Amsterdam were not the men to refuse the challenge, and they found useful allies in the Portuguese Jews who had been banished by His Catholic Majesty.

Events soon gathered momentum. No sooner had the failure of the Invincible Armada revealed the naval impotence of Spain than the Dutch ships were sailing distant seas. In 1595 Cornelis de Houtman was one of the first to put into the Cape, where he engaged in a few barter transactions in what to him seemed a favourable atmosphere; more important, he came away with the impression that the Portuguese position was less strong than it appeared. In 1601 another expedition was made. In 1602, a key date in the history of South Africa, the Dutch East India Company was formed. The unco-ordinated efforts of individuals now made way for a single driving force. The number of Dutch ships calling at the Cape grew rapidly: 117 between 1611 and 1621, and 461 during the next thirty years, according to Professor Boxer. Not all these ships were interested solely in trade: within twenty years the west coast of India, Ceylon, Malacca, Java and Sumatra became Dutch possessions.

Success followed success, with only one failure. From 1604 to 1607 the Dutch tried to capture Mozambique, a stronghold where the Portuguese were still solidly established, and on three occasions were driven back. About this same time, however, their pilots discovered that it was not necessary to follow the east coast of the continent in order to sail to the Indies from the tip of Africa. By taking advantage of the west wind it was possible to reach Batavia; by tacking, moreover, good navigators could reach the zone of the 20th parallel, and from there the south-east trade winds carried them to Goa. But it was essential to be able to put in at some point beyond St Helena. A glance at the map showed that the Cape was the ideal place. The Dutch were already using it as a posting stage; on their voyages to the East they hid letters in the hollow of a tree for collection by ships sailing for Europe. It was generally agreed that the air there was pure, the climate healthy and the land fertile.

The inhabitants, alas, seemed less attractive. Here are some extracts from ships' log-books: 'They are entirely naked, but for an ox-hide around them like a cloak, and a wide thong of leather round their waists, of which a cord hangs before their privities ...' 'They always stank greatly, since they besmeared themselves with fat and grease ...' 'Their colour is olive black, blacker than the Brazilians; their hair is curled and black as the Negroes of Angola. ... In speaking, they click with the tongue, like a hen.' And so they were not easy to understand: 'In seven weeks, the sharpest wit among us could not learn one word of their language.' In any case, what was the point in trying? It was hard to imagine 'a more heathenish people and more beastly ... very brutish and savage, as stupid as can be and without intelligence ... without religion, without laws or government. ... These brutes devote themselves to idleness, for they neither dig nor spin. ...' And the women! They wore no more than the men and had enormous sagging breasts! They were quite without modesty: 'Upon receipt of anything they return their gratitude by discovering their shame. ...'[1]

And in conclusion: 'It is a great pity that such creatures should enjoy so sweet a country'—a sentiment that was soon to inspire many an enterprise.

---

[1] 'A courtesy taught them by some ill-bred Boore [Boers]', observed a virtuous Englishman; 'our men, I hope, will have more civility.'

In 1648 the hazards of shipwreck compelled a Dutch crew to spend several months in Table Bay. The captain's report prompted a decision in Amsterdam, and the 'Seventeen'—the controlling body of the Dutch East India Company, which was both a trading corporation and a semi-sovereign power, a phenomenon common at this period—resolved to establish a footing on the Cape. Seizing this key to the route to the Indies seemed to them all the more urgent when, in 1651, the Navigation Act imposed rigorous conditions on the entry of foreign shipping into British ports.

Jan van Riebeeck, about thirty years of age, was put in command. Previous voyages had taken him, it appears, to the West Indies, Greenland, Japan and northern China. According to the historian, Theal, he was 'resolute, of unfailing energy and unbounded zeal', a judgement confirmed by a rapid glance through the eight hundred and thirteen octavo pages of the Journal which, to the great joy of historians, van Riebeeck kept throughout the ten years of his mission. He attached more importance to practical considerations than to idealism; indeed, it would be difficult to detect the slightest trace of evangelizing intent in the early years of South Africa.

The two-hundred-ton *Dromedaris*, carrying van Riebeeck and his fortune, his wife, son and two nieces, left the Texel on Christmas Eve 1651, followed by two smaller ships: in all two hundred crew members, of whom about a hundred were destined to remain in Africa. The duration of the voyage, three months and thirteen days, shows how much progress had been made since Vasco da Gama. On 6 April 1652 the 'commander'—such was his official title—gave the order to drop anchor in Table Bay.

The Company's instructions were precise. Van Riebeeck was to keep drinking-water, vegetables and fresh meat available for ships calling at the Cape; as a precaution, a fortress was to be built. All this was easier said than done. Water and vegetables posed no major problems. Rivers were not lacking, and there was little likelihood of a well remaining dry. To the great delight of the newcomers, many of whom had suffered from scurvy during the winter, the lettuce, cress, radish and sorrel that had been sown grew with surprising rapidity when the spring came. Even the fort was built, in spite of the difficulty of finding wood of good quality.

The real problem was cattle. Where could they be obtained, except from the natives? Two types of native population, scattered over a wide area, inhabited this part of the world. The Bushmen, originating in East Africa, possibly from the borderland of Abyssinia, are believed to have arrived in southern Africa at the end of the Stone Age. Professor Walker describes them in detail: '. . . . they were little sallow folk, barely five feet high, their heads adorned with peppercorn tufts of hair and lobeless ears, their triangular, fox-like faces almost innocent of beards. Their twinkling eyes were deep-set beneath upright foreheads, their noses broad and low-rooted, their jaws projecting; and their slender limbs and tiny feet seemed ill-fitted to bear the protuberant stomachs of the men or the pendulous breasts and fat buttocks of the women.' Was it their ancestors, or an even older race, that made the admirable wall-paintings in the caves of Domboskava,[1] which are comparable with those at Lascaux in south-western France? By the seventeenth century, however, the Bushmen were in decline and living a wretched existence as hunters.

These first arrivals had been the victims of invaders of much more recent date. It is thought that the Hottentots,[2] pouring down from the Great Lakes under pressure from the Bantu, reached the Atlantic coast several centuries before the Portuguese. Having already attained the stage of a pastoral life with a minimum of social organization, able to work iron and copper, and thus notably more civilized than the Bushmen, they had little difficulty in driving the latter out of the rich lands surrounding the Cape. It was the Hottentots who gave van Riebeeck and his companions their first experience of the native world, for there were as yet no pure-blood Negroes in this part of southern Africa.

At first, courtesy prevailed. The barter transactions—cattle in exchange for tobacco, pipes, brass wire, copper, glass beads and alcohol—were conducted according to a meticulous ritual. At the fortress gate the Hottentots were greeted by an official. Their chief, who was usually mounted on an ox, would dismount and, with his companions, be led into the commander's office. The guests squatted on carpets and their hosts sat wherever they could. Then the conversation would begin, usually by means of gestures and sometimes with the help of an interpreter. A Hottentot woman called Eva earned herself an undisputed reputation in this latter role.[3] The visitors were offered refreshments—bread, rice, cheese, sugar, wine—and, on special occasions, a little music. The exchanges began on the following day; the whole affair lasted two or three days.

This idyllic situation was short-lived. It was tempting for the Whites, who had the advantage of armed strength, to seize the cattle, and equally tempting for the Hottentots, armed with arrows instead of arquebuses, not to submit passively but to make reprisals. A 'cold war' atmosphere thus developed which became real war—much to van Riebeeck's dismay, since his instructions had been to establish good relations with the natives. He hoped to settle the matter by a policy of 'to each his own domain'

[1] Near Salisbury in Rhodesia.

[2] A traveller observed in 1682 that the word *Hautitou* occurred incessantly in their songs. Is this perhaps the origin of their name?

[3] She was baptized and eventually married a Dutchman. Great hopes were built on this union of the races. Alas, when Eva became a widow her conduct was an object of scandal. The sociologists concluded that the Hottentots were 'too unstable to admit of their adoption of civilization, otherwise than very slowly and gradually'.

surprisingly similar to present-day South African policy. He planned to cut a canal across the peninsula, leaving the natives to the north and the Europeans to the south. But this would have been a formidable undertaking, and he had to content himself with the construction of a few blockhouses supposed to serve as barriers. This static solution did not prevent the inevitable clashes. The Dutch proved the stronger and gradually the Hottentots were dispersed or brought into subjection.

Five years after his arrival van Riebeeck took two decisions of far-reaching consequences. The colony had been developing, it might be said, in spite of him. The increasingly frequent calls made by ships necessitated ever larger stocks of supplies. But vegetables and cattle could not be accumulated by relying on the handful of men who had landed in 1652 and by never venturing beyond Table Bay.

The problem of manpower thus presented itself. There was no question of immigration, for the 'Seventeen' still had no intention of making the Cape anything more than a revictualling station. As for the natives, no matter what they were given it was impossible, complained van Riebeeck, to persuade them to work. He suggested an economic solution: it would be much less costly to have all the work done by slaves who could be fed on ordinary fare—rice, fish, or even seal or penguin meat—and who would not be paid. The idea did not meet with disfavour. The first boatloads came from Java and Sumatra; then it became the custom to import Negroes from East Africa and Madagascar. This influx had two consequences. First, the inevitable miscegenation gave rise to the ill-defined category of half-breeds nowadays known as 'Coloured People'. Secondly, a great many Whites, surrounded by this abundant and servile labour force, lost the habit of working.

This was certainly not true of the nine employees of the Company who in 1657, under the name of 'free burghers' (which meant nothing, for they were neither 'free' nor 'burghers'), received concessions of land which they undertook to cultivate for twenty years. This modest essay in free enterprise was subject to numerous restrictions. The occupants were not entitled to grow tobacco (a monopoly), to trade with the Hottentots or to sell their produce except at the official prices. Yet the effects of the decision proved considerable. A first attempt at colonization, it had established organized agriculture side by side with the commercial centre of the Cape. Furthermore, this handful of men, left to their own devices and seeing unoccupied, fertile lands around them, would sooner or later heed the call of the open spaces and be tempted to discover what lay hidden behind the magnificent scenery that limited their horizon.

Van Riebeeck left the Cape in 1662. Perhaps his vision had lacked breadth, but he had accomplished what the Company had expected of him, and it is understandable that South Africans should still remember him with gratitude.

It is not worth dwelling on the next fifteen years or so, a period of tentative experiment and administrative instability (there were nine rulers of the settlement in seventeen years).[1] In 1679, however, Simon van der Stel was to play an important role. A fervent patriot—what was not Dutch was worthless in his eyes—as bold as van Riebeeck had been cautious, and not afraid of the responsibilities which his predecessor had been disinclined to assume, he anticipated the future awaiting the country. Two wars, against England in 1665 and against an Anglo-French coalition in 1672, had highlighted the strategic value of the Cape. By the time van der Stel took up his duties the restoration of peace had given less urgency to military considerations. One thing remained certain, however: without a minimum population the colony could not be defended. Moreover, the new governor was convinced of the economic possibilities of the region. He did everything he could to facilitate the arrival of immigrants and, for the first time since 1652, a policy of colonization was systematically pursued. His efforts were not in vain, for by 1688 there were some six hundred farmers on the Cape. In that same year, reinforcements of quality landed in Table Bay.

[1] The title of 'governor' replaced that of 'commander' in 1672.

2

The Arrival of the French Huguenots

Commenting on the flight of the Protestants to Holland after the revocation of the Edict of Nantes in 1685, Voltaire writes: 'There were some who settled as far away as the Cape of Good Hope. The nephew of the famous Duquesne, a naval lieutenant-commander, founded a small colony at this extremity of the earth, but it did not prosper; most of those who went there perished.[1] But there are still some remnants of this colony neighbouring upon the Hottentots.' This only proves that in France in 1751 little was known about South Africa, revealing the dangers of writing history too soon after the events. Clearly, the author of *The Age of Louis XIV* regarded as a failure of limited significance what was in fact a triumph of profound consequences.

It is important to attempt to establish the facts, although the sources are unusually fragmentary.

The exact number of Protestants who emigrated after 1685 is not known. Estimates vary between 2000,000 and 350,000. Out of this total, it is reckoned, some 40,000 to 60,000 headed for Holland. This high proportion (high in relation to the small area of the country of refuge) cannot be explained solely by geographical proximity. Emigration to the Reformed Netherlands had been continuous since the end of the sixteenth century, both from France itself and from the country that was to become Belgium, especially during the six years (1567–73) when Philip II's representative, the redoubtable Duke of Alva, had imposed his reign of terror there. It was quite natural that these unfortunate people, who a century later were forced to choose between their faith and their country, should settle in a land where they could count on a favourable welcome. Holland thus became the 'Noah's Ark of fugitives', in the words of Pierre Bayle, the French philosopher and critic.

[1] Voltaire can hardly have checked his information. The project was to settle some Huguenots on the Ile Bourbon (later renamed Réunion), under the protection of Holland. The States General granted their patronage in 1690. That same year the *Hirondelle* sailed by the Cape route; it called at the Cape, set down two passengers on one of the Mascarene islands (two years later, it appears, they landed on the Ile de France) and, on the return voyage, was intercepted by a frigate of the French royal navy and escorted back to La Rochelle.

If Louis XIV had revoked the Edict of Nantes twenty years earlier, the destiny of South Africa might well have been different. At first the directors of the Dutch East India Company had no desire to send emigrants to the Cape. Under the influence of Simon van der Stel, however, their policy changed. After 1685 it seemed the obvious course to seek colonists among the new arrivals in Holland, and they were all the more tempted to do so because of their anxiety at the growing numbers of Frenchmen settling in their country.

The Company made its decision in the autumn of 1687. The refugees were offered a free passage and free land for cultivation; they would be provided with farming implements, for which they would be expected to pay in due course. In return, they would have to sign a five-year agreement; even more important, they would have to swear an oath of loyalty to the States General and to the Dutch East India Company (an oath similar in all respects to that taken by Dutchmen). One can imagine how these texts must have been read and re-read by the French. About a hundred and fifty agreed to accept the challenge. Some were of Waldensian descent; their ancestors had lived in Provence, whose soft and golden light they remembered with nostalgia and hoped to rediscover in the Cape region.

The ships sailed at intervals over a period of four months, starting on 31 December 1687. At the last minute some could not summon the courage to face such a long voyage, one that would take them six thousand miles from the land of their forefathers. The others conquered their misgivings. These refugees were people of iron: they had already proved this and were now going to prove it again. They left in seven ships, which bore no resemblance to transatlantic liners. Conditions were extremely uncomfortable.[1] Worst of all, the passengers were condemned to a diet of salt meat; the consequent hazard of scurvy, combined with the threat of storms, fires and even pirates, hardly made the expedition a pleasure trip. Six of the ships were lucky, making the crossing in the usual time of three to four months. The captain of the seventh, the *China*, must have been a novice with no experience of coping with contrary winds, for he took a hundred and thirty-seven days to bring his passengers to their destination—by which time twenty of them were dead, including fourteen French.

And so these hapless creatures who had come from so far away reached their Promised Land. They were awaited with sympathy. 'We are so happy at their imminent arrival. . . . They will strengthen the colony wonderfully. . . . We shall help them as much as we can,' wrote Simon van der Stel (Dutch Governor at the Cape) to the 'Seventeen'. These

[1] 'She was between the decks so choked with filth, that some of my officers assured me, they had never seen so much dirt, not even aboard of any French ship,' an eyewitness remarked when a ship of the East India Company called at the Cape in 1774. It is hardly likely that hygiene was any better eighty-six years earlier.

were generous but rather fanciful sentiments. It is a great pity that none of the refugees set down their impressions in writing. Their immediate reaction was undoubtedly one of disappointment. One wonders why the Company had landed them on the Cape at the beginning of winter, when the rain and squalls did not help to make the place attractive. The Huguenots were utterly destitute. They were given biscuits, chick-peas and salt meat (again!) to stop them dying of hunger, and also some planks to build makeshift accommodation. It was all so miserable and inadequate that a relief fund had to be set up. Then they were taken to the land on which they were to live. The situation was magnificent, surrounded by high mountains in the valley of the Berg, about fifty miles from the Cape between Drakenstein and Stellenbosch. That the land was fertile was obvious even to the less experienced among them. But the Huguenots had another disappointment in store. The governor, although delighted to have this extra manpower at the Company's disposal, was afraid of separatist tendencies. His fears were by no means absurd, for the new-comers represented about one-fifth of the White population; he decided, therefore, that it would be wise to disperse them among the Dutch.

This did not exactly please the French. Although the refugees had renounced the *Roi Soleil*, they had not repudiated their origins. They wanted to stay together and speak their own language which, with their religion, was their only common link, since they hailed from different parts of France—some from the north, others from the south, mostly of modest extraction, a few from the bourgeoisie and nobility: 'M. de Savoye' was a wealthy merchant, and the surgeon, du Plessis, had Richelieu blood in his veins. They all regarded a school and a church of their own as essential. On the first point they obtained swift satisfaction, and by November their children, of whom there were not many, were having lessons from a bilingual teacher, Paul Roux. A pastor who had come with them from France took charge of their religious problem. The Reverend Pierre Simond was a colourful personality. 'He had a great strength of character and possessed all the qualities necessary to recommend him to his flock as a reliable guide . . . [His letters] prove that, if he cherished no sentiments of charity towards those who did not share his convictions, he could take pride in having suffered for his beliefs.' He occupied his leisure and enriched his faith with a projected translation of the Psalms of David. It was by his initiative that the registers in the church at Drakenstein, an invaluable source of information for the history of the Huguenots, were kept in French from 1694 to 1713.

At first the Reverend Simond's relations with the local authorities were satisfactory. Van der Stel agreed to be godfather to one of his sons. But the governor did not like the French character, even when tempered by Calvinism. He felt that the newcomers under his administration showed no sign of forsaking their 'fickle nature'; in a flush of biblical fervour he compared them to 'the children of Israel who, fed by the hand of God in the wilderness, longed for the flesh-pots of Egypt'. He could not believe his ears when, in November 1689, a delegation led by the Reverend Simond came to ask him to open a separate church. He nearly choked with indignation at the impertinence of such a request. 'They will be wanting their own magistrate, commander-in-chief and prince', he exploded. His refusal was categorical. The Huguenots then resolved on a heroic course: they would marry no more Dutchwomen! But there were some who did not agree with this Lysistrata tactic. Finally, it was decided to appeal to the 'Seventeen', who, less intransigent than their representative, authorized a compromise: sermons would be given in French on every other Sunday at Drakenstein[1] and at Stellenbosch; but the refugees' children would be obliged to learn Dutch.

This rough and ready compromise lasted only about ten years. At the beginning of the eighteenth century the Reverend Simond left for Europe and was replaced by a Dutchman. 'In this way,' the Company's directors wrote to the governor, 'French will in time be eliminated from the colony. . . .' Dutch became the only official language. Of course, this rule was not applied immediately, but it is estimated that, twenty years later, only twenty-five persons at the most were still speaking French. By the end of the third generation the process of assimilation was complete.[2] There remained, however, certain names which were never to disappear from South African history—du Plessis, de Villiers, Marais, Fouché, du Toit, Joubert, Malan and many others—and will appear frequently in the course of this book.

The influence of the Huguenots was profound and is still evident today. It is not just a question of the techniques which they taught the colony. If the wines of the Cape are of a quality comparable with that of French wines, this is due to the decision of Louis XIV. It has been said of these refugees that they arrived with 'a vine in one hand, the Bible in the other'. The image is in bad taste, but it is expressive. It is quite true that their religion was of a kind superior to that of the other immigrants. They had been shaped by their ordeal, and they had more than a touch of that intense, even fanatical faith which the English Puritans had brought to America sixty-eight years earlier. They thus contributed in large measure to the development of that spiritual toughness which was to ensure the survival of the Boers. They can also be seen as the ancestors of Afrikaner nationalism. They had cut themselves off from all links with their native land and, to an even greater degree than the Dutch, they came to regard South Africa as their country, their only country.

[1] Tradition has preserved the charming story of the three brothers who, having only one horse between them, used it in turns to go and listen to the Reverend Simond's sermons.

[2] When the naturalist François Levaillant came to South Africa in 1781, he visited the Huguenots' descendants. Only one old man could understand him.

A Frenchman would have to be totally devoid of imagination not to be moved at the sight of Franschhoek, the 'French corner', where the first French colonists settled, with its evocative farm names—Dauphiné, Rhône, Champagne, Languedoc, Bourgogne, La Motte, Cabrière. Against the line of mountains stands a majestic monument whose three arches, representing the Holy Trinity and crowned by a sun and a cross, the Huguenot emblem, seem to be protecting the statue erected below, the symbol of freedom of conscience. The inscription engraved on a plaque reads: 'Erected on this dedicated ground in 1943 by a grateful South African people in honour of the Huguenots at the Cape (1688) and their invaluable contribution to our nationhood.'

3

Clashes with the Bantu and Internal Difficulties

When one thinks of the intellectual upheavals that led in America to the independence of the United States and in Europe to the French Revolution, the contrast with South Africa is striking. Clearly, the Enlightenment had not radiated as far as this remote corner of the earth, the Cape Colony. The transformations that took place there at this period had little or no ideological origin. The Boers began what has been called, perhaps rather pompously, their 'Diaspora'; for the first time since the arrival of van Riebeeck, Whites and Blacks clashed, and rebellions showed how keen the feeling for independence already was; then, after being Dutch for a hundred and fifty years, the territory came under British sovereignty.

When, in 1699, Simon van der Stel left the post which he had occupied for twenty years, he was replaced by his son, Willem Adriaan. The policy of colonization continued, but in an atmosphere that was to lead to its abandonment. The new governor was full of his own importance and he had an excessive love of money, even for a representative of a company that was only too willing to allow its employees to enrich themselves in its service. Eventually his subjects were scandalized by his manœuvres to monopolize the most profitable contracts, and sixty-three French and Dutch colonists took the bold step of appealing to the higher authorities. The date of this incident, 1706, is worth mentioning, for it was the first demonstration against an autocratic administration. Willem Adriaan reacted vigorously, having the leader of the movement arrested and making two hundred and forty of his faithful supporters sign a counter-petition. But he lost the battle; recalled to Amsterdam, he was dismissed from the Company.

The 'Seventeen' had not been pleased by the affair and they used it as an argument for reverting to their earlier policy. See the trouble the Huguenots are causing, see the critical attitude which seems to be developing!—these colonists, they declared, can only be a source of annoyance and frustration; our predecessors were right: let the Cape become again what it should never have ceased to be, simply a revictualling stage. They decided to halt all immigration. From 1688 to 1708 the population had tripled, from 573 to 1,723. Inevitably, the production of cereals, vegetables and wine had risen accordingly. But outlets had remained the same, hence a periodical slump. Most important of all, the fixing of prices by the administration made an increase in profit impossible.

Briefly, the Colony was stagnating. Such a situation was hardly likely to please either the French Huguenots or their Dutch co-religionists. They, or their ancestors, had taken risks to reach the Cape, and they were determined to continue the adventure. And so they set out, in 'Western'-style wagons drawn by six, eight or ten oxen under the supervision of two or three drivers, vehicles sufficiently robust to carry considerable weights and yet sufficiently resilient to adapt themselves to a variety of terrain. Women and children piled into them with the provisions and furniture (when there was any). The men, on horseback or on foot, reconnoitred the ground. The advance of the trekboers[1] was obstructed neither by big rivers, by dense forests, nor by the danger of fever. The physical geography of southern Africa is much less daunting than that of Australia or Canada. The South African pioneers knew neither hunger nor thirst, which proved common hazards for the explorers who plunged into the Australian interior. They encountered the tsetse-fly and the mosquito only much later, when they reached the latitude of Delagoa Bay. Neither did they experience the rigours of the Canadian winter. Wild beasts and uncivilized natives presented the chief dangers. Animals abounded—elephants, lions, wildebeeste, leopards,[2] rhinoceros and, above all, 'horrible wolves'.[3] But firearms solved that problem, and the ivory tusks and skins proved valuable for barter transactions. As for the natives, Hottentots and Bushmen, clever at concealing themselves in the countryside, their ambushes were all the more menacing for being difficult to anticipate. However, both the Hottentots and, especially, the Bushmen proved wretched warriors by comparison with the Indians whom the conquerors of North America were encountering at this same period, or by comparison with the Bantu against whom battle would be joined some fifty years later.

At first the travellers followed the easily accessible coastal belt. But the barren, sandy region to the north and the frequent clumps of brushwood to the east obstructed the wagons' progress. The trekboers had to change direction and cross the mountains separating the Cape region from the territory called by geographers the 'Low Veld'. Unlike their American counterparts, obsessed by the Pacific, they had no fixed objective. What

[1] Boer means 'farmer', and trek means 'a journey by wagon'.
[2] The Dutch called them 'tigers', confusing them with the animals they had seen in the Indies.
[3] Wolves have never existed in southern Africa. They must have been wild dogs or hyenas.

they were looking for, rather haphazardly, was a place where they could support their families, as far away as possible from the harassments of officials of the Dutch East India Company. Their adventure transformed their way of life. These crop-growers became stock-breeders, changing their sedentary existence for a nomadic life. Why, at the cost of such great effort, should they cultivate the soil and grow produce for which they would find no market? Cattle now became their primary concern and, since pasture-land was soon exhausted, they were constantly having to move on. There was no lack of space, however, and their conception of the rights of property was inspired more by emotion than by reason.

The Dutch governors viewed these headstrong Boers with rather the same feelings as their French counterparts had entertained towards the Canadian *coureurs des bois*. They were disturbed by such initiative and, even more, by the problem of distance, for they felt themselves deprived of the means of controlling these remote subjects whom they considered to be still under their authority. They tried to instil in them certain juridical notions by making the possession of land subject to contracts of a variable nature. But to attempt to apply in the *veld* the system of law solemnly described by the experts as 'Roman-Dutch' was absurd. The only point on which officials and farmers were agreed was the area of the farm, which varied between 6,000 and 10,000 acres. The Boers had devised an ingenious method of measuring their land: from a fixed centre they would ride at foot-pace for half an hour towards each of the four points of the compass.

The inhabitants of these immense solitudes gradually lost contact with the rest of the world. At rare intervals they would travel as far as Cape Town, their wagons full of butter and soap, and would bring back alcohol, coffee and fabrics. The rest of the time, retiring within themselves and having occasion to speak only to their wives, their children and their Hottentot servants, they devoted their thoughts to practical problems. Their native country was so far away, the life they had led until so recently bore such little resemblance to their present existence, that the conscious-ness of their singularity forced itself upon them. Even their language reflected the transformation taking place within them: it seems that, by the end of the eighteenth century, Afrikaans was sufficiently different from Dutch to form a separate dialect. Thus, little by little, there emerged among these people a common store of memories, interests and hopes.

The Company did not foresee the long-term effects of this exodus, but it recognized its immediate results. The farther the *trekboers* advanced, the greater the risks of conflict with the natives. The governors did every-thing they could to halt the advance; prohibition followed prohibition, and frontiers, which were constantly being moved, were established with the intention of fixing the boundaries of the Colony. In 1778, during a voyage which enabled him to give his name to one of the most beautiful bays in the world, on the Indian Ocean, the governor van Plettenberg decided that the expansion of the Whites should not extend beyond the Great Fish river. At this time the Boers, who had been pushing forward continually for the past sixty years, found their path barred in all directions. To the north and north-west of the Cape, the deserts prevented them from going further; to the north-east, in the direction of the Orange river, the Bushmen still appeared aggressive enough to make colonization precarious; moreover, rain was rare in this region and the land infertile. Along the coast, on the other hand, a humid soil guaranteed the Europeans the pasturage they needed. And so everything induced them, in spite of van Plettenberg, to continue their march towards the country that was to become Natal. Here, however, they were to be confronted by Blacks.

Who were these 'Kaffirs', as they were called at that time, these 'Bantu', as they are known today, and where had they come from?[1]

These questions are difficult to answer, for the experts constantly contradict one another (theirs is, admittedly, a perplexing task). Historians often complain of being submerged by documents, but this certainly cannot be said of those writers who courageously attempt to bring Black Africa's past to life. Texts as such are non-existent. The historian must turn to ruins; but these are few and far between and have only recently been discovered; the archaeologists themselves admit that they have scarcely passed the stage of tentative investigation. There remains oral tradition, which is far from negligible, for the tribes seem to have handed on the adventures of their ancestors with surprising precision from generation to generation; nevertheless, one can hardly hope to reconstruct from these narratives more than two or three hundred years at the most. It must be added, however, that the evolution of the Blacks has been so slow that, by studying them today, there is some chance of being able to imagine them as they were in earlier times—an undertaking that would clearly be hazardous in the case of the White societies, whose more rapid evolution has continually accelerated.

One must therefore advance cautiously. It is generally accepted that, two thousand years ago, the Bantu inhabited the high plateaux of East Africa, the region of the Great Lakes. They were descended, say some writers, from a mixture of three races: Negroes from West Africa and the Congo, Hamites from North Africa, and a small number of Bushmen. In the second century A.D., according to the Greek geographer Ptolemy, some of them reached the north of Mozambique, but these must have been only isolated groups. The archaeologist Kirkman, writing seventeen hundred years after Ptolemy, suggests that the Bantu arrived at the coast

[1] The word 'Kaffir', of Arabic origin, means 'infidel'. The term 'Bantu' originally referred to a group of languages used by certain Negro tribes; eventually it came to be applied to the Black tribes of southern Africa as a whole, and for the sake of convenience it will be used in this sense in the course of this book.

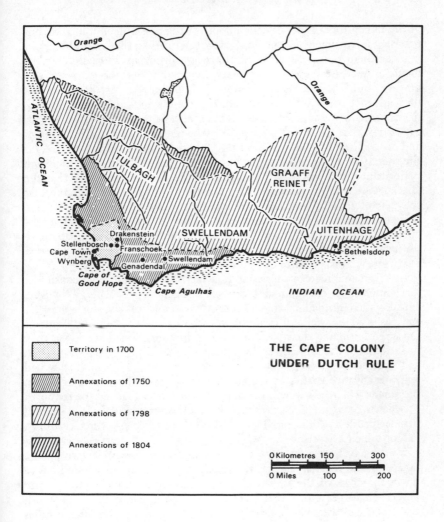

THE CAPE COLONY
UNDER DUTCH RULE

Territory in 1700

Annexations of 1750

Annexations of 1798

Annexations of 1804

0 Kilometres 150   300
0 Miles   100   200

of the Indian Ocean towards the middle of the first millennium A.D., but precisely how, when and where is not known. As to the reasons that had induced them to leave their native territory, historians show little agreement: an increase of population, wars between tribes, the exhaustion of grazing-land, invasions from Ethiopia? One thing is certain, however: their advance southwards continued. But the chronology of these movements remains vague. According to the recent studies of Professor Fagan, they arrived at the Zambezi 'by the early centuries of the Christian era and crossed the Limpopo some time after the fourth century A.D.'. Was this merely an advance party or a horde of invaders? On the pre-medieval period the information is less vague. There can be no doubt that the Blacks were numerous in the Arab kingdoms of the east coast, and that they had attained a sufficiently advanced stage of evolution to be capable of working iron and forging the weapons that were to make them redoubtable adversaries; it is equally indisputable that the ruins of Zimbabwe, to the north of the Limpopo, reveal a degree of civilization which a hundred years ago was hardly thought possible.[1]

At first it might seem surprising that the Bantu should have continued their migrations for so many centuries. Their way of life, however, explains their nomadic habits, for they were exclusively stock-breeders and pasture-land was indispensable to them. Yet they were ignorant of the art of fertilizing their pastures, which they abandoned as soon as they had exhausted the soil, and so they needed to seek out the regions of rain and rivers. A cautious people, they never began travelling until they had sent out advance parties to reconnoitre the terrain. The decision which they made when, possibly in the ninth century, they reached the far north of what is now the Transvaal reveals much of their methods. The land here seemed less promising. They divided themselves into three columns, one of which arrived at the Vaal river around 1700, it is thought, and thereafter advanced very slowly; the second, marching westwards, came up against the Kalahari desert; the third, by far the largest, made its way down the coast of the Indian Ocean, where rivers were plentiful, and pushed on to the Great Fish river. Thus, by the end of the eighteenth century, the Blacks were established, roughly speaking, a thousand miles from the Cape on the Atlantic coast; at about the same distance in the direction of what is today the Orange Free State; and some four hundred and fifty miles to the east.

It should not be imagined that the Bantu formed a homogenous group; there existed as many differences between their tribes as between the peoples of Europe. Yet they had enough in common to justify an attempt at a general description. First, their physique: of average height, well proportioned, often of an athletic sturdiness, and sometimes possessing a beauty not without nobility, their anatomy bore little resemblance to that of the natives to whom the Whites had been accustomed. They lived in

[1] The ruins were discovered in 1867.

circular huts the walls of which were made of wood or dried mud; poles supported a cone-shaped roof covered with thatch. When these dwellings stood fairly near to each other, they formed a *kraal*. The cultivation of the land, an activity of secondary importance, was left to the women. Only the men tended the cattle, mostly horned animals, which constituted the basis of social life. A candidate for marriage had to provide his future father-in-law with a certain number of animals:[1] this was the *lobola*, the sign of his wealth and the pledge of his fidelity; its chief purpose was to legitimize the children. Since monogamy applied only to the poor, the possession of large herds was highly desirable. A meticulous hierarchy existed among the chiefs' wives. The 'number 1' wife (chronologically, that is) was the 'wife of the right hand', the 'number 2' the 'wife of the left hand'; but neither could lay claim to pre-eminence. Only the 'great wife', superior to them in prestige, enjoyed the privilege of providing the heir to the throne. As she was often married late in life, and then for reasons of political convenience rather than physical attraction, the heir born of the union was often very young when his father died. At such times regencies were customary, creating just as much turmoil as the regencies of the queens of France.

The political régime was monarchic, but the Bantu potentates had not managed to establish a doctrine of divine right. Their power was both absolute and unstable—absolute because it permitted them to indulge the most cruel whims (some examples are mentioned in Chapter 6), and unstable because of a tendency towards fragmentation and the formation of rival clans. Moreover, the monarch did not take decisions on his own, but had at his side a sort of council of ministers, the *amapakati*, whose opinions he was in theory obliged to seek. An assembly of elders, a primitive form of representative régime, was consulted on important occasions. It would be absurd to interpret this system as exemplifying the theories of Locke or Montesquieu. It was all vague, ill-defined and constantly fluctuating. The flexibility and uncertainty of such régimes made negotiations and treaties difficult. Who had authority to speak in the name of the tribe, and, in particular, how could one be sure that a promise would be kept?

Then there were the redoubtable witch-doctors, who perhaps alone enjoyed true omnipotence. The metaphysics of the Bantu were confused. They talked readily enough of a Supreme Being with a variable and sometimes musical name, 'Umkulukulu'. Of a much more concrete kind, however, were the forces of evil, the restless souls of ancestors, perfidious demons ever ready to harm both man and beast. Sometimes they were embodied in living persons, who maintained mysterious and sinister relationships with them. To track down these sorcerers, to smell them out, was the function of the witch-doctors and the origin of their power. They devoted themselves to this liberating task with all the more enthusiasm because they were often prompted by secret motives: hunting out

[1] These customs still exist, as do the huts described above.

malevolent spirits was obviously an instrument of government. Except during periods of tyranny, however, everything was done in accordance with traditional ritual. Custom prescribed the penalty appropriate to each offence; the penalty was applied without mercy, but not arbitrarily.

Thus the Whites and Blacks, so different and yet so similar, confronted one another. Superficially, everything distinguished them—appearance, origins and customs; but they were alike in more than one respect.

In the first place, both Whites and Blacks considered that the land for which they were to fight each other belonged to them, and both had good reasons for making this claim. A hundred and twenty-seven years had passed since van Riebeeck, roughly the period extending from the accession of Louis XIV to the reconvening of the French States General. During this century and a quarter the Whites had taken root in the soil of South Africa. Neither Hottentots nor Bushmen had been able to resist their supremacy. Can the Whites be blamed for feeling first surprise, then vexation and resentment, when they found that the route along which their ancestors had guided them appeared to be blocked? To the east of the Great Fish river, however, in less developed but more instinctive minds, a similar notion was germinating. To the Blacks, accustomed to seeing only their own kind in these lands where intruders were now looming up, the Whites appeared aggressors. Again, could they be blamed?

Conflict was thus inevitable. It would have been of a different kind if an identity of interests had not exacerbated passions. History detests hypotheses. Nevertheless, it is tempting to wonder what might have happened if South Africa's mineral wealth had been known at this time. Only the Whites possessed the techniques that would have enabled them to exploit this wealth; the Blacks would have provided the labour; and so the relationship would have been established, no doubt difficult but on the whole peaceful, which was imposed upon them a century later by the Industrial Revolution. Unfortunately, in 1779 it was the soil, and not the subsoil, that offered riches. These cattle-farmers were seeking good land and rivers in abundance. What made them kill each other was not so much the difference in their colour as the similarity of their ambitions.

Is there any need to add that bravery was not lacking on either side? These Europeans were not milksops: their ancestors had crossed six thousand miles of sea, and they themselves were venturing into an unknown continent. But nor were the Bantu cowards, fighting with shields and javelins against bullets and cannon-balls. The struggle was to last nearly eighty years, a period which historians divide into nine active phases. It is now time to consider the early phases and their consequences.

Obviously, neither the Boers nor the Blacks sent trumpeters out to sound a declaration of war. Hostilities commenced, halted, resumed, slackened and accelerated without its ever being possible to determine whether they were spontaneous or planned. In any case, the cause was always the same—cattle. The first skirmishes took place between 1779 and 1781: the Xhosa,[1] looking for new lands, crossed the Great Fish river and pillaged the region known as the Zuurveld, where quite a large number of Whites had settled; the latter retaliated, adopting the well-tried 'commando' technique. The Boers, in theory with the authorization of the central administration, would assemble in groups whose numbers varied according to the purpose of the conflict.[2] Every man had to provide himself with a horse, saddle and bridle and take with him three days' food and ammunition; after that, rations and armaments were supposed to be supplied by the Company. Each commando chose its own officers. There was no uniform and little discipline. But these makeshift warriors were remarkable horsemen and first-class marksmen. (By the time of the Boer War their skills had been carried to perfection.) Under the command of Adriaan van Jaarsveld, a man clearly not to be trifled with, they routed the Xhosa, showing no leniency, and pushed them back across the river.

After eight years of armistice, guerrilla warfare resumed. This time there was a temptation in Cape Town to prefer negotiation to violence. The role of peacemaker was entrusted to Honoratus Christian David Maynier, who did not make himself popular among the Boers and is still not popular with certain Afrikaner historians. He has been portrayed as a disciple of Rousseau, a believer in the 'noble savage'. Was he not simply a zealous and inexperienced official? Maynier threw himself obstinately and innocently into the vortex of Black Africa, of which he obviously understood nothing. He hoped to make a good impression by showering the Xhosa chiefs with presents, but the Xhosa feared neither the Greeks nor their gifts. Once again it proved necessary to have recourse to commandos. After four years peace was restored on both sides of the Fish river.

There was no peace, however, between the Company's representative and his subjects. The latter were clearly in a bad humour. According to Professor Marais, they were demanding in particular that all Bushman prisoners and their children should be regarded as slaves, that Hottentot children born on their farms should be compelled to work there until the age of twenty-five, and that the runaways should be sent back to their lord and master. Maynier must have thrown up his hands in astonishment. On learning of his reaction the Boers of the two recently created districts, Graaff-Reinet and Swellendam, proclaimed their independence and declared that they no longer recognized the authority of the Dutch East India Company.

The Company, which had been in decline for several years, would have had great difficulty in imposing its will. However, the problem did not

---

[1] The Bantu tribe which had advanced nearest to the Cape.
[2] Ninety men, for example, in 1781.

arise. When the rebels started waving the banner of revolt on the eastern frontier, the Union Jack was already flying over the Castle of Cape Town.

What was a pen in the hands of Holland was in danger of becoming a sword in the hands of France, as a British naval officer shrewdly observed at the time. Since the conquest of the Indies the Cape position had obsessed British strategists. How could it be made another Gibraltar? At that time Britain knew how to seize its opportunities. Suffren's ships, anchored in Table Bay during the American War of Independence,[1] had given the Lords of the Admiralty some sleepless nights. In 1793 the Admiralty had hoped that Holland would agree to place its overseas territories under their 'protection'. French aggressiveness provided London with the solution to its problem. Even in the mild atmosphere of the 'Thermidorean reaction', the advance of the French revolutionary armies continued through the winter of 1794-5. Jourdan reached the Rhine; even more important, at the beginning of January Pichegru occupied Holland, which the frozen canals had placed at his mercy. For several years the local 'patriots' had been counting on a foreign intervention to free them from the authoritarian rule of their stadtholder, and so the troops of the friendly French Republic encountered a distinctly favourable reception. Like the exiled kings of 1940, William V fled to England. In March 1795 the proclamation of a 'Batavian Republic' brought the country under French control. At any moment the Cape might fall into the hands of the 'Jacobins'.

No time was wasted in London. In February the Prince of Orange, 'hereditary stadtholder of the States General of the United Provinces, hereditary governor of each province, commander-in-chief and admiral of land and sea forces', invited the colonial authorities to hand over their territories to 'His Grand Britannic Majesty'—on the understanding, of course, that the said territories would be restored to Holland 'as soon as the ancient and traditional forms of government have been restored there'. In June a British squadron anchored near the Cape. The Company's representative, the commissioner-general Abraham Josias Sluysken, was highly embarrassed. At first he temporized and then, on learning of the Franco-Batavian alliance, decided on resistance. But the struggle was an unequal one, and on 16 September he had to capitulate. The victors' terms were generous. Official properties were confiscated and the inhabitants were obliged to take an oath to their new master, but local laws and customs remained in force; no new taxation was to be introduced and freedom of trade became the rule.

The British occupation lasted eight years. It was accepted readily at the Cape and in the neighbouring districts, but provoked strong reactions in the 'republics' of Graaff-Reinet and Swellendam, which were not at all pleased by this change of sovereignty. The Xhosa took the opportunity to make new raids, provoking a third war (1799-1802) which did not

[1] See pp. 41-2.

improve feelings between Boers and Bantu. The British authorities, greatly embarrassed by their position, must have been relieved when the Treaty of Amiens restored the Colony to the Batavian Republic in 1803. This change was short-lived. Less than three months had passed since Trafalgar when another British squadron appeared off the Cape. Again a hopeless resistance was offered and followed by capitulation of the same kind as before (except for the oath). This time the British established themselves as the undisputed masters of the Cape. The last Dutch governor, Lieutenant-General Janssens, wrote a sort of political testament to his victors: 'Give no credit . . . to the enemies of the inhabitants. They have their faults, but these are more than compensated by good qualities. Through lenity . . . they may be conducted to any good.' Perhaps it is a pity that the new régime did not ponder on these remarks more often.

PART TWO

Britain Takes Possession
1806–34

List of Dates

4

South Africa at the Beginning of the Nineteenth Century

Looking at the maps, one might well imagine that the boundaries of the Cape Colony were clearly defined by the time it became British. In fact, nothing was less certain than the zone in which European authority supposedly prevailed. Only in one sector did geography offer the illusion of a frontier: in the official reports the Great Fish river separated Blacks and Whites over a distance of some sixty miles; but reality constantly gave the lie to this. In other places, one wonders on the basis of what information a line had been drawn which turned successively to the north-east, the north-west, the south-west and then north-west again, finally reaching the Indian Ocean. The following extremes of distance will give a clearer idea of the situation of this 'frontier': to the east, it lay a hundred miles beyond Port Elizabeth; to the north-east, about a hundred and twenty miles south of Bloemfontein; and to the north-west, seventy-five miles south of the mouth of the Orange. Administratively the Colony was divided into four districts: Cape Town, Stellenbosch, Swellendam and Graaff-Reinet. At the head of each was a commissioner (*landdrost*) assisted by a council of six members (*heemraden*).

According to the statistics, 25,757 Whites, 29,545 slaves and 20,000 Hottentots inhabited this territory in 1806. Seven-twelfths of the Whites, apparently, were of Dutch origin; the French and German elements each represented two-twelfths; the final one-twelfth, it seems, proved difficult to identify. The 'slaves' comprised Negroes and Malays, the latter of a distinctly superior cultural level and famous for their musical talent. The number of Hottentots, it will be noted, is approximate—a necessarily cautious estimate, for it would have been impossible to calculate exactly a population which was largely nomadic and had been decimated by epidemics of smallpox.

North America and southern Africa had been discovered at about the same time. The figures quoted above show how differently the two continents had evolved: three centuries after Vasco da Gama, there were no more than 26,000 Whites in southern Africa; in Canada, 250,000; and in the United States, over six million.

At the beginning of the nineteenth century the handful of immigrants whose arrival at the tip of Africa the Dutch East India Company had reluctantly tolerated were divided into three quite distinct groups. Some lived at the Cape and in the immediate environs. Others had settled in the region of Stellenbosch and Drakenstein, beyond the sandy zone separating the coast and the interior. Much farther inland, the *trekboers*, whose epic story was just beginning, constituted a perpetually mobile advance-guard.

Cape Town, notes Bernardin de Saint-Pierre,[1] was 'formed of neatly aligned white houses which from a distance look like little houses of cards. . . . The streets are well aligned, some watered by streams, the majority planted with oaks. . . . The fronts of the houses were shaded by their foliage; the doors were flanked on each side by seats of brick or turf where fresh, rosy-cheeked ladies sat. . . .' Other observers, less romantic than the author of *Paul et Virginie*, confirm the European aspect of this little town at the end of the world: wide streets intersecting at right-angles, brick houses of one or two storeys, white or green, with thatched roofs, flat, undecorated façades and gardens in front—the latter a useful precaution, sparing Bernardin's 'ladies' from being covered in dust, for most of the streets were mud. The general effect was one of cleanliness and monotony. Standing out in contrast with this uniformity were the more imposing Company buildings, the hospital and, in particular, the Castle, the glory of the town. The Castle, begun in Van Riebeeck's time, had been completed in the eighteenth century. The balcony of the Council Chamber, from which official proclamations and edicts were read, is traditionally attributed to a French architect. The Dutch governors had resided in this building, and their British successors naturally imitated their example.

Daily life must have been rather lacking in variety. Is this, perhaps, why meals occupied such an important place? 'At eight o'clock, tea or coffee; at mid-day, a copious dinner; at four o'clock, tea or coffee; at eight o'clock, a supper like dinner. These good people eat all day . . .' marvels Bernardin de Saint-Pierre. What did they do the rest of the time? 'Society' men held an official position or managed a business; in the former case they worked, at various levels, with the all-powerful governor. A seat on the Council of Policy, whose seven members were entitled to offer the governor their advice, was obviously the most sought-after office. Failing this, however, there existed a variety of highly desirable legal posts. Finally, the Senate, a modest essay in representative government, allowed a few 'burghers'—duly chosen by the governor—the illusion of having their say in things.

If regulating every aspect of life is the duty of a good administration, then the Dutch régime at the Cape should surely be awarded a prize, for

[1] He stayed there in 1771, but in those times countries did not change much in thirty years.

it did not neglect details. Professor Marquard points out that the regulations laid down 'whether or not a lady might wear a train or have silk and satin dresses; which ladies were allowed to use an umbrella or sunshade; how much money might be spent on a funeral or a bridal bed; how many servants people of different rank might employ and whether the coachman might wear livery. . . .' In such circumstances the role of the businessman was not an easy one—in fact the term 'businessman' is rather pretentious when applied to the few tradesmen and craftsmen who, without much success, were trying to earn their living.

Official authoritarianism certainly provided them with topics of conversation at the family table, which would otherwise have been a tedious affair. People read very little, for the simple reason that there were no bookshops. 'Education was provided by a few privately run institutions at which younger children were taught the elements of the three R's. Two attempts to establish a high school failed for want of support, and only a few of the wealthiest burghers could afford to send their children to Holland for further education,' writes Professor Marquard. Spiritual life was hardly more active. There were ten parish churches, and no one would have dared to miss the Sunday service, but this was not so much from conviction as from social convention. It is significant that, until 1792, no effort had been made to Christianize the Hottentots. One cannot help wondering what were the subjects of conversation in the burghers' houses. No doubt, incidents of etiquette were discussed: the Company, which clearly forgot nothing, had determined where everyone should sit in church or at official ceremonies, a source of countless disputes and enduring bitterness. Moreover, as in any small town, any gap in the conversation could be filled by resorting to gossip.

Everything changed on the arrival of a ship. As soon as a look-out had spotted it, a cannon-shot announced the event. The ship would arouse all kinds of expectations: everybody wanted news, for there was no regular postal service. The men wanted business: the technique of smuggling had been perfected, and no regulation could have prevented tradespeople selling their goods at the prices they thought desirable; furthermore, sailors have never been misers—money, and also the local wine, flowed so freely in the taverns that the Cape had come to be known as the 'Tavern of Two Seas'. For the women, the sight of a ship awakened hopes of a different kind: perhaps the visitors would break the monotony of their lives, and if warships were coming the governor might even give a ball!

Such feminine desires were gratified to the full on an unexpected occasion, the American War of Independence. At the end of December 1780, when the Netherlands were proposing to join a League of Armed Neutrality, Britain declared war on that nation. The possibility of seizing the Cape played no small part in this decision. At Versailles the danger was recognized and action swiftly taken. Three months later, after a review inspected by the Marquis de Castries, Minister for the Navy, and a grand rehearsal at which the decks were cleared for action and a cannonade was fired, a squadron of a hundred and thirty ships sailed for Brest. The larger part of the squadron, commanded by De Grasse, headed for the West Indies. Six men-of-war and eight transport-ships under Suffren took the South Atlantic route. In the meantime the British had not remained inactive. Commodore Johnstone had been entrusted with the task of seizing the Cape first. The two squadrons met at the Cape Verde islands. Although inferior in numbers, the French took the initiative by attacking first. They inflicted sufficient damage on their adversaries to immobilize them for several days and thus managed to overtake them. On 20 June 1781, Suffren dropped anchor in False Bay, on the east of the Cape Peninsula. There he landed the Pondicherry regiment and a part of the Austrasie regiment; two months later he set sail for the Indies, where he was to win immortal fame. On the eve of his departure the Colonel Comte de Conway, commander of French land forces, gave a supper and a grand ball in his honour. One can imagine the excitement of Bernardin de Saint-Pierre's 'fresh, rosy-cheeked ladies'. They had other joys in store, for the French kept them company for two years, until the signing of peace in 1783. According to South African historians, these Frenchmen created such a stir that Cape Town came to be known as 'Little Paris'.

Then life returned to normal.

The impressions that the population left on visitors varied strangely according to their nationality. On the whole the French were favourable. Here are some of their reactions.

In 1769, at the end of his voyage round the world, the navigator Bougainville wrote: 'We had every reason to be pleased with the governor and the inhabitants. . . . They lost no time in providing us with both the necessities and the pleasures of life. . . .' The 'pleasures' referred, in particular, to the hospitality they encountered: 'My friends and I went to dine with M. de Vanderspie, owner of the Haut-Constance.[1] He gave us a wonderful welcome, and we drank a lot of his wine. . .' And as they departed: 'Supplied with good food, wines and refreshments of every kind, we sailed from the Cape roadstead on 17 January. . . .'

Bernardin de Saint-Pierre was quite idyllic. 'This people, content with the homely happiness which virtue gives, has not yet expressed it in novels or in the theatre. There are no entertainments at the Cape, and people do not want them. . . . Happy servants, well brought up children, faithful wives—here is a pleasure that fiction does not offer.'

Barras,[2] writing ten years later, was a little more reserved: 'The Cape

---

[1] A local vineyard, the name being comparable with 'Haut-Brion'.
[2] Barras, the future member of the Directory, was an officer in the Pondicherry regiment and stayed at the Cape from June 1781 to March 1783.

had as its governor a fat Dutchman, M. Pletinberg [sic]. . . . His wife
thought that her own plumpness gave her the right to be no less insolent
than her husband. These two vain creatures, isolated in their palace, were
feared by the inhabitants. The second governor, called Hacker, had a wife
and two daughters who received strangers, and especially the French,
with affability. I was taken into the bosom of the family and treated with
friendliness and respect. Carriages and horses were put at my disposal.
The Fiscal,[1] M. Boers, a hard worker, administered this country; he was
just, tolerant, enlightened and courteous, and at his home he gathered a
select society. . . .'

On his return from the Indies in 1783, Suffren remarked: 'The good
Dutchmen here greeted me as their liberator.'

The 'good Dutchmen' clearly had no reason to cherish similar sentiments towards their conquerors of 1795. The British reciprocated their
feelings. To judge by the comments of Captain Robert Perceval, the first
officer to enter Cape Town, the men did nothing but smoke and drink,
'exhibiting a most lamentable picture of laziness and indolent stupidity'.
The women possessed at least one quality: 'they are most excellent house-
wives and managers'. But the furniture was invariably dreadful:
'. . . usually clumsy in the extreme and looks very awkward'. Lady
Anne Bernard[2] was usually more discriminating in her judgements,
though on one occasion she went so far as to castigate 'the known
dastardly spirit of the Dutch who run from a musket or a scarlet coat'. On
another occasion she was stupefied that some inhabitants should have
refused to take the oath of loyalty to His Britannic Majesty, calling them
'silly, bold, foolish people'. Most of the time, however, condescension
prevails over violence in her writing. The word 'tolerable', with its
suggestion of slightly scornful indulgence, recurs constantly. Describing
a ball which she attended, Lady Anne wrote: '. . . the Dutch ladies, all
tolerably well dressed. . . . I saw no real beauty though they were fresh,
wholesome looking . . . as for manners, they had none, and graces and
charm were sadly lacking, though they had most of vulgar smartness
which, I suppose, passed for wit. . . . The most exceptional thing about
them are their teeth and the size of their feet.' There was worse to come:
'Some of our Dutch ladies are not at all what they should be. The French,
I am told, corrupted them; the English have merely taught them to affect

---

[1] An administrative officer responsible for supervising finance and justice.
[2] A member of London's fashionable society, renowned for her wit and beauty,
and a friend of Pitt, Sheridan, Burke, Hume, Dr Johnson and Walter Scott, Lady
Anne found herself rather out of her element, although she by no means disliked her
new surroundings. She had obtained for her husband the post of Colonial Secretary
of the Cape and she must have been not a little flattered when the Secretary for War,
Lord Melville, invited her to write to him directly—which she did, with much talent,
from 1797 to 1801. Responsible for the household of the governor, Lord Macartney,
whose wife had remained in England, she had ample opportunity to exercise her
faculties of observation.

virtue.' Lady Anne heard it said that young women often had fine little boys only two months after their marriage, so much more quickly did things seem to happen out at the Cape!

Perhaps British principles finally bore fruit. One is tempted to think so on reading the descriptions of Lichtenstein[1] six years later. This German clearly possessed a certain psychological insight. Of the women at the Cape he wrote: 'I neither found them uniformly amiable nor, as many earlier travellers asserted, uniformly rough and insignificant. . . . He who comes into the Colony with all the recollection of the friends and acquaintances he has left in his highly civilized country can scarcely be pleased at first with the Cape beauties. . . . The women here are commonly very pretty and dressed in the very height of the European fashions whence strangers are led to expect a high degree of education and polish in their manners . . . and when reluctantly obliged to change their opinions in this respect they perhaps often go too far the other way. . . . It may be easily imagined that the African ladies cannot display any knowledge and have no opportunities of gaining any enlarged stock of ideas. . . . It is by no means impossible that they may take offence at modes of expression in fact very polite and well bred, because they do not understand them, while the rough jokes of an African youth, at which our ladies would blush and cast down their eyes, will be received with laughter and applause.'

Lichtenstein suggests that this was because 'their imagination is more tranquil, they are more secure against seduction. . . . They are very anxious to punish by the distance of their behaviour the error of these somewhat too squeamish foreigners. . . . No instance fell under my knowledge of the last favour being obtained. . . .' Those who expected too much would 'find parties dull and *ennuyeuses*'. But otherwise, observes Lichtenstein, one could not help being impressed by 'the universal cheerfulness, the *naïveté*' of the girls and by 'the strong sense of honour' of the young men.

It is not known if 'the very height of the European fashions' had reached Stellenbosch. In any case, life in this region was already very different from that of the Cape. The distance was not great—barely thirty miles to the main settlement and about sixty to the boundaries of the district;[2] but along the shores of the two oceans the view of the sea conjured up an atmosphere of mystery and movement; inland, by contrast, familiar and unchanging horizons created a sense of stability.

[1] Martin Heinrich Lichtenstein, the future founder of the zoological gardens in Berlin, stayed in the Cape Colony from 1803 to 1806, during the three years when it was reoccupied by the Dutch. He was tutor to the son of the governor, Janssens, and had an opportunity to travel round the country. The objectivity of his observations is remarkable.

[2] This meant at least three days' journey in an ox-wagon.

Apart from a few officials, the Whites were crop-farmers and often quite prosperous, depending for their livelihood on wine and maize. The vineyards of Constantia had acquired a reputation which they have never lost. The houses, in the 'Cape Dutch' style, presented a solid and sometimes elegant appearance, with gabled roofs covered with thatch and white walls reminiscent of the southern United States. Side by side with the building occupied by the landowner and his family stood the dwellings of the Black slaves and Hottentot servants, and also the workrooms essential for the functioning of the farm, which had to be self-sufficient. Oak trees offering their precious shade, orange trees that gave a brilliance to the countryside, and vineyards laden with grapes promising future delights, combined to create an atmosphere of calm and peace.[1]

These farms were not far enough apart to make contact between them impossible. Neighbours would visit each other; one week in the year was set aside for training in the militia; and there were always weddings and funerals. Every three months the inhabitants of the district flocked to Stellenbosch for the *nagmaal* or Holy Communion ceremonies, which lasted from Thursday to Monday: here the pastors made their reputation by delivering interminable sermons. Of a less exalted nature, but equally attractive, were the public auctions. 'Advertised well ahead of time,' observes Professor Marquard, 'these auction sales were great social gathering-places and people travelled many miles to attend them. Free drink and food were provided by the auctioneer, and sometimes a dance was arranged for the evening, all of which no doubt helped to keep the bidding brisk.'

Each group considered itself superior to the others. The people of Stellenbosch looked with equal contempt on the 'civilized' inhabitants of the coast and the 'barbarians' of the *veld*.

It is quite true that the dwellings briefly described above bore little resemblance to the windowless mud huts, with mud floors and thatched roofs, in which many of the *trekboers* lived. These zealous adventurers cared little about comfort. They slept on wooden beds or on mattresses on the floor, took their meals at tables made of planks precariously supported by trestles, and dressed in garments of crude cloth and leather made primarily to last. Rarely did they have the opportunity of renewing their wardrobes. From time to time a pedlar would call; the women would gladly have bought everything he had, but the men contented themselves with essentials. There were no shops, since villages did not exist. Individualists first and foremost, these pioneers regarded the family as the only social unit that mattered. They made no attempt to establish themselves in groups—it has been said that the very sight of a smoking chimney gave them the feeling of being overcrowded. They did not feel at all lonely, surrounded by their ten, fifteen or even twenty boys and

[1] The house of the governor Simon van der Stel still has this quality.

girls. The children were spared the trouble of going to school, for it would have been impossible to find a teacher for miles around. Sometimes an ex-soldier would perform this function; going from farm to farm, he would instruct his pupils in the rudiments of reading and writing for a few months. Usually the mothers assumed this task, but they were less concerned to see their offspring reading and writing than to hear them praying. They were always reading the Bible to them, and it was not uncommon, apparently, to find children capable of reciting the whole of the Psalms by heart. A French missionary recorded the fact that in every house 'we found large folio Bibles inscribed with the dates of birth and names of all the members of the family'.

The religion of the *trekboers* was sincere and fanatical. They all belonged to the Dutch Reformed Church and would tolerate no other denomination. Lichtenstein relates that, if it had been realized that he was a Lutheran, he would have been forbidden to take part in a religious service: 'They would have all deserted me with no less disgust than they now attended me with satisfaction.' They were imbued with a strange mysticism in which they found their justification and which isolated them from the rest of the world. The sky under which they lived evoked for them the memory of Abraham; they pursued a way of life similar to that of Abraham and they understood much better than could any European the image-studded language of the Hebrews, for it seemed to them to apply directly to their own mode of existence. Under the triple influence of faith, space and solitude, the Boers thus formed themselves, to quote the historian Carrington, into 'a sober, secretive, frugal race, outwardly calm and inwardly passionate, notable for shrewdness and subtlety, and a stubborn, unending courage'.

What did the travellers from Europe think of this race? Again, one finds a variety of contradictory opinions expressed. It would be impossible to ignore the oft-quoted Barrow,[1] although his book is so biased that it can be cited only with the strongest reservations. The author certainly does not mince his words. According to him, the Boers lived in mud huts amid a host of spiders, scorpions and ants; their stomachs must have been made of iron, for they ate enormous pieces of mutton swimming in grease; and their manners, in Barrow's view, were deplorable—a pipe always in their mouths, spitting everywhere and putting their elbows on the table! They did nothing all day, and their laziness seemed to infect their womenfolk. 'The women of the African peasantry lead a life of the most listless inactivity. The mistress of the family with her coffee pot

[1] John Barrow, one of the secretaries of Lord Macartney, Britain's first ambassador in China, arrived at the Cape in 1797 at the age of thirty-three, when his chief was appointed governor of the Colony. A few months later he set off to explore a country of which he knew nothing. His *Travels in South Africa*, published in two volumes in London in 1801 and 1804, and reissued in 1806, enjoyed a great success. Barrow, later knighted, became secretary to the Admiralty and was the founder of the Royal Geographical Society.

constantly boiling before her on a small table seems fixed to her chair like a piece of furniture, and it is the business of a little black boy or a Hottentot, wholly naked, to attend her with a small branch of a tree, or a fan made of ostrich feathers to flap away the flies. Most of the girls can neither read or write so they have no mental resources whatsoever.' In Barrow's opinion, the only extenuating circumstances in the Boers' way of life were the fact that, morning and evening, they would read a chapter of the Bible and sing Psalms, and, in spite of their uncouthness, their ability to excel in one particular virtue, that of hospitality to strangers.

In defence of the Boers, Lichtenstein writes: 'I was led almost daily to ask whether they were really the same African colonists which the celebrated Mr Barrow represents as such barbarians—as such more than half savages, so much did I find the reality in contradiction with his descriptions.' Obviously, different types of houses must have existed. Lichtenstein was greatly impressed by a visit to one Boer dwelling: 'There reigned a neatness and order in their house, a decency and propriety on expressing themselves with a friendship and kindness towards each other.... We never heard from the mouth of a colonist an unseemly word, an overstrained expression, a curse or an imprecation of any kind. ... The African colonists are a remarkably sober race. ... Out of ten colonists, three at least will not drink and the rest very moderately. ... However indolent and spiritless the African women may appear when seated at tea table they showed the utmost resolution in any time of danger and many striking examples of female heroism have been exhibited in Kaffir wars.' Lichtenstein came to the conclusion that, in their sense of dignity and moral behaviour, the lower classes of Europe were distinctly inferior to the South African peasantry.

In pronouncing judgement on the inhabitants of Graaff-Reinet, however, Lichtenstein is not so very far removed from Barrow: 'What is most deprecated in the character of some among them is the harshness with which they treat their slaves and Hottentots, and in others the bitterness and irreconcilable animosity with which they carry on their differences among each other.'

What conclusion is one to draw? Only that these Boers were simple and sometimes very primitive peasants, and that the British had no liking for them and made little effort to understand them. Britain thus found herself confronted with a problem in many respects similar to that which she had encountered in Canada since 1760 and which she had not yet managed to solve. Yet there was one fundamental difference between the two situations: the Indians in Canada never played as important a role as the Blacks in South Africa. At the beginning of the nineteenth century, South Africa can be imagined in the form of a triptych: in the centre the Boers, the first comers, at least at the extremity of the continent; to one side the British, more recent arrivals but utterly convinced of their superiority; and to the other side the Bantu, also with deep roots in the country and whose limited ambitions always remained the same: to ensure themselves pasture-land for the cattle on which their livelihood and their social structure depended.

5

Reform and Tentative Experiment

Between 1806 and the fall of Napoleon, Britain had worries other than the colony of which she had just taken possession. Later, it became customary in London circles to refer to the governorship of the Cape as 'the graveyard of reputations'. The men appointed to this post in the early nineteenth century were hardly there long enough to win or lose prestige. Between 1806 and 1814 six governors followed one another at the Castle, and four of these were only acting governors with mandates varying from two months to a year. Of the two titular governors one, Lord Caledon, remained in office just over four years, and the other, Lieutenant-General Cradock, two and a half years. The problems they encountered must have made them envious of the transient power of their predecessors.

With the exception of Caledon, all were officers who had acquired their military experience in India, in Egypt, or in the Peninsular War. Their education and careers had inculcated in them a superiority complex which they seemed reluctant to abandon. They knew nothing of the questions that were to fall within their jurisdiction, having only a vague idea of their magnitude and an even vaguer idea of the means of resolving them. But their national pragmatism proved an invaluable asset. It would be difficult to discern any guiding principles in the policy which Britain adopted towards her new colony. On the other hand, it is easy to distinguish in her policy that mixture of idealism and realism which contributed in such a large measure to the building of the British Empire.

Official preoccupations were dominated first by the Hottentots and then by the Bantu.

The Hottentots enjoyed the enthusiastic but unconsidered support of the Protestant missionaries who were to play such a great role in the history of the country. Until the end of the eighteenth century the Reformed Churches had hardly concerned themselves with the conversion of the heathen. There had been only one exception, the German community of the Moravian Brethren. As early as 1737 this small body of sincere and modest Christians had tried to establish a footing in southern Africa, but this first attempt had met with the opposition of the all-powerful Dutch Church. A second attempt in 1792 was more successful. The Genadendal mission, about fifty miles from Cape Town, soon gained great popularity; its directors, interested solely in improving the lot of the natives, had no intention of using their religious and social influence for political ends.

The London Missionary Society (hereafter designated by the traditional abbreviation L.M.S.) had more ambitious ideas. It had been formed in 1795 with the purpose of co-ordinating the activities of the different denominations. Its first representative, Dr Johannes Theodorus Vanderkemp, arrived at the Cape in 1799. Fifty-two years of age, Vanderkemp had enjoyed a full life, starting his career in the army. 'Proud and self-willed, he freely pursued his sensual pleasures.' Was this the reason for his resignation? Whatever the circumstances, he left Holland, settled in Britain and took a degree in medicine. His 'road to Damascus' had been an accident from which he had miraculously escaped; in his enthusiasm he had himself ordained a minister of the Church of Scotland. But he longed for a life of adventure, and so he offered his services to the L.M.S. The Society, which was looking for vocations, had no hesitation in accepting such a recruit and sending him to South Africa, where it considered his Dutch origins would make his task easier. If his instructions were to make himself talked about, he carried them out scrupulously. Those poor governors, first Dutch and then British, continually having to listen to complaints and answer criticisms! Dr Vanderkemp's defenders proclaim his courage, his ability and his disinterestedness, but do not deny his intransigence or his unwillingness to obey the authorities.

In 1803 Vanderkemp had founded a refuge for Hottentots at Bethelsdorp, about thirty miles from the present Port Elizabeth. The mission rapidly became the object of bitter controversy. According to some, the Gospel was taught there in all its purity, but the witness of others was more discriminating. A judicial commission which visited the local headquarters of the L.M.S. in 1812 declared that 'laziness and idleness and consequently dirt and filth grow there in perfection'. The Reverend John Campbell, the doctor's colleague, was no more flattering: 'Truth obliges me to confess that, had the founder of Betheldorf been more aware of the importance of civilization, there might at least have been more external appearance of it than there is now.[1] He seems to have judged it necessary to imitate the savage appearance rather than to induce the savage to imitate him.' Campbell's observation seems to find a certain justification in a startling description written by Lichtenstein a few years earlier. 'In the very hottest part of the morning we saw a wagon drawn by four meagre oxen . . . Van der Kemp sat upon a plank laid across it, without a hat, his venerable[2] bald head exposed to the burning rays of the sun. He was dressed in a threadbare black coat, waistcoat and breeches without shirt

[1] Vanderkemp had died the previous year.
[2] Vanderkemp was only fifty-seven at the time.

or stockings and leather sandals bound up on his feet the same as worn by the Hottentots. . . . He descended, a tall meagre yet venerable figure. . . . Instead of the usual salutations he uttered a short prayer.' Vanderkemp's eccentricity became more marked with age, leading him to marry one of his former slaves, an ill-assorted union which, according to Robert Moffat,[1] cast a veil of sadness over his last years. Dr Philip[2] confirms Moffat's disillusioned view of the marriage: 'His benevolence in this instance is more to be admired than his knowledge of human nature and he lived to see and regret his mistake.'

However, having a protector of this sort at least brought the Hottentots into the limelight. These natives had certain habits which the Boers found difficult to accept: they liked to work as little as possible and to move about as they pleased. Consequently it was quite a problem to keep them on a farm: here today and gone tomorrow, they were elusive people. To make them stay their masters often had recourse to strong-arm methods. The Hottentots were not slaves, but their condition was hardly more enviable; above all, their remuneration was miserable and constantly fluctuated. In 1809 the governor, Caledon, decided that the situation had to be put in order. To please the missionaries his Hottentot Proclamation laid down that all employers would be under an obligation to sign a contract specifying a regular wage and to render an account of these payments to the administration. The reason given for this decision was the following: 'It is necessary that the Hottentots find an encouragement for preferring entering the service of the inhabitants to leading an indolent life.' But—and this time the governor was thinking of the Boers—'every Hottentot shall have a fixed place of abode and will not be allowed to change his place without a certificate; otherwise he will be considered as a vagabond and treated accordingly'—and there is every reason to think that such treatment would not have been pleasant.

This half-measure did not meet with the approval of Dr Vanderkemp, and it pleased his colleague, the Reverend James Read, even less. As early as 1806 the latter had brought the attention of the L.M.S. to what he considered the intolerable condition of the Hottentots. In 1811 he reopened his dossier. The Secretary of State for War and the Colonies, Lord Liverpool, who at this time had other things to worry about, adopted the customary procedure of ordering an inquiry. The Colony was then under the governorship of an energetic man, Lieutenant-General Cradock. Anticipating these instructions, Cradock had already resolved to act on his own initiative. In 1812 circuit courts were ordered to judge the complaints which the Hottentots felt obliged to bring against their masters; the hearings would be public. The very idea of putting natives and Europeans on an equal footing incensed the Boers. Their anger knew no bounds when they learned that a report drawn up by Read would involve nearly a hundred highly respectable families.

[1] See p. 66   [3] See p. 59.

Some were accused of murder pure and simple, others of barbarous treatment, and many of non-payment of wages. Over a thousand witnesses were summoned. One can imagine the problems that the judges encountered in the search for the truth. They were of the same blood as the accused and, no doubt, knew some of them. Moreover, how could they evaluate the evidence of wretched Hottentots, who had no understanding of legal procedure and were torn between fear of their masters and fear of disappointing the missionaries? The verdicts seem rather moderate, and it could not be said for certain that they were altogether impartial. Out of sixty-two Europeans, eight were sentenced for 'violence' and several for withholding wages. One of the accused was sent to Cape Town where the High Court imposed the death penalty, but he was reprieved.

The court proceedings had taken place in an atmosphere of passionate feeling. Hitherto the relationship between victors and vanquished had raised no problems. The *trekboers* felt so remote from the rest of the world that it was a matter of indifference to them that they owed allegiance to His Britannic Majesty instead of the Dutch East India Company or the Batavian Republic. At the Cape a *modus vivendi* had been established without too much friction. Except for the heads of departments, the civil servants had remained in their posts; Dutch was in common use, and the courts continued to administer justice in accordance with local law. A certain sense of solidarity had emerged between the Dutch and British ruling classes: both were equally fond of hierarchy and stability. This identity of tastes had given rise to numerous mixed marriages (including that of the terrible Barrow!). The glamour of the red uniforms had played its part, and the officers had not been insensible to the charms of the girls 'who dance well, flirt readily and speak their broken English softly'. This state of harmony, though a little artificial, did not crumble all at once. Nevertheless, people now viewed each other with more suspicion. In the *veld* the repercussions were more rapid and profound: the judgments of the courts were seen as proof of deliberate hostility and an assault on liberty, a word which the Boers interpreted in a distinctly egotistical manner. The Black Circuit of 1812, as it is commonly known in South African history, may have been an act of justice; politically, however, its consequences proved disastrous.

On the other hand, in this same year the British took the initiative in one way which earned them a revival of popularity. The Kaffirs, an eternal problem, had infiltrated to the west of the Fish river, still the imaginary frontier of the Colony. Cradock decided to drive them back. Commandos and regular troops undertook the task in unison, with the participation of Hottentot regiments, and the operation proved a marvellous success. Then it was decided, yet again, to settle the problem once and for all. A double chain of blockhouses, each guarded by ten men, was built along the river, with a skeleton headquarters at Grahamstown, a small settlement only just beginning to take shape but destined to become famous.

When the post of governor fell vacant at the end of 1813, Lord Charles Somerset was appointed. Somerset, forty-six years of age, was a person of distinction. Descended from the Plantagenets, he bore an illustrious name[1] and was related to the greatest families in the realm. At the age of seventeen he had been sent on the traditional 'Grand Tour' of Europe, in the footsteps of Boswell. Then, still under twenty, he had abducted a girl of a family equal in rank to his own and had married her with the grudging consent of her parents. He naturally entered the army, but did not pursue an active military career; he received no commands outside Britain and made no appearance on the battlefields of Spain. This relative inactivity did not prevent him gaining rapid advancement: at the age of thirty-one he was already a major-general, six years earlier than his contemporary, the future Duke of Wellington. This was not the limit of his ambitions. As Gentleman of the Privy Chamber to the Prince Regent, he obtained some flattering and lucrative appointments: Comptroller of the Royal Household, member of the Privy Council, and Paymaster-General of the Armed Forces. In the House of Commons, to which he had been elected at the age of twenty-eight (as a Tory, needless to say), his advice was not ignored—initially because it came from a Somerset, but later because he was seen to lack neither judgement nor authority.

His professional commitments did not prevent him from leading the social life of a fashionable young aristocrat. He moved in the snobbish and corrupt circle centred on the Prince Regent, but he did not have a reputation for chasing women. His overruling passion was for horses and hunting: 'a jockey', his enemies were to call him; 'the greatest hunting family the world has ever seen', says one historian in speaking of the Somersets. Lord Charles was only really happy in his country house at Badminton, which had a hundred and sixteen bedrooms, a dining-room for two hundred people, innumerable servants and, most important of all, so many horses that it was impossible to keep count. On his official engagements the lord of the estate was accompanied by a retinue of gentlemen and an escort of cavalry. All this had accustomed him to giving orders and instilled in him a taste for splendour.

On his arrival at the Cape on 5 April 1814, surrounded by his wife, their four children and some twenty friends, secretaries and servants, the new governor is said to have likened his future residence to a dog-kennel. The prospects now awaiting him undoubtedly offered a striking contrast to

---

[1] At the end of the Wars of the Roses, Charles Somerset, natural son of the Duke of Somerset, was the only surviving Plantagenet. He founded the Beaufort family, and received a dukedom in 1682. The governor was the second son of the fifth Duke of Beaufort and the grandson of Admiral Boscawen, who had achieved fame in the War of the Austrian Succession and the Seven Years' War.

C

his previous way of life. Hottentot servants were obviously available in unlimited quantities, but they bore little resemblance to English footmen. As for the 'fresh, rosy-cheeked ladies', they doubtless did not lack charm, but they did seem insipid in comparison with the beauties of the European courts. Above all, it would have been futile to seek in Cape Town the sparkling conversation typical of Brooks's or White's, two fashionable London clubs of the time. But Lord Somerset was too well-bred to show his feelings. Moreover, he had that admirable notion of public service which made the greatness of the English aristocracy—and so he set to work.

Somerset certainly did not lack titles: governor and commander-in-chief of the Castle, the city, and His Majesty's settlements and their dependencies on the Cape of Good Hope, in southern Africa; vice-admiral; commander of the armed forces; and judge of the Court of Appeal—all this, admittedly, under the supervision of a very meddlesome Colonial Office. But to ask for instructions would have meant six months of patience, and when one belonged to the family of the Dukes of Beaufort and possessed an instinct for authority, action seemed preferable to waiting. Thus the arrival of Lord Somerset was in itself enough to bring colour to the years following 1814.

Other factors, however, gave this period a character which the preceding years had inevitably lacked. Since 1806 no one had known what would become of the Colony: if Napoleon were to seize it, might it not be handed over to a new Batavian Republic, or might not France appropriate it herself? Four months after the French Emperor's abdication, an Anglo-Dutch treaty ratified British sovereignty. Somerset's decisions thereby acquired a new weight; furthermore, he was to exercise his mandate for thirteen years and thus enjoy the continuity without which administrative action cannot be effective. New problems also presented themselves. The Boers, Hottentots and Kaffirs—those actors continually on stage—were joined by others as the first British settlers established themselves in southern Africa. Finally, the first murmurings of liberalism were heard when certain bold persons dared to demand the freedom of the press.

If, at the end of his life, Lord Somerset ever turned his thoughts to his stay at the Cape, he must have been struck by its contrasting phases: after six easy years and then twenty-three months' leave, there followed five years in which his problems multiplied. The main features of this period must now be considered.

The new governor probably had preconceived ideas about his subjects. A Tory of the old guard, an aristocrat to his fingertips and as English as anyone could possibly be, how could he have avoided looking with condescension on these Boer peasants who knew nothing of the sweetness of life? To do him justice, however, it must be said that his impartiality triumphed over his prejudices. At the end of his first journey into the interior he wrote to Lord Bathurst, Secretary of State for War and Colonies, saying that, after what he had read and heard, he had not expected to meet a race of men possessed of such energy and initiative, showing such courtesy to one another, and who accorded foreigners a welcome far surpassing anything one might have hoped for. This letter, written in 1817, is a revealing document. Two years earlier a lamentable incident had stirred up feeling. In 1815 a Boer by the name of Bezuiden-hout, accused of maltreating a Hottentot, was summoned to appear at court; he refused to attend and was sentenced to a month's imprisonment; when the police came to arrest him he took refuge in a cellar; the police, thinking that they could see him taking aim, fired and killed him. His brother and some friends swore vengeance and tried to secure the support of the Bantu. At the last minute they had second thoughts and most of them surrendered; a few fled, but were captured. Thirty-nine of them were charged with treason and five condemned to death. The governor refused to reprieve the five. The hangings were tragic: four of the five ropes broke and it was necessary to start again. Slachter's Nek, the place of execution, has remained famous in South African folklore as a symbol of British tyranny. But is this justified? The sentences were not at all excessive for the time. Moreover, these Boer rebels were no more than a handful. The best proof is the letter quoted above, which shows the friendliness of Somerset's hosts and that they bore him no grudge for this tragedy.

The governor's visit of 1817 had been prompted by a project likely to appeal to his subjects. For reasons of economy London had recalled a part of the troops which had been guarding the Fish river since 1812. The frontier was now less well defined than ever. Somerset tried the experiment of a treaty. The Xhosa were divided into two factions, one of which advocated resistance; Gaika, the leader of the second, had fifteen years earlier declared himself to be in favour of co-operation. It was decided to impress him by a show of force and splendour. The governor, in full uniform, took his place under an awning, surrounded by his troops. At first the Xhosa chief took fright and fled; he was caught but insisted that he would come back only if accompanied by hundreds of his warriors. Somerset greeted him as 'chief' of his 'nation'; his future ally must have had a sense of humour, for in reply he is supposed to have thanked his Lordship warmly and begged him to accept the same title. Then they discussed the perennial 'question'—the theft of cattle. Gaika eventually agreed to submit to an old Anglo-Saxon custom: whenever animals disappeared, the owners would follow their tracks, and the tribe to which the tracks led would be held responsible for restitution or compensation. In return the natives obtained permission to go twice a year to Grahams-town to barter ivory and hides for the iron and copper which they always coveted. Then they separated with interminable compliments, and Gaika received a fine grey horse and a sack of gifts containing footwear, hand-kerchiefs, buttons, knives, glass beads, mirrors and tins.

The agreement which had been reached required good faith on both sides, and it would be impossible to be sure that it was scrupulously observed. What could have been easier than to erase tracks or fake them? In any case, the arrangement did not last two years. In 1819 ten thousand Xhosa assembled on a hill overlooking Grahamstown and in wave after wave, shouting their war-cries, poured down on the town, defended by three hundred and fifty men and two cannon. Eventually the Xhosa lost heart, but they had delivered a sharp warning. Somerset tried another solution, persuading Gaika to accept the principle of a neutral territory east of the Fish river, where neither Europeans nor Kaffirs would have the right to penetrate. He was presuming that both sides would resign them-selves to immobility—a highly optimistic assumption.

The uproar from the frontier was muffled by the time it reached the Cape, where a little inflation and Napoleon's captivity on St Helena were creating a prosperity to which the Colony was not accustomed. It had become the market for supplying St Helena, and ships were always coming and going between the island and Table Bay. From one of these ships, in 1817, emerged the Count de Las Cases, Napoleon's secretary on the island, accused by Hudson Lowe of carrying on a clandestine corres-pondence. Somerset felt embarrassed: should he treat Las Cases as a prisoner or as a guest? For ten days, under the influence of his colleagues, he adopted the first solution. Then his natural courtesy prevailed, and he gave Las Cases and his son accommodation in one of his own residences. Here the Frenchmen discovered a drawing of the Emperor sketched by one of Lord Charles's daughters, and which they found sufficiently displeasing to add this vengeful inscription:

> Sous vos doigts élégants tout devrait s'embellir;
> C'est aux belles surtout à peindre le courage;
> Du héros des héros, du Mars de l'avenir,
> Comment avez-vous pu défigurer l'image?

('Under your elegant fingers everything should be enhanced; it is for beautiful women, above all, to portray courage; how have you been able to disfigure the image of the hero of heroes, the Mars of the future?')

Perhaps this doggerel irritated the governor. At all events, his guests were transferred to a private house about twenty-five miles from Cape Town, 'a veritable desert', wrote Las Cases in his Mémorial de Sainte-Hélène. They stayed there seven months, until their departure, at which Somerset was sincerely delighted.

Other, less controversial, visitors called at the Cape. Civil servants and officers were in the habit of taking a rest in this delightful climate on their way back from India, providing the governor with an excuse for some splendid entertainments. After being shattered for a time by the loss of his wife, who died in 1815, Somerset found his social instincts getting the better of him. Receptions helped him to relax after his hunting parties[1] and also gave him an opportunity to display his perfect manners. He made a great fuss of the women on these occasions: 'He talked to me all evening in a very personal manner and with an amiability that stems from his adoration of our sex. It is even said that he loves us a little too much . . .', observed a French lady. The master of the house was followed everywhere by a strange figure, his personal doctor, Dr Barry, small in stature, pale and with a long nose, raising himself on his high-heeled boots, in a uniform with epaulettes and an enormous sabre at his side. Out of doors he was accompanied by a gigantic native servant, who carried a sunshade to protect his master's complexion, and was followed by a black poodle called Psyche. On the servant's death fifty years later 'he' was discovered to be a woman. . . . But it is well known that the British aristocracy enjoyed disconcerting ordinary mortals.

In 1820 the health of one of his daughters induced the governor to apply for leave. He sailed on 12 January and did not return until 30 November 1821, with a new wife eighteen years younger than himself.[2]

Somerset must have been a model father to allow his family worries to persuade him to leave his post at the very moment when a project dear to his heart was in process of being realized. Three months after his departure four thousand British immigrants landed at Algoa Bay.[3] Lord Charles had proposed the idea on his appointment in 1813, but it is understandable that his government should not have followed it up at the time. Besides, the experience in the United States and then the difficulties in Canada had not made the idea of settlement colonies popular. India and the West Indies seemed more reliable sources of wealth. However, the economic crisis at the end of the Napoleonic Wars had altered the situation. Revolutionary murmurings could be heard among the growing numbers of the unemployed. Emigration seemed a partial solution to a problem that Britain was not yet ready to face squarely. The Cape Colony was obviously underpopulated: less than thirty thousand Europeans, barely a tenth of them of British origin; immigrants, it was thought, would have no trouble settling there and would help to offset

---

[1] For example: one Thursday morning he rose at two o'clock, was on horseback at three, rode twelve or thirteen miles, and started hunting at dawn (at twenty minutes to five); at half past eleven he was back in his tent; after allowing the hounds to rest until two o'clock, he set off hunting again until half past six. He dressed for dinner that evening and was up again at half past three the next morning.

[2] On the way to England he called at St Helena, where he tried to visit Napoleon, but the Emperor avoided him. Hudson Lowe commented that 'the great man' had behaved with his customary rudeness.

[3] Another thousand had arrived by the end of 1821.

the imbalance caused by the numerical superiority of the Boers. Moreover, once he was at the Cape, Somerset saw another advantage in the scheme: by populating the Zuurveld, the region to the west of the Fish river which had been a perpetual object of dispute between Whites and Kaffirs, it would be possible to give the Colony the defensive reinforcement which the numerically inadequate regular troops were incapable of providing.

In 1819 the decision was taken. The Colonial Office received ninety thousand applications. It had been laid down that the emigrants would travel in groups under leaders chosen by themselves. Sixty such parties were formed, ranging in number from fifteen to three hundred and forty-four, and comprising an incongruous medley of men and women from various walks of life: 54 per cent crop-farmers, 33 per cent artisans, 7 per cent tradesmen, 2 per cent officers, 2 per cent from the liberal professions and 2 per cent sailors. They had to deposit a minimum sum as security, but their passages were paid and they were promised, free of charge, a hundred acres of land, which seemed splendid to poor people used to small plots of ground. Rarely can the contrast between expectation and reality have been more striking. After an interminable crossing followed by a journey of varying duration in ox-wagons, the newcomers at last saw the place where they were destined to live. The land bore little resemblance to the descriptions in the prospectuses, which had omitted to mention the prolonged droughts and the sudden floods. Some looked for more favourable sites; and for a time they were obliged to possess passes, like common Hottentots. Bad luck also played its part. Lord Somerset and his acting governor, Sir Rufane Donkin, proved totally incompatible in temperament. On his return Somerset immediately set about undoing all Donkin's work. He was irritated, moreover, by the recriminations made by his new subjects, most of whom he regarded as 'radicals'. 'Their chief object,' he wrote to Lord Bathurst, 'is to oppose and render odious all authority, to magnify all difficulties and to promote and sow the seeds of discontent wherever their baneful influence can extend.'

These 'rebels' cannot have been very dangerous, for the failure of three successive harvests reduced them to heartbreaking penury. One traveller tells of 'a captain and his two sons without sufficient clothing to cover their naked limbs'. Another describes 'what had been once a fine hearty young woman, apparently 24 or 25, she and three children without shoes and stockings, the woman's dress, if such it could be called, consisted of the remnants of an old tent tied about her'. These wretched people took the bold step of appealing to London, where their petition was all the more favourably received because at this same time other criticisms were being levelled against Somerset. The governor, autocratic by nature, mistrusted the missionaries, whose irrepressible zeal prompted them to concern themselves with many other matters apart from the conversion of the natives. From 1819 the chief representative of the L.M.S. had been Dr John Philip, one of the most controversial figures in South African history. His defenders portray him as Whig by inclination, with a horror of extremism, a great admirer of respectability as understood by the middle classes, sensitive to the notice of persons in positions of importance, and respectful of established authority. According to his detractors, on the other hand, he was a deliberate agitator with a passion for polemics, a man of ambition, pride and violence who in his judgements was always ready to declare the Hottentots to be in the right and the Europeans in the wrong. He has been likened to John Knox, and his writings reveal enough fanaticism to justify the comparison. He was no more indulgent to the British immigrants than to the Boers. It was, in his view, a sad reflection on human nature that the British settlers had been in Africa only three years when they began to cherish similar, if not worse, feelings towards the natives as those whom they condemned had so rigorously. Dr Philip can be regarded (may his ghost forgive us!) as a forerunner of *apartheid*: it was his opinion that Whites and non-Whites should be separated, for he considered this the only means of ensuring the latter's development.

At first his relations with the governor were amicable, but their mutual tolerance was too artificial to last. From the Castle the Colonial Office began to receive reports which spoke of nothing but the insidious character of this dangerous man who, it was claimed, was always ready to shirk his responsibilities and to twist the facts, interfering in anything so long as he could gain some practical advantage. Since contrary reports were naturally arriving from Bethelsdorp, the government decided to send a commission of inquiry, which started work in July 1823. This was only the beginning of Lord Somerset's troubles. In London the Opposition, casting all restraint aside, even went so far as to question his honesty. In Cape Town he found himself in violent conflict with the editors of the two modest newspapers which had recently been launched. A mysterious poster appeared (and was quickly torn down) bearing embarrassing insinuations about his morals. At the same time the economic crisis, from which the Colony had not managed to recover since the manna of St Helena had vanished, was aggravated by a monetary reform that replaced the paper rix-dollar with British silver.[1] The governor was delivered the final blow in 1825. Without waiting for the report of the commission of inquiry, London decreed that henceforth his decisions would be subject to the approval of a Council of Advice, which admittedly was composed of his principal colleagues, but which nevertheless would be standing at his side with supervisory authority. His only consolation was that the lot

[1] In 1806 the rate of exchange had been fixed at four shillings to one rix-dollar. When British money became the only legal currency, the rate was changed to one shilling and sixpence per rix-dollar. The consequences are obvious.

of the immigrants had greatly improved since they had been permitted to change from crop-growing to stock-breeding, and since a large number of them had found jobs that suited their abilities in the urban centres.

At the end of 1825, Lord Charles resolved to return to England to vindicate himself. His departure was preceded by the kind of entertainments he loved so dearly. He embarked on 5 March 1826. The sun, which had been obscured earlier in the morning, shone with unusual brilliance, like the reputation of a man of duty which calumny can distort but never tarnish. Lord Charles and his officers were wearing full uniform. The crowd was enormous, and all the ships in the bay splendidly decorated. Nineteen cannon-shots greeted the governor.

On his arrival in London he received 'a gracious welcome from His Majesty', a newspaper declared three months later. Would he return to his post, or would he be dismissed? This question, which remained unanswered for eleven months in spite of passionate and confused debates in the House of Commons, was finally settled by the death of the Prime Minister, Lord Liverpool, in February 1827. The Tory Left wing assumed power under Canning and, since Lord Charles's friends were not among their number, he offered his resignation. The new government accepted it in a rather insolent manner, informing him that, although certain regrettable events had taken place in the Colony in recent years and had posed some embarrassing problems in the administration of his affairs, His Majesty saw no reason to doubt the purity of the motives that had inspired his conduct. It was left to Somerset to decide whether he had been incompetent or merely naïve. Did he understand the irony of the royal letter? This seems doubtful, for it must have been difficult for him to think that he was wrong. He died four years later.

6

Black Potentates

To the north-east, some twelve hundred miles from the Cape, tragedies
were being enacted whose horror verges on the unbelievable.

For fifty years the Whites had continually been pushing forward. The
Xhosa, who had slowed but never halted their progress, were only an
advance-guard. When, under pressure from invaders, they surged back,
they found themselves in territory occupied by a mass of other Bantu,
like them hungry for open spaces and fertile grazing lands. Was the
'explosion' that now occurred due to a fear of encirclement—to the west
by the barrier of the Drakensberg, to the east by the sea and to the south
by the Europeans? Or was it the result of the ambition of chiefs of exceptional bravery? Whatever the reason, the Blacks spent some fifteen years
killing one another with such passion that the number of casualties is
estimated by the experts at two million—though this is pure guesswork,
like everything relating to these massacres. The witness of a few traders
and missionaries, and an oral tradition which is occasionally reliable but
often inclined to fantasy, are the historian's only sources. In other words,
it would be hazardous to try to reconstruct these events in detail and
wiser to be content with a general description. The protagonist of the
tragedy was undoubtedly Chaka, king of the Zulu. At the beginning of
the nineteenth century the Zulu wielded little influence. The founder of
their future power came of good stock. The natural son of a chief, Chaka
was possessed by ambition. A quarrel with his father prompted him to
seek refuge with another tribe, led by a certain Dingiswayo, whose
confidence he gained. His protector—who is said to have learnt them
from some unknown European—taught him the rudiments of the military
technique that was to revolutionize the native wars, and his own determination and intelligence, not to say genius, did the rest. In 1818
Dingiswayo died and the army proclaimed Chaka his successor. Two
years earlier Chaka had made himself master of the Zulu and during the
next ten years he was to gather round these two tribes three hundred
clans over which he ruled with absolute authority. At the beginning of
his rise to power he had only five hundred warriors at his command and
his influence was limited to the territory of an average-sized tribe. On his
death his regiments numbered fifty thousand men and his sway extended

over the whole of present-day Natal and Zululand, from the Kei river to the Zambezi and from the Indian Ocean to Botswana.

The secret of this prodigious success was 'blood and iron'. The training of the young Zulu has been compared to that of the Spartans and Chaka's *impis* to the Roman legions. Without going back quite so far, and forgetting for the moment the savageries which will be described shortly, one finds something of Napoleon in this black potentate: the same concern with detail, the same sharp eye, the same thorough knowledge of the fighting man.

The future warriors were subjected to two or three years' training before being admitted to the honour of serving in the army. In peacetime the army was divided between various sites chosen for their strategic importance. The men lived in huts of the traditional type placed side by side in a circle to form a stronghold, which was protected by a thick hedge of dried thorny branches. The thorns, judiciously used, played their part in Chaka's achievement. Like all great military leaders, he had learnt that the mobility of an army is a factor in its success. His warriors wore sandals, but his own experience had taught him that it was possible to run more quickly with bare feet, and so he made them remove their sandals and spend hours manœuvring over ground covered with brambles. Once they had been sufficiently hardened, he would subject them to forced marches (an average of fifty miles a day for six days). Disobedience was out of the question, for the slightest infringement incurred harsh punishment. The great chief—the 'August One', as he was called—brought pressure to bear on his men by methods which he knew to be effective: none of his soldiers was allowed to marry before he had 'washed' his spear in the blood of an enemy.

The day of battle came; the army was divided into regiments of a thousand men which were distinguished from each other by the colour of their head-dress and shields. The battle-dress was uniform: round the head a band with multi-coloured feathers; on the body a skirt made from the skins of monkeys, civet-cats or genets; bracelets on the arms and legs, and flounces of ox-hide on the ankles. The bravest were entitled to wear glass beads, the symbol of their exploits. Weapons consisted of two types of assegai: one type was thrown immediately before the attack; the other, with a short shaft and a long, heavy blade, was used for hand-to-hand fighting—and to lose this assegai was the worst possible disgrace for a Zulu and meant certain sentence of death. A broad oval shield, which when stood on the ground reached to the shoulders, provided protection.

The only strategy that Chaka understood was the offensive, whatever the numbers and position of the enemy. But he did not attack without due preparation. He had an excellent intelligence system at his disposal. Moreover, the army was accompanied by a service corps of young boys (one to every three warriors, according to one historian), who provided the heroes of the following day with mattresses and blankets, lit wood fires if the temperature so required and, most important of all, made sure that meat was served in unlimited quantities. The men thus arrived at the battlefield fresh and well-fed. The deployment of forces followed a strategy that allowed of no variation: the one overriding aim was the encirclement of the enemy. The main body of warriors was preceded by two lines of scouts, both in front and on each side. The first line, composed solely of new recruits, went ahead of the army at a considerable distance; its task was to give warning of the enemy's whereabouts to the second line, consisting of more experienced men, who then reported to the chief. The centre of battle was occupied by only a part of the troops; on the flanks two wings of particularly swift-footed warriors were responsible for surrounding the enemy. Chaka always had large reserves of men behind him.

Here is an eye-witness account of one battle. 'At four spears' throw the deep majestic Zulu war chant rolled like thunder across the valley. . . . With the beginning of the chant the speed of the warriors slowed down to the rhythmic measured jog-trot of a death dance and at every tenth step there was a shaking step of the right foot carried out in perfect unison. At one spear's throw the chant ceased abruptly. There was a deadly silence for the time required to take a deep breath. Then the fearful Zulu war cry crashed out *Si-ji-di*, and the Zulus charged.' Seldom were their adversaries able to sustain the impact without disintegrating. Then the massacre started, followed by a merciless pursuit. The huts of the vanquished were systematically burnt down, and no man was spared; the victorious army would bring back with it women, children and cattle.

One can imagine the conquering hero back in his *kraal*. The beauty of Zululand has often been described: 'It is a country of alluring contrasts, where in the mornings the valleys are draped in blankets of mist and the sun blazes down on smooth, moist mountain slopes. . . . A miscellany of insect-chirping and bird-song vibrates. . . . Cascades of fountain water tumble crazily from the sides of the cliffs to the rocks hundreds of feet below. . . . There are vast, open expanses of lush pastures and stretches of bushveld. . . .' One does not know if Chaka was sensitive to the beauties of nature, but he does not appear to have been indifferent to the beauty of women. His courtiers knew well that, to flatter him, it was even more important to talk to him about his alleged amorous exploits than to mention his military victories. His harem is supposed to have numbered twelve hundred concubines who, for want of eunuchs, were supervised by the most repulsive men he could find. Alas, the days were long and the flesh weak. Eighty-five women were convicted of infidelity and did not die a pleasant death. To belong to the privileged class of concubine, moreover, offered no guarantee of security, for the master would pass on his women to his officers when he had grown tired of them and replace them with younger ones. Chaka had made it a matter of principle not to marry. Pampata occupied the position of official mistress; the bold Mbuzikazi succeeded in supplanting her for a time and even dared to insult her, but the king's heart lay elsewhere and he soon returned to his true loves.

The vain Chaka did not find these jealousies displeasing. He took an even greater delight in the ceremonial splendours with which he surrounded himself. He was tall and well-proportioned; so that everyone should be aware of the fact a ritual levee was held each morning at which he would perform his ablutions before an admiring public. In addition to this homage to his person there were the more solemn honours which his glory demanded. His troops were subjected to frequent march-pasts. One of these occasions is thus described by an eye-witness: 'Full war dress with the uniform colour of the shields of each regiment. The sea of tossing white shields and waving ostrich plumes of the veterans followed by the black and white shields of the younger regiments and the flashing of all the spears. . . . The rhythmic stamping of ten thousand feet made the earth quake . . . an ominous display which was heightened by the deep sonorous chant of the warriors.' The spectacle ended with a march past of three regiments of girls with miniature shields and javelins, 'in their almost nude and natural glory'. Then, as was the custom, spokesmen from each unit ventured to put questions to the king and even criticize him. It is true that when he was in a good humour Chaka did not dislike discussions, as the few Whites who approached him discovered. In 1824 Lord Somerset gave three of his fellow-countrymen, Francis Farewell, Henry Fynn and James King, permission to trade with Natal. Chaka received them with great pomp, assuring them that he was the greatest king on earth, contradicting them and making fun of their manners, all with great gaiety. Then, as a token of his friendship, he signed a treaty conceding them a large area round what was to become Durban. Everything was going well, indeed far too well, when the Zulu king decided to send an ambassador to his 'good brother' in Great Britain, George IV, with whom he professed his willingness to share the world. James King was entrusted with this mission; to endow him with the necessary splendour he was made chief of a regiment and dressed accordingly. The purpose of his journey was to obtain a mysterious 'elixir of life' which Chaka was anxious to acquire because he thought it would prolong his mother's life.[1] Matters were complicated when the 'ambassador' discovered that he would have to take with him 'six of the choicest and the most virginal harem lilies to be presented in their nude glory' to his sovereign. He feared the gift might be considered in doubtful taste at the Court of St James's and adroitly declined such an unusual retinue. Accompanied by more traditional Zulu, King was obliged nevertheless to set off on his journey, though he got no farther than Port Elizabeth.

[1] The author cannot vouch for the truth of this anecdote. The elixir, it seems, was a kind of hair-dye which Fynn had mentioned for some unknown reason.

After three months of waiting he had to admit that it was impossible to make use of his credentials. Chaka did not take offence, declaring to his friends (or so they seemed): 'The whites have knowledge . . . and knowledge is strength, and there is much we can learn from them.'

During their conversation Farewell and his companions had an unpleasant surprise. Suddenly, without the slightest warning, Chaka ordered that one of his guards should have his neck wrung. This was the most common form of execution, but many other methods were used: the victim might be stabbed, stoned, impaled, burnt alive, drowned or fed to the crocodiles. Even more ingenious means of revenge were employed: a sorceress, for example, supplied with a jagged spear, was put in a hut with a hungry hyena and devoured bit by bit. On the death of his mother, despair reduced the king to the most savage cruelties, which Fynn witnessed. Half a dozen women were found guilty and burnt alive. 'For hours and hours commenced the most horrid and dismal lamentations.' Seven thousand who had not wailed loudly enough were then massacred.

The end of the story is easy to foresee. In 1828, when he must have been about forty, Chaka was assassinated by two of his half-brothers, Dingaan and Mklangana. He delivered his own *Tu quoque, Brutus*: 'It is you, children of my father, who are killing me,' he cried. Then he made this prophecy which was to be fulfilled within ten years: 'You will not rule this country, the white people have already arrived.' Pampata spent the night alone beside his body. The hyenas were howling in the vicinity but did not dare come too near, for they were instinctively afraid, and the Great King's lover drove them back with a stick. Later she committed suicide.

In a gallery of the native chiefs of the period the king of the Zulu would have a place of honour. But there are others entitled to keep him company.

Mntatisi, for example, queen of the Mantati. 'It was said that a mighty woman, of the name of Mantatee [Mntatisi], was at the head of an invincible army, numerous as locusts . . . that she nourished the army with her own milk, sent out hornets before it. . . .' Her invincible tribe crossed Basutoland, nearly succeeded in penetrating Cape Colony, which was saved by the Orange River in spate, devastated the north of what is now the Orange Free State and the south of the Transvaal, and eventually disintegrated on the borders of Bechuanaland.

Then there was Msilikazi and his Matabele. Msilikazi was one of Chaka's officers. Having incurred the wrath of his chief, he had thought it wise to flee beyond the Drakensberg. Forming an army on the Zulu model, he laid waste and subjugated the high plateaux stretching between the Vaal and the Limpopo. At the height of his power he had twenty thousand soldiers under his command, and his influence extended over 300,000 square miles. The historian is quite well informed about

Msilikazi as a result of a visit which the missionary Robert Moffat made to his *kraal*, where he was courteously received. Moffat admits that he was 'surprised to find that this notorious conqueror was a soft spoken person whose bearing was far more dignified than any other potentate'. Msilikazi liked to call his visitor 'father' and to refer to himself as his 'child'. He was a very special kind of child: 'His stocky body, well smeared with fat, was draped in heavy columns of beads reaching to the ankles, and an otter skin, stuffed to form a solid roll and pressed firmly onto his head, was decorated with bundles of the beautiful plumes of the blue jay, his favourite bird. . . . He wore a kilt of multicoloured beads . . . a lion shield in his left arm and a butcher's knife clutched in his right hand . . . an impressive figure.' Like Chaka, Msilikazi had a taste for protocol. A drawing shows him sitting in an armchair and, beside him, a white man entitled only to a low chair—though the latter makes up for his inferior position by wearing a top hat.

Moffat was the guest of honour at a war dance. 'For ten long minutes, silence pervaded the royal *kraal*, not a word was spoken as the regiment stood rigid behind their shields. Suddenly a captain raised his face to the skies and bellowed a command. Immediately the floor thundered beneath the stamping of warriors' feet: some singing in harmony, others hissing and others imitating the groaning of dying enemies. A brief period of silence. Cheers rose in the farthest sections of the *kraal* and spread through the ranks of the warriors as Mzilikazi came swaggering into the dusty arena.' For most of the night the visitor heard the drums beating a monotonous rhythm and the Matabele chattering, whistling and dancing. They were obviously afraid of not showing enough enthusiasm by stopping too soon—to displease Msilikazi entailed the same consequences as a frown from Chaka.

Finally there was Moshesh, the only truly great chief, whose achievement has lasted to this day. 'He has a pleasant and intelligent physiognomy; his bearing is noble and confident; in his features one discerns the habit of thought and command, but this does not prevent him having much kindness in his smile,' wrote one of his first European visitors. He had been shrewd enough to establish himself in an impregnable fortress, Thaba Bosigo, the 'Mountain of the Night'. He then succeeded in bringing under his authority large numbers of natives who had fled to this region to escape the raids of extermination conducted by tribes stronger than themselves, such as the Zulu and the Matabele. In this way, in a region so mountainous that it has been called the Switzerland of South Africa, he gradually gathered round himself the nation of the Basuto. The missionaries so intrigued him that he tried to buy one, offering a large number of cattle in payment, but Dr Philip provided him with one free of charge. The Evangelical Mission in Paris accepted the challenge; with this body, and in particular with its first representative, Eugène Casalis, Moshesh maintained excellent relations, though he was

never converted. Christianity's presence in present-day Lesotho is thus
the achievement of Frenchmen.

Many other names could be mentioned and many other episodes
described, but to do so would be pointless since events invariably followed
the same pattern. These *mfecane* or wars of extermination between Blacks
had rapid consequences. Over vast territories to the north of the Orange
river an air of desolation reigned: it seemed that life had vanished from
the region. The land, however, was ready to welcome new settlers, and
the Boers, those perpetual seekers of adventure, saw an opportunity to
appropriate it for themselves. They were all the more tempted to do so
because their relations with the British authorities were becoming less and
less satisfactory.

7

Difficult Coexistence

When, on 22 June 1897, in London, during one of those magnificent processions of which England possesses the secret, Queen Victoria heard the acclamations that greeted the sixtieth anniversary of her accession to the throne, her thoughts must have turned to her coronation. So great was the contrast between the two epochs that she might well have imagined herself having ruled over two different peoples.

Now, in every part of the Empire, a unity existed around her dynasty and her person. When she had assumed power, however, a section of the French-Canadians, and even a handful of English-speaking Canadians, were in open revolt; the planters in Jamaica, embittered by the abolition of slavery, were actually talking of secession; and thousands of people were leaving the Cape Colony in search of territories where the Union Jack did not fly.

If, in 1837, it thus seemed that in certain British possessions overseas there existed the same mood of dissatisfaction that had led to the independence of the North American colonies, and if fifty years later, on the other hand, the imperial edifice appeared capable of defying time, Britain's conception of her role had itself changed totally. As the twentieth century drew near the country was sure of its destiny, eager for power and proud to bear the 'white man's burden'. Twenty years after the end of the Napoleonic Wars, however, it had still not overcome its shattering ordeal. On at least two occasions since Waterloo it had seemed on the brink of civil war. Attempted uprisings had been broken by ruthless repression. No solution had been found for the social problem. The emancipation of Catholics in 1829 and, in particular, the electoral reform of 1832 had revealed the existence of liberal tendencies that were timidly seeking to assert themselves. Yet even the greatest optimists had to admit that, since 1815, Great Britain had not managed to regain her equilibrium.

The colonies were suffering from this uncertainty and posed questions that were not easily answered. Should they be developed, or were they even worth keeping? Would not a Britain reduced to her island boundaries, the mistress of the seas and of international commerce, increase her wealth more surely than by exploiting territories where she encountered one obstacle after another? From 1827 to 1841 there were eleven successive holders of the office of Secretary for the Colonies—proof enough of wavering attitudes.[1] Canada and South Africa, in particular, were the despair of the experts, who were compelled to recognize that in these distant lands, Frenchmen and Boers, incomprehensible and obtuse, were stubbornly refusing to admit the superiority of British institutions. What was happening at the Cape, however, was much more serious than the situation in Quebec. In America the natives, decimated and reduced to impotence, posed no threat to British domination; moreover, the rigours of the climate had preserved the valley of the St Lawrence from the scourge of slavery. In Africa, on the other hand, the Blacks were constantly offering proof of their aggressiveness. 'Once embarked on the fatal policy of establishing a frontier in South Africa and defending it by force, there seems to be neither rest nor peace for us till we follow our flying enemies and plant the British standard on the walls of Timbouctou', groaned *The Times* in 1852. It could well have said as much twenty years earlier. No matter how often they were crushed and dispersed, the Bantu always reappeared, indomitable. The problems were not only military. The British accepted social injustice more readily at home than in their colonies. Was this because they felt that in the latter case others were responsible? At all events, the lot of the natives under Boer control seemed to them intolerable, as far as they could judge from the missionaries' reports. Their desire to remedy the situation was sincere, and it would be unjust to impute hypocrisy to them. The same can be said of their determination that their country should be the first to put an end to slavery.

It was only too easy for these humanitarian inclinations to become engulfed in contradictions. To protect the Bantu from the 'wicked' Boers, it would have been necessary either to halt the Boers' expansion or to follow them in order to control them. But such a policy did not square with Downing Street's desire for withdrawal and it also presupposed a military strength that would have involved further expenditure. At this time Britain, exhausted by the financial strain of twenty-three years of war, was obsessed with the need for economy. As a result she was to find herself adopting the most imprudent of policies—that which allows a disparity to exist between theoretical objectives and practical resources. All this was hardly likely to ease the problems of coexistence among Europeans with widely differing views on the native question.

In 1826 Dr Philip deemed it advisable to re-establish contact with London, where he soon acquired considerable influence. Confident that he was

[1] Lord Glenelg occupied the post for four years, and so there were ten appointments within ten years, some lasting only four, five or six months. At the age of sixty-six, that man of destiny, the Duke of Wellington, was himself in charge of the Colonial Office for five weeks in 1834.

speaking in the name of God, and able to combine lofty spiritual ideals with an exceptional flair for bargaining, he found an attentive audience among the 'Saints', the small group of naïve, enthusiastic and sincere reformers who had been given this flattering name. Thomas Fowell Buxton, who for several years had been struggling for the reform of the penal system and the abolition of slavery, proved a particularly staunch supporter.

The London Missionary Society decided that the moment had come to strike a major blow. Circumstances were all the more favourable because Major-General Richard Bourke, Somerset's successor, was by no means unwilling to appear an innovator. On 17 July 1828 the new governor took a decision destined to become famous—the most important since slavery had been introduced into the colony, it has been said. By the terms of the Fiftieth Ordinance, as this measure is known, the Hottentots found themselves placed on an equal footing with the Whites. The provisions of the Ordinance were unambiguous: 'No Hottentot or other free person of colour lawfully residing shall be subject to any compulsory service to which others of His Majesty's subjects are not subject.' The penalties for vagrancy were abolished. Should this statute be seen merely as a means of making the use of Hottentot labour more hazardous and that of Bantu labour easier, as Professor Macmillan suggests? Or should it be judged in the light of purely humanitarian aspirations? Whatever the case may be, the consequences of the Fiftieth Ordinance were far-reaching enough to lead, twenty-five years later, to the granting of the vote without distinction of colour in the Cape Province.

Bourke's initiative earned him the approval of the Establishment. The essentially practical Boers were less impressed. It was fortunate, for their inner peace of mind, that many of them were illiterate. Those who had the opportunity to read the eight hundred and fifty-three octavo pages of the Researches in South Africa which the indefatigable Dr Philip published that same year cannot have been in a good humour by the time they came to the end of the book. One of its aims was to throw light on the progress of the Christian missions and the civilizing influence of Christianity. In the opinion of Dr Philip, the Dutch Reformed Church and its followers were making very little contribution to this praiseworthy task—just the opposite, he claimed, quoting numerous examples of brutality. Not all his allegations were false, but neither were they all true. The persons he had accused felt an understandable satisfaction when he was ordered to pay £1,100 damages for defamation of an official. In the tense atmosphere prevailing at the frontier Dr Philip eventually became a scapegoat. Conflicting passions were thus crystallized, but nevertheless the problem was somewhat simplified.

Six years after the Fiftieth Ordinance another decision shook the Colony to its foundations. The campaign for the abolition of slavery had been initiated by Wilberforce in 1787, but at the time had made no great impression at the Cape. In fact, during the first British occupation of 1795–1803 'more slaves were imported into Cape Colony than during any previous period of equal length', observes Professor Marais. Nevertheless, the idea was gaining ground. In 1807 the British Parliament at last prohibited all slave traffic. This law was strictly applied in South Africa as elsewhere. It is estimated that there were 39,000 slaves in South Africa when, on 1 December 1834, they were declared free men,[1] as in the other British possessions. The principle of compensation was accepted: the governor proposed to fix the total at a little over £3 million, but the British government reduced this by £200,000; finally, the total indemnity did not exceed £1,250,000, payable in Britain, with losses ranging between 18 per cent and 30 per cent in discount paid to intermediaries. The inhabitants of the eastern borderlands were less severely affected by the decision than those of the Cape neighbourhood, where five-sixths of slave labour was concentrated. Yet British popularity was not increased by the measure.

Hottentots and slaves were a minor worry by comparison with the Kaffirs.

It will be remembered that Lord Somerset had hoped to solve the problem by creating a 'no-man's-land', prohibited to both Whites and Blacks, beyond the Fish river.[2] Although this solution brought the Colony a few years of peace, it was too unnatural to last. How could the natives, who were finding themselves increasingly short of space, be expected to observe an imaginary barrier? The infiltrations resumed. At the Cape the authorities waxed indignant, but once again they wavered. Sometimes they shut their eyes and sometimes they sent regular troops to intervene; occasionally it was left to highly skilled Boer commandos to remind the Xhosa that they must keep their word.

It is easy to imagine the mixture of irritation and alarm which the dispatches from South Africa must have provoked at the Colonial Office. Nearly all the officials of this department had spent a part of their careers in India. There, over immense and overpopulated territories, calm prevailed, and it seemed incomprehensible to them that things should not be the same in a colony where neither the population nor its area ought to have created problems. Starting from this premise, the conclusion of their reasoning was inevitable: the method which had succeeded so brilliantly in Calcutta must be applied at the Cape. There cannot have been a single official who was not familiar with the principles of this method, which were quite simple: to enter into treaties with the local chiefs which, while leaving them the semblance of power, in fact reduced them to a magnificent but powerless subjection; then to maintain British domination with the help of local troops commanded by European

---

[1] They remained, however, at the disposal of their masters for another four years as 'apprentices'.

[2] See p. 56.

officers. Around 1833 the experts were inclined to believe that this formula, transposed from one continent to the other, would prove equally successful. However, while they knew the Indians well enough, they appear to have been less well informed about the Bantu. The Xhosa chiefs were not maharajahs; they did not have behind them centuries of civilization which, though different, could provide faint bonds of mutual understanding between themselves and their conquerors; furthermore, the methods of their warriors in no way prepared them for the role of mercenaries which the sepoys of India had played.

At the beginning of 1834, Sir Benjamin D'Urban was made governor. This was the fourth appointment since the departure of Lord Somerset. The new holder of a post of which the difficulties ruled out a good many candidates was fifty-seven years of age. Inevitably, he had fought in Spain and had been rewarded for his services with honorary posts in Antigua, Barbados and Guiana. He was said to be of liberal tendencies, inclined to be influenced by missionaries, and in any case anxious that a distinguished career approaching its end should not be tarnished by problems of too difficult a nature.

Poor Sir Benjamin! What a disappointment! He did not like making hasty decisions and, in spite of alarming reports, did not judge it necessary to visit the eastern frontier during his first year of office. He contented himself with informing the native chiefs of his peaceful intentions, while warning them that he would not tolerate cattle-stealing. At the same time he authorized Colonel Somerset, in charge of the frontier troops, to eject any tribes that did not comply with his instructions. Colonel Somerset, son of the former governor, was heavy-handed in his methods. Perhaps he carried out his orders with too much brutality; perhaps the Xhosa simply decided that circumstances were favourable; or perhaps an abnormal drought had reduced them to famine. At all events, from 23 December onwards their raids spread terror throughout the districts adjoining the Fish river.

The alarm was given at the Cape on 31 December 1834. D'Urban was lucky to have as a colleague a man who might have come straight from a cloak-and-dagger novel, with a colourful career behind him and the banal name of Harry Smith. A second lieutenant at the age of nineteen, Smith had taken part in the Peninsular War, during which a dramatic incident had shaped the course of his life. Shortly after the British forces had captured Badajoz, he saved two girls from the clutches of some troopers; one of them, only fourteen years old, took his fancy and he married her. She was to follow him in all his campaigns, the idol, it seems, of both his fellow-officers and his soldiers. Wherever there was fighting her husband could be found: after Europe, the United States, where in 1814 he was present at the fall of Washington and at the battle of New Orleans. He fought again at Waterloo, where two horses were killed under him. The years of peace must have weighed heavily on him.

After spending three years as garrison commander at Cambrai, he was sent on expeditions to Nova Scotia and Jamaica. In 1828 he was posted to South Africa, where he formed a sympathetic and shrewd opinion of the Boers: 'Men of strong prejudices, most credulous in most respects, especially where the government is concerned, jealous to a degree of what they regard as their rights, constantly at variance with one another.' Smith saw the natives mainly as brutes, but he had no inclination to make martyrs of them. For both Boers and natives, whom he liked to call 'my children', he felt a condescending affection tinged with severity and a certain religious sentimentality.

On the night of the feast of St Sylvester, Smith decided that some of his 'children' were in need of correction. Not being a man to waste time, he got on his horse and, in a ride destined to become famous, covered the six hundred miles between Cape Town and Grahamstown in six days. D'Urban, who followed him twenty days later, was horrified by the extent of the devastation. His relations with Dr Philip, which had so far been good, were to be marred by what had happened. For the time being, as a good soldier, he concentrated on quelling the enemy, a task which, with the help of Boer commandos, he achieved in a few weeks. It was the Xhosa's turn to see their huts burnt down, their grazing-grounds laid waste and their cattle seized: some estimate the total dead at two thousand, others at four thousand. This disaster completely changed the governor's ideas. Some of his colleagues must have found it difficult to believe their ears when, on 10 May 1835, on the banks of the Kei river, they heard him proclaim that the aggressors, who had been defeated, punished and dispersed, were 'irreclaimable[1] savages' and that they were expelled 'for ever' from the territories to the west of the Keis which became the Colony's frontier. The only exceptions were a few thousand natives who had remained peaceful. Then, to give his words a judicial sanction, D'Urban awarded the name of Queen Adelaide Province[2] to the vast territory which, on his own responsibility, he had decided to annex.

At first everything went fairly well. Harry Smith had a task that suited his inclinations. At times he would show unlimited forbearance; at other times he would boast of having burnt two thousand seven hundred huts in three weeks and then, almost immediately, would admit that he would need a hundred thousand men to drive the Xhosa back across the Kei. Here he was speaking words of wisdom, for the forces at his disposal were obviously inadequate.[3] He made the best possible use of them by applying martial law (which clearly cannot have meant much in the

---

[1] The word 'irreclaimable' deeply offended the missionaries, since it denied them any hope of success.

[2] Queen Adelaide was the wife of King William IV.

[3] Less than two thousand White soldiers for the whole Colony, plus two to three hundred Hottentots.

prevailing local circumstances). But when D'Urban, smitten with legal qualms, proposed to abolish martial law, the colonel protested that there was nothing for it but to clear out: 'How am I to eat up Kaffirs according to Blackstone?'[1] A compromise was necessary. From September 1835 the 'irreclaimable savages' were permitted to stay where they were, under the supervision of officials who, with patience and gentleness, were supposed to make real British citizens of them. The governor then explained this volte-face to London in a report which he sent on 19 November.

Unfortunately he had forwarded an earlier report in June, after his dramatic exploit of May. At this stage the time factor must be taken into account, for only this explains the confusion caused by the crossing of dispatches between the Cape and London (each took three months to reach its destination). Charles Grant, Lord Glenelg, had just been appointed Secretary for the Colonies. Since he was of liberal sympathies, the annexation of the new province did not appeal to him at all; moreover, his chief concern was to avoid incurring the disfavour of his very powerful colleague, the Chancellor of the Exchequer. And so he equivocated, something by no means contrary to his nature. On 26 December he finally decided to acknowledge D'Urban's communication of June. His reply was hardly concise (it covered a hundred and fifty folio pages) its gist being a ruthless repudiation of the governor: the 'irreclaimable savages' had some excuse for their behaviour and, furthermore, there could be no question of adding a new province to His Majesty's possessions in South Africa. In short, there must be a return to the status quo ante.

A few weeks after D'Urban learned of the verdict, the arrival at the Cape of a colleague whom he had not himself chosen must have confirmed his realization that the mood of the British government was decidedly unfavourable towards him. Harry Smith was replaced by a lieutenant-governor, Andries Stockenstrom, who was made responsible for the eastern territories. The two men had very different ideas, especially with regard to the Boers. Stockenstrom, born at the Cape in 1792, was the son of a colonial official and had himself occupied the post of landdrost at the time of the Slachter's Nek tragedy.[2] Later, he had been promoted 'Commissioner-General of the East', an office he had held with various setbacks from 1828 to 1833. The testimony which he had given to the Aborigines Committee,[3] while on leave in London, had been ill received by his former subjects. His return was therefore unlikely to soothe their indignation, which had been intensified by the decision to capitulate. Stockenstrom certainly did nothing to make himself popular, for his aim was to accelerate rather than slow down the process of evacuation.

[1] Sir William Blackstone, the great eighteenth-century jurist whose Commentaries on the Laws of England was the first comprehensive survey of the English legal system.
[2] See p. 55.
[3] The term 'aborigine' infuriated the Boers because it seemed to imply the seniority of the Bantu.

Would things have turned out differently under another governor? Here the experts are confronted with a riddle for which they do not appear to have found the key. The sequence of events is in any case bizarre. In March 1836 D'Urban received Glenelg's dispatch disowning his policy. He contented himself with an acknowledgement expressing his profound regret that he had not been heeded. The passive attitude which he then adopted can be explained by his hope that the Colonial Office would have changed its view on the arrival of his revised report of 19 November. Two months passed and then, at the end of May, D'Urban had another disappointment: a further dispatch from Glenelg which, though more indeterminate, did not go back on his decision of December. This time D'Urban exploded, sending London a violent reply written in a tone which, remarks Professor Galbraith, is unusual for a subordinate to employ to a superior. Then he maintained silence, making no further attempt to justify himself. To find a successor was the only solution available to the British government, but the policy of 'wait and see' was as fashionable in London as in Table Bay. Sir George Napier was not appointed until October 1837, taking up his post in January 1838.

A relative calm prevailed at this time along the eastern frontier. The attention of the authorities was in any case directed to the north, from where alarming news was arriving of the hundreds of Boers who, two years earlier, had crossed the Orange in search of freedom.

PART THREE

An Attempt at Separate Development
1834-75

List of Dates

1835	Departure of Trigardt and van Rensburg.
Early 1836	Departure of Potgieter and Cilliers.
April 1836	Departure of Retief.
August 1836	Punishment Act.
September 1836	Departure of Maritz.
October 1836	Battle of Vetchkop against the Matabele.
April 1837	Adoption of the Nine Articles.
End of 1837	Arrival of the Boers in Natal.
6 February 1838	Massacre of Retief and his companions by the Zulu.
November 1838	Arrival of Andries Pretorius.
16 December 1838	Victory of Blood River.
December 1839	The British evacuate Natal.
October 1840	Organization of the Republic of Natal.
1841	United Republic of Transvaal and Natal.
December 1841	Napier decides to re-occupy Natal.
1842	Wool replaces wine as the chief export.
March 1842	Arrival at Port Natal of the *Brazilia*.
May 1842	British troops occupy Port Natal.
23 May 1842	Boer victory at Congella.
June 1842	Boers retreat on Pietermaritzburg.
1843	Natal becomes a British colony.
1845	Shepstone takes up his duties in Natal.
1846–8	Seventh Kaffir War, called the 'War of the Axe'.
1847	Sir Harry Smith, governor.
1848	Annexation of British Kaffraria. Treaties with the Griqua.
February 1848	Constitution of the Orange River Sovereignty.
August 1848	Defeat of the Boers at Bloomplatz.
1849	Incident of the convicts.
1850	Beginning of the Eighth Kaffir War.
1851	British troops driven back by the Basuto.
17 January 1852	Sand River Convention. Independence of the Transvaal.
1853	End of the Eighth Kaffir War.
1853	A representative government is established in Cape Town.
23 February 1854	Bloemfontein Convention. Independence of the Orange Free State.

1854	Sir George Grey, governor.
1856	Kaffir tragedy.
1857	Marthinus Pretorius, president of the Transvaal.
1858	First Basuto War.
1858	London rejects the Federation proposed by Grey.
1860	Arrival in Natal of the first Indians.
1860	Pretorius is elected president of the Free State.
1861	Founding of the London and South Africa Bank.
1861	Sir Philip Wodehouse, governor.
1862	Founding of the Standard Bank.
1863	Brandt replaces Pretorius as president of the Free State.
1864	British Kaffraria incorporated in the Cape Colony.
1865–6	Second Basuto War.
1867–8	Third Basuto War.
1869	Annexation of Basutoland by the Crown.
1870	Death of Moshesh.
1875	Marshal MacMahon decides in favour of the Portuguese on the Delagoa Bay question.

8

The Great Trek

If, today, one-fifth of the population of a country were to leave its national territory, the sociologists would not be able to find enough words to explain the 'motivations' of such an extraordinary exodus. Yet this is what happened in southern Africa in the nineteenth century. Around 1835 the Colony numbered some sixty-six thousand Whites, of whom fourteen thousand emigrated within ten years—a phenomenon whose magnitude, uniqueness and consequences are worth analysing and describing in some detail.

The convulsions of history are rather like mole-hills: the only visible signs of long periods of activity. These inhabitants of the Cape did not decide overnight to abandon the land which their ancestors had discovered and colonized. The Boers were simple people conscious of their rights. For fifteen years they had felt less and less understood by their conquerors. After 1820 their first shock had been the decision to create a 'neutral' territory to the east of the Fish river, a zone prohibited to all Whites; then exceptions had been made in favour of British immigrants and even Hottentots. When the news reached the farms in the east, indignation had broken all bounds and, since that time, had shown no sign of abating. In 1822, claiming that 'the moment appears favourable, as teachers have arrived from England to facilitate the acquirement of the English language to all classes of society', Lord Somerset[1] decreed that from 1 January 1827 only English would be permitted in official documents and in court proceedings. This was tantamount to condemning nine-tenths of the population to silence. Even Dr Philip was amazed;[2] in his opinion, to send instructions in English to a population that did not understand a word of it was an extraordinary example of the manner in which affairs were being conducted. Although modifications to this rule were made, it was nevertheless reaffirmed in 1828.

The year 1828 has been called by one South African historian the *annus mirabilis*, and 'astonishing' it certainly was in the extent of the reforms which it brought. Unfortunately—perhaps by the deliberate design of

[1] See p. 53.   [2] See p. 59.

the authorities, perhaps because of the Boers' inability to recognize the necessity of change—not one of these measures was likely to appeal to the Dutch population. The Fiftieth Ordinance[1] had been just in principle, allowing equality of rights between Whites and non-Whites; but its consequences had been deplorable, for there are hardly any historians now who do not admit that the freedom granted to the Hottentots resulted in a resurgence of stealing and vagrancy. No less equitable had been the decision to proclaim the freedom of the press—yet was it not a little cynical to affirm a principle of this kind, knowing that only a few citizens would be able to benefit from it?

The third and most important reform was the complete reorganization of the judiciary and the civil service. The judicial system undoubtedly needed remodelling, and the introduction of courts of the British type, especially the institution of a Supreme Court, reflects great credit on those responsible. It had not been proved, however, that methods which had been successful in Britain would necessarily be appropriate to South Africa. Admittedly, in the eastern borderlands all this appeared rather hypothetical. What seemed less so was the replacement of the *landdrosts*, nearly always Boers, by commissioners who were often British and, in particular, the abolition of the *heemraden*, which had more or less performed the function of municipal councils. Underlying all these reforms was the commendable but essentially theoretical notion of centralization and unification. It is surprising that British pragmatism should not have helped the government in London to understand more clearly the facts of the South African problem. To presume to impose English on a population less concerned with education than with survival revealed a curious lack of appreciation of realities. The same can be said for the illusion that commissioners, whose districts extended over areas ranging from five to ten thousand square miles, would be able to exercise effective authority over their subjects. Finally, it is easy to see why the processes of justice failed to make widespread progress when plaintiffs and accused sometimes had to travel two hundred miles or more to find a tribunal.

The *annus mirabilis* was thus not a popular year on the frontier. Neither was 1831, when the administration, smitten with scruples, announced that auction sales would replace the land-grants which hitherto had been awarded by a highly flexible interpretation of the law. The breaking-point, however, was reached only three years later—not as a result of the abolition of slavery, for the most hard-hit slave-owners lived near the Cape and had not left the Colony, but because the Kaffir invasion had exacerbated passions. An eye-witness, later a judge of the Supreme Court, calculated the extent of the disaster: 456 farms entirely burnt down or destroyed, 350 partially, 60 wagons missing, and thefts of 5,715 horses, 111,930 cattle and 161,930 sheep, the total valued at about £300,000.

[1] See p. 70.

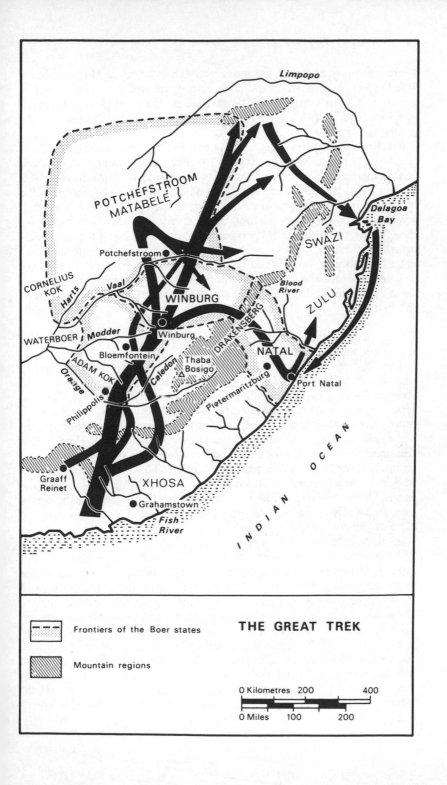

Limpopo

POTCHEFSTROOM
MATABELE

Potchefstroom

CORNELIUS
KOK

Vaal

Harts

WINBURG

WATERBOER

Modder

Winburg

Bloemfontein

ADAM KOK

Caledon

Thaba
Bosigo

DRAKENSBERG

Orange

Philippolis

Pietermaritzburg

Graaff
Reinet

XHOSA

Grahamstown

Fish
River

SWAZI

Blood
River

ZULU

Delagoa
Bay

NATAL

Port Natal

INDIAN OCEAN

THE GREAT TREK

- - -   Frontiers of the Boer states

▨   Mountain regions

0 Kilometres 200   400

0 Miles   100   200

There was no question of compensation. The victims might have felt a little happier, so powerfully did hope burn in the breasts of these pioneers, if they had been compensated with land in the new Queen Adelaide Province.[1] But British sovereignty there was something of an illusion and in any case lasted only a few months.

In other words, many Boers in 1835 felt that their expansion, sometimes rapid, sometimes slow, but sustained for fifty years, was now obstructed. Space, that unique wealth of unexplored continents, came to their aid. Their exodus has been described as 'that long series of flights from the incoming nineteenth century in British uniform'. It seems doubtful, however, that the brave farmers who decided to try their luck ever thought in terms of historical perspective of this kind. But if their imagination lacked breadth, they possessed an ample fund of common sense: what they wanted was to be themselves, to govern themselves, to preserve in lands of which they would be the masters the principles implanted in them by religion and heredity. To stay where they were would have been self-betrayal.

They soon made their choice—the north, for they knew the obstacles they might encounter to the east.

They had only a vague idea of their ultimate destination. They would stop, observes Professor Walker, wherever they found land, labour and security. In 1834 three expeditions had set out to reconnoitre. One had returned, disappointed, from the north-west. A second had brought back more encouraging news about the future Transvaal. The third, which had reached Natal, gave idyllic descriptions of that region. However, it had managed to pass through territory inhabited by natives only because its small numbers had not attracted attention. To repeat such an exploit in a body was impossible. Although the Promised Land lay beside the Indian Ocean, it was therefore necessary to start by heading for the north-east, apparently free of natives, and then cross the mountains separating the *veld* and the entrancing Natal.

As these bold men and women prepared for their journey, what kind of landscapes awaited them? First, the Orange river, a canal in a desert of sand, as it appeared in times of drought, and impossible to cross in the rainy season. Beyond lay the *veld*, three hundred miles of plateau broken up by ravines to the south and its horizons increasingly monotonous to the north. As one approaches the Vaal, the scenery changes: this pleasant river, less irregular than the Orange, flows through fertile lands. Beyond it begins the High Veld, rising gradually to between 5,000 and 6,000 feet. To the east, green savannahs interrupted by rivers; to the west, a brownish soil covered with bushes and shrubs. The mass of the Zoutpansberg conceals the approaches of the Limpopo. To the east and south-east the countryside becomes less and less attractive with its unusable rivers,

[1] See p. 73.

gorges ideal for ambushes, and everywhere mosquitoes and tsetse flies. The *voortrekkers*[1] knew Natal to be free of such hazards. Between them and the Indian Ocean, however, stood the Drakensberg range, about a thousand miles long, its highest peaks rising to 12,000 feet. A nineteenth-century traveller described 'the appearance of innumerable pyramidical hills thrown together in the most grotesque and disorderly manner; one peak jutting beyond, one soaring above the others as though precluding the possibility of any human foot, much less any wheeled vehicle, from passing over'.

The barrier was not insurmountable to the determined Boers. When they set out on their journey they knew nothing of these formidable mountains, but they were aware that a varied and difficult terrain awaited them. The 'trek wagon', the brother of the American 'covered wagon', was known for its combination of toughness and flexibility: about three feet wide and over fifteen feet long, it had four wheels each protected by an iron band at least half an inch thick. The floor consisted of wooden boards; the roof was supported by two perpendicular planks, one fixed to the rear of the frame, the other pivoting on the front axle. The various parts were held together by straps and plates so that they could be dismantled, and also to prevent the wagon from breaking up in the event of an accident. A dozen hoops supported two canvases placed one above the other: the first covered with a thick coat of paint to make it water-proof, the second coloured white to give an effect of coolness. A box at the front served as a seat; two more boxes at the sides and one at the back contained provisions and ammunition. The well-to-do emigrants some-times set off with three wagons: one loaded with bedding and clothing, the second for storing food and the third for weapons and powder. But most families had only one wagon, which was filled with everything it would hold, a small space on the floor being left for the women and children. When the men were not on horseback, driving herds of oxen, sheep and goats, or following the caravan on foot, they rested on a rather uncomfortable board placed under the wagon.

The wagon's load could be as much as two tons, which meant that the animals pulling them had to be strong, and so the teams consisted solely of oxen. Moreover, the choice of the oxen was influenced by the colour of their hides: red and white, or black and white, were considered preferable to all white or slate grey. Four to eight pairs were commonly used and were controlled by two drivers, one in front, the other sitting on the box-seat, calling each animal by its name and brandishing an enormous whip; in an emergency a few well-placed blows with a steel whip recalled the beasts to their duty. Over flat ground the teams of oxen could cover about three miles an hour for seven or eight hours. Engravings exist which depict the improbable spectacle of these wagons

---

[1] Literally the 'trekkers in front'. The word came into use only forty years later. Originally the Boers called themselves 'emigrants'.

D

climbing or descending steep slopes and moving along precipices where the slightest error could send them hurtling down.

During these perilous crossings the women and children would get out of the wagons and the men would cling to their vehicles, pushing them or holding them back. The Boers were exceptionally sturdy, often over six feet tall and powerfully proportioned; their cowboy-style clothes gave them great freedom of movement. The women were similarly sturdy. Wearing ample linen dresses and flannel underclothing, with shawls wrapped across their bosoms and bonnets fastened under their chins, they rarely fulfilled the requirements of a modern beauty contest. But they were healthy, strong and courageous, and they also possessed a will of iron. 'The Dutch African women have their say in things,' wrote a French traveller of the time; 'it is they who make their husbands do whatever they do.' They never used their influence to encourage laziness. A British officer who happened to meet a number of them, at a time when their cause seemed lost, was astonished by the poverty and misery he discovered. But he also observed that the large majority of the women refused to accept British domination; many of them had been living in comfort not long ago; their present situation was more than uncertain and subject to innumerable inconveniences; the savages had killed their husbands and their brothers; yet, in spite of everything, these women contemptuously rejected the idea of returning to the colony. The wife of a pastor must have expressed their unanimous feelings when, in the depths of distress, she uttered this poignant cry: 'We are footsore and weary with wandering and suffering, but we shall march once more across the mountains to liberty or death.'

The Boer womenfolk certainly needed to be tough in spirit in order to face the dangers to which the trekkers were exposed. There were other hazards apart from the nature of the terrain. Visitors to the Kruger National Park, that jewel of South Africa, will have little difficulty in imagining the variety of wild beasts that inhabited the plains and mountains crossed by the *voortrekkers*. The rivers were full of crocodiles and hippopotamuses; on the *veld*, lions, elephants, rhinoceros, buffaloes, zebras, kudus and antelopes abounded. The antelopes provided the travellers with the fresh meat they needed; and these delightful animals were defenceless; this was not so in the case of the lions, which were only too often ravenous.[1] With good rifles, however, such problems could be overcome. Confronting the natives was a more complicated matter, and in these supposedly uninhabited lands they appeared from all directions. It will be seen later what fearsome adversaries the Matebele proved— although getting the better of these people was child's play by comparison with the implacable Zulu.

[1] Livingstone had the unpleasant experience of being knocked down by a lion, which lay on him, then changed its mind and moved off. When asked to describe how he had felt, the missionary replied: 'I was thinking what part of me he would eat first.'

Fighting tactics were perfected, at first for defence and then for attack. For defensive purposes the wagons were used to form a stronghold. The Boers made a habit of camping on high ground from which they had a chance of spotting the enemy; here, the wagons were arranged in circles or squares, the shafts of each vehicle being firmly fastened under the next. This was called forming a *laager*. When numbers permitted, a double line of defence was provided: behind the inner line the women and children were placed, and the rifles were passed to them to be reloaded; the space between the two lines was packed with horses and cattle, the horses hobbled, producing a cacophony of mooing, bleating and neighing which mingled with the sounds of firing and the cries of the assailants. Branches of thorn-bush were placed between the wagons to bar the way. The Boers were outstanding marksmen, the best in the world according to one historian. From the shelter of their barricades the accuracy of their fire, and in particular the use of the *roer*, the rifle loaded with a heavy charge of shot which they used for hunting elephants, eventually enabled them to get the better of the enemy. The fatal danger was to let themselves be taken by surprise; the later part of this chapter describes some of the massacres that resulted from a failure to take precautions. Gradually the *voortrekkers* realized that they, too, could catch their adversaries unawares. Their horses were tireless, capable of travelling sixty miles in a day, adapting their speed to the slightest pressure applied by their riders, standing motionless while their riders fired, then galloping off again, an impossible target for an enemy who had to rely on his own two legs and his assegai.

As the moment of battle approached, prayer was obligatory. They would all bow their heads and listen to a passage from the Bible or a psalm. If the outcome of the battle was favourable, hymns of thanksgiving would rise from the *laagers*. The religion of these Boers was sincere, and to call their faith in doubt would be totally to misunderstand their simple, burning passions. Professor van Jaarsveld has given a lucid analysis of the mysticism which inspired them, a mysticism permeated with pride rather than resignation. They expressed themselves in biblical terms, calling the natives 'children of Ham and Canaanites'; the king of England was 'Pharaoh' (because of his oppression they had been forced to leave the Cape Colony, which had become another Egypt); they were on their way to the Promised Land, a chosen people inspired by God, the Creator of all things, in His infinite wisdom. What happened to them could not possibly be otherwise. The Afrikaners had been called by Divine Providence to go from place to place as pioneers of civilization. To them had fallen the awesome task of conquering Africa for King Jesus.

These men had leaders worthy of them. First, Piet Retief. Fifty-four years of age when he decided to go into exile, and with Huguenot blood flowing in his veins, Retief had known both riches and poverty. Born of a family of farmers who had settled several generations earlier around Swellendam, he had been lured by the world of business. Total failure, following a brilliant success, had brought him back to earth. Since 1824 he had been living not far from the Kaffir frontier, experiencing hardships which gradually made him resentful towards a government incapable of protecting him. Not that Retief was wholeheartedly hostile to the British; but eventually he despaired of making them understand his fellow-countrymen. He was the Thomas Jefferson of the Great Trek. Before setting off, he published a manifesto that could well be called the Boer Declaration of Independence: '. . . . as we desire to stand high in the estimation of our brethren,' the Boers would, wherever they found themselves, 'uphold the just principles of liberty'. There was one reservation, however, dictated by a candour not to be found in the more uncompromising but also more theoretical American documents: '. . . whilst we will take care that no one shall be held in a state of slavery, it is our determination to maintain such regulations as may suppress crime and preserve proper relations between master and servant'—an allusion, directed at coloured people, the terms of which were clearly going to be open to interpretation. The manifesto ends with the following conclusion, the origin of a misunderstanding that proved difficult to dispel: 'We quit this colony under the full assurance that the English Government has nothing more to require of us, and will allow us to govern ourselves without its interference in future.'

Gerrit Maritz probably took no great interest in these political and philosophical concepts. Much younger than Retief (thirty-nine against the latter's fifty-four when they went into exile), Maritz was one of the richest men of the Trek and is said to have set out at the head of a hundred or so wagons—a figure that is not at all unlikely, for he had made his fortune constructing these vehicles. The energy and tenacity of the two trekkers were equal, but assumed different forms. Retief was more easy-going, preferring persuasion to coercion; it is said that a certain gleam in his expression was enough to win over the hesitant. Maritz was a man cast in a simple mould, impetuous, domineering and impatient of contradiction.

Indeed, these were qualities he shared with the majority of the trekkers. The Boers were people of a violent nature, and the intensity of their passions explains why they threw themselves into such a prodigious adventure; on the other hand, it was also responsible for the squabbling that repeatedly paralysed their ability to act. Andries Potgieter, for example, was capable of remaining silent for hours on end—but if something displeased him, what an explosion! He was a man made for battle, in which he would conduct himself like a hero, and at the same time the father of a family who was always ready to spoil the thirteen children borne him by his four successive wives. It is difficult to imagine him making a joke; singing psalms was probably his only form of relaxation, and even then they had to be carefully chosen, for Potgieter was a Dopper, a member of the most fanatical Calvinist sect.[1] This did not prevent him from associating himself with the least intransigent of the Boers, Sarel Cilliers, who, like Retief, came of French stock. In essentials Potgieter and Cilliers resembled each other: both were men of few words and great faith. Cilliers loved theological discussions and sermons (especially, perhaps, when he had written them himself) and was always seeking divine aid. The first words of his diary are revealing: 'It is my desire that by higher Hand I may be placed in the position to write the truth, for our God loves the truth!'

There were many others. 'Old Father Smit' (he was fifty-nine) was the brother-in-law of Maritz, whom he accompanied as his private chaplain—the Dutch Church, disapproving of this mass exodus without 'the guidance of an Aaron or a Moses and without the divine assurance of a Canaan', had left the trekkers to the ministrations of this unordained mission teacher. The 'Reverend' Smit could hold the attention of his audience with sermons two hours long, but the opposition of the Potgieter clan prevented him from being recognized as official minister of the Trek. The Uys family, on the other hand, appears to have been universally popular. In the first place, it had numbers in its favour (there were a hundred people or so bearing this name). Moreover, two members of the family enjoyed great prestige. Jacobus, the 'patriarch', had been presented by the British of Grahamstown with an enormous Bible bearing the following inscription, which was no mean compliment: 'Offered by subscription to Mr Jacobus Uys and his departant fellows by the inhabitants of Grahamstown and its vicinity in a farewell token of their esteem and heartfelt regret at their departure.' Piet, the old man's son, had other claims to the confidence of his companions, for he had been the first to tell them of the wonders of Natal and had influenced Retief's decision to head for the Indian Ocean. Although better educated than the majority of the *voortrekkers*, Piet Uys relied less on learning than on will-power to reach the Promised Land.

Finally, Andries Pretorius, perhaps the most famous—it was he who was to enjoy the honour, fifteen years later, of signing the Transvaal's first treaty of independence—but not the greatest of the Boer leaders. He was the equal neither of Retief nor even of Gerrit Maritz. His experience was more limited. He was a well-to-do farmer from the environs of Graaff-Reinet and nothing more. His stock of knowledge was slender, and he knew hardly anything about what was happening in the world outside his native country. He was not lacking in sense, but in a crisis his judgement was in danger of deserting him; then he would try to get by with blustering. Circumstances smiled kindly both on Andries Pretorius and, perhaps to an even greater degree, on his son Marthinus, thanks to

[1] The Dopper sect finally broke with the official Dutch Reformed Church in 1859.

whom the capital of the Republic of South Africa bears the family name.

Almost as soon as the curtain had risen the Great Trek assumed tragic dimensions.

The first departures took place in 1835. Initially they were limited to two groups, under Louis Trigardt and Hans van Rensburg—in all some twenty men, their wives, about sixty children, a few colourful characters travelling independently who included a widow with a Rabelaisian tongue and an old soldier (or so he claimed) from the Napoleonic Wars, and some Bushman servants. Trigardt deserves a place of honour, for he was the only one, apart from 'Old Father Smit', to keep a diary, a document invaluable for its matter-of-fact account of the perils, obstacles, hopes and joys which he shared with all the trekkers. The two families travelled together whenever they feared an attack by the Blacks, though in the early stages they were unmolested. The first part of the journey passed without mishap, between the Orange and Vaal rivers. On Sundays they would stop to observe the sabbath. If the spot chosen seemed agreeable, the halt was extended for a few days and the opportunity was taken to attempt barter transactions with apparently peaceable natives.

Then they would move on, but no one quite knew where, and so arguments would arise which, inflamed by the Boer temperament, finally caused the two teams to part on very bad terms. Van Rensburg opted for the east and Delagoa Bay, but he and his family were massacred in the valley of the Limpopo. Trigardt enjoyed a longer run of luck. Continuing northwards, he reached the Zoutpansberg region, where he spent a year. But he could not stay there indefinitely, as provisions and ammunition were running out and the cattle were being attacked by mysterious diseases, and so he had to look elsewhere. Like van Rensburg, Trigardt was tempted by Lourenço Marques, the only known White town on the Indian Ocean. Now began the dramatic part of the adventure. The Portuguese governor, with whom the trekkers had succeeded in making contact, sent them two guides, and under their leadership the party entered the Drakensberg mountains in 1837. At first they found themselves travelling over sandy ground where the wagons got stuck, then ravines and precipitous slopes even more dangerous to descend than to climb. When the gradient was too steep they used only two oxen for each wagon, more for holding it back than pulling it, removed the rear wheels and allowed the vehicles to slide by fits and starts, the men clinging to them to stop them hurtling down—all this amid frequent storms and torrential downpours.

Exhausted and drastically reduced in number, the expedition finally arrived on the coastal plains, where it found the tsetse fly and malaria. The generous welcome accorded them by the Portuguese was not enough to save these wretched people, and they died one after another. Only one man survived, the son of Louis Trigardt; no less adventurous than his father, and not at all discouraged, he pursued his explorations as far as Mozambique and possibly even into Abyssinia. Twenty-six women and children were finally repatriated from Natal in 1838.

Did Louis Trigardt have the joy of learning before his death that his example had been followed by thousands of his compatriots and that a Boer Republic, his dream for so many years, was to be set up on the shores of the Indian Ocean?

The years 1836 and 1837 saw mass emigration. The Potgieter–Cilliers team left first, comprising some two hundred persons who included an eleven-year-old boy, Paul Kruger. The waters of the Orange were too high for the river to be forded; the men often swam across, and the wagons were carried on rafts; at these solemn moments, it is said, the women would sing with hymn-books in their hands. The early stages of the journey confirmed the emigrants' impression that the *veld* had been abandoned by the Blacks. At most they would come across a few starving natives who were only too glad to hand over land for contracts which in their eyes meant nothing. This was the first example of a misunderstanding that was repeatedly to have tragic consequences. The Whites, always anxious to justify themselves with legal procedures, would draw up texts which even the most meticulous lawyers would have endorsed and which they presented to the tribal authorities, who then solemnly marked them with a cross as their signature. However, since Bantu tradition forbade a chief to dispose of his patrimony, the document had little value. It sometimes happened, moreover, that the same territory was assigned to different persons, which provoked indignation among the Europeans, who were apparently incapable of understanding that legal practices varied from one continent to another, and resentment among the Blacks, who were intensely irritated by such formality.

Potgieter's party, having first obtained the 'authorization' of the natives, settled itself around the Vaal. Pushing farther afield, Potgieter himself explored the region north of the river where, in June 1836, he briefly met Louis Trigardt and even made contact with some Portuguese traders about sixty miles north of the Limpopo. On his return he was greeted with disastrous news. In August the Boer intelligence service had been shown to be inadequate: not only was the *veld* still inhabited by Blacks, but these natives were proving at least as aggressive as the Kaffirs. A party of hunters had been taken by surprise and annihilated. On 16 October Msilikazi's terrible Matabele encircled a *laager* hastily organized near a place called Vechtkop. The assailants gradually drew nearer—'the countryside was darkened by their mass'; squatting behind the wagons, women and children wept. Then the order to attack was given. 'The warriors were in full uniform: a thick skirt of fur composed of three rows of cats' or monkeys' tails hanging down their knees; white cows' tails covering their shoulders and torsos, with others attached as ornaments to the knees, wrists, elbows and ankles; a shield and five or six small spears.' The natives tried to clamber over the wagons or to crawl through the branches blocking access to the *laager*; they tried to hit the occupants by hurling their assegai into the air—'the canvases of the wagons looked like balls of wool bristling with needles'. The battle lasted over three hours. When the attackers retired they left behind them four hundred and thirty dead, the corpses piled on top of each other and forming a wall round the camp. The Boers had won a resounding victory and their losses were insignificant (two dead, fourteen wounded). The Matabele did not risk a second onslaught. In 1837 the Boers took the offensive and in two commandos pushed their enemies back across the Limpopo, into present-day Rhodesia. But Vechtkop had been a Pyrrhic victory, for it had been impossible to prevent the natives taking a hundred horses, five thousand cattle and fifty thousand sheep.

Potgieter and Cilliers saw the hand of God in the arrival, shortly afterwards, of large reinforcements: seven hundred emigrants, this time, including two hundred men led by Gerrit Maritz. They had left the Colony in September.

The increasingly frequent departures of trekkers were beginning to worry the Cape authorities, who wondered if there was any legal basis for prohibiting them. The Ministry of Justice was consulted and offered this judicious advice: 'Would it be prudent or just, even if it were possible, to prevent persons discontented with their condition to try to better themselves in whatever part of the world they please? . . . the same sort of removal that takes place everyday from Great Britain to the United States.'[1] (The author of this note is unlikely to have had any promotion.) On 13 August 1836 an extravagant text was published which aimed to extend British law to all territories, occupied or not, as far as the 25th parallel.[2] Five hundred miles from the Cape this symbolically titled Punishment Act cannot have made much impression on the Boers, assuming they even heard of it. Besides, they felt themselves sufficiently numerous to organize their own government. They had not read Montesquieu and they were content with simple ideas. The 'people' elected a Council of seven members, the *Volksraad*, which combined the executive, legislative and judicial functions. It was not specified whether this body's decisions would be final. Two personalities were obvious choices: Potgieter, the first to arrive, and Maritz, who had the larger following. Maritz became president of the *Volksraad* and Potgieter military commandant—a duality of powers which, with such uncompromising men, was to degenerate rapidly into conflict.

The arrival in January 1837 of Piet Retief, at the head of a hundred and

[1] 318,000 British subjects (237,000 from Ireland and 81,000 from Britain) emigrated to the United States between 1820 and 1830.

[2] That is, to the northern region of the present-day Transvaal.

twenty men and a hundred wagons, temporarily eased the tension. Retief wielded great influence and his judgement was respected. A new election was held: Potgieter lost office, but Maritz continued to hold his judicial and legislative functions; the two titles awarded to Retief—head of the government and commandant-general—indicated clearly to whom the real power belonged. This change of régime was accompanied by a solemn ceremony: in June the emigrants assembled on the banks of the Vet at the site of the future village of Winburg and decided to form themselves into a community, the *Maatskappy*, to which everyone would swear an oath of loyalty. Those who refused would be excluded from the future Promised Land, which was baptized 'Free Province of New Holland in South-East Africa'. Of the Nine Articles adopted, one is more revealing than all the rest: it vowed that there would be no dealings with the British missionary societies. History has no record of Dr Philip's reactions to this resolution.

This was all very well, but the two thousand men who had just entrusted their fate to Retief wanted to know what direction to take. The problem was not made easier by the arrival of the Uys family, which joined the group after the adoption of the Nine Articles and, being independent by nature, refused to subscribe to them. A fierce clash occurred between those in favour of the northward route and those who preferred the eastern route. Potgieter led the first section, maintaining that the region between the Vaal and the Limpopo fulfilled all the emigrants' requirements fertile land and, after the flight of the Matabele, no more natives; furthermore, it would be possible to establish contacts with the Portuguese of Delagoa Bay and thus have access to the Indian Ocean; finally, was it not advisable to move as far away as possible from the British authorities, of whose intentions very little was known? History has shown how well-founded were such arguments, for the epic of the Great Trek was to culminate, after many a tragedy, in the very region recommended by Potgieter. The fascination of Natal, however, proved stronger than all reasoning: Retief, Maritz and Uys favoured this second route, and so the emigrants found themselves heading east across the mountains.

The *voortrekkers* were not unaware of the existence of the Zulu and must surely have heard of Chaka's military exploits. If so, it seems strange that they did not have misgivings. Did they tell themselves that the Zulu king had won battles only against other Blacks? Did they think that Chaka's successor was of inferior calibre? Or had their victories over the Matabele given them too much confidence? Whatever the reason, Retief appears to have been convinced that negotiations with the natives would make peaceful settlement possible. The journey began in September 1837. Potgieter followed, resigned to the decision. Retief led the advance party, crossing the Drakensberg farther to the south than Trigardt had done and over less dangerous terrain. When he and his sixteen men arrived at the top of the last mountain pass 'they saw the magnificent prospect of Natal with bush-clad ravines, fertile plains, towering peaks and ranges of hills undulating . . . the earth was carpeted with flowers'. In October they reached Port Natal.

At this time Port Natal was only a small settlement, periodically occupied and then abandoned by British traders and missionaries, the first seeking to obtain ivory, buffalo hides, cattle and maize from the natives, the second dreaming of converting the heathen. The sentiments of the Reverend Gardiner, an ex-naval officer whose only relic of his past life was the monocle he wore, were typical of the sincere and fanatical faith that inspired these missionaries. Although traders and missionaries differed in their point of view, on one question, however, they agreed: such a magnificent bay and such a beautiful hinterland should belong only to Britain. In 1834 a hundred and ninety inhabitants of the Cape had signed a petition to this effect after seeing an enthusiastic report drawn up by two men who had explored Natal. The governor contented himself with sending the document to London 'for information'. The request was rejected as out of the question. A year later Gardiner broached the matter again. This missionary should have been a courtier, for he decided to rename Port Natal after the governor, D'Urban, and name the surrounding region 'Victoria', in honour of the British princess. Then he had his decision endorsed by thirty signatures and asked the Cape authorities to appoint a governor and arrange the election of a Legislative Assembly. He received an icy reply from the Colonial Office, declaring that His Majesty's government was so convinced of the inadvisability of engaging in any programme of colonization in South Africa, or of acquiring new territories there, that it found it impossible to give the slightest encouragement to this project.

By the time Retief and then the rest of the *voortrekkers* (about a hundred wagons) arrived in Durban, Gardiner had nevertheless obtained from London various ill-defined powers over his British compatriots; a treaty with the Zulu, moreover, was supposed to guarantee him possession of the territory. But it was all so vague that the missionary must have been extremely naïve to imagine that he had achieved anything constructive. White solidarity operated to the advantage of the Boers, to whom the British accorded the warmest of welcomes, either because their experience led them to believe that they would be able to dominate the newcomers, or because they needed them in order to present a stronger front to the natives, of whose numbers they were fully aware.

To remain in Natal without the consent, voluntary or enforced, of the Zulu, established some fifty miles from Durban, was clearly out of the question. Dingaan, who had ruled the Zulu since he had murdered Chaka in 1828, had at first played the part of constitutional monarch, then had realized that this role did not suit him. As a tyrant in the manner of his predecessor he felt more at ease. His *kraal*, Umgungundhlovu ('the place of the elephant'), was situated about twenty hours away on horseback from the mouth of the Tugela. Here he lived in royal splendour, surrounded by a hundred concubines, calling himself the 'Great Elephant', the 'Lion's Paw', the 'King of Kings', allowing no one to spit or cough in his presence and only receiving visitors on their knees. These privileged persons were greeted by Dingaan seated in glory in an old armchair that served as a throne, his face covered with a light red veil held by a fringe of strings through which he scrutinized his guests. A missionary, the Reverend Owen, had been admitted to his intimate circle and was hoping to reveal to him the spirit of Christianity.

Retief obtained two audiences. He attended the second accompanied by a hundred or so men. Dances were performed by both sides, the Zulu striking the ground in rhythm and brandishing shields and assegai, the Boers on horseback firing rifle shots. The atmosphere was friendly. Dingaan willingly made his cross on a document which a lawyer would have found it hard to fault and in which he ceded a part of Natal to the 'South African Dutch emigrants'.[1] Then he invited the Boers to celebrate the occasion around pots of beer. Retief was full of confidence, in spite of the warning given him by a young Englishman, Owen's servant. He agreed to go to the appointed place with his men unarmed, since he had been assured that this was required by custom. It was about 100° F. in the shade. The guests were again honoured with dancing. Then suddenly Dingaan shrieked: *Bulalani Abatageti!* ('Kill the wizards!') A massacre followed and the corpses were dragged on to a hill above which the vultures soon started to wheel. The Reverend Owen had watched the slaughter of 6 February 1838 in horror; he managed to leave the *kraal a* few days later.

Then began the darkest days of the Great Trek. The Boers, waiting for Retief to return, were scattered and taking few precautions. An attack at Blaauwkraus, on 17 February, a moonless night, caught the Boers completely unawares, and not a single man, woman or child escaped. Gradually Maritz managed to organize resistance, and the Zulu, faced with *laagers* of the traditional type, grew weary of attacking, though not before they had inflicted heavy casualties: forty men, fifty-six women, a hundred and eighty children and two hundred Hottentot servants were killed, and twenty-five thousand head of cattle stolen. Should the Boers admit defeat and go back across the Drakensberg? Many of them would have been incapable of the journey, for they had no oxen to pull their wagons. Moreover, such a decision would not have been in keeping with the Boer character. The women, in particular, refused to give up. 'Old Father Smit' invoked the Lord, and Retief's widow declared that her husband had found his reward in heaven. It was decided to stay and counter-attack.

[1] Roughly the same territory that he had granted to Gardiner.

Potgieter and Uys were put in charge of the operation, but Uys was killed and his companion did nothing to add to his glory in a fruitless assault on the Zulu positions at Italeni on 6 April 1838. This time Potgieter, who had favoured the Transvaal, had had enough; reminding his fellow-Boers of his opposition to the Natal route, he proceeded to lead his group towards the calmer regions of the Vaal. At about this same time, the news that the Blacks had seized Port Natal and driven out the few remaining British inhabitants did not strengthen the arguments of the optimists. Many felt ready to admit that the Zulu were invincible: Retief and Uys had been killed, Potgieter had left, and the loss of these leaders was aggravated by the illness and death of Maritz. In mid-winter the attackers returned, and it took two days to force them to retire. The situation was made worse by epidemics, shortage of food and, above all, the agonizing fear that the stocks of gunpowder would soon be exhausted.

But will-power can achieve miracles. In the spring these forlorn people, who had plumbed the depths of misery, heard some wonderful news. Their own disappointments had not discouraged their fellow-countrymen, and wagons were still pouring across the Orange. In particular, Andries Pretorius, one of the wealthiest men of the Graaff-Reinet region, had decided to join them. Pretorius was known to be loyal, determined and imaginative. On his arrival on 22 November he is described as under forty years of age, tall, solidly built and armed from head to foot with a rifle, pistols and a heavy sabre. He was immediately elected commandant-general, and within a week everything had changed. Six days after assuming command, Pretorius set off at the head of about five hundred men; he was preceded by scouts well in advance of the convoy. Every night a *laager* was formed, whether or not danger threatened, and Sarel Cilliers recited prayers morning and evening. On 7 December, Pretorius and Cilliers made their companions swear that, if their efforts were crowned by victory, they would build a church.[1]

On 15 December the Boer scouts warned that the enemy was near. A *laager* of sixty-four wagons was immediately formed, under the protection of two cannon. Then they waited. In the mist the silence was broken only by the husky voices of the Boers singing hymns and psalms. Lanterns had been hung on tall poles to avert the danger of a surprise attack. As the mist cleared from time to time, the enemy's fires could be glimpsed. By five o'clock on the morning of the 16th the sun was shining in a cloudless sky. The attack was launched by a force of ten to fifteen thousand warriors. Pretorius had given orders that firing should not begin until the Zulu were only ten paces away. Within three hours four waves of Zulu had been dispersed by the defenders' fire. At about eight o'clock Pretorius sensed that the enemy was exhausted and ordered a sortie on horseback.

[1] The church was built at Pietermaritzburg.

The panic-stricken natives took to their heels and some three thousand are said to have been massacred. A river flowing nearby was so reddened with their blood that the victors dubbed their triumph the 'Battle of Blood River'. The Boers had suffered only three casualties: two dead and one wounded, Pretorius himself, who narrowly escaped death in a hand-to-hand struggle. Shortly afterwards they occupied Umgungundhlovu, no more than a pile of ashes—Dingaan had fled, destroying everything before he left.[1] Yet the Zulu resistance had not been totally crushed: eleven days after Blood River they were still capable of holding off a commando which attempted to recover some of the cattle stolen at Blaauwkraus and elsewhere.

For the time being the route to the south was free, and the Boers set off on the final stage of the Great Trek. At first they found themselves travelling under a blue sky, then in the oppressive heat of midday; in the afternoon a cold wind blew up, followed by storm after storm, and torrential rain, which poured all night, throughout the next day and the following night. Finally the sun shone. 'The women of the party gathered flowers all around,' the Reverend Smit writes. 'It is more and more indescribably beautiful.' Then the rain started again, continuing for three days on end and making the ground so slippery that the oxen could go no farther. At last, however, the Boers arrived at their haven, Pietermaritzburg,[2] barely a village but destined to become the capital of the Promised Land.

Pretorius had a disappointment in store. Twelve days before his victory British troops had landed at Port Natal. D'Urban's successor, Sir George Napier, who had arrived at the Cape at the beginning of 1838, had been comforting himself with the illusion that he would be able to bring the Boers back into the British fold. He tried to render them powerless by blocking their supplies of arms and munitions, but they solved this problem by smuggling. His attempt at negotiation proved no more successful, for the Boers politely replied that they had no confidence in Her Majesty's government. For the sake of peace and quiet Napier resolved to occupy Port Natal and temporize. He was lucky that the officer entrusted with this mission, Captain Jervis, was a man of sang-froid who succeeded in establishing peaceful coexistence with the Boers and avoiding incidents. But this patchwork solution lasted less than a year. Eventually the Colonial Office, still opposed to the undertaking of new responsibilities, ordered evacuation, which was put into effect on Christmas Eve 1839.

There remained the Zulu. A quarrel brought about Dingaan's end. Dingaan had killed his brother, Chaka, and now he was in turn betrayed by his brother Panda. According to historians, Panda was something of a

---

[1] The Boers discovered Retief's remains and, miraculously, the text of his treaty, which is now preserved in the Pietermaritzburg museum.
[2] So named in honour of Piet Retief and Gerrit Maritz.

bon vivant.[1] He had built himself a reputation for indifference, incompetence and fine manners—a missionary described him as 'a Kaffir gentleman'. Then he revealed his true self: taking seventeen thousand warriors with him, he offered the Boers an alliance which the latter did not refuse. But Panda did not really need their support, and early in 1840 his troops overwhelmed Dingaan[2] and his faithful warriors. Panda must still have felt uneasy, for he repeated his desire to co-operate with the Whites, and so he was adorned with flowers, recognized as ruling prince of the emigrant Zulu and then proclaimed king—but of a territory which Pretorius had reduced by about a half.

Now that the British and the Zulu no longer posed problems, had the dream become a reality? Had independence at last been won? The 'emigrants' had reason to believe this as they hoisted the blue flag of the new Republic of Natal, but in fact their troubles had only just begun.

[1] Perhaps they are right. The French explorer Adulphe Delegorgue was received at Panda's *kraal*. Early one morning he paid the chief a visit. The guard at the door of the hut allowed him to enter. The Frenchman was not expecting what he found there: 'On mats laid on the floor lay ten naked girls with firm and velvety contours; one was supporting his head with her body, a living pillow whose breathing induced a sleep of opium dreams; another supported his right arm; a third was still grasping his left hand and resting his temple on her large bosom; another supported the right leg and a fifth girl was lying across the left leg. They were all asleep . . .'

[2] Dingaan fled and was murdered three years later in Swaziland.

9

Years of Expectation and Confusion

The fifteen years following the Boers' arrival at the Indian Ocean is probably one of the most confused periods in the complex history of South Africa.

The Republic of Natal had a brief existence, terminating in British occupation and a Great Trek in reverse; two Kaffir wars brought further devastation to the eastern frontier; beyond the Orange, two half-caste settlements received their independence; the Blacks were concentrated in territories where they clung to the illusion of being answerable only to their chiefs; and, finally, Britain found herself compelled to grant sovereignty to the Transvaal and the Orange Free State. By the middle of the nineteenth century South Africa comprised three British colonies (the Cape, Natal and British Kaffraria), two Boer states (the Transvaal and the Orange Free State), two Coloured states (territories of Adam Kok and Andries Waterboer), and six large native agglomerations (Swazi, Zulu, Pondo, Tembu, Basuto and Bechuana).

The term 'balkanization' has been used to describe this process of fragmentation. But would it not be more exact to say that, consciously or not, the rulers of the country were trying to practise the policy of 'to each his own domain' which van Riebeeck had favoured two hundred years earlier and which is the basis of the present-day doctrine of 'separate development'?

Space, a commodity which the Boers always coveted, was not lacking in Natal; and so, after staying together for a time, they dispersed. They might well have adopted a new motto—'In the matter of land, possession is nine points of the law'—for they settled wherever the soil was fertile and rivers abounded. Seven to ten thousand acres once again became the normal area of their farms, where they often lived in huts made of wood and reeds and plastered with cow-dung. Sometimes there was no track for thirty to sixty miles around, but this did not worry them; they had found, or so they imagined, what they most wanted: the opportunity to do what they liked in conditions of their own choosing.

Although they were all individualists, their republic needed a minimum of government. The problem of local administration was easily solved

by reverting to the Dutch system of districts under the control of a *landdrost* assisted by *heemraden*. The organization of the central power created more difficulties. All were agreed in recognizing the principle of the sovereignty of the people, and so everyone (women excluded) participated in the election of a legislative assembly of twenty-four members (the *Volksraad* or Council of the People). It is curious, however, that these men who had undergone every possible tribulation should not have been more aware of the necessity of a powerful executive. In time of war the post of commandant-general was maintained; but, in time of peace, no one person was entitled to speak in the name of the Republic.

The drawbacks of such an ill-balanced constitution did not reveal themselves immediately. On the first problem that presented itself, the native question, the Boers were unanimous and their ideas clear-cut: they intended to make use of local labour by maintaining, in accordance with their traditional formula, 'proper relations between master and servant'—in other words, an unquestioned and paternal authority. To prevent vagrancy the servants were subject to a system of pass laws, like the Hottentots in earlier days. Although the Blacks were necessary, however, there must not be too many of them, and so to north and south lines of demarcation were fixed—always rivers—which they were forbidden to cross under pain of death.

Andries Pretorius was the power behind the Republic. He had saved his fellow-countrymen and knew their weaknesses. If Natal really seemed the Promised Land, was there not a danger that the British might return there sooner or later? The Boers would be in a better position to resist if they were more numerous. Pretorius therefore made contact with Potgieter who, established in his 'capital' of Potchefstroom to the north of the Vaal, remained convinced that the future was on his side. Potgieter did not, however, refuse to take part in negotiations, which resulted in 1841 in an ill-defined union of the two Republics. Pretorius was to remain commandant-general in Natal, Potgieter in the Transvaal; but the *Volksraad* at Pietermaritzburg would be increased by twelve members representing the emigrants west of the Drakensberg. As always, no provision was made for arbitration in the event of a dispute.

History does not reveal the identity of the wise man who suggested that it might be advisable to inform the British authorities of these decisions, a proposal which the *Volksraad* implemented in courteous terms, expressing its hope that it would please Her Majesty to recognize the Boers as a free and independent people. The new governor, Sir George Napier, was a simple person incapable of understanding how sensible men could be unwilling to live under the British flag. He asked the applicants for independence to clarify their position, and in reply they proposed an alliance, promising to seek the protection of the British navy in the event of aggression by sea, undertaking not to attack the tribes between Natal and the Cape Colony (except in an emergency), and guaranteeing

the rights of the British residents—assurances that ill concealed their longing for total sovereignty.

The policy of Downing Street hovered between opposing influences: the fear of a new native war and the obsession with economy. All expansion was therefore regarded with disfavour. If the Boers had followed Potgieter's advice, the Colonial Office might have grown weary of disputing their right to independence. But they were occupying Natal. South Africa was of little importance to Britain except as a stage on the route to India. To allow a foreign state to be established beside the Indian Ocean, to see it fall under the influence of a European power, was to risk jeopardizing the mother country's communications with the jewel of her colonial possessions.

Napier was convinced of the gravity of the problem; in other words, the emigrants' claims were not passed on to London with a favourable recommendation. He still needed a pretext to intervene, which the Boers supplied him with their customary imprudence. One of their commandos had set out on a punitive expedition against a tribe to the south of Natal. The avengers killed some thirty Blacks and brought back three thousand head of cattle and seventeen 'orphans' to whom they awarded the highly equivocal status of 'apprentices'. The missionaries immediately protested at what they called 'slavery', and the governor condemned the raids as an act of flagrant cruelty and injustice. With the agreement of the British government Napier sent a garrison to the region where the raid had occurred. Then, in December 1841, he announced his decision to reoccupy Port Natal; so as to leave no doubts of his intentions, he told the Boers that, having refused to be recognized as British subjects, they had placed themselves beyond the protection of the law.

It is easy to imagine the feelings which the announcement provoked. The advocates of intransigence and of compromise argued one against the other. All were agreed, however, in making a solemn protest in a document of touching sincerity which recalled their reasons for leaving the Cape; its thirteen octavo pages make one wonder if it was read with the attention it deserved. As the weeks passed and no redcoats appeared, the Boers comforted themselves with the hope that the British government had changed its mind. Having lived in a vacuum for several years, their illusions were great, and these were given full rein when a Dutch ship, the *Brazilia*, called at Durban in March 1842. The sight of its blue, yellow and red flag, bearing the arms of the House of Orange, awakened in them an ancestral patriotism which time and distance had partially numbed. The shipping merchant's representative, Johan Smellekamp, was given a triumphant welcome, toasts were drunk to the king and thanksgiving offered to the Lord. The visitor was delighted with his reception, especially since his instructions were to establish trading relations with Natal. He was promised all sorts of wonders. For his part, Smellekamp gave his hosts to understand that The Hague had not forgotten them, and, knowing of what was happening in the world, they had no difficulty in believing him. Matters assumed an official character when he persuaded the *Volksraad* to sign a treaty by which the emigrants entrusted their fate to the Netherlands. Then he left, insisting that the royal approval would be a formality.

Alas, not two months had gone by when Captain Thomas Charlton Smith appeared before Port Natal at the head of two hundred and fifty men. A little stage-setting was essential. The drums began to beat, with the troops marching past as on a parade, the infantry in red uniforms, with fixed bayonets, the sappers and artillerymen in blue and gold, the cavalry in dark green tunics and brown trousers. The Republican and Dutch flags, flying side by side, were lowered. The commander of the detachment gave the order to present arms, and the Union Jack soared upwards, flapping in the wind.

What was to be done—resist or surrender? Resistance was so much a part of the Boer character that, in the heat of the moment, this course of action met with no objections. For fifteen days the two sides watched each other, the British near the sea, the Boers farther inland at a place called Congella. On 23 May, Smith decided to attack. This first encounter between British troops and Boers did not turn out well for the British, whose casualties included seventeen dead, thirty-one wounded and two cannon lost. Then Pretorius took the offensive. The encircled British garrison seemed to have been driven to the point of surrender when it was saved by a feat of valour: one Dick King, whose name became a legend, managed to escape, jumped on his horse and, accompanied by a Zulu, covered in ten days the five hundred miles or so separating Durban and Grahamstown, where he gave the alert. A month later reinforcements arrived; the Boers had to give way before the enemy's superior numbers and withdrew to Pietermaritzburg.

This was the beginning of the end. Three years passed. For a time the fanciful hopes of the emigrants were prolonged by an administrative fiction: their *Volksraad* continued to function, but under British supervision. Then the *Brazilia* reappeared on the horizon. The British would not allow it to anchor—thereby sparing the vanquished Boers one more disappointment, for the king of the Netherlands had hastened to inform London that he completely disowned the grandiose schemes of the presumptuous Smellekamp. In 1843, Napier made up his mind to settle things once and for all, and on 12 May the district of Port Natal was declared a British colony under the authority of a High Commissioner, Henry Cloete. Three principles were to guide the new administration: no more slavery, equality of Whites and natives, and the prohibition of commandos.

The Boers made one last effort. From beyond the Drakensberg nearly a thousand of them arrived to display their solidarity, launching protest after protest. But words and demonstrations of feeling were futile—the game was over. The victors allowed the *Volksraad* to function for another two years, though it was now stripped of all power and, moreover, no longer represented anything: the *volk*, the 'people', had gone and their wagons were once more crossing the mountains, but in the opposite direction. The Promised Land had collapsed under the emigrants' feet, and yet their dream had not faded: they were trekking into the setting sun to find their brothers in lands where they would hear no more of the British government. For the time being they felt, quite justifiably, that they had been the tool of Her Gracious Majesty.

Sir George Napier left his post in 1844 and was succeeded by another general, the son-in-law of the Duke of Richmond, Sir Peregrine Maitland, a worthy and irascible Irishman of sixty-seven who probably had no other ambition than to reach his retirement without mishap.

Events gave him no such opportunity. Hardly had he arrived than the insoluble Xhosa problem assumed a new urgency. The solution of appeasement imposed by Glenelg in 1836 had satisfied no one: neither the Boers who had remained in the Colony and who considered themselves the victims of an injustice, nor the Xhosa whose success had not diminished their marauding instincts. In short, the classic process of raids and reprisals persisted. The new governor showed little imagination, deluding himself that by arranging three more treaties he had brought the Pax Britannica to the eastern borderlands; just to be sure, however, he ordered the completion of a fort which had been started by Napier to the east of Fish river.

One incident was enough to demolish this diplomatic and military house of cards. In March 1846 a native, convicted of killing a Hottentot and stealing an axe[1] in European territory, managed to escape. The British authorities demanded his extradition, but the Xhosa refused—they probably had little idea what the word meant. Thereupon Maitland, who had a fondness for protocol, formally declared war and invaded the enemy territory at the head of regular troops, Boer commandos and loyal Xhosa—in all some fourteen thousand men, the most powerful army that had ever been assembled on the frontier. Order was soon restored, but by severe methods. 'The effect of the peaceful penetration of Hottentot and Bantu land by the earlier Boers was indeed as nothing to the systematic havoc wrought among the Amaxhosa,' observes Professor Macmillan.

Some reconstruction was now necessary. Lord Grey, son of Fox's successor, occupied the post of Secretary for the Colonies. The detailed instructions which he sent to the Cape at the end of 1846 gave him an opportunity to clarify his own ideas. 'An enlightened regard for the real welfare of our uncivilized neighbours not less than for the welfare of the

[1] Hence the name 'War of the Axe' often given to this Seventh Kaffir War (1846-8).

colonists, requires that the Kaffir tribes should no longer be left in possession of the independence they have so long enjoyed and abused.' Reverting to the policy of D'Urban, the new minister was thus affirming his determination to deprive the natives of the former Queen Adelaide Province—not to annex it, but to make it a protectorate under a British Resident and with a few garrisons at strategic points. 'I should propose to grant to the more friendly and trustworthy of the native chiefs some small stipends and to assign them such distinctions, titles and ornaments as would enlist their vanity in our support.' It might also be desirable to form Kaffir regiments which, under the command of British officers, would be sent to the western provinces where they would serve as hostages. In conclusion Lord Grey declared that 'experience has fully shown the futility of such treaties. . . . It would be probably better to trust to a general understanding that the British authority is to be supreme and to be in all cases implicitly obeyed.'

After an interlude of eleven months, during which the fate of South Africa—'the British Algeria', as it was known in London—had been entrusted to Sir Henry Pottinger, an expert in Far Eastern affairs, the inimitable Sir Harry Smith returned to the scene, this time as governor.

Sir Harry arrived from India on 1 December 1847, basking in the glory of his victories over the Sikhs. Cape Town, which had been illuminated for the occasion, gave him an enthusiastic welcome. He had not changed in the past ten years: he was still as extravagant a figure as ever and, if one is to judge by his letters, just as much in love with his *alma mia*, as he called his wife. Indecisiveness was not one of his weaknesses: ten days after taking up his duties he was in Kaffirland, assembling the native chiefs and organizing the sort of theatrical display at which he excelled. Nearby he had set up a trek wagon of the traditional type. 'Look at this wagon,' he shouted at the stupefied gathering. At a signal from him the wagon exploded: 'That is what I shall do for you if you do not behave!' Then he picked out the most notorious of the rebels, forced him to lie down in front of him, put his foot on his neck and, brandishing a sabre, announced: 'This is the way I shall treat the enemies of the Queen of England.' More dead than alive, the victim got up to join his companions, whom the governor proceeded to inform of his decisions after first making them kiss his hand. The western part of the territory was attached to the Cape Colony under the name of Victoria East. The rest, the former Queen Adelaide Province, between the Keiskamma and the Kei, became a British possession as British Kaffraria. The audience was then treated to a little lecture on constitutional law and Christian morality. 'No more treaties', proclaimed the governor; and, to make himself understood, he tore a piece of paper into tiny shreds. He informed the natives that they were now British subjects, an honour which also involved responsibilities, and told them to get rid of their witch-doctors, dress themselves like everyone else, forget their dialects, learn English and, most important of all, stop practising polygamy. It is a pity that a photographer could not have caught the expressions of the natives as they listened to this tirade—assuming they could understand it.

Sir Harry Smith then headed for the Transorangia district, where no less serious problems awaited him. The confusion of races was infinitely greater in this region than in Kaffirland. The south was inhabited by the Griqua, a people of mixed blood, half-European and half-Hottentot. Since they held the territory between Cape Colony and the north of the continent, their strategic position would in itself have made it impossible to ignore them. Furthermore, armed with rifles and practising a way of life similar to that of the less civilized Europeans, they were not at all inclined to let themselves be assimilated or dispersed as their Hottentot ancestors had been. Sir Harry Smith, imitating the example of his predecessors, therefore concluded a treaty with them which guaranteed them a measure of independence over a vaguely defined territory.

This was only one stage in the governor's plan for a more far-reaching solution. Near the Griqua were the Basuto, occupying the Drakensberg mountains under the great chief Moshesh. Then there were the Boers who, scattered everywhere and convinced of their superiority, did not make coexistence among the races any easier. Always tending to quarrel among themselves, they were divided into three factions. One, led by Michiel Oberholster, comprised those Boers whom the British modestly called the 'well-disposed'; the die-hards had as their spokesman Jan Mocke; and the idea of compromise was embodied in the person of Jacobus Snyman. Smith was too typically British not to be confident that the only way to reconcile these irreconcilables was to place them all under the sovereignty of his queen. On 2 February 1848, after obtaining the qualified approval of Moshesh, he proclaimed the whole of the territory between the Orange and the Vaal a British possession under the name of the Orange River Sovereignty, 'for the maintenance of a just peace, the improvement of the condition of the people and the advancement of the blessing of Christianity, civilization and habits of industry and honesty which will elevate and civilize the barbarians and support and uphold the Christian community'.

On 1 March this expert at annexations returned to the Cape, highly satisfied with his achievement. He felt sorry for the Boers; he had met some of them in the Drakensberg, 'exposed to a state of misery which I never before saw equalled, except in Masséna's invasion of Portugal'. He was sure that he was acting for the good of his 'children', as he persisted in calling the emigrants. In a triumphant tone he communicated his feelings to Lord Grey. 'I am induced to believe that, as the case I have described "Great Trek", so the measures stand alone as regards the peculiarity of their nature.' The jealousies that were tearing all these racial groups apart 'are at once banished by the establishment of the paramount power of H.M.' As for those men 'over whom a succession of singular circumstances have exercised their baleful influence and led astray', Smith guaranteed their 'loyalty and good faith' for the future. The Colonial Office acquiesced, but with the reservations dictated by its constant concern with economies: 'The country must not be held in any way responsible for the protection of the persons who have chosen to establish themselves in these wild and distant regions and . . . they must be contented with such rude institutions and such means of defence as they can themselves provide and afford the means of paying for.' In other words, don't cause us any more trouble, and don't count on us to help you! If the intention was clear enough, its implementation removed all possible doubts: Smith left behind him only sixty or so cavalrymen to patrol a territory of roughly fifty thousand square miles.

The governor imagined that Pretorius was himself ready to rally to the Union Jack. It would have been asking a great deal of this Boer to expect him to accept British sovereignty in Transorangia, when this was the very reason that had induced him to leave Natal. Conversations between the two men led only to misunderstandings. Smith grew impatient. Was it not scandalous that reasonable human beings endowed with immortal souls should want to deprive themselves of the benefits which he was bringing them? He called Pretorius a 'demagogue'. This was a declaration of war. Pretorius began by holding a series of public meetings, always with the same programme: a prayer, a recollection of the Great Trek, a reading of the texts instituting British sovereignty, then an appeal to everyone to form a single Republic, from the Orange to the Zoutpansberg, perhaps including Natal. But words were no longer enough. Once again, the squabbling among the Boers damaged their cause. Potgieter, firmly anchored in 'his' Transvaal, refused to lend his support, and so Pretorius had to act alone. At first fortune smiled on him: with a few hundred men he took possession of Winburg and then, on 17 July 1848, captured Bloemfontein, forcing the small British garrison to surrender.

When the news reached the Cape a few days later, the governor could hardly believe his ears. But Smith preferred actions to words, and so he set a price of a thousand pounds on the capture of Pretorius, appealed to his Griqua allies, assembled all the troops at his disposal and, on 29 August, presented himself before his enemies at Bloomplatz, to the north-east of Philippolis, at the head of a thousand men. The battle did not last long, for the British artillery and cavalry quickly got the better of the Boers. Then Sir Harry assumed his haughty manner: on Sunday 2 September he entered Bloemfontein and celebrated his victory with a march-past and a religious ceremony at which he read the service himself. On the 7th he was at Winburg, where twenty-one cannon-shots saluted the restoration of British sovereignty; the conquering hero, in full uniform of blue and gold tunic and white trousers, was flanked by his Griqua ally, Adam Kok, and his Basuto ally, Moshesh, who had dressed himself for the occasion in a general's old blue coat and gold-laced trousers. No sooner had the fire been extinguished in one place than it flared up in another.

In the spring of 1850 some alarming news reached Cape Town. The Xhosa, clearly impervious to the benefits of British Christian civilization, were again showing signs of insubordination. Smith was all the more worried because the forces at his disposal had been reduced by two thousand men since the end of the 'War of the Axe'. But he was confident that his presence would settle everything. Leaving for Kaffirland on 15 October, he there deposed in his absence a chief to whom he had taken a dislike and returned to Cape Town on 24 November, no doubt tempted to borrow Caesar's *veni, vidi, vici.*

Alas, as had happened in 1834 and 1846, the Xhosa revolted en masse on Christmas Day. This was too much. The governor now looked on them as nothing but cruel, treacherous and ungrateful savages. His indignation reached its peak when a group of Hottentot troops deserted. All this had happened at a particularly inopportune moment, for the government in London was growing increasingly weary of these problems which were supposed to have been solved but were always recurring. It was fashionable at the time to criticize these wars as 'ignominious if unsuccessful, inglorious if successful'—wars which in neither case settled anything. The slowness with which the situation was taken in hand gave the august *Times* occasion to indulge in some ironical comment. 'It is delightful, doubtless, to regulate in an office in Downing Street the domestic affairs of the antipodes, but the people of England must remember they purchase this intellectual treat by a needless annual outlay of some two million, with an occasional bonus of another two million on the cost of a Kaffir war.' If they do not want us, the Colonial Office eventually informed Smith, all we can do is leave—and the sooner the better. Poor Sir Harry! What a contrast to his glorious days of 1848! He clung stubbornly to his position, but so did the Xhosa. Smith suffered his crowning humiliation when Lord Grey, recalling him at the beginning of 1852, accused him of not having shown 'that foresight, energy and judgement which your very difficult position required'. His successor, Sir George Cathcart, knew the limits of his mandate as soon as he was appointed: it was made clear to him that, apart from the very limited territory necessary for the security of the Cape as a naval base, the only motives for British activity in South Africa were the protection of Britain's faithful subjects and the philanthropic desire to promote Christianity and civilization.

The 'inglorious' war[1] dragged on into 1853, when it was brought to an

---

[1] Not always inglorious. A troop-ship, the *Birkenhead*, ran aground on a reef and began to list dangerously. To prevent it keeling over and to save the women and children on board, the officers lined their men along the deck, all on the same side of the ship. The troops remained standing at attention right to the end (357 out of 506 were drowned). The king of Prussia ordered that at every parade this feat of arms should be brought to the knowledge of his regiments.

end. Even beyond the Kei river European officials were installed side by side with the tribal chiefs. The natives were concentrated in territories whose density could be as much as sixty inhabitants per square mile, whereas ten or twelve should have been the absolute limit in view of their methods of stock-raising. But comfort was taken in the hope that they would learn to use the plough.

By immobilizing nearly all the troops on the eastern frontier, the Kaffir War did not ease the task of Major Warden who, with a handful of men, was supposed to maintain British supremacy in the Orange River Sovereignty. Warden considered himself quite capable of confronting Moshesh, but in June 1851 the Basuto chief showed him that his tribe's fighting qualities had not diminished. Warden had to make a rather pitiful retreat and ask for reinforcements. London finally granted his request, but with the greatest reluctance, reproaching its representative for having acted without instructions.

The Boers were presented with an opportunity when Moshesh and then the Zulu in Natal offered them an alliance. To join up with Blacks against Whites, however, would in any circumstances have been contrary to all the *voortrekkers*' principles. Pretorius preferred to act alone. The situation was dreadfully complicated. As always, the bickering among his compatriots prevented him from speaking in the name of all. Even north of the Vaal three 'republics', which have justly been compared to the Italian cities of the Middle Ages, had been established. In 1845, when British ambitions in the Orange district had been proclaimed, Potgieter had judged it expedient to move as far away as possible from an authority which he was less than ever inclined to recognize. By crossing the 25th parallel, the limit of the extravagant Punishment Act,[1] he thought he would be safer. Moreover, he was hoping to establish contacts with the Portuguese and thus have access to the Indian Ocean. He started by founding a new 'capital', Ohrigstad, about two hundred and fifty miles north-east of Potchefstroom. The climate here was unhealthy, however, and three years later he moved to the foothills of the Zoutpansberg where, from another settlement named Schoemansdal, he claimed by right of priority to govern the whole of the Transvaal. Wanting to hear no more of the British, he withdrew into a policy of 'splendid isolation'.

A second group of Boers, who had come from Natal and settled at Lydenburg in the eastern Transvaal, were not far from sharing the same attitude, though their leader, J. J. Burger, was playing a balancing game between the two great men, Potgieter and Pretorius. Eventually Pretorius emerged triumphant, maintaining that the independence of his fellow-countrymen would remain an empty word as long as it had not been ratified by the British government. A part of the population of the Orange River Sovereignty appealed to him to intervene. Pretorius, it will be

[1] See p. 92.

recalled, had been outlawed, which did not make negotiation easy. In September 1851 he nevertheless decided to make contact with Warden, without consulting a *Volksraad* whose authority no longer existed except on paper. Smith felt that the circumstances hardly permitted an attitude of intransigence, and the British government, more impatient than ever of being haunted by the South African problem, sent two plenipotentiaries to negotiate with the ex-rebel, who had previously been granted an amnesty.

British and Boers met on 17 January 1852 at a farmhouse to the north of the Sand river, in the Winburg region. Both sides were anxious to bring matters to a successful conclusion. 'If we could obtain co-operation of men trained in and accustomed to bush warfare,' a British document shamelessly stated, 'the Kaffirs would no longer appear such dangerous enemies. No time should be lost to repair the errors that have made these men our enemies instead of friends and invaluable allies.' It is not difficult to imagine the feelings of the Boer leader, Pretorius. How glorious it would be to pass into history as the founder of the independent Republic of the Transvaal!

One day of talks was enough. The sovereignty of the Boers beyond the Vaal was recognized without reservation; the British undertook to sign no treaties with the natives of the region and not to supply them with arms or ammunition. One provision sanctioned a principle dear to the *voortrekkers*: 'In the matter of master and servants, every master shall have the right to maintain discipline properly among his servants.' The only qualifications were the prohibition of ill-treatment and slavery. When he put his signature to the Sand River Convention, as history has designated this agreement, Pretorius must have felt that, all in all, the Great Trek had not been in vain.

There remained the question of the Orange River Sovereignty. Sir George Cathcart, regardless of some unhappy experiences, tried in his turn to bring Moshesh to his senses, accusing him of repeated thefts—in which he was probably right—and ordering him to return a thousand horses and ten thousand head of cattle within three days. The Basuto chief would not commit himself, suggesting an extended time-limit and adding this warning: 'Do not talk of war.... A dog when beaten will show his teeth.' Then he handed over a third of the animals demanded. Cathcart considered it beneath his dignity to be satisfied with this; gathering together two thousand five hundred men, he marched on Thaba Bosigo, his adversary's impregnable capital. What followed added nothing to his reputation, for after suffering a series of attacks he had to beat a retreat. Moshesh showed that he was as good a diplomatist as a strategist: pretending to be incapable of resisting any longer, he assured the governor of the purity of his intentions and, for good measure, even delivered a few cattle-thieves to the British. This was more than Cathcart could have hoped for, and he returned to Cape Town determined never to come back to this hornets' nest.

The incident proved decisive, confirming the Colonial Office's conviction that this 'sovereignty' was only costing money without ever yielding a return. At the same time, the European horizon was darkening, and the possibility of a war against Russia could no longer be dismissed. The Whigs, who had just returned to power, decided to entrust a special envoy, Sir George Clerk, former governor of Bombay, with the task of conducting an inquiry on the spot. Downing Street was inclined towards the relinquishment of the Sovereignty, but a part of the White population, in particular some speculators who had recently arrived, protested against this policy with such vigour that Clerk was left with the responsibility for making a decision. He judged the situation with perspicacity: 'The sentiments of the majority continue to be what they ever have been; they are averse to British administration and envy their fellow-exiles across the Vaal living contentedly and peacefully under self-government.'

The government in London, which was really only interested in the sea route to the Cape and Natal, must have read Clerk's report with relief rather than displeasure. Furthermore, two buffer-states instead of one might protect the Colony more effectively against the 'barbarians', as it was now customary to call the 'aborigines' of earlier days. On 23 February 1854, at Bloemfontein, a Convention was signed which in its broad lines resembled the Sand River Convention. The Orange Free State was born.

In less than twenty years many changes had taken place on the territorial map of southern Africa. It is now time to consider changes of a different nature and of no less far-reaching consequences.

10

Economic and Constitutional Transformations

The distance from the tip of the continent to the loop of the Limpopo is about twelve hundred miles, and to the mouth of the Tugela about a thousand miles. These figures indicate the extent of European expansion in South Africa towards the middle of the nineteenth century. But the country was still underdeveloped and the conquest of its political liberties only just beginning.

From the outset the great weakness of the Colony had been its lack of natural resources. Canada had flourished first with its furs and then with its wood. The representatives of the Dutch East India Company and their British successors enjoyed no such opportunities. For a time it had seemed that ivory might become a fruitful source of trade. Elephants were plentiful around Table Bay when van Riebeeck settled there; but as land was cleared they disappeared, and the hunters had to travel farther and farther to find them, so that an elephant-hunt became more like an exploration (the Orange was crossed for the first time in 1760 by an elephant-hunter). In the Colony itself there remained enough animals for the trade in hides to develop of its own accord. It is understandable, however, that the Dutch governors should not have been content with exporting hides only, even when supplemented with a little wheat and a few other products. It seemed that wines could usefully be added to their exports to Europe.[1] Preferential duties and then the Continental System opened up the British market, and during the first quarter of the nineteenth century wine represented half of the Cape's foreign trade. Nevertheless, whatever the quality of the vineyards of Constantia, they could not hope to compete indefinitely against those of Bordeaux and Burgundy. In 1831 buyers of French vintages obtained a considerable reduction of the advantages accorded to the Colony. This marked the beginning of a progressive fall in wine exports, which by 1860 had almost come to a standstill.

Thus, a hundred years ago the problem of foreign trade had not yet

[1] Professor Serton quotes a typical example of a cargo in 1792: wine, wheat, talc and aloes.

been solved. Chronic overproduction followed by a slump remained the pattern of South African economic life. Two products, however, offered hope for the future: wool, which had been in production for a long time, and sugar-cane, which had begun to be cultivated quite recently.

Home-bred sheep, such as those reared by the Hottentots, were useful only as butcher's meat. It had been necessary to import other breeds. The early experiments proved disappointing, but everything changed when two governors, Caledon in 1808 and Somerset in 1818, introduced merinos. Wool production then grew with startling rapidity: 20,000 lb exported in 1822; 200,000 lb in 1832; 1,372,000 lb in 1842, at which time wine dropped to second place; then an even swifter increase—twenty times as much within twenty years, leading to a total of 25 million lb in 1862.

The Orange Free State territory and the Cape Colony were the principal centres of this new activity. Along the coastal region of Natal, where the climate was favourable, sugar-cane was developed. The planters, however, had no labour at their disposal. The Bantu had no desire to leave their reserves and, when they were eventually persuaded to come nearer to the sea, they proved unsuited, as always, to occupations other than cattle-raising. On the island of Mauritius, it was said, coolies were working wonders, and so the South African planters decided that they too would use Indian labourers. The first landed in 1860, mostly from the Madras region (83 per cent Buddhists, 12 per cent Muslims and 5 per cent Christians). The maximum proportion of women was fixed at 50 per cent. When this experiment proved highly successful the arrivals of Indians multiplied, reaching thirty thousand by the end of the century. An economic obstacle had been surmounted, but a new racial problem had been created.

Neither sugar nor wool provided enough exports to pay for the raw materials and manufactured products which the country needed. Its development was therefore an extremely slow process until the discovery of diamonds and gold, the miraculous consequences of which will be described later.

At the time of the constitution of the Boer Republics, exports stood at £1,330,000 and imports at £1,558,000. This deficit could be made good only by an outflow of bullion, for the credit system was still primitive. The cost of money could be as high as 12 per cent, even on sureties of real estate, and when the Cape Colony or Natal dared to ask for a loan the City made them pay 6 per cent interest. The absence of a banking system did not make things easier. Until 1831 only one such institution, the Lombard Bank, was in operation, and even then under government control. Subsequently, various private enterprises led to the creation of numerous establishments whose geographical distribution twenty-five years later is revealing: seventeen in the Colony, two in the Free State, one in Natal and none in the Transvaal. But it was not until the opening of the London and South Africa Bank and the Standard Bank in 1861 and 1862 that South Africa could boast of finally having established a credit machinery.

The construction of railways had followed an equally slow pace: in 1863 only two lines existed, one of about sixty miles from Cape Town to Stellenbosch and Wellington, the other running along the peninsula to Wynberg, twenty miles from the capital. Everywhere else people travelled on tracks or on the few existing roads (the first roads were not begun until after 1840). It was not until the 1850s that postal communications became regular in the Cape Colony and that a monthly link was established between Cape Town and Britain. The incomparable Table Bay, moreover, was still dangerous during the winter months, when ships had to anchor there without the protection of a jetty and without docks; these were not built until after 1860.

The enormous advances that were soon to be made show that the spirit of enterprise was not lacking. But the numerical insufficiency of the White population proved an even more serious handicap than the shortage of natural resources. It is estimated that about 250,000 Europeans inhabited the country in 1865; their distribution indicates how underpopulated certain regions must have been: 180,000 in the Cape Colony, 35,000 in the Orange Free State, 20,000 to 30,000 in the Transvaal and 18,000 in Natal. The growth of the population had been almost entirely due to the birth-rate. Between 1820 and 1860 the average number of immigrants did not exceed seven hundred and fifty per year. The only appreciable influx of immigrants took place between 1840 and 1850, when four to five thousand workmen were imported to build roads, followed a little later by another six thousand, the majority of whom soon left South Africa for the goldmines of Australia; apart from five thousand German Legionaries who settled in the East London region after the Crimean War, that was all. During this same period, observes Professor Marquard, 'hundreds of thousands of Britons settled in New Zealand, Australia, and Canada. During the years 1841 and 1842 alone, when Boers were leaving the Cape Colony in large numbers, 62,000 Britons emigrated to Canada, 80,000 to the United States, 18,600 to Australia and New Zealand, and 340 to the Cape.'

This low population density and the territorial fragmentation described in the previous chapter inevitably had their effects on political development.

During the first half of the nineteenth century the Colony remained under the authority of an autocratic régime subject to various controls. The efficacy of these depended on the personalities of the governors, who, all military men with the single exception of Caledon, were more concerned with discipline than with liberty. Nevertheless, even though it lay so far from Europe and the United States, democratic doctrines gradually penetrated into southern Africa. Lord Somerset, it will be remembered, had been obliged to accept that his most important decisions be ratified by a Council of Advice (which admittedly was appointed by himself). But the British Crown's representative continued to concentrate all powers in his own person. The institution of a Supreme Court in 1827 deprived him of the right to make judicial decisions. Seven years later the principles of Locke were timidly applied for the first time. By accepting the creation of two Councils, the British government pretended to sanction the separation of the executive and the legislature, but this concession to doctrine was encumbered with so many fine distinctions that it remained a dead letter. The Excutive Council was supposed to fulfil the function of a cabinet of ministers; however, the Crown appointed its members, and the governor was empowered to ignore its recommendations in an 'emergency', a highly flexible concept at a time when it took several months for a reply to arrive from London. The Legislative Council was hardly representative of the people: the officials were in a minority of five, against five to seven colonists, but both groups were chosen by the governor, who made sure that a balance was maintained between the two, reserving the casting vote for himself. Sir George Napier, with typically military frankness, made it clear what both he and his colleagues thought of this so-called Legislative Council: on one occasion he advised the opposition not to waste its breath, as the important decisions were taken elsewhere.

From time to time the more liberal elements in the Colony demanded that the régime be made more democratic. But the British government had no difficulty in countering their requests with two equally valid objections. One, concerning the racial question, was unequivocally formulated by Lord Stanley in 1842: no one envisaged universal suffrage; but, he pointed out, how should a suffrage based on property-qualification be conceived? If a high minimum of property were specified, nearly the whole of the African-born population would be excluded. If the government were more generous, there would be the risk of arousing strong misgivings among the Europeans. Lord Stanley declared that this proposal had not been given mature consideration. Downing Street offered another reason for these delaying tactics. The Boers were in a majority in the western part of the Colony; the British, mostly settlers of 1820, had established themselves in the east where, since the Great Trek, they represented a large proportion of the White population. Since the two groups mistrusted each other, how, it was argued in London, could power be handed over to people divided by feelings of hostility, many of whom were even demanding separate capitals and administrations?

In 1849 an unexpected incident, which could be said to be the first manifestation of South African nationalism, revealed that the two groups were quite capable of uniting. There was no more room in British prisons, packed with thousands of Irishmen whom the tragic 'potato famine' of 1848 had provoked to acts of desperation. It had become the practice to send the overflow of convicts to Australia, but using only that country for the purpose had its disadvantages. Between 1839 and 1845 three Secretaries for the Colonies, Russell, Stanley and Gladstone, had asked the governor of Cape Town if he would object to South Africa sharing the privilege with Australia. The first two replies had been negative; the third, less uncompromising, hinted at the possibility of acceptance on the understanding that the newcomers would be strictly supervised and would not be freed on their arrival. In 1848, Sir Harry Smith, still bubbling over with zeal, thought it advisable to put himself in the position of applicant. This was more than London could have expected, and immediately the *Neptune* set sail for the Cape with two hundred and eighty-eight convicts on ticket of leave, which allowed them considerable freedom of movement.

The storm of feeling in the Colony was extraordinary: eight public meetings, the creation of an Anti-Convict Association led by John Fairbairn (who twenty years earlier had achieved fame by obtaining the freedom of the Press), mass resignations and boycotting of official invitations, including a governor's ball! In dismay, Smith forbade the landing of the convicts. The *Neptune* remained in the roadstead from September 1849 to February 1850. when the British government resigned itself to ordering the captain to make for Tasmania. Lord Grey must have read and re-read the governor's comments: this was, Smith told him, the first occasion on which Dutch and British had united in common opposition; they had shaken hands and were standing side by side.

The British government took four years to learn the lesson offered by this sudden expression of the popular will. Since the Durham Report,[1] however, liberal ideas had been fashionable. To give the colonies—'these wretched colonies' in Disraeli's words—the right to govern themselves would be in keeping with British tradition; it would also mean handing over to them a financial burden which the mother country was more and more loath to bear; and it would release military forces whose presence in Europe was required by the diplomatic situation. Under the combined pressure of these influences the Cape was endowed, on 11 March 1853, with a constitution which it was to retain until the Act of Union of 1910.

This decision coincided with the recognition of the Boer Republics, which now organized their own political systems. This sudden profusion of constitutions, though doubtless desirable from a democratic point of view, was hardly conducive to the unity of the country.

[1] Lord Durham, sent to Canada after the rebellions of 1837, had pronounced in favour of representative government.

In the Cape Colony two assemblies were provided, both elected on a property-owning franchise. The minimum property required for voting in the elections to the lower house or House of Assembly was fixed at the very low figure of £25 which, it has been calculated, corresponded to an annual rent of 30 shillings; this meant that 80 per cent of the male population enjoyed the right to vote. Any qualified elector could seek election. The selection of the upper house or Legislative Council, on the other hand, was subject to strict conditions: to become a member a man had to be at least thirty years of age and in possession either of lands worth at least £2,000 or of a fortune of £4,000 free of all debts. The two houses formed the Parliament. Like the Parliament at Westminster, it could not initiate government expenditure. All proposed legislation was submitted for its approval, but under conditions that placed it in a position very different from that of its British counterpart. About a third of the supplies voted, for the salaries of officials, religious worship and the surveillance of the frontier, was regarded as having been granted once and for all. The governor had the right of veto, and for a period of two years the government in London retained the power to rescind any legislation that it considered undesirable. Above all, the fundamental principle of parliamentary government had been ignored, for the queen's representative continued to be responsible only to the Crown.

In 1856 Natal was also awarded a constitution, but one even more limited than that of the Cape Colony: a single assembly, two-thirds of its members elected and one-third nominated by the governor; a stricter property-qualification than in the Colony; and even more rigorous safeguards for the prerogatives of the Crown.[1]

The Boer Republics, on the other hand, proposed to apply the doctrine of the sovereignty of the people without reservations. The Free State took its inspiration from the American example which, as Professor de Kiewiet observes, had come to the knowledge of its legislators by the merest chance. They seem to have made the most of their opportunity, for one historian is of the opinion that theirs was the most well-balanced and liberal of the republican constitutions. As in the United States, a president was elected by universal suffrage, but for five years; he was assisted by a cabinet, some of its members chosen by himself, the rest by the assembly or *Volksraad*, to which the legislative power was entrusted and which was also elected by universal suffrage. The *Volksraad* voted laws, and the nominations of top officials were submitted for its approval; its decisions were final, for the president did not enjoy the right of veto. The office of commandant-general, the source of so much controversy, existed only in the event of war. In theory all this was by no means ill-conceived, but in practice it was to prove less satisfactory. Was the Boer of the old guard right when, on learning of the complicated texts that

[1] The institution of a Supreme Court in 1857 deprived the lieutenant-governor of his judicial powers.

would regulate his existence, he is said to have exclaimed: 'Wasn't the Law of Moses enough, then?'

In the Transvaal, also, it was the Great Trek rather than the Book of Exodus that provided inspiration. The Transvaalers were fanatically individualist and religious. In the constitution of 1858 even greater stress was laid on the sovereignty of the people than in the Free State; moreover, all the official posts were reserved for members of the Dutch Reformed Church. As in the sister republic, a single assembly was elected by universal suffrage, as was the president. On the other hand, the Transvaalers did not dare abolish the post of commandant-general, thereby allowing a dangerous duality of powers to subsist.

Dissimilar in many respects, the four constitutions differed chiefly in the provisions they made for the native population.

In the Cape Colony the equality of races, as recognized in 1828 by the Fiftieth Ordinance,[1] had been strictly respected and no form of discrimination had been envisaged. On the contrary, the fixing of the property-qualification at a minimum of £25 enabled a great many coloureds to assert their rights. Even the illiterate were allowed to vote; they did not need to be able to write, making their choices known by word of mouth. Was this why so many non-Europeans failed to take advantage of their privilege? Was it through indifference or, rather, from timidity? At all events, although the Coloureds represented 55 per cent of the population, it has been observed that there exists no proof that the votes of the Coloured people had any real influence on the election of a single member of the first Parliament.

In Natal, at first, a similar respect was accorded to egalitarian principles. But, as a policy of segregation was being practised there in an attempt to isolate the Blacks from the Whites, this attitude had little practical effect; it was in any case modified as the increase in the native population gradually led to their becoming more inextricably intermingled with the Europeans. In 1865 it was laid down that inhabitants regulated by special laws—which meant the Blacks—would be excluded from the electorate, but that the other non-Europeans would retain their privileges (at the time there were only a few hundred Indians on the sugar-plantations).

The Boer Republics did not bother themselves with such fine distinctions. The Orange Free State gave the Whites an electoral monopoly, not forgetting to take precautions: no Arab, Chinese or coolie, nor any coloured Asiatic, could reside in the state for more than two months without permission. In the Transvaal a principle was categorically asserted and the appropriate conclusions drawn: the 'sovereign people' did not recognize any equality between Whites and coloured people, either in the Church or in the State; consequently, no native would be permitted to settle near the agglomerations, to the detriment of the

[1] See p. 70.

inhabitants, without the express authorization of the whole Assembly; and every native must carry a pass supplied by his master, by a missionary, by a *landdrost* or by the chief of his tribe—this was to protect settled workmen against vagabonds.

Not many years had passed before it became clear that the Great Trek had resulted in the juxtaposition of two White South Africas—one still permeated with colonialism but priding itself on its humanitarian preoccupations, the other obsessed with republicanism and unconcerned with equality, and both still seeking a stability which they had not been able to achieve.

II

The Beginnings of the Boer Republics

The history of the Transvaal begins with a scene straight from a boy's adventure story. Potgieter had never seen eye to eye with Pretorius, even going so far as to suspect his rival of having 'sold' the country to the British. Three months after the Sand River Convention, the two men decided to talk things over. Each was accompanied by his followers, who were all armed. Potgieter and Pretorius withdrew into a tent and the rest waited, fearing the worst. At last the order was given to raise the flap of the tent, and the former adversaries could be seen holding their hands crossed over a Bible. The 'people' breathed again. But the reconciliation was to bear no fruit, for Potgieter died before the end of the year and Pretorius survived him by only a few months. The latter's dying words are said to have been an exhortation to his fellow-adventurers: 'Do nothing for your own exaltation, but in everything let your aim be the glory of God and the welfare of country and people. . . Whatever you undertake, do it with the Lord.'

A vague feeling for dynastic continuity induced the Boers to replace the 'founding fathers' with their sons, Pieter Potgieter and Marthinus Pretorius. Hereditary rivalry had no time in which to manifest itself, for Potgieter was killed by the Blacks. Pretorius II thus stood alone, and in 1857 he was elected president. He possessed his father's qualities of strength of character and courage, but unfortunately the art of diplomacy was foreign to him. A man cast in a simple mould, impulsive and inflexible, Marthinus Pretorius was to be the cause of many an upheaval. In 1857 he was guided by a single passion, which he shared with all his followers: 'Isolation' could well have been the Boers' password—alone they had longed to be for the past twenty-five years, and alone they were determined to remain.

Their desire to make themselves different from others was symbolized in a series of decisions. First they gave their new country a name full of promise for the future: the South African Republic. Then they chose a capital, Pretoria, and a flag with three horizontal bands, red, white and blue, and a vertical band of green. Finally, they made Dutch their official language. This last measure was hardly likely to facilitate contacts with foreigners, but they were resolved not to share with other Europeans a sovereignty which they had for so long struggled to achieve. An incident revealed their aversion to compromise. Livingstone, sent out by the London Missionary Society, had been in Africa since 1840. Nine years after his arrival he had discovered Lake Ngami and made contact with the Blacks on the Zambezi. As a result, trading links had been established between the station of Kuruman, to the north of the Cape frontier, and a hitherto unexplored part of the continent. As soon as the Transvaal became independent it decided to put an end to a traffic by which, it was claimed, arms were reaching the Blacks. But did not the 'Missionaries' Road', as this route was known, lie outside the Transvaal territory? The question was all the more debatable because, apart from the Vaal frontier, no boundaries had been fixed for the new state. The Boers, however, were not the kind of men to bother themselves with subtle distinctions. A commando, taking it upon itself to enforce their point of view, came across a hut, partly destroyed, which Livingstone had built for himself in this locality. Whether the commando confined itself to observing the damage, or actually contributed to it, is a matter on which no two historians are agreed.

The Boers' relations with the natives also raise a great many questions. In Britain it quickly became fashionable to talk of a restoration of slavery, though it seems that no proof was ever advanced. But the masters of the Transvaal certainly regarded the Blacks as inferior beings over whom it was quite natural and desirable that they should impose their unconditional authority. Inevitably, everyone interpreted this principle in his own way. Some reduced their servants to a state of extreme subservience, though not to slavery. Others, more concerned to exercise a paternal influence, succeeded in maintaining a less rigorous discipline. On two points, however, all were agreed: they would have preferred to isolate themselves from the natives and, at the same time, they could not manage without their labour—the eternal problem of South Africa. Moreover, one must remember that in these boundless open spaces there existed as yet only three or four villages, if one can so term the handful of settlements that had gradually taken shape. Everywhere else there were only scattered farms dozens of miles apart. In the event of an uprising a massacre would be inevitable. And so in 1854, to show that they were the stronger, the Boers delivered a terrible warning. After twenty-three of their number had been killed in an ambush, a commando swooped down on the tribe responsible; the panic-stricken natives took refuge in caves and nine hundred were slaughtered as they tried to make their way out. 'The number of those who died inside from starvation or thirst is much greater,' writes the historian M. Nathan.

When the Orange Free State was recognized, another problem presented itself: should not the two sister Republics be united?

Conditions were different in the Free State. As in other parts, the Whites were divided into conflicting groups. Those of British stock cherished nostalgic longings for the Union Jack. Even among people of Dutch or French ancestry, many looked to Cape Town rather than to Pretoria, since opportunities to improve a highly unstable economic situation only existed in co-operation with the Cape Colony. Yet the Orange Free State enjoyed a twofold superiority over the Transvaal: although their proximity was quickly seen to pose a threat, the natives were not intermingled with the European population; moreover, an administrative unity had been achieved in the Free State, and it was hoped to make Bloemfontein the capital of a future South African Empire.

Although the centrifugal force of Boer individualism remained powerful, the impetuous Pretorius decided that the time had come to broach the question, which he did with incredible ineptitude, asserting that the lands south of the Vaal belonged to him by right, 'in virtue of a cession of all emigrant lands made to his father by the Queen'. This argument failed to impress the president of the Free State, Jacobus Boshof, who, judging by his portraits, cannot have been of an easygoing character. Both sides eventually raised commandos, which watched each other for a time across the river, and then common sense finally prevailed. The two Republics concluded a treaty of friendship, but they remained separate.

Their fusion would in any case have encountered the opposition of two men in important postions. Theophilus Shepstone (later Sir Theophilus) was Secretary for Native Affairs in Natal and the real master of the country. The son of a missionary who had arrived in South Africa with the 1820 settlers, Shepstone had started his career at the age of seventeen as an interpreter in the Kaffir War of 1834. A year later he had been awarded the impressive title of 'Diplomatic Agent' to the frontier tribes. He spoke the natives' language fluently and soon earned their affection. Transferred to Pietermaritzburg in 1845, he was to remain there for thirty years. Shepstone achieved the remarkable feat of maintaining peace throughout this period in a territory where the Blacks outnumbered the Whites by ten to one. At the same time, he was too intelligent not to be aware of the ever-present dangers: Natal was encircled, to the north by the Zulu, to the west by the Basuto and to the south by the Kaffirs. A man of far-reaching imagination, he envisaged nothing less than a gradual extension of the territories under his control and the establishment there of the Pax Britannica. He had opposed the Sand River and Bloemfontein Conventions as soon as they were signed—and since he had been so loath to accept two Boer states, he was even more reluctant to tolerate a single, united Republic.

The views of Sir George Grey, governor since 1854,[1] were less simplistic, but in some respects led to similar conclusions. Both men thought only in terms of a British South Africa: Shepstone, as he was to show in

[1] His predecessor, Cathcart, had received a command in the Crimea, where he was killed at the battle of Inkerman.

the Transvaal, proposed to achieve this end by the brutal method of annexations; and Grey, by means of a federation of which the British government would be the driving force. The new High Commissioner,[1] governor of South Australia for four years and then of New Zealand since 1845, had earned himself a flattering reputation by bringing the Maori people to heel and then attempting to assimilate them. His firmness of purpose and taste for responsibility had not been blunted during his governorship of countries where it sometimes took a year to receive a reply from London. In other words, he was not inclined to play a passive role at the Cape. A tragic episode made it easier for him to pursue his enterprises. His predecessors had been haunted by the nightmare of the eastern frontier, but a mass suicide by the Kaffirs freed Grey of this obsession. In 1856 a young Kaffir woman, Nongquase, had visions and heard voices which the witch-doctors interpreted: the dead were announcing that they would shortly return and, with the living, would drive the White Man away. On the day of liberation, predicted for February 1857, the rising sun would be blood-red and, instead of following its course to the west, would return to the east; a hurricane would dispose of any Europeans who might have escaped slaughter by the warriors. Abundance would then reign, for the risen ancestors would come back to earth with more cattle and grain than was needed. But the Kaffirs must have confidence in them and put themselves at their mercy, which meant killing all animals and destroying crops. The great chief, Kreli, made no attempt to prevent this collective madness. The missionaries pleaded with the natives to reconsider their decision, but in vain. The majority of these poor creatures obeyed the injunctions of the spirit world, and twenty-five thousand are said to have died of starvation; thirty thousand took refuge in the Cape Colony, their warrior might broken for ever.

Grey was thus able to concentrate his attention on the Basuto, who had lost none of their fighting spirit. Moshesh was still their leader; he approached his sixtieth year but was just as active as in his youth. On special days his attire became Europeanized: a top hat covering his turban, a double-breasted coat and military-style trousers with broad stripes, a cape round his shoulders, a scarf round his neck and a walking-stick in his hand. His moustache and pointed beard suggested a vague resemblance to the Saxe-Coburg-Gotha family. In the portrait from which this description is derived his half-closed eyes reveal an expression sparkling with intelligence. Moshesh still surrounded himself with French missionaries—it has been said that they even thought and wrote for him. He proved a brilliant pupil. Artful as a peasant, shrewd as a diplomat and with the courage of a Stoic, he possessed the true statesman's ability to seize opportunities and adapt himself to compromise. Above all, he was

[1] This title had been conferred on the governor of the Cape since 1847 to indicate that henceforth his responsibilities would extend beyond the Colony.

endowed with a sufficiently strong sense of continuity to bind together a multiplicity of small, isolated groups.

From the outset Moshesh and the Free State had regarded each other with mutual fear. A year after acquiring its independence the Free State appealed to Grey to intervene. The governor agreed to the request all the more willingly because it would enable him to flaunt his rank as High Commissioner. His intervention did nothing, however, to halt the raids across a theoretical frontier which enabled the Basuto and the Boers to steal each other's cattle in turn. Of course, it was always the 'others' who had started it. Relations became sufficiently bitter for a state of war to be officially proclaimed in 1858. Operations lasted only a few weeks. The Boers were too few in number to get the better of the Basuto. Moreoever, it was no longer a matter of fighting an enemy armed with assegai and shields, for Moshesh's warriors were now supplied with firearms and horses. The Boers disintegrated in their assault on the fortress of Thaba Bosigo. From the Transvaal came only a few volunteers, among them the thirty-year-old Paul Kruger. Boshof had launched an appeal to his compatriots in the Cape Colony, to which Grey replied with a declaration of strict neutrality. The Boers had to negotiate under the governor's auspices, the Basuto receiving a strip of fertile land between the Orange and the Caledon rivers.

Grey considered that the time was ripe to realize his 'grand design' and began blocking another attempt to merge the Republics. Pretorius had made union a condition of his support. The Free State, sensing that it faced defeat, had finally accepted. An agreement was on the point of being concluded in June 1858 when a letter from the governor announced that, if it were signed, the Conventions of independence would *ipso facto* be terminated. The risk was too great for the Boers to ignore, and so Pretoria and Bloemfontein remained separate capitals. Grey wasted no time. By September he was in the Free State, wooing an audience weary of so much uncertainty with the guarantees to be obtained from a federation with the Cape Colony. By a majority vote the *Volksraad* gave its assent.

A few months earlier, Grey had informed the Colonial Office of his views in categorical terms. 'Nothing but a strong federal government which unites within itself all the European races in South Africa can permanently maintain peace in this country and free Great Britain from constant anxiety for the peace of her possessions here.' The governor was exactly fifty-two years ahead of his time.[1] He thought that the support of the Free State would strengthen his argument, and so in November 1858 he sent to London a dispatch of fifty-nine folio pages which has remained famous as much for its length as for its insight. But in London his words fell on deaf ears. A federation, argued the experts, meant either enormous expenditure or independence. 'South Africa is a vast section of a continent and a federation connected by the slightest ties to Great Britain would be

[1] The Union of South Africa came into being in 1910. See Chapter 21.

only in fact a new United States.' The Secretary for the Colonies, Sir Edward Bulwer-Lytton, explained the official view. His having published some twenty years earlier *The Last Days of Pompeii* had no doubt made him sceptical of the workings of the human mind. He had no objections to a federation comprising only the British colonies, but Grey's report seemed to him a vague and impracticable plan. 'In a federation with these Dutch republics,' he wrote in criticism of the document, 'we have much to risk and nothing to gain. . . . It would thrust their Dutch nose into all sorts of black squabbles from which the British giant would always have to pull him out with the certainty of more kicks than halfpence.'

Grey persisted and was recalled in 1859. A change of government brought him back to the Cape in the following year, but he did not stay long, since troubles in New Zealand required his presence there.

Sir Philip Wodehouse succeeded him. Wodehouse was a civil servant, not an army man. He had behind him thirty-three years of colonial service: twenty-three years in Ceylon, three in Honduras and seven in Guiana. He showed himself to be honest, sincere and hard-working, but his maladroitness and prejudices overshadowed his qualities. The historians say that he was the most unpopular of South Africa's governors. His experience had in no way prepared him for the task of perfecting a system of representative government that had been functioning only a few years. His clashes with the House of Assembly resulted in the paralysis of the administrative machinery, so much so that in 1872, after his departure, a genuinely parliamentary system had to be introduced. If the elected members proved so recalcitrant towards the governor, it was, perhaps, because they knew what he thought of them. It was no secret that Lady Wodehouse had one obsession—to leave the country as soon as possible. With a curious imprudence her husband expressed similar sentiments in his letters to his son, whose indiscretions in London doubtless led to their contents being divulged. For example, on 5 January 1865 Wodehouse wrote: 'Your mother will give you by this mail a full description of her wrath and wrongs against the Cape people; really they do not deserve much better.' In another letter: 'Some of them are animals of queer description.' And he would apply a variety of blunt epithets to those who opposed him: Brand, the president of the Free State, was 'a confounded fellow' and Saul Solomon, proprietor of the newspaper *The Cape Argus*, was 'that little rascal'. Such intemperate language earned him a number of enemies. On the other hand, it must be said in Wodehouse's defence that he was unlucky in two respects: his predecessor had been very popular, and, secondly, the ten years of his mandate coincided with one of the economic depressions to which South Africa was chronically liable.

Although he could not get on with those under him, Sir Philip at least had the satisfaction of not finding himself in conflict with his government. The Colonial Office had had enough of 'those nomads', as it chose to call the Boers. In the years following the signing of the Conventions of independence, London had assumed an air of total disinterestedness. 'Since there was nothing else to be done, let's say no more about it' was a sentiment that must have been heard frequently at cabinet meetings. Around 1850 the experts began to have doubts. 'Was a mistake not made?' The question mark soon became an exclamation mark: 'These treaties are intolerable!' But no one quite knew how to undo them. At all events, during Wodehouse's governorship a policy of territorial expansion and latent opposition to the Republics was substituted for the projected federation.

Shortly after his arrival the new governor received authorization, 'for the safety of the settlers' (the word 'annexation' was not used), to bring under his control a part of the present-day Transkei, between the Kei and the Bashee. Shepstone, for his part, saw no objection to moving 'his' frontier twenty or so miles southwards, thus reducing the distance separating 'his' Natal and the Cape. This first decision admittedly proved premature, for the Kaffirs, even though drastically reduced in number, still presented a threat. Their chief, the redoubtable Kreli, was described as 'pacing up and down the Bashee's banks as some caged beast'. It was considered advisable to give him back a little space, and so in 1864 the Transkei was evacuated; but two years later British Kaffraria, a Crown possession, was incorporated in the Cape Colony, which could well have done without such an expensive gift.

These were minor problems compared with those presented by the Orange Free State and the Transvaal. At Bloemfontein there was a feeling of bewilderment; an attempt at union with the South African Republic had been vetoed by the governor, and a federation with the Cape, which the Free State had accepted, had been rejected by London. Pretorius devised another solution—a personal union. In 1860 he had himself elected president of the Free State, hoping that his duality of function would eventually bring about unity of power. This only showed how little he knew the Boers beyond the Vaal, the virulence of whose factions eventually persuaded him to relinquish his first title in favour of the second. He must have been singularly lacking in political sense, for this concession, which failed to solve the Free State's problems, could not prevent a civil war beginning in the Transvaal. In 1863 he reverted to a less artificial situation, forsaking his three-year presidency of the Free State to return to the office to which his compatriots had called him after independence. At Bloemfontein the choice of president fell on a man who was to prove a figure of major importance, Johannes Brand. Born in Cape Town forty years earlier, Brand was the son of the president of the Cape Assembly where he himself, a lawyer by profession, represented a constituency. In other words, he inclined, both by heredity and occupation, towards the Colony rather than the Free State. But he was one of those South Africans—of whom there are so many today—who seek in the achievement of their ancestors not so much grounds for antagonism as reasons for mutual understanding.

Brand assumed power in a dire situation. His country was on the verge of bankruptcy, and the elusive, stubborn Moshesh, from his inviolable fortress of Thaba Bosigo, was causing the sword of Damocles to tremble. Brand appealed to Wodehouse to intervene. The governor, convinced like his predecessors that the decision of a representative of the Queen was the equivalent of a Gospel utterance, confirmed the frontier endorsed by Grey in 1858. As there were neither soldiers nor customs officers to give a little reality to this imaginary line, the Basuto continued to cross it with an easy conscience. As long as they confined their raids to cattle, a precarious peace existed. In 1865, however, a series of skirmishes precipitated a conflict into which the men of the Free State, realizing that their survival was at stake, entered with the energy of despair. Paul Kruger came to their aid with a commando from the Transvaal. Even in the Colony and Natal a certain feeling of White solidarity operated in their favour. Wodehouse hastened to declare himself neutral, confiding his secret feelings to his son in a letter of 28 July 1865: 'I shall be very sorry if they [the Boers] succeed.'

The military operations were conducted with a determination not lacking in savagery. The Boers' attacks once again crumbled against the impregnable Thaba Bosigo, but their flying columns spread terror. Moshesh, a master of the art of adapting himself to circumstances, sued for peace. In reply the Boers demanded half of his territory, forty thousand cattle, six thousand sheep, five thousand horses and the appointment of a High Commissioner who would govern in his name. The old chief refused and then, playing a double game, asked Wodehouse to recognize him as a British subject. The governor would willingly have agreed, but the attitude of the Colonial Office had not yet changed sufficiently. The war continued. The Free State, more determined than ever on extreme measures, began by expelling the French missionaries who, not without reason, were suspected of bias. At the same time, in the summer of 1866, the commandos set about a systematic destruction of the natives' crops. This time the struggle was too unequal: the victors, symbolically, dictated their terms at Thaba Bosigo itself. Half of the Basuto's arable land was ceded to them, and Moshesh now found himself ruling a territory of largely stony ground equally unsuited to stock-raising and crop-growing. Threatened with famine and stricken with disease, the tribes began to disintegrate; many natives crossed the frontier in search of domestic employment.

Wodehouse was worried: would this Boer victory reduce his plans to nothing? His rival in the field of annexations, Shepstone, was no less annoyed. The *Natal Mercury* vented its spleen: 'It is mad policy to deprive the Basutos of their land, to destroy their crops and to convert them into a race of bandit desperadoes.' This sudden fit of virtue proved favourable to British interests. The French missionaries had no intention of conceding defeat and appealed to the London Missionary Society, to the British government and even to Napoleon III, who had other problems. Most important of all, they restored the confidence of the Basuto. In 1867 Moshesh repudiated the treaty and demanded annexation to Natal. Immediately raids and commandos resumed.

It has been said that the Colonial Office always reacted more by instinct than by reason. Its traditionally intuitive approach induced it to take a decision which, though doubtless designed for the immediate situation, was to prove far-reaching in its consequences, authorizing the annexation of Basutoland by Natal. The Colonial Office explained its position in a memorandum to the cabinet: it was a question not of an extension of territory, but of the security of Britain's South African possessions. In other words, let the colonies make sure that we hear no more of Moshesh! Shepstone saw only one way of achieving this: the complete incorporation of Basutoland as it existed before the Treaty of Thaba Bosigo. One can imagine how the people of the Free State must have felt when they found themselves on the point of being dispossessed of conquests that had cost them so much blood and effort. Wodehouse intervened. He certainly had no love for the Boers, but he was jealous of Shepstone. On his own responsibility he decided that Her Majesty's new subjects would come directly under the Crown. His offer of resignation prevented London disowning him. In 1869 the Treaty of Aliwal North[1] reduced by half the territories snatched from Moshesh three years earlier. But this compromise satisfied no one—neither the French missionaries, convinced that their protégés were being unjustly treated, nor the Basuto, crammed into an area too small to provide them with sustenance, nor Natal, robbed of its prey, and even less the Orange Free State, whose *Volksraad* declared that the High Commissioner had hurt the country 'in its honour, its dignity and its most cherished interests'.[2]

The government in London must now have looked at the maps. Between the Indian Ocean and the Free State lay a solid line of British possessions. The barrier was particularly strong to the south-east of Bloemfontein, with mountains from five to ten thousand feet over which the Union Jack now flew; beyond lay a strip of land inhabited by the Griqua, who in 1862 had made their own Great Trek from Philippolis to the southern foothills of the Drakensberg. The Free State, forbidden all access to the sea, was condemned to suffocation.

There remained the Transvaal. Pretorius had been congratulating himself on being as far as possible from the Cape, but he did not feel similarly about the obstacles separating the Transvaal and the Indian Ocean. Geographically the distance was not great: less than three hundred miles

---

[1] Sir Harry Smith, who when in India had beaten the Sikhs at Aliwal, had given this name to a locality south of the Orange in 1849.

[2] Moshesh died in 1870 and Wodehouse left the Colony that same year.

as the crow flies from Pretoria to Lourenço Marques. In those days, however, malaria made the journey almost impossible, as Louis Trigardt had discovered (see p. 90). Yet it was only in this direction that the South African Republic could hope to find the access to the sea that would guarantee its independence. In 1861 Pretorius obtained from the Zulu a cession of territory which moved his frontier eastwards. Britain retaliated immediately. In 1823 a certain Captain Owen had thought he was doing the right thing by hoisting the Union Jack on the south coast of the wonderful Delagoa Bay, where the Portuguese occupied the north shore. At the time the Colonial Office had been unimpressed by this symbolic gesture. Thirty-eight years later, however, it seemed expedient to recall the incident by annexing to Natal an island in the middle of the gulf. Matters might have gone no further if a series of events had not confirmed the anxiety of the British strategists. In 1864 an imaginative Scotsman persuaded Pretorius that it would be possible to use a more or less navigable river, the Maputa, and thus skirt the malaria zones. All that emerged from this project was the intensification of the Transvaal's ambitions. In 1868 the president of the South African Republic created a sensation when, with the stroke of a pen, he annexed vast territories to north and west, where gold had just been discovered,[1] and appropriated a narrow corridor sufficient to link Pretoria with Delagoa Bay. Immediately, British hopes and Portuguese memories were crystallized. Both sides feared not so much the weak Transvaal as all-powerful Germany, which seemed to be showing signs of colonial aspirations. London and Lisbon agreed to submit their rival claims to arbitration and to place themselves in the hands of France which, after her defeat of 1870, seemed inoffensive enough. In 1875 Marshal MacMahon pronounced in favour of Portugal on all counts, little suspecting that he had just decided the fate of the Transvaal.[2]

[1] See p. 153.   [2] See Chapter 13.

PART FOUR

Economic Revolution and Political Tension
1867-99

List of Dates

1867	Discovery of the first diamond.
1870	Working of the 'dry diggings'.
1871	Keate Award.
1871	Annexation by Britain of the Diamond Fields.
October 1871	Cecil Rhodes arrives in Kimberley.
1872	Election of Burgers as president of the Transvaal.
1874	Disraeli comes to power.
1876	War with Sekukuni.
12 April 1877	Annexation of the Transvaal.
May 1877	Kruger's first mission to London.
1878	Kruger's second mission to London.
1879	Zulu War.
1 June 1879	Death of the Prince Imperial of France.
1880	Gladstone comes to power.
December 1880	Beginning of the first Anglo-Boer War.
27 February 1881	Boer victory at Majuba.
1881	Pretoria Convention.
1883	Arrival of a German warship at Angra Pequena.
1883	Kruger is elected president of the Transvaal.
1884	London Convention.
1884	Annexation by Britain of St Lucia Bay.
1885	Annexation by Britain of southern Bechuanaland.
1885	Northern Bechuanaland becomes a protectorate.
1886	Working of the Witwatersrand goldfields.
1887	Founding of the Goldfields of South Africa Company.
1887	Natal assumes the administration of Zululand.
1888	Formation of the De Beers Consolidated Company.
1888	Customs union between the Free State and the Cape. Leyds appointed Secretary of State in the Transvaal.
1889	Creation of the British South Africa Company, which receives a royal charter.
1890	Cecil Rhodes becomes Prime Minister of the Cape Colony.
1892	Completion of the Cape Town–Pretoria railway. Charles Leonard founds the National Union in Johannesburg.
1893	Formation of Rand Mines Limited.
1894	Completion of the Pretoria–Delagoa Bay railway.

December 1894	Rhodes goes to London.
1895	Sir Hercules Robinson, High Commissioner of the Cape Colony.
June 1895	Joseph Chamberlain becomes Secretary of State for Colonies.
October 1895	Closing and reopening of the Vaal drifts.
29 December 1895	Jameson Raid.
2 January 1896	Jameson surrenders unconditionally.
3 January 1896	The Kaiser's telegram to Kruger.
12 January 1896	Rhodes resigns.
April 1896	The Johannesburg conspirators are sentenced.
July 1896	Jameson is sentenced.
1897	A commission of inquiry meets in London.
1897	Renewal of the treaty of alliance between the Free State and the Transvaal.
1897	British naval demonstration at Delagoa Bay.
1897	Annexation of Zululand to Natal.
1897	Sir Alfred Milner, High Commissioner of the Cape Colony.
1898	Kruger's fourth re-election.
1898	Leyds appointed envoy extraordinary to Europe.
1898	Secret Anglo-German treaty.
1898	Kitchener reconquers the Sudan.
1898	The Fashoda Affair.
March 1899	Milner sends to London a petition signed by 21,684 uitlanders.
4 May 1899	Milner's telegram about the 'helots' of Johannesburg.
9 May 1899	The British government accepts the petition.
31 May– 5 June 1899	Bloemfontein Conference.
9 October 1899	Kruger's ultimatum.
11 October 1899	Beginning of hostilities.

12

The Discovery of Diamonds

On a fine summer's day in 1867, a small boy was gathering pebbles beside the Orange river. His attention was caught by a particularly shiny one, which he took home with others. When a neighbour showed interest, the child's mother reacted with lordly indifference, telling him that he could keep the stone. Her neighbour did not refuse the offer, and the find was submitted to experts who declared it a genuine diamond. The first to be discovered in South Africa, it was bought for £500 by Sir Philip Wodehouse.

The following year other stones of similar brilliance were found in the valley of the Vaal. Rumours multiplied, reaching fever-point a few months later. In 1869 a Griqua shepherd brought a magnificent white diamond of astounding purity to be examined by a possible buyer. He must have trembled with excitement as he demanded, in exchange, five hundred ewes, ten oxen and a horse, and one can imagine his surprise when what to him seemed an extravagant price was immediately accepted. The stone was weighed: uncut, the famous 'Star of South Africa' was 83·5 carats; it was sold for £11,200 and then re-sold for £25,000 to Lord Dudley.

When the news reached London a diamond-dealer, who could not believe his ears, considered it advisable to consult an expert. He was unlucky in his choice, although the person to whom he referred the matter seemed to offer every guarantee of reliability, a professor of the University of London, James R. Gregory, for whom mineralogy was supposed to hold no secrets. Gregory agreed to investigate, but on condition that he could go out to study the locality. His verdict was unequivocal: 'The whole story of the Cape diamonds discoveries is false and is simply one of many schemes for trying to promote the employment and expenditure of capital in searching for this precious substance in the Colony.'

Not everyone showed the same scepticism. When experience revealed that the valley of the Vaal, to the north of its confluence with the Orange, was particularly promising, people rushed there on foot, on horseback or in wagons. The diggers did not clutter themselves with equipment, taking just a pickaxe, a shovel and, most important of all, a sieve for separating sand and stones. In a few months this barren and uninhabited region was teeming with life. A German missionary has left a colourful description of the scene. 'Both sides of river covered from hilltop to water's break with canvas tents, carts, wagons, and a few iron buildings. . . .' All day long could be heard the noise of seven hundred sieves, perhaps more, being tirelessly shaken by their owners. Wheelbarrows and wagons were going to and fro continually. 'By night, when these canvas towns were lit up, music of all kinds was heard from the banks and from small boats on the Vaal.' Two settlements grew up, Pniel on the south side of the Vaal, Klipdrift on the north. Pretorius II, who was decidedly fond of acting on his own initiative, paid an official visit to Klipdrift in the middle of 1870, and a dance was organized in his honour, in a tent. About a hundred and fifty dancers took part in every imaginable form of dress, from tails to a well-cleaned miner's costume. Sixteen women added a little feminine grace to the gathering. There was no roof, and the floor was made of the finest gravel that it had been possible to find. A few tallow candles gave a dim light, and the moon did the rest. Behind the bar stocks of alcohol and cakes of all sorts had been piled up; by lifting the bottom of the tent, uninvited intruders were able to help themselves, distributing the refreshments to their friends. An accordion, a fiddle, a flute and a big drum provided the music.

The fame of Pniel and Klipdrift proved transient. At the end of the year the Vaal flooded its banks and the two camps were almost totally destroyed; they were already largely abandoned, for most of the diggers had moved southwards. The experts were confronted with one surprise after another. At first they had thought that the diamonds, washed along by rivers, would be found only on their banks, mixed with other stones; then discoveries were made far from any river, and eventually it was realized that the richest deposits lay deep in the substrata of the land. The lunar landscapes where prospecting proved most fruitful have been described a hundred times: immense, flat-rimmed craters resembling a gigantic glass and, rising from their depths like exclamation marks, columns of every shape and size, full of the petrified volcanic substance that produced the diamonds. The era of sieves was past and had been succeeded by the age of machines. Gradually the first forms of collective organization replaced the spontaneous activities of individuals.

At the origin of the colossal achievement soon to be realized was that inevitable mixture of daring and luck which gives rise to great enterprises. The beginnings of the De Beers Company are typical. For about two years a certain Richard Jackson, like so many others, had been looking for diamonds beside the Vaal, but had found very few. A native spoke to him of a mysterious white man who, farther to the south, was discovering precious stones all day long. At first Jackson was dubious, but then he said to himself, 'Why not?' He set off with three comrades, not knowing quite

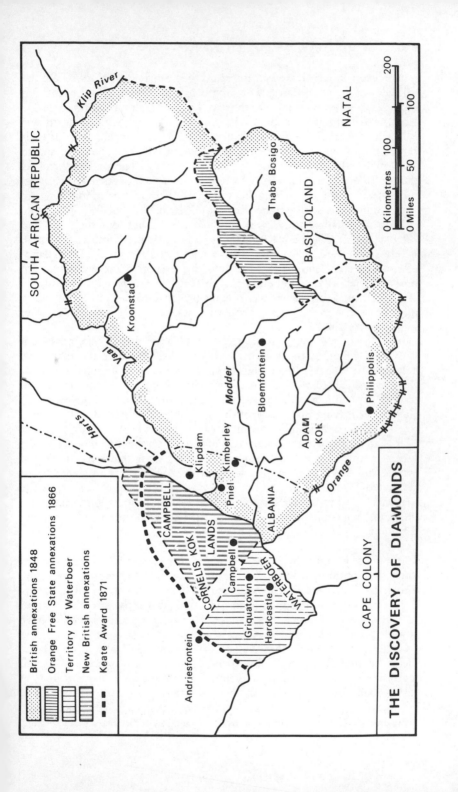

THE DISCOVERY OF DIAMONDS

Legend:
- British annexations 1848
- Orange Free State annexations 1866
- Territory of Waterboer
- New British annexations
- Keate Award 1871

SOUTH AFRICAN REPUBLIC

NATAL

BASUTOLAND

Klip River

Kroonstad

Vaal

Harts

Modder

Klipdam

Kimberley

Pniel

Thaba Bosigo

Bloemfontein

ADAM KOK

Philippolis

Orange

CAMPBELL

CORNELIS KOK

LANDS

ALBANIA

Andriesfontein

Campbell

Griquatown

Hardcastle

WATERBOER

CAPE COLONY

0 Kilometres   100   200
0 Miles   50   100

where he was going. It was summer and they nearly died of thirst. On the third day of their expedition they caught sight of a white tent. On making inquiries they learnt that it was the dwelling of Diedrich and Johannes De Beer, who had settled in the region in 1860. What they had heard was true: there were more diamonds here than anywhere else. Back at their camp, they tried to keep their information secret, but the news spread like wildfire. In May 1870 the first rush took place. The De Beer brothers thought they were being clever by selling for £6,000 a farm that had cost them only £50; but within a little over fifty years diamonds worth £90 million were to be mined from their land.

Two months later there was another rush. Other 'dry diggings' had been started at Colesberg Kopje (later to become the Kimberley Mines), barely a mile away. This time it was a native cook who made the chance discovery, conscientiously informing his master. The same pattern repeated itself—a race to be the first to reach this second Promised Land where, before long, stakes were being driven into the ground to mark off, somewhat ineffectively, properties whose legal foundations were highly uncertain.

In the matter of personal property, luckily for the diggers, possession was nine points of the law, and no one disputed that the diamonds belonged to whoever had found them. Their sale was arranged in one of three ways. Those who had made a strike could set off for London to dispose of their stones themselves; but the journey was expensive, and it also meant leaving one's competitors a clear field. Another solution was to go to Cape Town and secure an advance from a broker. But the attraction of an immediate gain induced many to sell on the spot. The would-be buyers admittedly cut an impressive figure, with their smoothness of tongue and dressed with a splendour designed to inspire confidence: a hat decorated with ostrich-feathers, a velvet jacket, gaudy cravat, white waistcoat, leather breeches, carefully polished high boots, glittering spurs and, most important of all, fastened to the belt, a bag supposed to contain a fortune.

In the mostly uninhabited, wide open spaces of southern Africa at this time, the notion of frontier was a vague one. In other words, until now people had not been much concerned to know who could claim sovereignty of lands presumed to be unproductive. When the miracle occurred it was a very different story, and the ensuing squabbles would have warmed the heart of any lawyer.

Pretorius maintained that the lands between the Vaal and the Harts[1] belonged to him by right, by virtue of treaties with the natives and, even more important, the Convention of 1854 which, in very general terms, had made the Vaal the only boundary of his territory. The

[1] The Harts is a tributary on the right bank of the Vaal, into which it flows about a hundred and twenty miles upstream from the junction of the Vaal and the Orange.

argument was rather specious, for it could have been applied to all the land north of the Vaal between the South African Republic and the Mediterranean. Brand had a stronger case. To the south of the Vaal his rights were difficult to dispute. During the six years when the Union Jack had flown over Bloemfontein, the British Resident, by making concessions of land as far as the Orange, had recognized that this region came under his authority—and it was here that Kimberley[1] lay. The Orange Free State could base its claim on this precedent. Moreover, in theory any territory between the Vaal and the Orange came under its jurisdiction. In other parts, however, its argument was more questionable. In what were called the Campbell Lands—the area extending westwards and straddling the river—Brand based his claim on a recent cession: in 1861 the Griqua chief, Adam Kok, had ceded this region to the Free State before setting out on his 'Great Trek',[2] but no one quite knew where the transferred territory began and ended.

Kok's neighbour and rival, Nicholaas Waterboer, another Griqua chief, saw in this confusion an opportunity to reopen the question. He had already tried to do so before the discovery of diamonds, and that event had not curbed his enthusiasm. Perhaps no one would have paid him much attention if he had not had the intelligence to entrust his case to a skilful Cape Town lawyer, David Arnot, whose opinions the authorities were not inclined to ignore. Arnot, a sort of miniature Rhodes, was fascinated not so much by diamonds as by British expansion, dreaming of a Colony that would stretch as far as the Zambezi. From this point of view the Kimberley region was of the utmost importance, for through it passed the famous 'Missionaries' Road' (the 'road' was barely more than a track), later renamed the 'Road to the North'. It skirted the Boer Republics to the west and was to provide the British with access to the heart of the continent. By defending the interests of his client, Arnot was undertaking to fight for the greatness of his country.

At first, direct negotiations were attempted. A conference between the three contending parties, in August 1870, only served to exacerbate passions. Waterboer and his faithful Arnot then decided to appeal to the Cape authorities. Brand and Pretorius, for their part, annexed unilaterally the territories which each had been claiming. For the Free State things went smoothly, and it even seemed that it had won the struggle. The South African Republic was less fortunate. Its president contrived to grant a twenty-one-year diamond-prospecting monopoly to three close friends and then dispatched a representative to the locality, thinking that everyone would submit to him. No sooner had he arrived, however, than Pretorius's ambassador was unceremoniously conducted back across the

---

[1] This name was soon given to the two combined settlements of De Beers and Colesberg Kopje, in honour of the Secretary for the Colonies, Lord Kimberley.
[2] See p. 127.

Vaal. Then the diggers formed the 'Independent Republic of Klipdrift' and elected a president, Stafford Parker.

They could hardly have chosen a more colourful character. The new standard-bearer of free democracy had been born in England thirty-seven years earlier. Having enlisted in the American navy, Parker had thought it wise to change his career after an unfortunate duel in Hong Kong. He had then tried to find a less strictly disciplined life at sea. A cargo-boat took him to San Francisco where he stayed for a while, at the time of the Gold Rush, and then he set out on a tour of America which took him as far as Boston, where in 1858 he joined a ship bound for the Cape of Good Hope and England. When the ship called at a South African port, the crew was told that it had been requisitioned to sail to India, where the Mutiny had broken out. This new destination did not appeal to Stafford Parker, and again he deserted; after spending some time as a pedlar, he was recruited as a captain in a recently formed mounted police force but, disliking discipline, he soon grew weary of this. He was the perfect example of the born diamond prospector. His official position as president lasted only a few months, but this did not prevent him from making a fortune. A little later he could be seen in the streets of London wearing a white top hat which soon became legendary and presenting to whoever would accept them visiting-cards with gilt corners which read: 'Stafford Parker, President of the Executive Council of Kimberley'.

The exploits of Stafford Parker were hardly of serious significance. At the Cape the news of the mines provoked growing irritation. Confronted with such a disagreeable situation, the acting governor, Lieutenant-General Charles Crawfurd Hay, displayed a thoroughly British self-control. His principal colleague, Richard Southey, showed less patience. As the implacable enemy of the Boer Republics, he considered, like Shepstone in Natal, that the only solution was an extension of British sovereignty. He found no difficulty in obtaining support for his views from Wodehouse's successor, Sir Henry Barkly, who took up his duties at the end of 1870. The new governor's career had been in the classic mould: five years in Guiana, three in Jamaica, seven in Australia and seven in Mauritius. Those twenty-two years had instilled in him a feeling for authority, but his previous posts had hardly prepared him for the problems posed in South Africa by the coexistence of two types of Whites. However, the new Secretary for Colonies, Lord Kimberley, had made sure that Barkly was aware of the 'great dissatisfaction of H.M.'s government' concerning any extension of the territory of the Boer Republics, which 'would open to the Boers an extended field for their slave dealing operations'. There was no mention of diamonds.

Although his ideas were firmly fixed in advance, Barkly nevertheless decided to visit the disputed territory in January 1871. His first act was to appoint a British administrator to replace Brand's representative in the region. Hostilities nearly broke out, but a show of strength intimidated the Free State. Then the governor suggested that the presidents of the two Republics should submit their claims to arbitration. Pretorius, inconsistent as ever, accepted, but the more cautious Brand agreed only on two conditions: the arbitrator must be a foreigner—for example, the president of the United States or the king of Holland—and the Kimberley district must be excluded from his terms of reference. Barkly considered these two demands excessive and referred the matter to the lieutenant-governor of Natal, Robert Keate.

This choice made the outcome certain. In August 1871 the governor asked the Colonial Office for permission to annex the Diamond Fields should the occasion arise. Lord Kimberley granted the request in terms which showed little respect for his predecessors: 'We are reaping the fruits of our folly in our abandoning the authority over the Orange River Territory.' The verdict was known in October. The claims of the Transvaal and the Free State were rejected. Waterboer and his Griqua were proclaimed British subjects, and their new status entitled them to protection. The Diamond Fields were annexed to the Crown, like Basutoland four years earlier. Yet Barkly was less skilful, or less lucky, than Wodehouse: this time the Cape Parliament spurned a gift which London, still obsessed with economies, would willingly have granted it.

Even in Britain the arbitrary nature of the Keate Award aroused criticism. At Klipdrift, 'President' Parker accepted the decision with good grace. In the Transvaal, however, Pretorius was forced to resign by his indignant fellow-citizens. The more popular Brand was able to bide his time. Five years later, some farmers from the Free State who had been settled in the annexed territory—henceforward commonly known as Griqualand West —contested Waterboer's rights. The matter went before the Supreme Court, which pronounced in their favour, thereby depriving the Keate Award of all legal basis. Kimberley's successor, Lord Carnarvon, extricated himself from this awkward situation by granting the Free State, which badly needed the money, an indemnity of £90,000—at the very least an admission that it was entitled to damages.

In the meantime, the production of diamonds had risen with enormous rapidity. In 1872 it was already six times greater than that of Brazil, hitherto the largest market. The population of Kimberley, a town of canvas, dried mud and tin, glittering in the evenings in a barren plain, was second only to that of Cape Town itself. Apart from the hopes it nurtured, however, the place must have been quite devoid of attraction, judging by the impression it left on Anthony Trollope, who found it difficult to imagine greater ugliness: not a tree for five miles, not a tuft of grass, the roads consisting of holes and dust, the atmosphere of dust and flies. The De Beers Company had brought the use of native labour to a fine art. The Blacks lived in compounds, vast enclosures surrounded by a double barrier of corrugated iron; from the top of the inner barrier ran a horizontal grating extending outwards for several yards to prevent anything from being thrown out. The workmen did not leave the compound during the three months of their contract. Every evening they were undressed and minutely searched. They were given blankets in which they wrapped themselves for the night, while their working clothes were also carefully examined. 'The precautions which are taken a few days before they leave, their engagement being terminated, to recover which [diamonds] they may have swallowed, are more easily imagined than described,' wrote one visitor.

The colourful diamond-buyers of the early days had made way for businessmen of a more traditional but no less shrewd kind: Jules Porgès in Paris, Anton Dunkersbuhler in London, and in South Africa itself Alfred Beit, Julius Wernher, J. B. Robinson, Barney Barnato and countless others whose forceful personalities were to shape this new country. In October 1871 one newcomer passed almost unnoticed: an eighteen-year-old planter from Natal whose affairs had not gone well. An eye-witness describes him as tall, gangling and frail in appearance. Soon it was learnt that his family had sent him to South Africa to recover his health. He said that he had crossed the Drakensberg alone in a cart, with a suitcase of classical authors. This last detail aroused curiosity, and on being asked his name he replied: 'Cecil Rhodes'.

13

Annexation and Liberation of the Transvaal

Political sense was hardly one of the qualities of the Transvaalers during this period. Marthinus Pretorius may have committed one blunder after another, but he was almost a Talleyrand by comparison with his successor. When, in 1872, he found himself compelled to resign, the 'people' chose as his replacement a thirty-eight-year-old clergyman, the Reverend Thomas F. Burgers. This gentleman's skirmishes with the official Church had tainted him with liberalism, which was not likely to please the majority. But he was known to be an ardent patriot; and, moreover, the charm of his eloquence proved irresistible. To these unconscious romantics, the children of the *voortrekkers*, he held out the promise of a dazzling future that would justify their parents' ordeals. One historian has said that the Transvaal had chosen a Cicero when it needed a Caesar. This Cicero was certainly full of good intentions; but, alas, he proposed to transform those intentions into reality by grand and impossible schemes.

The new president was unlucky, for he had been in office only two years when Disraeli came to power. The British Prime Minister was also a man of imagination, but he possessed the invaluable gift of being able to cross the no-man's-land which lies between thought and action. He dreamed of a Great Britain that would be mistress of the seas and of an empire whose subjects would instinctively bow to her pre-eminence. In other words, he found it difficult to believe that a handful of Boers, isolated in a land that had not yet revealed its hidden wonders, could defy his country. Further-more, the transformation of attitude at the Colonial Office was now complete:[1] whenever South Africa was discussed, the only differences of opinion concerned the means of ensuring the Queen's supremacy there.

The Secretary of State, Lord Carnarvon, wanted to implement the idea of a federation advocated by Grey twenty years earlier. He had occupied the same post in 1867, at the birth of the Canadian Confederation. He had extolled that event in an enthusiastic speech and saw no reason why a solution adopted in North America could not be transposed to South Africa. But he could not have chosen a worse moment. The annexation of

[1] See p. 125.

the Diamond Fields had filled the Boers with a bitterness and a mistrust that were far from subsiding. Even at the Cape, moreover, it was felt that, if there was to be federation, the initiative must be taken locally and not in Britain. Carnarvon's first attempt in 1875 was rejected out of hand. Not allowing himself to be discouraged, he called a conference in London the following year. The reaction was disappointing: the Transvaal refused to take part; the Orange Free State agreed to talk about anything except federation, and the Cape Colony did likewise; only Natal and Griqualand West rallied to the 'grand design'.[1]

This was obviously not enough. Those who had been advocating extreme measures seized their chance, insisting that time was being wasted. These Boers must be taught to respect the British, advised Knatchbull-Hugessen, the Under-Secretary of State for the Colonies. Governor Barkly went one better, declaring that Great Britain had only to make her will known simply and firmly, and people would submit to it. Clearly, the Conventions of independence no longer meant much in the eyes of the British experts. Yet they did not dare attack the Free State, where Brand was keeping the flag flying high. The Transvaal, on the other hand, seemed temptingly easy prey: the recklessness of its new president, the quarrelling among the inhabitants and the native threat all offered arguments in favour of its annexation.

Burgers made impressive noises but seemed reluctant to act. A glance at the map was enough to convince him that, without access to the Indian Ocean, the South African Republic was under sentence of death. Like Pretorius, he made one of his priorities the construction of a railway to Delagoa Bay. But he had no experience of international negotiations. The financiers in London reduced the question to essentials: no federation, no money. Burgers then turned to Amsterdam, all the more readily because he had surrounded himself with advisers from the Netherlands and because he dreamed vaguely of a Dutch Republic of South Africa of which he would be the George Washington. This time he had more luck—not enough for the project to bear fruit, but enough to reveal it as an illusion. He needed £300,000 and obtained £90,000. He then proceeded to put the cart before the horse: instead of devoting the money to laying track, he used it to buy rolling stock, including a presidential carriage which was doomed to rust slowly at Lourenço Marques.

These discussions abroad lasted more than a year. When Burgers returned to his duties in May 1876, his optimism must have been sorely tested. The public coffers were almost empty, and the factions were squabbling with their customary ferocity. Even more disturbing was the news that a Black chief, Sekukuni, had raised the banner of revolt in the north, for it was feared that the Zulu, always a menace, might seize the opportunity to invade the country from the east. The classic solution of

[1] The project was finally abandoned in 1880, after an unfavourable vote in the Cape Parliament.

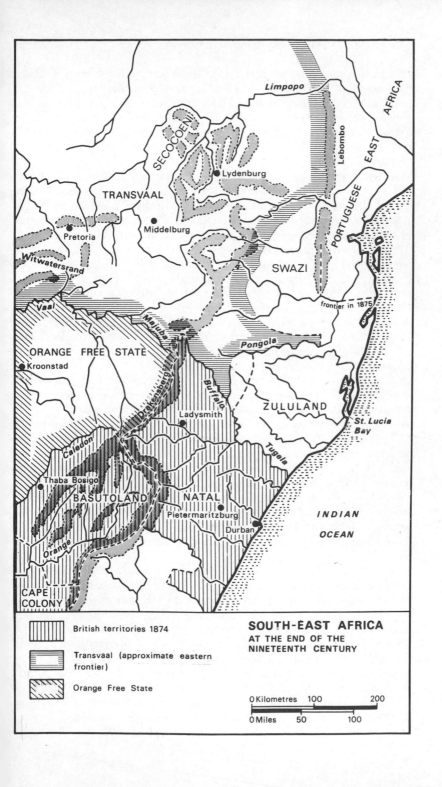

SOUTH-EAST AFRICA
AT THE END OF THE
NINETEENTH CENTURY

commandos was tried, but perhaps the Boers were weary of these punitive expeditions: according to some historians, a thousand of the fourteen hundred mobilized men returned home rather too quickly. It was necessary to have recourse to volunteers who, under the leadership of a former Prussian officer, von Schlickmann, and an Irish refugee, Alfred Aylward, reduced the Blacks to submission by methods of singular brutality.

In August 1876 a report signed by the governor, Barkly, was sent to London. Its terms were straightforward: 'Army of President totally routed. Deserters pressing into Pretoria. Sekukuni pursuing in force. Annexation demanded during meeting at Lydenburg.'[1] This tendentious communication was more than the Colonial Office could have hoped for. The message was received on 14 September. Carnarvon, whose mind was already made up, acted swiftly; the following day he asked Disraeli for permission to intervene: 'By acting at once we may prevent a war, and acquire at a stroke the whole of the Transvaal Republic, after which the Orange Free State must soon follow and the whole policy in South Africa for which we have been labouring be completely justified.' The Prime Minister made no objections. The government had the good luck to have the ideal man on the spot in London: Shepstone, who was said to know both Boers and natives better than anyone, happened to be on a brief visit there. Eight days later he was on his way back to South Africa.

Shepstone's instructions were shrewdly formulated, prescribing annexation as the ultimate objective, but on condition that the people approved. In other words, the operation was to be carried out smoothly and painlessly. A few troop-movements were arranged to strengthen the position of the negotiator. This military deployment, however, was undertaken with extreme caution, for it was feared that the Zulu might get the impression that it was designed to protect the Boers. Such was certainly not the intention of the Colonial Office. 'No assistance should be offered to Transvaal unless we saw our way clear to taking over the country,' Shepstone was informed by Lord Wolseley, then commander-in-chief in Natal; to avoid all misunderstanding Wolseley added: 'Its difficulties are our opportunity.'

The envoy extraordinary had no need of advice. Indeed, Shepstone displayed remarkable ability. Arriving in Pretoria at the end of December with a minimum escort (twenty-five armed men) and seven assistants, he quickly saw where the weak Republic was most vulnerable. The financial situation, he declared, would 'ripen the pear'. But it was important that the process should not be unduly prolonged. Social life came to his aid: historians fond of statistics have pointed out that, in eleven weeks, fifty-nine receptions were held in his honour or arranged by him. The people with whom he talked presented him, perhaps out of courtesy, with a very distorted picture of the situation. Shepstone listened to them criticizing

[1] The request for annexation had been made by some British gold-prospectors.

their president and concluded that to transfer their allegiance from a discredited régime to a highly respected Crown—a course on which he was already resolved—would suit them perfectly. Burgers's unpopularity, moreover, seemed an excellent reason for keeping him in office, since it would put him in a weak position. The two men thus reached a tacit agreement to avoid consulting the people, a course that might well have brought to power the *bête noire* of both parties, Paul Kruger, who had been making his poor health an excuse for refusing social invitations.[1]

After two months of conversations which consisted largely of hints, Shepstone decided that the 'pear' was beginning to 'ripen'. On 26 February 1877 he informed the *Volksraad* unofficially of his intention to annex the country. His victims were hardly a match for him. An eye-witness—an Englishman, admittedly—has left a pitiful description of the local legislators. 'The members, as a rule, are insignificant in appearance, dirty, oddly and poorly dressed, and crowded together in a most uncomfortable manner.... The brains of the majority became more and more cloudy with the multitude of words.' Her Majesty's representative let them have their say and, when they suggested compromise, replied sadly that it was too late. Then he reminded them of the Zulu peril, which in his view was imminent, and assured them that the Queen's only concern was to preserve the Transvaal, 'without any desire whatsoever to add to Her dominions'. Once again Burgers's eloquence exerted its baleful influence. His last speech was nothing but 'a flow of contradictions'. Although the members of the *Volksraad* despised him, they rallied round him in a last bid for unity. But their fellow-Transvaalers were weary of upheavals. On 12 April the flag of the South African Republic was lowered and the Union Jack hoisted. 'There was not a blow struck, not a shot fired.... A memorable day for the Transvaal and for me,' Shepstone noted in his diary. 'This afternoon my proclamation declaring the Transvaal British territory was issued and read by Mr Osborn on the steps of the Post Office.' The nations of the world remained indifferent, except for Portugal which, according to Carnarvon, showed some annoyance. Bismarck, on meeting the British ambassador, took him aside and asked 'what we meant by seizing other people's territories at such a moment'.[2] The ambassador came up with an unexpected rejoinder: 'It was necessary for us to secure the approaches to Egypt'—which must have made Bismarck think. Shepstone was appointed as Administrator. The troops saluted him and his assumption of office was greeted with *God Save the Queen*. 'For a few months,' writes Professor Uys, 'he lived in a fool's paradise.'

There were, however, certain ominous signs. Not a month had passed

---

[1] See Chapter 15.
[2] The war between Turkey and Russia began twelve days after the annexation of the Transvaal. The Tsar's ambitions were well known, and the Chancellor was obviously afraid that he might use Britain's action as justification.

when Kruger, accompanied by the attorney Jorissen, left for London. The new High Commissioner, Sir Henry Bartle Frere, was one of the few British officials to form a lucid judgement of the man who was to become a formidable adversary of Britain. It was Frere's opinion that Kruger concealed 'considerable ability and shrewdness under his somewhat clownish appearance'. Disraeli dismissed him as 'an ugly customer'. Carnarvon, for his part, extricated himself from an awkward situation with some fine-sounding words. The Boers, he said, had already been assured that 'they would enjoy the fullest legislative privileges compatible with the circumstances of the country and the intelligence of its people'. (Were they to take these latter words as a compliment?) The Secretary of State told his visitors that he would do everything he could to create 'a feeling of satisfaction' and, in particular, that Dutch would be recognized as an official language on the same footing as English.

On their return the two delegates found an utterly disillusioned country. Shepstone had adopted a passive policy in the conviction that time was working in his favour. If he had convoked the *Volksraad* in April he might have obtained its resigned acquiescence, but he allowed the weeks to roll by and his enemies to gather strength. He had led London to believe that the population was behind him; in an unofficial referendum, however, 597 voted for annexation and 659 against (there were about 1,000 abstentions). Kruger set out for England again, taking with him this time not a lawyer but an army man, Joubert. There were more conversations and another disappointment. When the negative results became known, three thousand burghers, at one of these confused and impassioned meetings to which they were accustomed, openly insisted on a return to independence.

For several months the native threat overshadowed their demands. On the south-east frontier the Zulu were growing restive. In 1872 Shepstone had thought he was ensuring the security of Natal by recognizing as supreme Zulu chief Cetewayo (or Cetshwayo), son of Panda and nephew of Chaka and Dingaan. The new king, however, was not at all inclined to be a puppet in the hands of the Whites and managed to assemble an army of forty to sixty thousand men, ably commanded, well equipped and, most important of all, instilled with the discipline which had shown its effectiveness on so many battlefields. For several years Boers and Zulu had been quarrelling over an intermediate territory, a problem which the British now inherited. Since annexations were fashionable in London, the experts suggested: 'After the Transvaal, why not Zululand?' Was not the best method of reconciling the contending parties to subject them both to the same sovereignty?

The affair nearly ended in tragedy. In December 1878, Cetewayo received an ultimatum ordering him to disband his army and pay reparations for insults to Whites. When he made no reply, three columns left Natal to invade his territory. The time of year was unfavourable: torrential rain and flooded rivers obstructed the conquerors' advance through country covered with wooded hills ideal for ambushes. The detachment was commanded by Lord Chelmsford, who had fought in the Crimean War, taken part in the suppression of the Indian Mutiny and led a punitive expedition in Abyssinia. His portraits reveal a quiet assurance and a certain naïvety. The decisions which he took show that he must have considered it inconceivable that Black Africans could be capable of standing up to British soldiers. On 20 January he pitched camp on the hill of Isundhlwana, about thirty miles inside enemy territory. He took no precautions, neither a reconnaissance in the European style nor a *laager* of the Boer type. Everything seemed quiet enough when suddenly, around four o'clock in the afternoon, 'there appeared as if by magic, from one edge of the ridge to the other, a long line of black men in skirmishing order. . . . It was a grand sight and they never uttered a word.' This was merely a warning. The sun was setting and the vision disappeared. Chelmsford made the mistake of setting off in pursuit with a detachment of troops. Thirty-six hours later the Zulu returned in force: eight hundred dead and nearly a thousand rifles and four hundred thousand cartridges lost were the outcome of this pitched battle between natives and Europeans. Reinforcements arrived, however, and Wolseley was put in command. Cetewayo, hard pressed, took to his heels. The war was drawing to its end when, on 1 June, the death of the Prince Imperial of France cast a shadow on the British successes.

The twenty-three-year-old son of Napoleon III, an officer in a British artillery regiment, had insisted on rejoining his comrades in South Africa, despite the expostulations of the Empress Eugénie. The British government had also tried to dissuade him, but with no more success. He had arrived at Lord Chelmsford's headquarters on 3 April 1879, bearing a letter from the Duke of Cambridge. 'My only anxiety in his conduct,' wrote the commander-in-chief of the British army, 'would be that he is too plucky and go-ahead.' It was difficult to know what to do with this rather embarrassing volunteer. At first he was appointed as a staff officer to the Royal Engineers and then, at his own insistence, to the reconnaissance service.

On 1 June a sergeant, five cavalrymen and a Kaffir left on an expedition under 'Lieutenant Napoleon' and a Lieutenant Carey, who was to keep an eye on him. The mission was in Zululand, a region of tall grass ideal for ambushes. On the way back, at about three o'clock in the afternoon, the officers decided to halt in an abandoned *kraal*[1] near the Ityotyozi river. No precautions were taken: no scout was sent out and no sentry posted.

Just as the detachment was preparing to move off again an hour later, the Kaffir guide, in a state of great excitement, announced that he had glimpsed the head of a Zulu in the brush. Lieutenant Carey leapt on to his horse, but the prince waited calmly until everyone was ready. Fifty or so

[1] See pp. 28–9.

natives surged forward, shouting their war-cry, *Usutu*. There was total panic: the cavalrymen galloped off, except for two soldiers, whom the Zulu threw to the ground and slaughtered, and 'Lieutenant Napoleon', who was trying to master his rearing mount. Then his saddle-girth broke, leaving him to the mercy of the assailants—they were the first to admit that he had fought 'like a lion'.

At his court-martial Carey claimed that he had not immediately noticed that the prince was not following him. When he became aware of his absence, he maintained, he had realized that going back on his tracks would simply have meant getting his men killed. Although Carey was acquitted, his career was ruined when a letter which he had written to his wife on the evening of the incident was published, in which, under the stress of emotion, he had admitted his moral responsibility.

The Prince Imperial's mutilated body was found stripped of his clothes; all that remained, twisted round his neck, was a thin gold chain with a medal of the Virgin Mary and a replica of the Emperor Napoleon's seal. He had received seventeen wounds, all indicating that he had died facing the enemy.

His body was taken back to England. The following year the Empress Eugénie went on a pilgrimage to the scene of the tragedy, where a cross had been erected on a pile of stones.

The last king of the Zulu finally placed himself at the mercy of his vanquishers. Cetewayo, according to an eye-witness, 'looked utterly exhausted and could hardly walk, the insides of his thighs were chafed raw with walking and running'. But, if he had lost nearly everything, he still retained his dignity. He was received with great ceremony at the British headquarters. 'At the head of the procession was Major Master followed by his trumpet and orderly, accompanied with a body of officers all with drawn swords. Following them was a company of dragoon guards with accoutrements flashing in the brilliant sunlight. Then, between two officers with swords at the salute, the king carrying a long stick, the symbol of his chieftainship. As he marched slowly forward between files of men all with fixed bayonets, he presented a strikingly impressive figure, every inch a king.' Cetewayo learned that he was deposed, considered a prisoner of war, and his kingdom divided into thirteen districts, under the nominal authority of a tribal chief and the effective control of a British Resident.[1]

The Boers' refusal to give the British any assistance had not increased their popularity. Sir William Lanyon, Shepstone's successor as Administrator of

---

[1] The ex-king obtained permission to go to England in 1882. He had an audience with the Queen and the Prince of Wales. Victoria presented him with a photograph bearing this dedication: 'I respect you as a brave enemy who will, I trust, become a firm friend.' He was allowed to return to his own country and to exercise a limited authority there. He died in 1884. Zululand was finally annexed to Natal in 1897.

the territory since the beginning of 1879, believed in strong-arm methods. He was convinced that Her Majesty's new subjects were 'like children who have yet to be taught the lesson of obedience'. Governor Frere was not far from sharing this view. When he came to conduct his own inquiry, the Transvaalers told him that they wanted a return to the Sand River Convention, to which he retorted that they 'might as well ask to go back to the Garden of Eden'. Wolseley, in true military style, did not mince his words. Three proclamations within a few months presented his point of view in the simplest possible terms. In the first he declared that the Transvaal would remain British as long as the sun shone; in the second, 'Transvaal shall continue to be forever an integral portion of Her Majesty's dominions in South Africa'; and finally: 'Under no circumstance whatever can Britain give back this country. Facts are stubborn things. It is a fact that we are here; and it is an undoubted fact that we shall remain here.' To show that he was not joking he had Pretorius put in prison, though he found himself rather foolishly having to release him not long afterwards.

Resistance was still being organized. Shepstone had promised all kinds of wonders, but changing its flag was not enough to make the poor Transvaal a rich country. The financial situation was still weak, and the Boers, naturally disinclined to fulfil their fiscal obligations, made it worse by refusing to pay taxes. A change of government in Britain gave a boost to their hopes. At the beginning of 1880, Gladstone and the Liberals replaced Disraeli and the Conservatives. When Leader of the Opposition, the new Prime Minister had condemned his predecessor's policy with some eloquent phrases. From one of his resounding speeches these words were remembered: 'We are in the strange predicament of the free subject of a monarch going to coerce the free subjects of a republic.' But Downing Street must have been his road to Damascus, for he now proceeded to reverse his position and resorted to this sly argument to justify his *volte-face*: 'To repudiate the annexation of a country is one thing, to abandon that annexation is another.' Clearly only force could settle the dispute. In December 1880 the revolt became quite open. Paul Kruger, Piet Joubert and Marthinus Pretorius formed a triumvirate. The *Volksraad* of 1877 was recalled and the national flag was hoisted over Heidelberg, the provisional capital of the 'insurgents'. The first shot was fired by the British on 16 December, the forty-second anniversary of Pretorius's victory over the Zulu at Blood River.

Perhaps this coincidence intensified the determination of the six thousand burghers who had taken up arms. At all events, they gained one success after another. The war lasted less than three months. The decisive date was 27 February 1881: on that day two hundred Boers took by storm the apparently impregnable hill of Majuba, held by over five hundred British soldiers. The accuracy of the assailants' fire is evident from the losses sustained on each side: the Boers had one killed and five wounded, whereas the British had ninety-two killed (including their general) and a hundred and thirty-four wounded.

The government in London had the sense not to persist. An immediate cease-fire was followed by a peace treaty signed at Pretoria in August. The British negotiators certainly knew their job. The Transvaal recovered its independence, but at what a price! A British Resident would have a right of inspection for laws concerning the natives; the new state could not sign treaties without the approval of its suzerain, the Queen; its western frontier was adjusted, and to the east it lost control of Swaziland; and in time of war Britain reserved the right to send troops through its territory. Kruger summed up Britain's attitude in a colourful image: 'First you put your head quietly in the noose so that I can hang you, then you can kick your legs as much as you please.' The agreement was ratified by the *Volksraad* only under the threat of renewed hostilities. The small group of British settlers in the Transvaal complained of treachery and formed an association which called history to its aid by claiming that Great Britain 'evinced a state of national degradation comparable to that which existed at the time of the second Charles'.

What must they have thought three years later! In 1883 a German warship cast anchor in the bay of Angra Pequena, about a hundred and fifty miles from the mouth of the Orange in the Atlantic Ocean. The territorial designs of Berlin could not have been more clearly indicated. The Colonial Office, already alarmed by French, Italian and Belgian ambitions in Africa, judged it prudent not to provoke an adversary whose calibre had been demonstrated at Majuba. Kruger, elected president that same year, took advantage of the opportunity. In 1884 he went to London and negotiated a new Convention infinitely more favourable to the Boers. Britain henceforth would be represented only by a consul instead of a Resident; the Transvaal—reverting to its name of South African Republic —recovered the right to legislate as it thought best in native matters; the only restriction of its sovereignty was the condition that its treaties, except those with the Orange Free State, would remain subject to the Queen's approval; finally, British subjects, now authorized to settle freely in the new state and to possess land and conduct business there, could not be taxed more heavily than the rest of the population. This was a far cry from the fanfares that had greeted Shepstone's assumption of office.

The years immediately preceding and following 1880 proved decisive in the history of South Africa.

In the first place, they marked the end of the conflicts between White and Black which had started on the banks of the Fish river in 1779 and had continued for a century. Henceforward, there were to be revolts and bloody encounters, but no more wars, properly speaking, such as those which the Boers and then the British had been obliged to fight against the Kaffirs and the Zulu. Futhermore, the upheavals set in motion by the discovery of diamonds, and precipitated by the discovery of gold,[1] were to bring about radical changes in the lot of the natives. From agricultural labourers, continuing even under a European master the way of life to which they had been accustomed, they were to become workers in mines and factories—a condition very different from that of their ancestors and which, imperceptibly but irresistibly, would undermine the tribal customs and structures round which they had hitherto maintained their cohesion.

No less important in its consequences was the awakening, during this same period, of an Afrikaner nationalism, whose origins and long-term effects have been skilfully analysed by Professor van Jaarsveld. This doctrine had been slow to emerge. It was not until they had suffered many ordeals that the Boers, born individualists, finally acquired a sense of solidarity. The Great Trek had divided rather than united them; they had fought side by side against the natives, but, once the danger was past, their desire for solitude had prevailed. The Transvaal had given them the illusion of a Promised Land; there they had found the great open spaces that they had known sixty years earlier, when they had made up their minds to leave the Cape region. Only occasionally finding themselves called together to form commandos, the purpose and duration of which were in any case always limited, they knew no unity other than the family and, moreover, they wanted no other.

When Britain recognized the independence of the Free State and the South African Republic, the result was distintegration rather than unification. Left to their own devices the Boers, especially in the Transvaal, succumbed to the factious, and even anarchic, tendencies which they had displayed on so many occasions. At this same time, those of their fellow-Boers who had remained in British territory were offering only a mild resistance to a process of anglicization which, all the signs suggested, would be irreversible.

British imperialism saved the Afrikaners. It will be remembered that towards 1870 the Colonial Office had changed its policy. For the past thirty years it had tended to take little interest in South Africa, but around this time it decided, on the contrary, to establish British power there permanently. It believed that it had found a panacea in a federation similar to that which appeared to have solved the Canadian problem. It then proceeded to indulge in a fever of activity: the annexation of Basutoland, the annexation of the Diamond Fields and finally—the decisive stroke—the annexation of the Transvaal. The Free State, the sole survivor, was now merely an island in a British sea.

Confident that it was winning the game, Britain had in fact just lost it. The Boers suddenly realized that they had not taken full advantage of their independence—they had to be deprived of freedom in order to appreciate its value. The series of meetings that preceded the outbreak of hostilities, and even more their military successes, had made them aware

[1] See Chapter 14.

of a national consciousness. The inhabitants of the Free State, on the other hand, now discovered the blood ties that linked them with their brothers beyond the Vaal. Even in distant Cape Colony there emerged the dream of a South Africa united under a single flag, whose union was not imposed by a foreign power but fashioned by the inhabitants themselves.

Afrikaner nationalism had taken shape. Finding its roots in the cult of the past, its strength in the mystical notion of the 'chosen people', and built around the idea of a 'motherland' that would finally welcome her scattered sons, it was to grow slowly but surely. The Boer War was to cement this feeling with blood, and nearly a century after Majuba it is more vigorous than ever. South Africa would be incomprehensible without a knowledge of the slow, powerful evolution which has reached its culmination in the country of today.

14

The Discovery of Gold

History offers no comparable phenomenon. For two hundred years southern Africa had been vegetating; it was barely known to the rest of the world and it seemed doomed to mediocrity. Then, suddenly, twice within twenty years, its earth revealed treasures; all eyes turned towards it, and the obstacles along the road to its future seemed to have vanished as if by magic.

The discovery of gold, however, was not quite as unexpected as that of diamonds had been. Without going as far back as Solomon and the queen of Sheba, the possibility of finding the most precious of metals in the African continent had long fired imaginations. The Portuguese, it will be recalled, had built great hopes on the empire of the Monomotapa, but had encountered only disappointment. It was not until the middle of the nineteenth century that these age-old dreams became a reality. The beginnings proved modest. In 1868 a German geologist affirmed the existence of gold reefs in the south of present-day Rhodesia; three years later a similar verdict, this time followed by mining, was reached at Lydenburg, about a hundred and twenty miles north-east of Pretoria; but the rock was hard and the results proved poor. In 1884, at last, it seemed that a strike had been made. In the course of their travels the Barber brothers discovered gold not far from the Portuguese frontier, in the direction of Delagoa Bay. Within a few months a mushroom-town had sprung up on the site, and by 1886 Barberton had over two thousand inhabitants. The experts, however, questioned the value of the deposits and they were not mistaken: in less than three years Barberton had dwindled to nothing.

The search for gold-bearing land thus aroused a curiosity tinged with scepticism. When, in 1885, Frederick and Henrik Struben assured the *Volksraad* that they had found large deposits in the Witwatersrand,[1] which were all the richer for lying deep in the earth, there was no lack of doubting Thomases. Everyone knew this ridge of mountains rising to some six thousand feet, thirty miles from the capital, mountains which change colour with the time of day; rosy at dawn, bluish in the afternoon

[1] *White Waters Rand*, the 'ridge of the white waters', commonly abbreviated to 'the Rand'.

and golden in the sunset. But if their beauty was unquestionable, their bare, barren earth held little appeal for the Boers. That land unsuited for cattle-raising could be a source of wealth ran counter to their whole way of life and way of thinking. Furthermore, they were mistrustful of this new type of land exploitation which threatened to attract unwelcome strangers. In 1852, a year after independence, one of their number had thought he had discovered gold in the Witwatersrand, but the authorities decided to prohibit the circulation of this information under pain of death.

This time the pressure of reality proved too great, and in September 1886 the government had to give way. It decreed that mines could be worked only with official permission. A settlement began to take shape, at first consisting only of canvas tents, but soon huts of wood, corrugated iron and mud appeared; it adopted the name of Johannesburg (the president of the Republic and the Director of Mines both bore the Christian name of Johannes). By the beginning of 1887 it already numbered three thousand inhabitants. People arrived on foot, on horseback, but mostly in convoys of ox-wagons. The place did not attract those who liked their comfort, for it had neither water nor lighting, and the streets were dusty in winter and muddy in summer. A semblance of town-planning could be found in Market Square, a large rectangular space where the oxen were unyoked and the wagons unloaded, and in Commissioner Street, the fashionable district, where there was more corrugated iron than canvas. Frequent epidemics of typhoid were the price for sanitary conditions which it is not difficult to imagine. The only relaxations were gambling and the bars, one of which was run by a German woman who, according to her customers, was 'brisk, accommodating and charming . . . a pleasant and good-natured maiden whose favours were impartially distributed'. As for contacts with the rest of the world, it was best not to be in a hurry: a letter took four to five weeks to reach London and at least four days to reach Kimberley, about three hundred miles away as the crow flies.

If the beginnings of the Rand are reminiscent of the American Gold Rush, what followed was quite different. A little luck and a sieve were for a time all that was needed to make a fortune in California. The prospector's equipment was limited to a shovel, a crude cradle to remove the topsoil, and one or two wooden bowls for washing off the sand. Some prospectors contented themselves with scraping the bottom of the stream with a knife (some of the nuggets carried along by the current came from a region of gold-bearing veins in Nevada). In South Africa the problems were quite different. It was soon realized that the tools of the individual prospector were useless, for the gold was embedded in rocks which had to be broken to get to the vein, protected by a matrix of extremely hard quartz. A nugget of variable dimensions might then be found, or sometimes just grains. Techniques became more and more sophisticated when it was observed that the richest deposits were nearly always the deepest. Shafts were then sunk which soon descended to a depth of over six thousand feet, giving the countryside a fantastic appearance, and later a network of tunnels was excavated, extending over several miles. Thus, from the outset, machinery and capital were indispensable. It was all very tempting. The proximity of coal-mines and the area of the Rand (170 miles long and 100 miles wide) guaranteed large profits. It was now twenty years since diamonds had been discovered. At Kimberley there had suddenly emerged a group of newly rich businessmen with a flair for obtaining the maximum return from any enterprise, and they now arrived at Johannesburg, bringing with them their experience and ambition, their optimism and greed.

Among them was J. B. Robinson, forty-six years of age, the son of an 1820 settler. He had fought in the Basuto wars and was one of the first to become a big diamond-dealer. The prospect of gold attracted him all the more strongly because his financial situation had been causing him grave concern. He obtained a loan and then, with characteristic intuition, bought lands that were soon to multiply a thousandfold in value, conducting his affairs with a ruthless determination that made him a number of enemies.

Friedrich Eckstein, barely thirty years old and born in Stuttgart, had tried his luck in the Indies, then South Africa had lured him. Unlike Robinson, he was capable of sentimental weaknesses, and was about to marry a very pretty girl. Was it for her that he took such great care of his appearance? Only in the most torrid heat would he agree to wear a colonial-style helmet in place of his London bowler hat, and he was always immaculately dressed, even on the dustiest days. The cut of his beard and moustache was impeccable. He claimed to resemble the Prince of Wales, and indeed his photographs do suggest a similarity. But he did not allow his Beau Brummel manner to interfere with his business activities. On 11 October 1886 he wrote to his brother: 'I have been away six weeks to Johannesburg; the journey was very tiring; I often did not get out of my clothes for four days and nights, sleeping out of doors or on terrible floors in rooms full of vermin. I fell, with horses or without but, thank God, without any damage. I lost ten pounds and feel fit and well.'

'Jim' Taylor, twenty-seven years of age, was always seen in tweeds with a flower in his buttonhole, his supreme luxury. He would only change his garb to put on riding-breeches and boots, which accentuated his country-gentleman appearance, though it was not agriculture that interested him. Like his friend Eckstein, he was conscious of his responsibilities, for both men represented Alfred Beit, one of the Kimberley magnates. Beit was also a German, of Jewish ancestry and Lutheran religion, native of Hamburg and thirty-six years of age. He had learnt his trade with Jules Porgès, who had come to Paris from Prague and become an international diamond-dealer. His employer had sent him to South Africa with one of his compatriots, Julius Wernher, three years his senior. When Porgès retired from business his two disciples followed in his footsteps and the firm of Wernher, Beit and Company acquired a worldwide reputation.

Cecil Rhodes was not one of the pioneers in the development of the Rand. When he heard the news of the discoveries he remained, for a time, more interested in diamonds than in gold. At Kimberley he had established himself in a prominent position which he was determined to transform into a monopoly; in any case, he attached more importance to the gold deposits of the region which was to become Rhodesia than to those of the Transvaal; his political ambitions, moreover, made him reluctant to move too far from the Cape. Yet he was not the sort of man to miss an opportunity. He went to Johannesburg and took options which he would have exercised immediately if he had not learnt of the illness of a friend. This future empire-builder allowed his sympathy to get the better of self-interest, leaving everything to go to the sick man's bedside, where he remained until his death. Once his friend was gone, the plans made a few months earlier began to take shape again, and in 1887, with his Kimberley associate, Charles Rudd, Rhodes founded the Gold Fields of South Africa Company.

This was only a minor achievement by comparison with his grand design. At this time only one man was still opposing him on the battle-fields of the diamond industry. But what a man! Barney Isaacs was born in 1852 in Whitechapel, the poor Jewish quarter of London. As a young man, together with his brother, he had made himself a reputation as a clown, juggler and boxer in the popular music-halls. He adopted the name Barnato, which he thought sounded better.[1] At the age of twenty he was beginning to wonder where his theatrical talents would lead him. Fascinating rumours were coming from South Africa. His elder brother, Henry, decided to go out to verify the rumours, and Barney followed him not long afterwards. The future diamond king arrived at the Cape in 1873, with a box of cigars which a far-sighted sister had given him for business purposes, and about forty pounds, five of which he spent on the hire of an ox-wagon to Kimberley. It was an awkward time to arrive there, for the diamond market was going through a crisis. Barnato decided that, for the time being, it would be advisable to revert to his former activities. Once again he was seen in the boxing ring and on the music-hall stage, but at a rather more refined level: *Othello* became one of his successes, and it is said that he used to like reciting Hamlet's monologue standing on his hands.

These were merely curtain-raisers. Barnato had not sailed from the north to the south Atlantic to seek applause in the theatre. He proceeded to make a thorough study of the diamond market and, when the situation improved, started buying and selling, his instinct always telling him where

[1] One of his biographers say that the name 'Barnato' originated from 'Barney too', an expression which the two brothers used to refer to their exploits together.

the best deposits lay. Thus began a rise to stupendous heights. Soon he controlled a multiplicity of firms which he was continually merging with others. Twelve years after landing at the Cape, what must he have thought when he looked back to his days in Whitechapel!

It would be difficult to imagine two men more different from each other than Cecil Rhodes and Barney Barnato. Rhodes was lanky in build, with long, stiff arms, his figure slightly bent, moving with a heavy step and looking older then he really was. Barnato, on the other hand, was small and squat, with a round nose, chin and head, his whole body possessing an athletic agility and suppleness and brimming with health, whereas Rhodes, according to one doctor, had less than six months to live.

The moral and intellectual differences between the two rivals are even more striking than the contrast in their physique. Rhodes, a lone wolf, sought the company of a few friends only; he detested the noise and bustle of a crowd, and took no interest in women. He was moved by a single idea, or rather a single obsession: the creation of a British Empire which, under English or, if necessary, Anglo-Saxon leadership, would unite the peoples of Africa and, eventually, the whole world; not, however, in the Roman manner, but in federations which, by respecting national traditions and identities, would ensure liberty and progress for all, under the protection of the Union Jack. To this glorious objective Rhodes was determined to devote a life which he sensed would be short. For this dreamer, who was certainly not out of touch with reality, money was a means rather than an end in itself. If he put so much energy into its acquisition, it was primarily *ad majorem Britanniae gloriam.*

Barnato did not concern himself with such vast and remote visions. He loved life, gambling and women, bars and race-courses, wherever he found gaiety, desire or intrigue. To make more and more money, to breathe an atmosphere of power, to bask in flattery, were enough to justify an existence whose only goal was success and wealth.

When the struggle began, Rhodes seemed likely to be the loser. Everybody knew that he did not have the same means at this disposal as his rival.[1] On the other hand, he lacked neither tenacity nor shrewdness. He managed to convince the Rothschilds in London and Wernher and Beit in Pretoria; with their assistance he acquired control of the French Diamond Company, thus finding himself in a position to negotiate on equal terms. But he was not satisfied with this. To put his imperial schemes into effect he needed to find a way to merge the rival concerns into a single firm with himself in control. Barnato was avoiding him, but Rhodes guessed his weak spot. He is supposed to have said to his adversary: 'This is no mere transaction; I propose to make a gentleman of you.' In more concrete terms this meant that Rhodes would get him into the Kimberley Club (the local Jockey Club) and ensure his election to

---

[1] According to some sources, the De Beers Company, which he controlled, was worth only a third of Kimberley Mines, of which Barnato was majority shareholder.

Parliament, of which Rhodes had been a member since 1881. Barnato must have trembled with excitement: a position in society and political influence were just what he lacked. Rhodes kept his promises, and the aristocracy of the diamond world admitted this rather too flamboyant upstart to its circle. As for the electors, the clubman found a way of charming them. Barnato conducted his campaign in a grey frock-coat and a top hat, with a red flower in his buttonhole. He could be seen descending from a carriage adorned with his monogram in gold letters, drawn by four dappled horses with riders dressed in red, and escorted by six more horsemen in equally gaudy livery, the procession being led by a gigantic postilion blowing a horn. How could the electorate resist him?

Before his triumph, however, the future member of Parliament had been obliged to bow to Rhodes's supremacy. De Beers Consolidated Mines Limited was formed in March 1888. Barnato had agreed to his enterprises being merged with those of Rhodes, on condition that he received a cheque for over five million pounds and a governorship for life in the new company. It had never occurred to him that De Beers Consolidated could have any other purpose than making profits, and he soon discovered that he was mistaken. He and his nephew, Wolf Joël, were invited to the house of the most popular doctor in Kimberley, Dr Jameson. There they found Cecil Rhodes and Alfred Beit. Rhodes began to speak. De Beers Consolidated would not restrict itself to sinking shafts and selling diamonds: its strength would enable it to prospect in the north, a region with a fabulous future. Joël protested that this was all fantasy, but Rhodes proceeded to prove his point by spreading out maps, quoting names and invoking statistics. After eighteen hours Barnato, exhausted, gave in—it was four o'clock in the morning. 'You want the means to go North if possible, so I suppose we must give it to you.' Later, he is said to have remarked of Rhodes: 'You cannot resist him, you must be with him.'

Was this the reason why, fleeing the seducer, Barnato went several months later to Johannesburg, where he had not yet been seen? His arrival did not pass unnoticed; after being greeted with a fanfare and bunches of flowers, he delivered a sensational speech in the course of which he declared: 'I look forward to Johannesburg becoming the financial Gibraltar of South Africa.' Then he set about buying land, forming companies and speculating on the Stock Exchange, the latter sometimes rather noisily, judging by this report sent to London by Eckstein: 'Barnato is making as always a great show. He fought with Lilienfeld in the Exchange. . . . Pending his apology, we have forbidden him entrance.' But this was a minor incident, and within three months there had appeared Barnato Consolidated Mines, Barnato Bank, Mining and Investment Corporation, and Johannesburg Consolidated Investment Company, not forgetting the Barnato Building where—perhaps in revenge?—a new Stock Exchange was to be installed. At the Corner

House[1] this flurry of activity caused a certain amusement, but it also aroused anxiety.

It would be tedious to relate in detail the ensuing battles of the giants, which always displayed the same boldness, the same passion and the same success. In 1889, however, it seemed that Johannesburg would suffer the fate of Barberton. A quarter of the population, it is estimated, left the city. In sinking shafts the mining engineers had eventually struck ore from which it proved so difficult to extract the gold that few firms could cope with the extra expense. As has happened more than once in its history, luck was on South Africa's side: its mines were saved by the discovery that, by using cyanide, even the most refractory rocks would yield ninety per cent of the metal. Furthermore, this temporary collapse had the advantage of eliminating fifty or so of the less solidly based concerns. The boom got under way once more, and in 1893 the Corner House achieved its greatest glory, the establishment of the famous Rand Mines Limited, a gigantic enterprise combining Eckstein, Beit, the Rothschilds of both London and Paris, and Cecil Rhodes.[2] Six years later it was distributing a dividend of one hundred per cent.

Ten years after its foundation Johannesburg had become an American-style city with straight, intersecting streets, parks, gardens, a residential district away from the city centre and a business quarter with Stock Exchanges, clubs and offices that emptied every evening. The Black workers—about 34,000—lived near the mines in enclosures similar to those at Kimberley, but apparently less strictly supervised.

In 1896 a census was taken which revealed that, out of 47,000 Whites, only 6,000 were born in the Transvaal. In the rest of the Transvaal the proportion was obviously reversed. Nevertheless, it remained a fact that, within a few years, an industrial city populated by foreigners had sprung up in the midst of a Boer civilization still predominantly pastoral. It is now necessary to go back and describe the preliminaries to the great drama which was precipitated by the arrival of so many newcomers.

---

[1] The Corner House was the headquarters of the gold magnates. The name became proverbial in Johannesburg.

[2] Of the first 300,000 shares, Eckstein held 200,000, the Rothschilds 60,000 and Rhodes 30,000. Barnato, who was now acting alone, committed suicide in a fit of madness, throwing himself into the sea from a liner that was taking him to England, in 1897, for the sixtieth anniversary of Queen Victoria's coronation. He was forty-five.

15

Rhodes and Kruger

To sum up the fifteen years following the liberation of the Transvaal with the names of Rhodes and Kruger is to reduce the problem to its essentials. These two men dominated the period. They both knew what they wanted and both were as tough as steel. This was a meeting of the giants which was to have far-reaching consequences and without which the present Republic of South Africa would not exist.

The personality of Cecil Rhodes has been briefly outlined in the preceding chapter. In the course of the events described here, he will be seen asserting himself with an extraordinary single-mindedness, employing different means but pursuing a single objective. Kruger was no less tenacious a personality, but his touch lacked subtlety. Above all, he found himself driven into a defensive position, whereas his adversary enjoyed the advantages of the offensive.

Stephanus Johannes Paulus Kruger was fifty-eight when his fellow-countrymen voted him to power. 'One of their entrails,' a contemporary wrote of Hugues Capet, referring to the Franks. This description of the first Capetian fits to perfection the man elected first president of the Transvaal in 1883. It would have been difficult to be more 'Boer' than Paul Kruger. One of his ancestors, a native of the Berlin region, had entered the service of the Dutch East India Company at the beginning of the eighteenth century and, like most of his kind, had then become a crop-farmer. The Krugers followed the classic route, settling first in the environs of the Cape and then pushing farther and farther into the *veld*. When Paul Kruger was born in 1825, his parents were living to the south of the Orange. Their way of life was typical: an isolated farm, cattle to tend, excursions on horseback and hunting expeditions that often proved hazardous (folklore has preserved the memory of the future president's encounters with bad-tempered lions). Education was almost out of the question: a few months of school from time to time, which never went beyond instruction in the rudiments; but every day, morning and evening, there were readings from the Bible, which was accepted in its most literal sense,[1] and on Sundays psalms were sung. This apprenticeship

[1] According to one of his biographers, Kruger believed that the sun moved round the earth.

produced rough, tough men of narrow horizons, remarkable horsemen and excellent marksmen, accustomed to open spaces, danger and solitude. They married young. By the age of seventeen Paul Kruger was engaged; history, or perhaps legend, says that he would ride nearly two hundred and fifty miles to court Maria du Plessis, a girl of French stock. The marriage lasted only four years. A widower at twenty-one, Kruger then married Maria's cousin, Wilhelmina. This second union lasted fifty-four years, producing sixteen children and a hundred and twenty grandchildren.

When the Great Trek began, the Kruger family was among the first to leave, joining Potgieter's party. This marked the beginning of a great adventure for an eleven-year-old boy who quickly grew into a young man. During the Trek he attracted attention by his extraordinary vigour: he is said to have been able to run as fast as a horse, and in a long-jump competition, the story goes, he won the prize with a leap of twenty-five feet. His courage also created a sensation. It has been suggested by some writers that he was one of the survivors of the massacre in which Retief and his companions perished.[1] He was always in the forefront of commando expeditions, and the natives learned to fear his skill and his brutality. A background of this kind guaranteed his military and political career. He was at the side of Pretorius in the negotiations which in 1852 resulted in the first independence of the Transvaal. With his customary ardour he involved himself in the internal strife that subsequently tore his country apart, but always adopting the cause of unity rather than that of fragmentation. His appointment as commandant-general showed him how highly he was esteemed by the majority of his fellow-Transvaalers. His role at the time of the annexation and then the liberation of his country has already beeen described.

The man who had thus risen to supreme office was a giant in stature and heavy in proportion, weighing over fourteen stone; he had prominent lips, a large nose with wide nostrils, firm eyes that were almost black and suggested that they knew no fear, framed by thick brows and bags which became puffier with age; big ears, hair pushed back, side-whiskers, no moustache but a long curly beard that looked as if it might have been combed. People were fascinated merely by looking at him. 'This is Jehovah himself,' someone innocently remarked on one occasion. He spoke with a deep voice which he used to stunning effect, roaring like a lion, bellowing like a buffalo or trumpeting like an elephant when he was angry—which happened frequently, for 'Oom Paul' or 'Uncle Paul', as he was affectionately known, was a man of a violent temperament which he knew how to turn to his advantage. Those who witnessed his fits of rage never forgot them. He would pace up and down, disconcerting noises issuing from his mouth, and his surroundings at such times seemed to make little impression on him. The story goes that at a session of the *Volkrsaad* he tore off the green sash, the emblem of his office, in

[1] See p. 95.

exasperation, stamped on it, then grabbed two of his most outspoken opponents by the shoulders and shook them so fiercely that they nearly lost their balance.

Presidential audiences were thus something of an adventure, for no one knew in what frame of mind he would find 'Oom Paul'. This man of passion was also an eccentric. Only in exceptional circumstances would he deviate from a rigid timetable. He would rise before dawn and begin the day with a reading from the Bible and a cup of coffee. At eight o'clock he had breakfast with his family and then set off for his office. At first he would go there on foot, invariably dressed in a black frock-coat and a top hat; later, protocol and the possibility of an attempt on his life compelled him to travel in a carriage, surrounded by an escort of horsemen. He would spend an hour talking with his colleagues and going through his mail. At ten o'clock he appeared at the *Volksraad*. He dominated the assembly by the superiority of his character and the intensity of his eloquence; his speeches resembled sermons, delivered with a rapidity that made objections impossible and interspersed with biblical quotations and comparisons drawn from animal life which were designed to appeal to an audience of believers and landowners. At midday he was back in his spacious but simple house. Mrs Kruger, or 'Tant Sann', kept herself in the background, a stout woman in the tradition of the Scriptures whose only rule of life was *Kinder, Kirche, Küche*. At two o'clock her husband would leave again for his office, returning home at four. This was the time usually set aside for audiences, though sometimes visitors were summoned at four or five in the morning. As soon as the weather permitted, the president preferred to hold these audiences on his terrace. He would drink the traditional coffee with his guest, drawing clouds of smoke from his pipe and aiming at his spittoon with more persistence than success.[1] These occasions ended at twilight. Then the family would gather for a Bible reading and the evening meal. At nine o'clock, whatever the season, the lights went out and silence fell.

Amusements were out of the question, for Kruger was intolerant of human weaknesses. As a rule, feminine tastes meant nothing to him—dancing and an interest in clothes were, in his eyes, simply manifestations of Eve's determination to act as the messenger of Satan. In 1889 a Johannesburg club which had requested his patronage for a ball received a withering reply from his secretary: 'His Honour informs you that he considers a ball as Baal's services, for which reason the Lord ordered Moses to kill all offenders, and as it is therefore contrary to His Honour's principle, His Honour cannot consent to the misuse of his name on such occasion.' When his responsibilities required his presence at official

---

[1] Witness a letter written by the wife of one of his colleagues. Kruger had paid her husband a visit at four o'clock in the morning: 'I lay in bed lamenting for my tablecloths and chairs, since you know that not only wise words issue from Oom Paul's mouth and indeed I found the expected surprise. . . .'

receptions in Europe, he was disconcerted and pained by fashions of dress for which 'Tant Sann' had not prepared him. The story goes that on one occasion, in Holland, he did no speak a single word throughout the meal to the lady sitting next to him, because her neckline was too low for his liking.

Should one smile? Perhaps, if such narrow-mindedness had not been compensated by a burning, almost irrational patriotism which made Kruger a great man. He has been reproached for constantly referring to 'my government', 'my people', 'my country'. But his conception of 'his' Transvaal was a possessive, almost sensual idea; he was a part of 'his' land —in it he found his strength and his *raison d'être*, and to preserve it was his sole ambition.

Is it surprising, then, that Kruger and Rhodes found such difficulty in understanding one another? Kruger's horizon was limited to the *veld*, whereas Rhodes allowed his ambitions to roam across the world. One wanted only to survive, the other to dominate. 'Oom Paul' clung to the past, not foreseeing that he would shape the future; the 'Colossus', as Rhodes was ironically called, wished to mould the generations to come, and consequently his achievement has less resonance than that of his adversary. The two men met for the first time in 1885. Kruger had been president for two years, and Rhodes was beginning to control the diamond market. Was it the difference in age? Kruger was sixty, Rhodes thirty-two. At all events, the older man mistrusted the younger. 'That young man is going to cause me trouble,' Kruger is said to have prophesied. His opinion never varied. 'He goes too fast for me,' he admitted on another occasion. 'I cannot understand how he manages it, but he never sleeps and he will not smoke.' Kruger had a more serious criticism: 'You cannot come to an agreement with a man who never goes to church.' At another time he remarked: 'Only four people I fear, God, the Devil, De la Rey[1] for his enormous strength and quick tongue and that Englishman Rhodes.' The sentiments of 'that Englishman' were more complex, alternating between admiration and condescension: 'I regard him [Kruger] as one of the most remarkable men in South Africa, who has been singularly unfortunate . . . I pity him,' Rhodes once said. Secretly, he found Kruger no match for himself; above all, he was determined not to be hindered by the Boer. At first he tried charm; but, in embracing his rival, his purpose was to destroy him.

In the year in which Kruger became president, Germany, it will be recalled, had hoisted its flag at Angra Pequena, to the north of the Orange. It was tempting for the Transvaal to establish contact with the forces of a sympathetic power. Admittedly, Pretoria lay more than seven hundred miles, as the crow flies, from the Atlantic, but distances did not frighten the Boers. No sooner had they recovered a conditional independence than

[1] The future general of the Boer War.

they attempted expansion to the west. If they succeeded, they thought, they would have erected a barrier to British expansion, which was threatening to encircle them. To act officially was dangerous. But the technique of using 'volunteers' is not a monopoly of the twentieth century. As early as 1882 commandos—at the request of zealous natives, it goes without saying—took possession of the rich lands in southern Bechuanaland and proclaimed the two 'independent republics' of Stellaland and Goshen. There was great agitation in London, and even more so in Cape Town. Should the *fait accompli* simply be accepted? The missionaries erupted in virtuous indignation, but Rhodes doubted the effectiveness of such methods. He was now beginning to wield a certain political influence and obtained the appointment of a commission of inquiry. On principles he remained intransigent: 'Don't part with one inch of territory to Transvaal,' he urged Prime Minister Scanlen; 'they are bouncing. The interior road[1] runs at present on the edge of the Transvaal territory; you part with that and you are driven into the desert.' Yet, secretly, he would not have been opposed to a compromise on the method of procedure. The Boers, however, were avoiding the issue, and a reckless act precipitated a solution: in September 1884, Kruger placed the contested territories under his protection. London issued threats and Pretoria quickly gave way, but not soon enough, and four thousand Imperial troops occupied the region. In 1885 Bechuanaland was divided in two: the south, between the Orange and the Molopo, became a Crown Colony; to the north, as far as the 22nd parallel, a more flexible régime was provided. The western frontier of the South African Republic was now firmly sealed and contact with the Germans prohibited. Of more serious significance was the fact that this decision gave the Boers new grounds for bitterness.

Rhodes deplored the decision; he would have preferred a willing victim. Nevertheless, he was not a man to let an opportunity pass. Ruskin's address to the students of Oxford reverberated in his memory: 'Will you, youths of England, make your country a royal throne of kings, a sceptred isle, for all the world a source of light, a centre of peace?' Rhodes dreamed only of grand enterprises. 'His plans,' writes the most recent of his biographers, 'were always on an immense scale; to monopolize the diamond industry, to paint the map of Africa red, to restore the United States to an enlarged British Empire, to "square the Pope", to found a secret society which should control the world, to annex the planets, even, in a moment of frustration and euphoria combined.' In 1885 the north was his obsession: 'up yonder', to use his own phrase, he sensed that new riches awaited him. Above all, there was emerging in his imaginative and yet realistic mind the majestic vision of a Union Jack flying without interruption from the Cape to Cairo.

It took him only four years to establish a hold over the country that was

---

[1] The famous 'Missionaries' Road' (see p. 120). It was eventually nicknamed the 'Suez Canal of South Africa'.

to become Rhodesia. The Matabele had fled to the regions north of the Limpopo after the Boers had driven them from the High Veld. There they lived under the paternal and despotic rule of Lobengula, son of the great Msilikasi.[1] Lobengula was an astounding fellow, over six feet tall, said to weigh twenty stone and dressed in nothing but a loin-cloth. Unhappy memories of the Whites were just beginning to fade when these tiresome creatures reappeared on the scene, arriving from both east and south. The Boers were the first to show themselves, and in 1887 Lobengula, who had no idea what it was all about, concluded a treaty of alliance with them, agreeing to receive a consular representative in his *kraal*. This was more than Cape Town could endure. Rhodes did not like the missionaries, but was not averse to making use of them. Ten months later the Reverend Moffat persuaded Lobengula to repudiate his treaty and promise not to make another without the approval of the British government.

This negative result was soon transformed into something more positive. The time had come for serious talking. Instead of a churchman, Rhodes this time sent a businessman, his associate Charles Rudd. This diamond expert worked wonders, reassuring Lobengula that no one had any intention of taking his lands, but just his subsoil, which was utterly useless for cattle. The king of the Matabele put yet another cross below his name, ceding to the foreign visitor the right to exploit all the minerals and metals that might be found on his domains. In exchange he would receive a hundred pounds a month, a steamboat on the Zambezi and—most precious of all—a thousand rifles and a hundred thousand cartridges.[2] Lobengula resigned himself to all this; then, having second thoughts, he decided to send a protest to the British Queen. 'The white people are troubling me much about gold. If the queen hears that I have given away the whole country, it is not so. I have no one in my country who knows how to write. I do not know where the dispute is as I have no knowledge of writing.' It is not said who held the pen for him. In any case, this appeal, which seems to have taken nearly four months to reach Cape Town, had no effect.

It remained to obtain official sanction and take possession of the territory. Rhodes took upon himself the first and more difficult task. He had enemies in London, but the magnetism of his personality reassured everyone. In 1889 the British South Africa Company, which he had just founded, received a royal charter: over a territory that extended as far as Lake Nyasa, and which was estimated at roughly twelve hundred miles from north to south and over five hundred miles from east to west, it obtained a twenty-five-year monopoly of sovereignty and exploitation reminiscent of the big companies of earlier days. Getting rid of Lobengula

---

[1] See pp. 65–6.
[2] A British high official in Bechuanaland was delighted by this arrangement. 'The use of firearms in modern warfare has notoriously diminished the loss of life,' he observed.

was child's play, and it was now that Jameson first achieved fame.[1] He began with a courtesy visit, followed by eleven companions, 'the apostles of Rhodes' as they were known. Later, making a native raid his excuse, he decided on military occupation. On consulting Rhodes, he received this laconic reply: 'Read Luke, XIV, 31.'[2] In acknowledgement Jameson wrote: 'All right. I have read Luke.' He then invaded the territory of the Matabele, who were annihilated by machine-guns in two encounters. Lobengula fled and died shortly afterwards. The Union Jack was hoisted above his capital, Bulawayo. A year later Mashonaland, farther north, was also occupied and Fort Salisbury was built, in honour of Robert Arthur Talbot Gascoyne-Cecil, third Marquess of Salisbury, Prime Minister and Foreign Secretary.

The Transvaal's northern frontier was in its turn firmly sealed. At the same time, precautionary measures had been taken in the south: in 1884 the annexation of St Lucia Bay, half-way between Natal and the Portuguese possessions; in 1885 a 'protectorate' along the whole coast; and in 1887 the administration of Zululand by Natal (the final annexation took place ten years later). Only one door remained open to Kruger: Delagoa Bay, to which Pretorius and then Burgers had also been anxious to gain access.

In 1890 the High Commissioner entrusted the post of Prime Minister of the Cape Colony to Cecil Rhodes. Since the Colony had been endowed with a parliamentary system, five governments had followed one another in eighteen years, none of them of any great brilliance. The same could not be said of the new Prime Minister: president of De Beers Consolidated and of the Goldfields of South Africa Company, absolute master beyond the Limpopo, regarded with a favourable eye by the Queen[3] and the Prince of Wales, and associating with the greatest names of the English aristocracy on the board of his company, Rhodes was unique. 'When he stands on the Cape of Good Hope, his shadow falls to the Zambezi', Mark Twain was to say of him when he visited South Africa a few years later.

The time seemed ripe to realize the first stage of his mighty project: a customs union and a political federation. A few basic principles served as his guidelines. Rhodes assumed power on 17 July, and on 6 September he

[1] Dr Jameson had arrived in Kimberley in 1878, at the age of twenty-five. He practised medicine there successfully, but he was not satisfied with the life of a doctor. Exactly the same age as Rhodes, he became one of his most faithful friends.

[2] 'What king going to make war against another king settleth down first and consulteth whether he will be able with ten thousand to meet him that cometh against him with twenty thousand?'

[3] Rhodes knew how to please her. In November 1890 Victoria wrote in her Journal: 'He said Great Britain was the only country fit to colonize, no other succeeded. He hopes in time to see the English rule extend from Cape to Egypt. He thought everything would be arranged and the difficulties got over.'

expressed his intentions unambiguously: 'I am not prepared at any time to forfeit my flag.' The Union Jack was thus to be the symbol of the new order, within which the Cape would play a dominant role. Rhodes made frequent declarations to this effect before Parliament. On 8 September 1888, when he was still an ordinary member: 'Let us leave the Free State and the Transvaal to their own destiny; we must adopt the whole responsibility of the interior.' On 30 March 1891: 'If your ambition or policy is a union of South Africa, then the Cape Colony must keep as many cards as it may possess.' A little later (23 April), referring to the charter which his company had recently been granted, he promised the members that, if their sons and their merchandise were sent to the north, they would enjoy privileged treatment.

At this stage Rhodes had not yet despaired of including the Boer states in 'his' federation. He was on the best of terms with the leader of the Afrikaner Bond, Jan Hendrik Hofmeyr. The two men had been drawn to each other. Nearly the same age (Hofmeyr was the older by eight years), they thought along similar lines. Both wanted a form of union that would allow a diversity of ideas and customs to continue to exist around a common objective. The flag was a problem which they hoped that time would solve. Hofmeyr admired Britain and was steeped in British culture. Whatever would bring British and Boers closer together seemed to him constructive; whatever would divide them, destructive. For different reasons Rhodes thought roughly the same at this time. 'Africa first' could well have been one of his mottoes. When, in 1884, the Great Powers assembled in congress to assign themselves spheres of influence on the Dark Continent, he criticized their methods: he had had enough, he told his electors (who were probably delighted to hear it), of this manner of redrawing maps. His opinion was that the development of South Africa rested with that or those countries whose progress showed that they were the best qualified—in other words, the Cape Colony and, by courtesy only, its northern neighbours. Rhodes was particularly suspicious of Germany; on one occasion he declared with great passion that, as an Englishman, he had an intense horror of the German government.

He must have regretted those words, for they were hardly likely to promote a closer understanding with Pretoria where, however naïvely, so much was expected from Berlin. On the other hand, Rhodes's views on the Blacks must have found a favourable response among Kruger's circle. Both as an ordinary member of Parliament and as Prime Minister, he made frequent utterances which even the most orthodox Boers would not have disowned. In the Cape Parliament, on 23 June 1887, he had said: 'Does this House think it is right that men in a state of pure barbarism should have the franchise and the vote? . . . Treat the natives as a subject people as long as they continue in a state of barbarism. . . . Be the lords over them and let them be a subject race, and [this was a mine-owner speaking] keep the liquor from them.' On 28 September 1888, Rhodes insisted that the real key to the South African question was the supremacy of the white race, not on a colour basis, but by virtue of its civilization. On 6 January 1894, after four years of power, he proclaimed: 'The natives are children and we ought to do something for the minds and brains the Almighty has given them. I do not believe they are different from ourselves.' Since these children must be treated with a proper severity, a class legislation and compulsory passes were necessary—spare the rod and spoil the child. In 1891, by agreement with Hofmeyr, Rhodes introduced a bill providing for punishment by whipping. The House of Assembly would not accept the bill, but a year later, at his suggestion, it raised the property-qualification from £25 to £75, which was obviously not intended to spread the vote among the Coloureds. Should Rhodes, then, be seen as the founder of the present-day policy of separate development? At all events, it certainly seems that he was the first to think of setting up reserves in which, as in the Transkei of today and the Bantu states of the future, the natives would learn to govern themselves.

For four years relations between the president of the South African Republic and the Prime Minister of the Cape Colony had been mistrustful but correct. Their last meeting in 1894 was, it appears, a stormy occasion. The failure of a customs union, a tariff war, the rivalry of the railway companies and the tension between Boers and immigrants had induced Rhodes to renounce all hope of a closer relationship and to contemplate henceforth only solutions by force.

As soon as they had secured independence the Free State and the Transvaal, cut off from the sea, had asked the Cape and Natal to assign them a part of the customs duties which these two more favoured provinces were levying on foreign goods. But the rich are not always the most willing lenders. Neither Cape Town nor Durban considered it necessary to come to the aid of Pretoria and Bloemfontein. Instead, they tried to tempt the Boer states with the advantages of a customs union that would provide a wider market for their agricultural produce. Interminable negotiations began which it would be tedious to record in detail. In 1888 the Orange Free State, torn as always between its political aspirations and its economic needs, finally agreed that there would be no tariff barrier between itself and its southern neighbour.

Kruger, however, remained adamant. Was he wrong? If common markets have a function, it is as a stepping-stone to political union, and this was something that the Transvaal did not want at any price, for in what would have been an association of the weak and the strong it might sooner or later have lost an independence which it had struggled hard to regain. Its president, moreover, was concentrating his attention on the Indian Ocean. Kruger has been criticized for not taking an interest in the north; but with such a sparse population (a little over sixteen thousand voters at the presidential elections), did he have the means at his disposal to take charge of those vast territories? And in any case, where would expansion northwards have led him? On the other hand, to advance to the sea, or at least to secure access to it, would broaden the Transvaal's rather narrow horizons and provide the opportunity for international contacts which, with a little more adroitness, could have proved fruitful. After the discovery of gold a policy of isolation was no longer conceivable, and there remained only one direction in which the Transvaal could usefully turn: concentrating on the east was as much a necessity as a choice. The relative distances provided another argument: 1,000 miles from Johannesburg to the Cape, but only about 500 to Durban and 400 to Delagoa Bay.

Like the Boers in Natal,[1] Kruger was counting on the Netherlands. His chief adviser, Dr Leyds, was a Dutchman whom he had appointed Secretary of State in 1888, at the age of twenty-nine. Many other Hollanders followed in his footsteps. When it was decided to initiate the 'grand design'—to link Pretoria and Lourenço Marques by rail—it seemed only natural to turn to Amsterdam. In 1887 a company formed with the help of German capital, but administered largely by Dutchmen, obtained a monopoly for building the railway. Efficiency does not appear to have been its strong point. In the Cape Colony and Natal other companies were working at greater speed. By 1890 the railway ran from Table Bay to Bloemfontein, and an extension to the Vaal river soon followed. A year later a line starting from Durban had reached the frontier of the South African Republic; it was completed in 1895. In the meantime, in December 1892, the station at Pretoria saw trains arriving from the Cape. At last, in October 1894, the Netherlands Railway Company managed to finish its task, and its locomotives whistled triumphantly as they entered the capital.

This was a day of glory for Kruger, but the following weeks brought humiliation. To compete with the new line the Cape Company lowered its rates. In retaliation the Transvaal raised its own on the Vaal–Pretoria section. In exasperation Rhodes paid Kruger a visit, but the conversation led nowhere. The experts then decided to have recourse to the ox-wagons of earlier days: goods would be unloaded on the south bank of the Vaal, in Free State territory, and then transported by road to the Rand. On certain days, it is said, one could witness the unlikely spectacle of more than a hundred wagons crossing the river, creaking under their loads. In August 1895 Kruger, believing himself to be in a strong enough position to stop this traffic, ordered that the drifts be closed. The reaction was violent. Alerted by the High Commissioner, Sir Hercules Robinson, the recently appointed Secretary for Colonies in the Salisbury ministry, Joseph Chamberlain, immediately showed his displeasure. A veiled ultimatum was dispatched to Pretoria, and the South African Republic submitted, bitter and humiliated.

[1] See pp. 101–2.

Rhodes had played a part in the adoption of this forceful attitude. At this same time, the internal situation of the Transvaal provided him with the opportunity to prepare a move which he hoped would be decisive.

It is a pity that Kruger's knowledge of history was limited to the Bible. If he had been familiar with ancient Greece he would have known that, twenty-five centuries earlier, Athens had found itself in a situation comparable to that of Johannesburg. In that city, too, there had been an influx of foreigners; these newcomers had owned a large part of its wealth and had been denied the civic rights reserved for nationals. Between the 'metics' of ancient Athens and the *uitlanders*[1] of Johannesburg the similarities were numerous. But the appropriate lesson was not drawn from the experience of Pericles. At first, relations between farmers and gold-seekers were by no means bad. Kruger visited the Rand in 1887 and again in 1888; his reception was lukewarm on the first occasion, courteous on the second. The august *Times* even awarded him a medal for good conduct, praising his good sense and the skilful and liberal manner in which he treated the immigrants. The honeymoon did not last long; Kruger grew alarmed at the increasing numbers of new arrivals. His biographers attribute to him this astounding prediction: 'Every ounce of gold taken from the bowels of our soil will have to be weighed up with the rivers of tears, with the life-blood of thousands of our best people in the defence of that same soil.'

Authentic or not, these words reflect the Boers' anguish at the prospect of becoming a minority in the land of their choice. They thought they would increase their chances of survival by clinging to their customs and their rights. In 1888 they proclaimed the primacy of their own language: official texts would be drawn up in Dutch,[2] and court proceedings, including the pleading of cases, would be held only in Dutch. This measure was hardly calculated to facilitate relations between business circles and the structure of administration. Then an attempt was made to settle the problem of citizenship. The laws of the Transvaal were, in many respects, extraordinarily liberal: anyone who chose could settle in the country. But with what status? In 1890 a complicated regulation was introduced, requiring fourteen years' residence before a citizen received the right to vote.

According to most historians, many *uitlanders* were not greatly concerned about taking part in elections: some, British by birth, because they felt that to renounce their nationality would have been sacrilege; others, the magnates, because they were shrewd enough to realize that their power did not depend on a voting paper; and a third group who considered themselves only passing visitors and were more interested in

---

[1] The Afrikaans name for the immigrants ('outlanders').

[2] Admittedly, a translation in a foreign language was to be added, but English is not mentioned once in the text of this law.

quick profits than in constitutional privileges. But the adoption of these restrictive measures coincided with the crisis mentioned in the previous chapter,[1] and they thus became the focus of a latent discontent. Furthermore, Kruger himself did not make things any easier. He must have been in a bad mood when he paid his third visit to Johannesburg, for he began an open-air speech with the words: 'Burghers, friends, murderers, thieves, and robbers'. The consequences are not difficult to foresee: the house in which he was staying was nearly taken by storm and, of more serious significance, a republican flag was removed by an angry group.

The situation went from bad to worse. There were plenty of reasons for friction. The businessmen complained about the customs duties and the rates charged by the railway; they could not forgive Kruger for making dynamite a monopoly which, they claimed, increased the cost of production excessively; they maintained that the government was not helping them to recruit labour and that, by allowing the consumption of alcohol, it was reducing the natives' efficiency; they accused the officials of corruption; and, finally, they complained that they were bearing the burden of taxation—which was hardly surprising considering their profits. The heads of firms did not, however, take the initiative in opposing the government. It was, it seems, a lawyer of talent and eloquence, Charles Leonard, who assumed this task by founding a National Union in 1892. Leonard then organized a succession of meetings and petitions demanding the right to vote—13,000 signatures in 1893, 35,000 twelve months later.

The year 1894 proved decisive when Kruger, a victim of his own impassioned logic, made another blunder. To combat a native uprising in the north the government conscripted British subjects on the same footing as nationals. Some refused and were enlisted by force. Cape Town appealed to London, and the British government, only too pleased to intervene in the affairs of the Transvaal, sent Sir Henry Loch[2] to Johannesburg. When Kruger went to meet him he was greeted with *Rule Britannia*; then the crowd unharnessed the horses of the official carriage, with the president seated beside his visitor, and dragged it to the High Commissioner's residence; a demonstrator took the driver's place, brandishing an enormous Union Jack. Kruger preserved an unruffled calm, but the incident had made him more intransigent than ever: the use of pressure by the British in a street demonstration had been hateful to him, and he refused to make a single concession. His opponents also hardened in their attitude. There was one revealing sign: the Chamber of Mines, the stronghold of the *uitlander* aristocracy, had remained passive; at the same time its president, Lionel Phillips, had resolved to give his support to Leonard's National Union.

Clearly, something was afoot.

---

[1] See p. 159.
[2] Robinson's successor since 1889. Robinson resumed office in 1895.

16

The Jameson Raid

A visit to London by Rhodes and Jameson in December 1894 appears to have been decisive. Rhodes won the esteem of the Prince of Wales, who thought him wonderful and his explanations lucid. Even more important, he impressed the Queen—and with good reason: 'Since I had seen him last, he has added 12,000 miles of territories to my dominions,' the precise Victoria noted in her journal. He assured her that the Transvaal—'which we ought never to have given up', the Queen commented—would be restored to the Empire. But prompt action was essential. Rhodes confided his thoughts to William Stead, the influential editor of *The Review of Reviews*, insisting that it was no use waiting for 'Oom Paul' to disappear; the Transvaal must be entrusted to more progressive hands —in other words, more docile hands. Rhodes never favoured annexation: an anglicized South African Republic, incorporated in a federation under the Union Jack, always remained his goal.

This does not mean that he ruled out the use of pressure. In fact he now made two specific requests in this connection. First, he needed a High Commissioner who could be trusted. Sir Hercules Robinson had occupied the post from 1881 to 1889 and he also had close links with De Beers; he seemed the ideal man, especially since it was thought that his seventy-odd years would make him fairly easy to handle. On this point Rhodes obtained satisfaction, and the new High Commissioner arrived at the Cape four months later. His other request met with a more cautious response. Rhodes would have liked the protectorate of Bechuanaland to be transferred to his Company, but he was promised only the cession of a strip of territory to the west of the Transvaal. Even this partial concession he considered an appreciable achievement, for he was more and more tempted by the idea of concentrating in this area a force that could be used for a surprise attack.

The situation which he found on returning to South Africa at the beginning of 1895 was much to his liking. Poor Kruger! Indiscretions seemed to be a part of his simple and passionate nature. Celebrating the Kaiser's birthday on 26 January, he had offered a most unnecessary and compromising toast. Immediately rumours had gone round Pretoria: the more sober-minded inhabitants talked of the imminent arrival of German officers, while the hotheads said they had already seen them in the flesh. These illusions were all the more dangerous because they proved not altogether unfounded: a year later German uniforms were to be seen on a ship of the Imperial Germany navy in Delagoa Bay; and everybody knew that the Secretary of State, Dr Leyds, was *persona grata* at the Wilhelmstrasse.

When Rhodes heard this news, distorted or not, he was by no means uninterested, for to make the Transvaal appear the vanguard of Berlin's ambitions was the best way of ensuring the support which he needed from London. The moment seemed favourable. When one thinks of the distances that Rhodes and his colleagues had to travel and the slowness of transport, one is confounded by the activity which they displayed during the next few months. In May, Alfred Beit, who preferred business to politics, but who, like so many others, found himself unable to resist the power of Rhodes's personality, arrived at the Cape after a stay in London and was dispatched without delay to Johannesburg; his meetings with Leonard and Phillips[1] enabled him to bring back encouraging news: the *uitlanders* were not ruling out the possibility of an uprising, although they made it conditional on military support from outside. Here geography had an important part to play. To organize an invasion of the Transvaal from the north would have been the easiest solution, since the expedition would have started from territories over which Rhodes exercised supreme authority (and which that same year assumed the name of 'Rhodesia'). But the distance from the Limpopo to Pretoria was over two hundred and fifty miles as the crow flies, whereas only about a hundred and fifty miles lay between the Transvaal capital and the eastern extremities of Bechuanaland; by approaching from the west the supporting troops would therefore have more chance of arriving in time.

The adoption of these tactics, however, presented a major difficulty: they required the co-operation of Britain, which exercised sovereignty over this region. In June, Salisbury and the Conservatives replaced Rosebery and the Liberals. For a time Rhodes was anxious. The new head of the Colonial Office, the redoubtable Joseph Chamberlain, of whose ambitions and personal authority he was well aware, puzzled him, and he was only partially reassured by a telegram which read: 'As far as I understand your main lines of policy, I believe I am in general agreement with you.' On receiving this equivocal message Rhodes decided to explain his ideas more clearly. He dispatched to London a secret agent, Dr Harris, secretary of the British South Africa Company. Harris arrived in July and saw the minister on 1 August—in the presence of a witness, for Chamberlain was suspicious. The subject of this conversation later became a matter of controversy. However, its outcome cannot have been discouraging, since a month later Jameson himself went to the Transvaal. This time details were discussed. The visitor said he was ready to lead an

[1] See p. 171.

expedition of fifteen hundred men, with machine-guns and field artillery; five thousand rifles and a million cartridges would be brought secretly to Johannesburg. The programme was outlined: an ultimatum to Kruger, who would ignore it; an uprising, the constitution of a provisional government and the seizure of Pretoria; if the Boers resisted, Jameson and his mercenaries would soon bring them to their senses. To prevent further bloodshed, Rhodes would then ask the High Commissioner to intervene; Robinson would make haste to Pretoria and order the election of a *Volksraad* chosen by the entire male population; Kruger would then simply have to resign and his successor would accept the inevitable.

In the third week of October 1895 the conspirators went to Cape Town. The finishing touches were put to the plan at a meeting at Rhodes's residence attended by his brother, Colonel Frank Rhodes, Lionel Phillips, Charles Leonard and John Hays Hammond, an American engineer employed by the Goldfields of South Africa Company. 'I hesitated at first,' Leonard later admitted, 'but gradually was drawn under by the singular magnetic power of Rhodes.' As throughout this shady affair, it is not known exactly what was said at this meeting. Did the Prime Minister of the Cape give his visitors the assurance, desired by some, that the Transvaal would retain its national flag? Did he give them to understand that High Commissioner Robinson was in agreement? Even at this stage Robinson showed little enthusiasm, judging by his remarks to his secretary, Sir Graham Bower, after a visit by Rhodes: 'The less you and I have to do with these damned conspiracies of Rhodes and Chamberlain, the better.'

Did the Secretary for the Colonies know the details of the 'grand design'? In any case he took a decision that was to make its execution much easier. On 5 November Rhodes sent him a telegram: 'I, of course, would not risk everything as I am doing excepting for the British flag.' Perhaps this assurance was enough for Chamberlain, for on the following day the territories which Rhodes needed, to the west of the Transvaal, were put at his disposal on the pretext of building a railway. Jameson then established himself there and started cleaning his weapons. Several British army officers joined him; if in fact the Colonial Office knew nothing of their involvement, this would suggest a lack of liaison surprising for a government as well organized as that in London. Moreover, truth does not come only from the mouths of children; during this same month Mrs Chamberlain wrote a mysterious letter: 'The newspapers far and wide, and on all sides, are ringing with praise of the policy of the Secretary of State. . . . He feels the encouragement and it helps his interest and energy. He says a "smash" must come.'

Jameson must have disliked staying in one place for long, for on 16 November he was back in Johannesburg, where he met the leaders of what was known as the Reform movement. These men gave him an undated letter that would justify his intervention and in which they appealed to him to protect the *uitlander* women and children, whose lives, the letter claimed, were imperilled by the prevailing atmosphere of terror. Two conditions, however, were laid down: only Jameson was to have knowledge of the document, and he was not to cross the border until he received a formal request.[1] On the same day Phillips delivered a violent speech against Kruger. The uprising was provisionally fixed for 28 December. Three weeks passed. The government in London was amazed, and Chamberlain remarked to Meade, Permanent Under-Secretary at the Colonial Office: 'It seems to me that either it should come at once or be postponed for one year or two at least.'[2] Maguire, vice-president of the British South Africa Company, warned Rhodes: 'The sooner the better the revolt came off.' On 26 December the Secretary for Colonies considered it advisable to report to the Prime Minister, Lord Salisbury, who apparently knew nothing of the whole affair: 'I have received private information that a rising in Johannesburg is imminent and will probably take place in the course of the next few days. . . . If it is successful it ought to turn to our advantage.' That same day a manifesto, bearing a strong resemblance to an ultimatum, was issued. Kruger, who had been touring the provinces, had just returned to Pretoria; a few days earlier he had been asked why he had not nipped in the bud a movement which had made so little attempt at secrecy. His reply had been typical: 'You must give the tortoise time to put out its head before you can cut it off.'

To everyone's surprise the 'tortoise' failed to emerge from its shell at the specified date. Secretly the conspirators were uneasy: they had lived too close to the Boers not to fear the fighting qualities of their possible adversaries, and their anxiety was all the greater because only a small proportion of the promised arms had actually reached them. Besides, business was going better than ever: would it not be absurd to throw away certain profits in exchange for hypothetical rights? They therefore thought it wise to wait. Jameson was advised of their decision in the agreed code: 'The polo tournament is postponed for one week as it would clash with races.' Deciphered, this meant: 'We shall raise the banner of revolt on 4 January'—and before then, the conspirators thought, anything could happen. There then followed an extraordinary confusion of telegrams crossing one another. Rhodes, who had not yet been informed, sent this message to Flora Shaw, the journalist of *The Times* who acted as his go-between in London: 'Today the crux is I shall win and South Africa will belong to England.' Chamberlain, who had learned of the delay, told High Commissioner Robinson: 'Intimate to Rhodes he would not have

---

[1] Neither condition was respected. Rhodes made a copy of the text and subsequently telegraphed it to the British newspapers. The circumstances of Jameson's intervention will be described shortly.

[2] The British government was afraid of a war with the United States. Cleveland, invoking the Monroe Doctrine, had dared to intervene in a frontier dispute between Venezuela and Britain concerning British Guiana.

my support and point out consequences that would follow.' Leonard, who
was in Cape Town, sent a telegram to his friends in Johannesburg saying
that Dr Jameson had been informed.

In fact the impetuous Jameson[1] had made sure that he would know
nothing. On the morning of 29 December he had sent two telegrams, one
to Rhodes, the other to the conspirators. The text was brief: 'Shall leave
tonight for Transvaal.' Then he cut the telegraph lines and set off. It was a
Sunday, and the message did not reach Rhodes until about one o'clock in
the afternoon. Those who saw him on that day all describe him as crest-
fallen: in a flash he had foreseen the disastrous consequences of an isolated
move made at the wrong moment. 'Kipling, who loved magic, maintained
that Rhodes and Jameson communicated by telepathy. This time it did
not work,' wrote André Maurois. The 'Colossus' was not, however, the
kind of man to lose heart. Shortly afterwards he left for London, cherishing
few illusions about the disavowals and denials which he was likely to
encounter there. The reaction of the Cape Afrikaners must have grieved
him, for he had based his policy on their co-operation. Jameson's blunder-
ing shattered an already fragile understanding. Hofmeyr experienced the
feelings of a man 'who suddenly finds that his wife has been deceiving
him'. His Boer heredity stifled his British culture; as soon as he was
informed he telegraphed to Kruger: 'I hope your burghers will acquit
themselves like heroes against Jameson's filibusters.'

In Johannesburg there was chaos. News of the attempted *coup* did not
reach the city until Monday the 30th. The railway station was crammed
with people trying to get away. About eight o'clock in the evening the
conspirators formed a Reform Committee, a sort of provisional government. The situation gave the young *uitlanders* a chance to show their
riding skills; a Frenchman staying in the city at the time, Pierre Leroy-
Beaulieu, described them as 'galloping through the city, wearing
sombreros with the left brim turned up, their tunics fastened at the
waist, glittering high boots, enormous spurs, rifles slung across their
backs. . . .' But these dazzling horsemen, instead of reassuring the people,
only made them more alarmed. The telegrams sent by the French consul
bear witness to the general disorder. On 1 January, at 5.20 a.m.: 'Dr
Jameson, with an armed force of the British Company, has entered the
territory of the Transvaal on his way to Johannesburg, where a revolution
is to be feared. . . . It is said that the wires have been cut. The present
situation appears grave. . . .' The previous day his colleague in Pretoria
had recommended a military initiative: 'We are presented with a favourable opportunity to establish a strong influence in the country by sending
a warship to Delagoa Bay.' Two days later he was even more bellicose;
having learned that the German consul was demanding 'the dispatch of
regular troops to protect his nationals against rioting', he suggested that the

[1] 'Anyone could take the Transvaal with half a dozen revolvers', he had prophesied
in a moment of euphoria.

French Foreign Office do likewise, which only shows how rapidly panic was spreading: it is difficult to see when and how European armed forces could have intervened, unless they had been prepared to arrive too late, like the carabiniers in Offenbach's *Les Brigands*.

For two days an armistice was tacitly agreed between Kruger and the Reform Committee. The president was still waiting for the 'neck' of the 'tortoise' to become sufficiently visible. The Committee did not know what to do: on the 30th it sent a telegram to the High Commissioner, Robinson, to come immediately; then, the following day, at the insistence of the American engineer, John Hays Hammond, it swore an oath of fidelity to the Transvaal flag, a ceremony that must have disconcerted many of its supporters. In the meantime Jameson and his faithful band were marching on the city: they had hoped to number fifteen hundred, but barely a third of this number had been assembled. Their leader made this miserable band, ill-equipped and inadequately armed, cover a hundred and fifty miles in three days. On 1 January 1896, exhausted after hardly sleeping or eating, it arrived within some ten miles of its objective. The Boers were waiting. The next day, after a short battle at Doornkop, Jameson had to surrender unconditionally—the raid had been a total fiasco. 'Heaps of flowers are withering at the door of the Goldfields of South Africa. . . . The conspirators are only too eager to deny . . . the man whom they were ready to acclaim and who, for his part, is calling them cowards,' the French consul in Johannesburg telegraphed two days later.

A king of Macedonia is supposed to have been the first to say: 'My God, preserve me from my friends! As for my enemies, I shall attend to them myself!' On 3 January 1896, Kruger might well have applied this aphorism to himself, for on that day he received from Berlin a sensational and embarrassing telegram in which Wilhelm II congratulated him on having overcome the danger without having recourse to the assistance of friendly powers. In straight language this meant: 'If you need me, I will come quickly.' Berlin, in fact, was trying to escalate the whole issue. At a diplomatic reception on 1 January the German Foreign Secretary had taken the French ambassador aside and asked him to pay him a visit. In the course of the conversation that took place the same afternoon the minister gave the ambassador to understand that Germany would be only too happy to come to an agreement with France with a view to curbing 'the insatiable appetite of the British'. The same suggestion was made to the Tsar a few days later in a personal letter from the Kaiser, but it was cautiously received both in St Petersburg and in Paris; the impulsive character of its author was well known in both capitals, and neither Russia nor France wanted to be drawn into a policy of which the methods and objectives were equally unclear. Wilhelm II thus had to act alone; the dispatch of a modest cruiser to Delagoa Bay confirmed his intentions and at the same time made the limits of the possibilities open to him even more obvious.

The British government found good reason to rejoice in the situation. 'The blunder of the raid was almost at once minimized by the blunder of the Kaiser,' writes Professor van der Poël. On hearing the news Rhodes is said to have declared that the Kaiser's action had justified his position. In any case, Whitehall saw this as a suitable opportunity to fan the flames of a nationalism that was ready to burst into a conflagration. 'Soon, the blame will lie entirely with the Transvaal,' wrote the French consul in Cape Town at the end of January 1896. While waiting for revenge, it was necessary to wind up as smoothly as possible an enterprise that had turned out badly. The conspirators had also surrendered unconditionally. Kruger, the undisputed winner, now displayed greater sagacity than was his custom. First he decided to hand over to the British government the hot-headed doctor and thirteen officers—an embarrassing gift. On 21 January the heroes of the most brilliant defeat known in colonial history —as *The Cape Argus* described them—left South Africa for England. There they found themselves accused, with certain other persons, of having illegally prepared and equipped, in Her Majesty's Dominions and without her authorization, a military expedition against a friendly state. On 20 July, Jameson and his chief accomplice were sentenced to fifteen years' imprisonment;[1] the rest received five or seven months' imprisonment.

Justice had been dispensed more promptly in Pretoria. On 28 April, after four months of captivity in conditions which appear to have been far from idyllic, the four leaders of the Reform Committee, including Cecil Rhodes's brother, were sentenced to death and immediately reprieved. The other fifty-nine were given two years in prison and fined £2,000. The suicide of one of them, however, resulted in the others' early release. At the beginning of June, after confessing to their misdeeds, expressing their repentance and paying their victors ransoms that eventually amounted to £222,000, they all found themselves free men again.

---

[1] Jameson was released after four months for reasons of health. He was to become Prime Minister of the Cape Colony in 1904.

17

On the Brink of Catastrophe

A redoubled mistrust on Kruger's part and an ill-concealed rancour on Chamberlain's part, even greater obstinacy in Pretoria and incomprehension in London, Afrikaners and British more antagonistic to one another than they had been since the Great Trek—such were the psychological results of the lamentable Jameson Raid. The fundamental problems had not moved one step nearer to a solution.

The Secretary for the Colonies had lost none of his self-assurance: six weeks had not passed since Jameson's surrender when Chamberlain sent a memorandum to the Transvaal endorsing the demands of the *uitlanders*, and then proceeded to sing Rhodes's praises to the House of Commons. Rhodes had decided, in spite of everything, that he had better restore a little brilliance to his somewhat tarnished reputation, and a Matabele rebellion provided him with the opportunity. After resigning as Prime Minister of the Cape Colony, he set off for 'his' Rhodesia, travelling via Egypt where he was received by Kitchener, commander-in-chief since 1892. It is a great pity that a shorthand reporter could not have recorded the conversation between the two men. On arriving in Rhodesia the founder of the British South Africa Company observed that the guerrilla war was dragging on interminably. Baden-Powell, the future founder of the Boy Scouts, had proved highly effective there, but the loss of eight thousand dead did not appear to have cooled the natives' ardour. Rhodes preferred his supreme weapon, negotiation. He secured peace, with the help of an astute old native woman, stepmother of the great Lobengula[1] and, according to the English historian Carrington, the only woman Rhodes ever respected. Then he returned to London, where there was talk much about a commission of inquiry.

The commission began its investigations on 5 February 1897. The year that had just come to a close had been disappointing. Chamberlain had hoped to persuade Kruger to come to London, but the Boer had avoided him. Kruger's success had reinforced his habit of judging situations only from his own point of view. When Jameson fell into his hands, he believed himself to be in a strong enough position to dictate his own terms, even to the British government. He wanted to insist on the total abrogation of

[1] See p. 165.

the Convention of 1881, the return and conviction of Rhodes, and even the dissolution of the British South Africa Company. Such pretensions, which he did not dare to express officially, must have made the experts at the Colonial Office smile, if in fact they knew of them. But they were certainly upset when the Orange Free State renewed and strengthened the treaty of alliance which it had made with its northern neighbour in 1889. Their embarrassment was not alleviated by the news of the measures for internal order which the president of the Transvaal had taken: three laws controlling the entry of foreigners, defining the circumstances in which they could be expelled and giving the government the right to ban newspapers whose content might be considered contrary to morality or dangerous to order and peace. The right to take such decisions was undoubtedly inherent in the principle of sovereignty, but was the Transvaal a sovereign state? Although the 'suzerainty' of the Queen had not been explicitly confirmed in the London Convention of 1884, was it not still implicitly valid as defined three years earlier in the Pretoria Convention? This legal question was to become the subject of endless debate, but in it Chamberlain found sufficiently solid grounds on which to base his policy, a position from which he refused to budge from 1896 until the final drama.

The commission of inquiry published its conclusions in July. Rhodes's testimony had lasted six days; he succeeded in giving an impression of good faith, but was nevertheless severely censured. The officers of the Jameson Raid were accused of grave dereliction of duty (Colonel Frank Rhodes had to resign, but was later reinstated). The Colonial Office, on the other hand, was fully exonerated. Chamberlain must have been amused; however, he had no need of such encouragement to resume a haughtiness which he had never really lost. In the spring of 1897 he had decided that a naval demonstration would remind the Boers of the fragility of their victory, and eight British cruisers arrived at Delagoa Bay. The chancelleries trembled. As the Marquis de Noailles, French ambassador to Berlin, was leaving his office on 12 April, he met 'the Emperor Wilhelm crossing the Pariser Platz on horseback. His Majesty, seeing me, stopped and talked to me for a few moments. . . . He seemed very preoccupied and was afraid that Delagoa would be taken by the British fleet.' Even more alarmed was the captain of the modest gunboat La Surprise, whom the French government had entrusted with the task of showing the red, white and blue flag in the waters of Lourenço Marques. When he asked anxiously what he should do in the event of a British blockade or a landing, the French Foreign Office recommended caution and forbearance. The captain had no occasion to display these very necessary qualities, for shortly afterwards the British squadron that had been the cause of the alarm raised anchor.

Chamberlain probably did not want to commit himself fully until a new High Commissioner had taken office. The government's choice had fallen on Sir Alfred Milner. It would have been difficult to find a man more completely moulded by the glories and the limitations of Victorian Britain. He was forty-five when he assumed office in May 1897. Of middle-class origins, although his ancestry on his father's side could be traced back to the early fifteenth century, Milner had been educated at Balliol College, that inner sanctum of the temple of Oxford, where his successes gave him no grounds for an inferiority complex. He began a career in journalism on the *Pall Mall Gazette*, an influential newspaper which advocated a foreign policy of liberal imperialism founded on the missionary role of the British Commonwealth and a domestic policy of rational socialism. He was soon drawn to politics, not so much the world of parliamentary assemblies as the upper reaches of the civil service. For two years he was private secretary to the Chancellor of the Exchequer. In 1889 he was appointed Under-Secretary for Finance in the 'Egyptian government' (since 1883 Egypt had been to all intents and purposes under British control); he wore a fez, in deference to his subjects, and pondered on the nature of British influence: 'It is a force making for the triumph of the simple ideas of honesty, humanity and justice,' he wrote in a book published at the end of his term of office. In 1892 he returned to England, where he served as chairman of the Board of Inland Revenue. But he found this an uninspiring task: the sober satisfactions of well-established fiscal policies seemed tame compared with Empire-making. It was therefore with great enthusiasm that he accepted the perilous High Commissionership of the Cape. His departure was the occasion of a banquet in the course of which Chamberlain proclaimed Britain's determination to maintain in their entirety the rights which it enjoyed by the terms of the Convention and its position as 'paramount power'[1] in South Africa.

The guest of honour must have discreetly joined in the applause, so closely did the speaker's sentiments accord with his own. Milner wrote so much[2] that it is possible to form some idea of his personality. 'I am an imperialist because I am a British race patriot. . . . It is the British race that built the empire and it is the undivided British race which alone can uphold it.' It should not be assumed from this that in 1897 the new High Commissioner was resolved on war. But that the Boers would not recognize the superiority of his fellow-countrymen seemed to him contrary to both divine and human law—and there can be no question of accusing Milner of bad faith. Besides, it would have been asking too much of him to have expected him to understand Kruger. 'Milner's method was to treat Kruger as a nineteenth-century up-to-date diplomat instead of a slow-thinking, suspicious seventeenth-century farmer', the economist John Hobson astutely observed. How could a man who had spent several years at Balliol avoid being slightly patronizing? Not that Milner treated his

[1] The phrase recurs constantly in British official documents.
[2] His official and private papers, annotated by his biographer, occupy two octavo volumes of about six hundred pages each.

subjects with anything but the most perfect courtesy. His receptions, to which he welcomed persons of Dutch ancestry as well as his British compatriots, soon became popular. Nevertheless, the epithets that he applied to the Cape Afrikaners were hardly flattering. He mistrusted de Villiers, thought Merriman 'a crank' and Sauer 'a beast'; Schreiner was 'not to be despaired of', though Milner probably changed his mind when Schreiner, as Prime Minister, began to cause him a great deal of trouble. His attitude is summed up in this comment: 'At present [September 1897] the politicians are all dwarfs except Rhodes who is really a *big* man.'[1]

In any case, for the time being his instructions urged him to show a patience dictated by circumstances. To Chamberlain, on 28 August, he wrote: 'This country [the Transvaal] is in a terrible mess, social, political and financial. . . . We should be very patient.' In the first place, the weakness of the British military presence ruled out all acts of force. Also, after the Jameson affair, Kruger had made a few concessions in spite of everything. Johannesburg had been promised a municipal council, the British schools there had acquired legal status, and, as a welcoming gift to the new High Commissioner, the *Volksraad* had decided to annul the measures restricting immigration. Moreover, the celebration in June of the sixtieth anniversary of Queen Victoria's accession to the throne had been the occasion of festivities of unparalleled splendour which nobody would have wanted to spoil with rumours of war.

The controversy was revived at the end of 1897. The Transvaal, having dared to suggest that the matters in dispute be referred to Swiss arbitration, found itself sharply reminded that it was still under the suzerainty of the Queen; any foreign interference was therefore out of the question. This indicated a hardening of attitude which became more marked in the ensuing months. Kruger's triumphant re-election for the fourth time, on 1 February,[2] infuriated his adversaries, as did a speech 'studded with biblical quotations' which he delivered on that occasion and which was 'received in Cape Town with a disappointment feigning contempt,' according to the French consul-general. The somewhat arbitrary manner in which, shortly after his success, the re-elected president rid himself of the judge Kotze, president of the Supreme Court, did not ease the tension. Then the appointment of Leyds[3] as envoy extraordinary to Europe and his replacement by the former president of the Free State, Francis Reitz, who did not have the reputation of being an anglophile, gave the impression of a double act of defiance. The cabinet in London hastened to inform the European governments that they did not recognize the new ambassador in any official capacity, which greatly embarrassed the governments—

---

[1] Rhodes had returned to the Cape on 20 April. 'If one is to believe the London papers, he was given an enthusiastic welcome', noted the French ambassador to Britain.

[2] 12,764 votes against Burger's 3,716 and Joubert's 1,943.   [3] See p. 169.

French, German, Russian, Portuguese, Belgian and Dutch—to which Leyds was accredited. Where was he to set up his offices? 'For my part, I see no special advantage in M. Leyds establishing himself in our country', thought the sagacious political director of the French Foreign Office. Berlin showed even greater reticence: at first the Kaiser refused an audience, then granted a twenty-minute interview during which he talked of anything but the Transvaal. Finally, Kruger's ambassador chose Brussels as his headquarters and there proceeded to engage in a laudable but largely futile activity.

Leyds was grieved but hardly surprised by Germany's coolness. All the chancelleries had heard talk of a secret Anglo-German treaty. Its terms were a mystery even to the best informed, but it was known that it concerned a share-out of the Portuguese colonies and that this proposed aggrandisement of the German Empire would be conditional on its tacit renunciation of the Transvaal. Did Milner possess private information? Whether he did or not, in 1898 he grew pessimistic and even aggressive. To Selborne, Under-Secretary of State for the Colonies, he remarked: 'Two wholly antagonistic systems, a medieval race oligarchy and a modern independent state, cannot permanently live side by side in what is after all one country.' To Chamberlain: 'They [the Boers] are armed to the teeth and their heart is black.' On another occasion he declared: 'No way out in the Transvaal except reform or war.' To a friend he commented: 'The Lord of Hosts, believe the pious parsons of the Dutch Reformed Church, is always on the lookout and will get them out of any tight place. But I have my private heresy and doubt whether He will always do it.'

In November the High Commissioner decided the time had come to re-establish contact with his government. He found it in an optimistic mood. The *rapprochement* with Germany had not been Britain's only success: the weakness of Russia had enabled it to acquire a naval base at the entrance of Korea Bay, facing Port Arthur; Kitchener had at last re-conquered the Sudan, the nightmare of the Colonial Office for nearly twenty years; and, most important of all, the humiliation inflicted on France at Fashoda[1] had supplied a powerful argument to advocates of strong-arm methods: if a great state had bowed to the will of Britain, how could a handful of uncouth peasants, isolated in the heart of Africa, hope to resist? An incident highlighted this attitude. During the night of 18–19 December a Johannesburg *uitlander*, who had obviously had too much to drink, nearly killed a man who had been arguing with him and then barricaded himself in his house; a Boer policeman followed him there, forced the door, received a blow on the head with an iron bar, drew his revolver and killed the man in self-defence. The jury acquitted the policeman and the judge commended him. On hearing this several thousand

---

[1] Captain Marchand, on his way to the Red Sea from the Congo, had planted the French flag there on 10 July. Kitchener, moving up the Nile, reached Fashoda on 18 September. A British ultimatum persuaded France to give way.

British demonstrators assembled, urged their fellow-countrymen to rally round the flag and drew up a petition to the Queen. The affair would doubtless have gone from bad to worse if the acting High Commissioner, General Butler, had not preserved perfect sang-froid. He had the courage to doubt that the Transvaal was always in the wrong in its conflict with Britain; moreover, he was convinced that South Africa needed 'rest and not a surgical operation'. He therefore refused to pass on the *uitlanders'* protest, and gradually the tension subsided.

Milner returned to his post at the end of January 1899, confident that he would not be disowned at the critical moment. For a few weeks the advocates of compromise found new hope; official negotiations between Boer civil servants and a group of 'kaffir kings', as the big industrialists of the Rand were called in London, nearly led to an agreement, but the secret leaked out and denials were promptly issued in both Pretoria and Johannesburg. On the surface, the dispute still centred on the same issues: the franchise (Kruger was suggesting a nine-year residential qualification, but the *uitlanders* were insisting on five years); the dynamite monopoly (the 'kaffir kings' wanted its abolition, but Kruger would only consider lowering prices); and the administration of the Rand (the industrialists would have liked to run the territory's affairs themselves— Pretoria reminded them that the discovery of gold had not affected the sovereignty of the land in which it lay).

The same ideas were still being debated in the same phraseology, but in reality the nature of the problem had changed. For the Transvaal, not to give way had become a matter of life or death; for Britain, not to enforce its will would have been a blow to its prestige. The shrewdest observers sensed that in the spring of 1899 the situation had taken a new turn. It is worth reading the dispatches sent by the French ambassador, Paul Cambon, an incomparable judge of British affairs. On 5 May: 'It seems that the European powers have tacitly or openly given Britain *carte blanche* in the South African Republic. A diplomatic and military move against President Kruger appears to be in preparation, and perhaps even in the process of being carried out. . . .' A few weeks later, on 29 July: 'Britain is less preoccupied with the *uitlanders* than with restoring its prestige in the eyes of the entire population of southern Africa.' Identical opinions were reaching the French Foreign Office from the Cape. The French consul was received by Milner on two occasions. At the first interview, on 7 August, he told Sir Alfred that, in his view, questions of reform had been transformed into questions of prestige. Milner admitted that it was the prestige of the British Empire that was at stake. In the course of the second conversation, on 6 September, the High Commissioner explained that people were beginning to grow weary in Britain as well as in South Africa, and that it was ridiculous that a little country like the Transvaal should be holding Britain at bay—it was Britain's prestige in the eyes of all her colonies that was in jeopardy.

As these pronouncements were being made, the crisis was drawing nearer. During the year tension had been steadily mounting. In March, Milner, who considered Butler 'a violent Krugerite', had no hesitation in sending on to London a new petition, signed this time by 21,684 British. The number of signatories surprised the French consul-general in Pretoria: three years earlier, he observed, there had been only 16,000 British in Johannesburg, and this increase seemed to him distinctly rapid. The South African League, a nationalist association founded in England shortly after the Jameson fiasco and which numbered some 2,500 members, entertained no such misgivings and gave the document maximum publicity.[1] Milner endorsed it without reservations. On 4 May the situation prompted him to send a two-thousand-word dispatch that was to become famous. In a grandiloquent style he described 'the spectacle of thousands of British subjects kept permanently in the position of helots,[2] calling vainly to Her Majesty's government for redress'. The government did not ignore the appeal. 'Our response will be a very strong one. You will consider it quite firm enough, I think', Chamberlain telegraphed to Milner on the 9th. In fact, London accepted the *uitlanders'* petition, relying on the argument that any government had the right to protect its subjects in a foreign country, especially when that country did not enjoy full sovereignty. As Professor van Jaarsveld has emphasized, a new situation had been created: it was no longer Johannesburg, but Great Britain and her Empire that now opposed Pretoria.

The Cape Afrikaners made a last attempt at conciliation, and at their entreaty Kruger and Milner met on 31 May at Bloemfontein, the capital of the Orange Free State. The talks lasted five days. The High Commissioner was polite but unyielding. 'He is as sweet as honey, but there is something in his very intelligent eyes that tells me he is a very dangerous man,' a twenty-nine-year-old advocate, Jan Smuts,[3] wrote to his wife (the president of the Transvaal had appointed Smuts state attorney the previous year). The future Boer War general was not mistaken. Milner refused to discuss anything but the franchise. In vain Kruger tried to bargain. Would the Transvaal at least obtain the annexation of Swaziland, an adequate indemnity for the Jameson Raid and recognition of the principle of arbitration? There was no reply. ' "It is my country you want!" ' Kruger finally exclaimed, 'tears streaming down his old wrinkled face', writes the historian Carrington.

[1] A counter-petition signed by 23,000 *uitlanders* (American, German, French, Dutch and British), rejecting the idea of foreign intervention, did not enjoy the same circulation.

[2] 'The helot wore his golden chains with insolent composure and demeanour as he feasted in the sumptuous rooms of the Rand and the New Clubs or lolled in the rickshaw which bore him to his luxurious home,' wrote an English visitor, who can hardly have earned the High Commissioner's good favour.

[3] Smuts had renounced his British nationality after the Jameson Raid and had settled in Johannesburg.

Such lack of self-control was hardly likely to impress Milner, who on 5 May declared the conference closed. Chamberlain published a bluebook and allowed a few weeks to pass, during which the Cape Afrikaners feverishly made another attempt at mediation. On 26 June, in Birmingham, the Secretary for the Colonies delivered a speech which sounded very much like a threat. 'We can wait no more. . . . I believe that we have reached a critical and a turning point in the history of the Empire.' The Queen was sufficiently pleased by the speech to ask to have it read aloud. In Pretoria the worst was expected. Chamberlain can at least be given the credit for frankness. Paul Cambon, who still did not believe in the likelihood of war,[1] met him five days after his speech and was disturbed by Chamberlain's words: 'You consider the use of force inevitable, and your speech was merely a veiled ultimatum?' Cambon asked him, to which Chamberlain tersely replied: 'Yes.' The Boers, added the Secretary for the Colonies, must be taught to reckon with a great nation like Britain.

Events gathered momentum, with emissaries rushing to and fro between Pretoria and Cape Town; proposals and counter-proposals were put forward, but neither side trusted the other any longer, and it would be futile to retrace in detail a succession of moves which, as often as not, were intended only to gain time. The British military strength was inadequate, and London did not want to engage troops until reinforcements, already on their way to South Africa, had reached their destination. The Boers, for their part, had long ago embarked on an armament programme, but it was still far from complete; moreover, they were counting on the spring rains to fertilize the pasturage necessary for their cavalry. July and August went by. Whenever Kruger took a step forward, Chamberlain would move one step back. At moments Milner would let his enthusiasm get the better of him: 'Loyal British South Africa has reason for its long degradation. . . . It's a great thing to be, even for a few brief days or weeks, the leader of the people possessing their utmost confidence.' In his less emotional moods he advocated firmness: 'They [the Boers] will collapse if we don't weaken, or rather if we go on steadily turning the screw.' The Secretary for the Colonies must have had this suggestion in mind when he made another speech on 26 August: 'Mr Kruger procrastinates . . . He dribbles out reforms like water from a squeezed sponge . . . The issues of war or peace are in his hands . . . The sands are running down the glass . . . If forced to make further preparations we shall not hold ourselves limited by what we have already offered, but we will, once for all, establish which is the paramount power in South Africa.' Thus threatened, Kruger retaliated by rescinding his own recent concessions. On 8 September a special meeting of the cabinet was held in London. Foreign

[1] His military attaché was even more sceptical, having prophesied a few weeks earlier: 'The British government knows . . . that it has only to wait a few years to see the old race of Boers disappear completely.'

diplomats concluded that the situation must be grave, a view shared by the British officials, one of whom told the French ambassador that never in living memory had a cabinet meeting been called at this time of year. An ultimatum was considered but a decision postponed. On the 15th Queen Wilhelmina of the Netherlands wrote to her 'dear aunt', begging her to use her influence to avert a war. By the end of the month the excitement had reached the streets; on the 26th Paul Cambon wrote to the French Foreign Office: 'I was curious enough to attend a meeting organized in Trafalgar Square by the Society for International Arbitration. Not one of the speakers in favour of peace managed to get a hearing.' Four days later he observed: 'Passions have broken loose . . . and reason no longer has any say in the matter.'

The French consulates in South Africa formed similar impressions. Pretoria, 30 September: 'The entire country is breathing gunpowder. Only a spark would be needed. . . .' Cape Town, 1 October: 'The *Volksraad* of the Orange Free State has unanimously approved a motion promising to support the Transvaal. . . .' Pretoria, 6 October: 'Hostilities are imminent.' Cape Town, 9 October: 'In the city alone the number of refugees from the Rand cannot be lower than 15,000. They are arriving crammed together in cattle-wagons; it is a pitiful sight. . . .' By the time this telegram was sent, the die had been cast. A British ultimatum was to be sent to Pretoria on the 11th, but Kruger forestalled his adversaries: on the 9th a peremptory note invited Britain to withdraw the troops that had arrived in South Africa since 1 June and to halt the dispatch of reinforcements. No government could have accepted such a demand, and it was answered with a brief refusal. Two days later a state of war existed between Britain and the South African Republic. The Secretary for War, Lord Lansdowne, wrote to his colleague at the Colonial Office: 'I don't think that Kruger could have played your cards better than he has.' Lansdowne must have been an optimist. Milner was more cautious. To Selborne he wrote on 11 October: 'We have a bad time before us and the empire is about to support the greatest strain put upon it since the Mutiny.'[1] This was a pathetic example of political distortion: to the High Commissioner, the national upsurge that had induced the Boers to risk their independence on the battlefield, rather then preserve only its appearances, seemed nothing more than a rebellion of the Indian kind.

---

[1] The Indian regiments had revolted in 1857, and it had taken a year of fighting and ferocious repression to quell the movement.

PART FIVE

Towards Unification
1899-1910

List of Dates

11 October 1899	Outbreak of the Boer War.
November 1899	Wilhelm II visits London.
November 1899	Winston Churchill taken prisoner by the Boers.
Nov.–Dec. 1899	Series of Boer victories.
December 1899	Appointment of Roberts and Kitchener.
February 1900	Beginning of the British offensive.
27 February 1900	Cronje surrenders at Paardeberg.
1 March 1900	The Boers forced to raise the siege of Ladysmith.
24 May 1900	Annexation of the Orange Free State.
1 September 1900	Annexation of the South African Republic.
October 1900	The 'Khaki Election' in Britain.
November 1900	Kruger arrives in Europe.
1901	Activity of the Boer guerrillas.
	Fruitless meeting of Kitchener and Botha.
	Reprisals intensified.
	Organization of concentration camps.
	Report of Miss Emily Hobhouse.
	Smuts's raid into the Cape Colony.
March–April 1902	Last Boer successes.
31 May 1902	Treaty of Vereeniging.
August 1902	The Boer generals travel to Europe.
December 1902	Chamberlain goes to South Africa.
1903	Inter-colonial conference.
1904	Arrival of the first Chinese in the Transvaal.
1904	Jameson becomes Prime Minister of the Cape.
1905	Founding of *Het Volk*.
	Selborne replaces Milner.
1906	The Liberals come to power in Britain.
	Smuts goes to London.
	Zulu revolt in Natal.
6 December 1906	Self-government granted to the Transvaal.
January 1907	Selborne Memorandum.
1907	Botha attends a colonial conference in London.
5 June 1907	Self-government granted to the Orange Free State.
1908	Merriman replaces Jameson.
	Talks between Smuts and Gandhi.
12 October 1908	Assembly of a National Convention.
11 May 1909	Closure of the National Convention.
1910	Herbert Gladstone, governor-general.
31 May 1910	The Act of Union comes into force.

18

South Africa at the End of the Nineteenth Century

It is now time to pause a moment and have a look at the South Africa that was about to experience the greatest upheaval in its history.

The territories over which the Whites, within two hundred years, had established their ascendancy comprised an area of roughly two million square miles (about twenty-five times that of Great Britain), if one includes the immense and ill-defined lands of the British South Africa Company from the Limpopo to Lake Nyasa. Considering only those regions subject to the sovereignty, direct or indirect, of a state, one observes that the Union Jack flew over some 800,000 square miles, and the flags of the Boer Republics over about an eighth of that area. In British territory the native zones represented more than half of the total. The Cape Colony over-shadowed Natal in sheer size (220,000 square miles against 20,000), and the Transvaal or South African Republic was nearly two and a half times the area of the Orange Free State (115,000 square miles against 50,000).

The most varied types of government were to be found in a country that was still no more than a geographical expression. There were two free republics: the White population of the Orange Free State enjoying unlimited freedom, that of the Transvaal subject to restrictions which had become a dangerous bone of contention. The Free State allowed all adult White citizens to vote; the Transvaal, it will be remembered, reserved this privilege to the burghers. Both states excluded from the franchise Blacks and Coloureds, whatever their origins, and in both the personality of the president played a decisive role. The parliamentary system had been in operation in the Cape Colony since 1872 and in Natal since 1893. The governor represented the Queen and appointed the Prime Minister, who was responsible to the Assemblies. The latter were elected on a franchise which in the Cape claimed to be liberal, though in practice it excluded the vast majority of Coloureds, and which in Natal had gradually drawn closer to the exclusiveness of the Boer states. In the Cape Colony the Afrikaners controlled the legislative power, with a majority of eight votes in the lower house; texts were published in English, but debates could be held in Dutch. A very different situation prevailed in Natal, which the British had made the country of their choice and where they felt completely at home. The other territories were subject to systems of government ranging from direct rule to the protectorate. Only Basutoland, over which lay the shadow of the great Moshesh, enjoyed relative independence. Elsewhere, treaties of alliance or *de facto* occupation had reduced the native chiefs to partial or total subjection.

The last pre-war census, taken in 1891, had recorded a population of 3,984,514. Such a precise figure, however, gives grounds for caution. It would be just as well to take into consideration only the four territories endowed with an organized administration: the Cape Colony, Natal, the Transvaal and the Free State. A population of 1,527,228 in the Cape and 588,570 in Natal gave British South Africa a total of 2,125,798 inhabitants —say two millions in round figures. The Boers had 809,560 in the South African Republic and 207,503 in the Free State—say a total of roughly one million. It should not be assumed, however, that there existed one Boer for every two British. The non-Europeans—Blacks, Coloureds and Indians—were numbered at 1,663,054 (!) in the Cape and Natal, and at 779,347 (!) in the Boer states. The White population of British allegiance can thus be estimated at a little over 400,000, and that governed by Pretoria and Bloemfontein at 230,000 (how many *uitlanders* and how many 'burghers' were there?—the estimates vary so much that none can be taken as reliable). If to these highly arbitrary statistics are added those concerning the native territories, it would seem that at the dawn of the twentieth century there existed in South Africa roughly 700,000 Whites and a little over 3,200,000 non-Europeans, the latter enjoying a superiority of about five to one.

The large majority of this population lived in the country areas. Apart from the two great urban centres—Cape Town with 80,000 inhabitants and Johannesburg with approximately the same—towns were few and sparsely populated. It is possible to obtain a fairly accurate idea of their appearance and atmosphere from travellers' descriptions. Since the discovery of diamonds and gold, South Africa had been in the fashion. The journey from Europe took eighteen days at the most, and so large numbers of British, American and, in particular, French visitors, either for business purposes or simply out of curiosity, set off to discover a country which only recently had been unknown.

Their accounts naturally differ, but on one point they are agreed: the beauty of Table Bay, which is constantly compared with Rio de Janeiro, San Francisco or Naples. Cape Town itself aroused less enthusiasm. Lord Bryce found it disappointing. One of his fellow-countrymen thought it 'in no way striking'. The Frenchman Pierre Leroy-Beaulieu probably gives the most vivid description: 'Narrow streets at right-angles, full of dust and mud; little two-storey houses with terrace roofs, built of light-coloured or whitewashed stone, above which tower a few large new buildings, the new Post Office, the Parliament; it is all rather banal. . . . In the back streets one still finds old Dutch houses with wide flights of steps. . . .' Fortunately, the people made up for the place. 'The popula-tion is more interesting, more colourful. . . . Every possible shade of human skin is represented, from the fair and fresh Dutchwomen, straight from a painting of Rubens, to the pure black of the Kaffirs. . . .' The Malays, in particular, attracted attention. 'Their women enliven the streets with their full, bright dresses of pink, green, lilac or blue, with a bodice of a different colour, and their heads covered with a scarf of a third shade. . . .' The cabs of Cape Town, according to one visitor, differed from those in London in that the roof of the vehicle was white and the driver's face black.

The city was surrounded by cornfields, vineyards and orchards amid which stood comfortable-looking white houses. Wynburg and Stellen-bosch were especially popular: '. . . proteas and other flowering trees, pretty cottages in genuine Dutch style two storeys high, long lines of dark green oaks shading the foot walks'.

From Cape Town visitors often went by sea to Durban, calling at Port Elizabeth and East London. The swell on the Indian Ocean did not make the passage an easy one. Even arriving at their destination had its hazards: a sand-bar prevented ships from mooring alongside the quays, and so the passengers, in twos and threes, had to take their places in baskets which a crane held swinging in the wind until, by a skilful manœuvre or a stroke of luck, they could be lowered into a dinghy—it was more like being rescued at sea than disembarking. Once ashore, however, visitors dis-covered in these two towns, both of British origin, a forward-looking, dynamic atmosphere. A traveller proudly described Port Elizabeth as 'the Liverpool of South Africa'.

But Port Elizabeth and East London were nothing by comparison with Durban, the enchantress. Mark Twain thought it a well-kept, clean town, and one of his compatriots went one better by calling it 'a colonial paradise'. 'A tremendous style,' remarked a Frenchman, 'with its pretty gardens and motley population.' The British, in particular, were delighted to find so far from Britain and the Indies an atmosphere both reminiscent of their own country and pervaded with an exotic quality. 'Never have we been struck with the appearance of contentment and brightness any-where more than in Durban,' observed a clergyman, admittedly some-thing of a chauvinist: 'The whole place had a healthy English air about it.' At the same time the rickshaws, drawn at great speed by coolies dressed all in white, gave the illusion of being in Asia—but a very comfort-able Asia, with wide, well-kept streets, beautiful public buildings and comfortable private residences. The only snag was the sand, which in some parts of the town still reigned supreme.

Rhodesia presented a quite different picture, for there civilization and savagery existed side by side with no clear boundaries to divide them. In two places, however, British supremacy was undisputed. Fort Salisbury had existed for only five years when Lord Bryce stayed there in 1895: 'Several churches . . . very pretty country residences in the style of Indian bungalows . . . street lamps light paths where four years ago lions were still encountered.' Bulawayo offered even greater surprises. Bryce, the celebrated author of *The American Commonwealth*, also stayed here. In a town which, two years earlier, was still Lobengula's capital, he found cricket fields and a racecourse! But these were trifles compared to the miracle that had transformed an African *kraal* into a European town within a few months. Moreover, it was rumoured that gold existed in the environs: 'It has filled everyone with a delightful sense of the power of civilized man to subjugate the earth and draw from it boundless wealth!' —a sentiment so typical of the times.

Johannesburg provoked similar ecstasies. What magic wand had raised this city from the dust? Fifteen years earlier it had been a wilderness; now it had a population of nearly one hundred thousand.

'A busy, eager, restless, pleasure-loving city.' Above all, a city of contrasts: 'Squalor and luxury, dirt outside and cleanliness within; funny little shanties built of biscuit tins nailed together and palatial business and private residences; low, dirty stores, and shops which would not be out of place in Regent Street; black men and white, eager busy men and listless loafers.' The growth of Johannesburg had clearly not been the result of town planning: the most bizarre and disparate styles could be found in the same buildings. However, the city had emerged from its temporary state; one visitor was impressed in particular by the solid, permanent character of its edifices.

The diamond capital, on the other hand, gave the impression of being unfinished. Kimberley, observed a Frenchman, 'has in most respects preserved the appearance of a mining camp in the early stages of its existence; the horrible corrugated iron still predominates. . . . The streets twist and turn among old huts with disjointed sheeting . . . ragged little negroes swarm everywhere, playing in the dust or the mud, disturbed from time to time by enormous wagons.' A similar impression is recorded by another Frenchman: 'The temporary has become permanent. . . .' The clergyman whose patriotic good humour has already been noted saw Kimberley in a different light: he found it 'bright, clean and pretty . . . the whole town gives an idea of prosperity and neatness'. It also appealed to Lord Bryce: 'streets wide, most of the houses built like Indian bungalows'. But it is probably Pierre Leroy-Beaulieu who delivers the most reliable judgement: 'The only curiosity is the mine. . . .'

The Boer capitals reflected none of the glitter of diamonds or gold. There people were not ravaged by passions, but lived in moderate comfort. A traveller who visited Bloemfontein, the only town in the Orange Free State, twice in twelve years found black and white houses and a bracing freshness pervading avenues lined with thick oaks and furrowed by clear, swift-flowing streams. The description given by Lord Bryce is more precise but similar in tone: 'A bright and cheerful little place . . . one of the neatest capitals in the world . . . a spacious market square with a good club and an excellent hotel . . . trees everywhere which make the whole place seem to swim in green . . . the most idyllic community of Africa, no poverty, no extreme wealth.' Pretoria, which seemed a sleepy town, left the same visitor with less favourable memories: 'Streets wide but so muddy after rain that they are almost impassable.' Admittedly, the government buildings were 'stately and sumptuous'. Activity was concentrated, notes another observer, round the one and only square where the post office, the branches of the principal banks, the law courts and the seat of the government were to be found. The most attractive part of Pretoria was the residential quarter: 'white bungalows with a very few large, handsome single or double-storeyed modern houses'; the streets, laid at right-angles, were planted with weeping willows, eucalyptus trees and enormous peach trees, and the gardens were adorned with geraniums, verbenas, dahlias, resedas, chrysanthemums and sunflowers. But seventy years ago there were none of the marvellous jacarandas which today strew the pavements of Pretoria with their pink and violet blossom and give its streets their splendour.

South Africa was embarking on a period of growth which, less than a hundred years later, was to make it an economic power.

Although it had only just been started (less than three thousand miles), a network of railways provided essential communications. The main line, beginning at Cape Town, divided into four branches: the first, heading east and then north, crossed the Orange Free State to reach Pretoria; the second, the beginning of the Cape to Cairo line, went up through Kimberley and Mafeking to Bulawayo and Rhodesia; a third and fourth led to Port Elizabeth and East London. Three other lines gave the interior access to the Indian Ocean: from Durban and Delagoa to Pretoria, and from Beira (about four hundred miles south-west of Mozambique) to Fort Salisbury. Everywhere else the traditional ox-wagons remained the means of transport for both people and goods, with one exception: round the Cape, as if in anticipation of modern times, some excellent roads had been laid which today are a cyclist's paradise.

Diamonds and gold were becoming the principal sources of wealth. The production of the Kimberley mines since the discovery of diamonds there is estimated at £80 to £90 million, and in less than fifteen years the Rand had obtained similar results. The subsoil was also providing coal (two million tons a year in the Transvaal and a million and a half in Natal over a period of ten years), copper in the north-west of the Orange Free State, and a little manganese in the Cape Colony. A few marble, lime-stone, sandstone and granite quarries just about complete the list of what the land was producing apart from crops and livestock.

Agriculture remained the predominant activity. If South Africans ever went to Canada they must have looked with envy at the greenness of that country. They had nothing like it in their own land, none of those splendid forests with their numerous species of tree; timber played an insignificant role, and exporting it was out of the question. Cereals were also in short supply: it is estimated that only one-thousandth of the land was cultivated; wheat was grown, but in such insufficient quantity that it had to be imported; maize was a little more common, especially 'kaffir corn', a sort of millet which provided the natives with their staple food. The fruits and vineyards around the Cape proved much more productive. Although it was fashionable in Britain to assume a supercilious air when drinking the wines of Constantia, and although the vineyards had suffered the ravages of phylloxera, production had been growing steadily: by the end of the nineteenth century it is estimated to have reached six million gallons. The almost tropical climate of the Durban region guaranteed the success of sugar-cane. Some planters, encouraged by this experience, tried to repeat it with cotton, tea and coffee, but the modest results merely earned Natal the nickname of 'a colony of samples'.

Grazing land occupied pride of place. Lord Bryce gives some figures which can be a little bewildering for non-specialists: two million head of cattle in the Cape Colony, 900,000 in the Free State, 800,000 in Bechuana-land and 725,000 in Natal. Sheep numbered fourteen million for the Cape alone, and the annual value of wool exports reached at least £4 million. Angora goats supplied a mohair that appears to have been highly prized for the manufacture of cloth. Finally, the increasingly numerous ostrich farms (225,000 birds, according to Lord Bryce) found a regular clientèle among women of fashion in Europe and America.

Since the end of the Kaffir and Zulu wars, the native problem seemed to have ceased to exist. The Boers treated the Blacks with a strict paternalism which allowed of no discussion. The attitude of the British was instinc-tively one of condescension, based not so much on contempt as on a superiority complex which, they imagined, no one could possibly consider unjustified. Both British and Boers agreed that the natives must be kept 'in their place'.

Sir Alfred Milner was soon made to realize this. He was not married, and the wife of one of his colleagues, Lady Hanbury Williams, acted as his hostess. On one occasion, when he happened to take a Negro boy in his arms and hug him, he incurred the disapproval of all present. The High Commissioner learned his lesson from this incident. He had not been in office six months when he wrote to Asquith: 'You might unite the Dutch and English by protecting the Black, but you would unite them against yourself and your policy of protection.' No one, in fact, was dreaming of doing anything of the kind when the first rifle-shots were fired. It was to be some time before their echoes died away.

19

The Boer War (I)

It is difficult to imagine the power of Britain seventy years ago. The United States of today provide only an imperfect comparison, for their atomic power is counter-balanced by the Soviet Union. At the end of the nineteenth century no fleet was capable of resisting the British navy, the undisputed mistress of the seas. The only real rival with which London had to reckon was Berlin. Germany was daily becoming a more dangerous economic competitor; but it was futile for Germany to pride itself on possessing the strongest army in the world, since it still remained powerless to attack a country protected by an impenetrable barrier of battleships. France, torn apart by internal conflict, had not yet acquired the international position which in 1914 was to enable it to enter upon war with a chance of success. The greatness of Russia was still a potent myth, but those who knew that country well had already discerned the weaknesses which its struggle against Japan and a first revolution were soon to uncover. As for the United States, their victory against Spain had recently reminded the world of their existence; but no one imagined that they could play a part in a conflict in which they were not involved.

In short, Britain accepted Kruger's challenge almost with a smile. Apart from the small group of isolationists who had been opposing expansion for fifty years, the country rallied round its government. Two statements by members of the Opposition illustrate clearly enough, by their very difference, what the majority of their compatriots were thinking. Sir Edward Grey[1] declared that a 'just war' had been forced upon Britain, while Sidney Webb[2] spoke of the war as 'unjust but wholly necessary'. Music-hall militarism ran riot. The French ambassador was present at the station where Sir Redvers Buller[3] boarded the boat-train. 'He was accompanied,' writes Cambon, 'by the Prince of Wales, the Duke of Cambridge and a large number of eminent persons. He was cheered with an enthusiasm rarely seen on such occasions.'

The fervour of the Boers was all the more extreme because they believed

[1] Secretary of State for Foreign Affairs in the Liberal cabinet of 1905.
[2] One of the founders of the Fabian Society, which was to lead to the formation of the Labour Party.
[3] See p. 208.

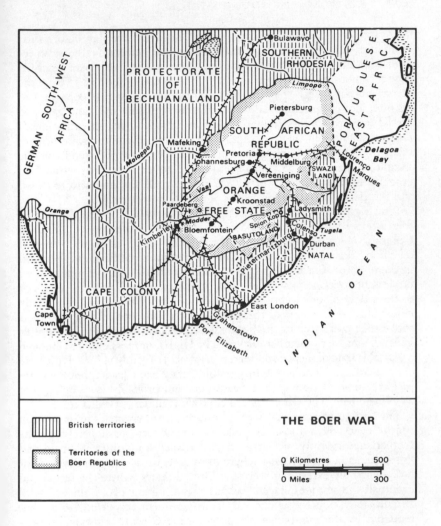

GERMAN SOUTH-WEST AFRICA

PROTECTORATE
OF
BECHUANALAND

SOUTHERN
RHODESIA

Bulawayo

Limpopo

PORTUGUESE EAST AFRICA

Pietersburg

SOUTH AFRICAN
REPUBLIC

Mafeking

Moloppo

Pretoria
Johannesburg
Middelburg
Vereeniging

SWAZI
LAND

Delagoa
Bay

Lourenço
Marques

Vaal

ORANGE
Kroonstad

FREE STATE

Paardeberg
Kimberley
Modder
Bloemfontein

Ladysmith

Spion Kop
BASUTOLAND
Colenso
Tugela

Durban
NATAL

Orange

Pietermaritzburg

CAPE COLONY

East London

Cape
Town

Grahamstown

Port Elizabeth

INDIAN OCEAN

British territories

Territories of the
Boer Republics

THE BOER WAR

0 Kilometres   500
0 Miles   300

they were being guided by the hand of God. On the day before their ultimatum expired a military march-past had celebrated the seventy-fourth birthday of the president of the Transvaal. A participant describes how magnificent it was to see commando after commando pass before the commander-in chief, everyone brandishing his hat or rifle according to his own idea of a military salute; then they formed a mass and galloped up the slope where Piet Joubert sat on horseback under an embroidered banner; standing in their stirrups, they shouted until they were hoarse; when night came, the singing and general hubbub reverberated from one camp to another until dawn. In Pretoria the government concentrated on practical matters; most of the *uitlanders* had gone, the mines were closed and the Bantu labourers had been taken back to their tribes.

'The loyalty of Natal has been splendid,' observed Winston Churchill a few weeks later.[1] He formed a quite different impression of the Cape Colony: 'A considerable part of the Colony trembles on the verge of rebellion.' Perhaps one should allow for a certain youthful exaggeration in these words. But the Afrikaners undoubtedly found themselves in an unpleasant position: should they give priority to their British allegiance or to their Boer blood? Many of them made angry noises, but few actually left. Milner did not make things easy for them, and in any case their spokesmen were lacking in boldness, according to the French consul-general, who on 25 October wrote: 'The High Commissioner has initiated a veritable state of silence and terror'; and on 31 October: 'The Dutch are very excited and would certainly revolt if they had a leader, but the latter [*sic*] are afraid of risking their heads and will probably keep quiet.' On 22 November: 'The whole of Cape Town is under surveillance.'

The foreign governments were also rather embarrassed. Public opinion nearly everywhere took the side of the Boers—passionately in the Netherlands, warmly in Germany and France, cautiously in Spain and Portugal, and even in Russia where, however, the *vox populi* counted for little. The only exceptions were the United States (where the mood was eventually to change); Japan, which was thinking of an alliance with Britain; Italy, which was divided, its government favouring Britain but hindered by the misgivings of the Vatican; Greece, traditionally pro-British; and the Scandinavian countries, especially Denmark, 'dominated by the fear of compromising its position in the butter market', to quote the slightly ironic words of Jules Jusserand, at the time representing France in Copenhagen. Expressions of sympathy took the form of small volunteer groups and the dispatch of field hospitals, but they had no influence on governments, which prudently took refuge in neutrality.

Chamberlain, however, took precautions with regard to the unpredictable Wilhelm II. Cecil Rhodes had arrived in Berlin in March, 'like the stormy petrel', wrote Prince von Bülow, then Minister of Foreign Affairs. Rhodes's indifference to etiquette—he wore a cutaway instead of

[1] See p. 209.

full dress at an Imperial luncheon—upset the protocol department, but on others he made an impression of naturalness, calm and strength. Above all, he knew when to keep quiet: the Emperor held forth without stopping, allowing him to get hardly a word in. Rhodes achieved his purpose, obtaining permission to lay a telegraph line across German East Africa. Six weeks after the declaration of war, more important conversations took place: on 20 November the Kaiser was received officially in London. He was feasted, guaranteed the Samoa islands in the Pacific, to which he attached great value, tempted with concessions in West Africa and, most important of all, given to understand that he would have a free hand in Asia Minor and that the 'Berlin-Baghdad' line might one day become the counterpart of the Cape to Cairo Railway.

On 11 October 1899, at five o'clock in the afternoon, British and Boers found themselves face to face. It is now time to study the terrain on which the opposing armies were about to join battle, their respective strengths and their commanders.

The most striking feature of the terrain was the immensity of the distances: some twelve hundred miles from the Cape to the Limpopo and about five hundred from the Kalahari desert to Delagoa Bay. Over these vast lands there were few urban settlements, and so the combatants were to find themselves almost invariably compelled to bivouac. Railway lines were also rare and highly vulnerable owing to the number of bridges and tunnels; consequently, tracks had to be used, often of the most primitive kind, for troop movements and supplies. The problem was particularly great in the east: between the Transvaal and Natal, the Drakensberg, a hundred and fifty miles long and over sixty miles wide, descended towards the Indian Ocean in precipitous terraces intersected by gorges along which flowed rivers which in the rainy season were transformed into torrents. Bearing in mind the perils which the trekkers had faced in this region, one can imagine the obstacles it would present to an army of the British type. To the west the *veld*, gradually curving towards the Atlantic until it met the Kalahari desert, was more suited to military operations: a gently undulating country of pasture-land and savannas, dotted here and there with flat-topped hills, the famous *kopjes*. The lack of trees and the exceptionally bright light would make it almost impossible to conceal a body of soldiers on the march, unless they had an inborn familiarity with the terrain.

At the outbreak of hostilities the Boers probably had a numerical advantage. Their forces are estimated to have been about thirty thousand, while the British had twenty to twenty-five thousand at their disposal.[1] However, if the armies were roughly equal in numbers, it would be difficult to imagine two more dissimilar bodies of men.

[1] The 10,000 soldiers already in South Africa at the beginning of 1899 had just been joined by another 12,000 drafted from India.

The principle of the 'nation in arms', so dear to the socialists of the *Belle Époque*, was never more vividly put into practice than by the Transvaal and the Orange Free State. The British were certainly to have good cause for bewilderment. The Boer states had no standing army: just a police force and a few artillery batteries, bought from Krupps and from Le Creusot and manned by uniformed professionals, often foreigners. When their country was in danger, all able-bodied men between the ages of sixteen and sixty were liable for call-up. They had to provide a horse (many arrived with two), a saddle, a harness, a rifle, thirty cartridges and rations for eight days (usually bread, dried meat and sausages). A bag containing a blanket and a rainproof cape, and a small kettle for coffee, were generally attached to the saddle, but these luxury articles were not obligatory. There was no question of uniform, and everyone dressed as he chose. Some even used umbrellas or sunshades. For the less whimsical, clothing was nearly always the same: boots or thick shoes, corduroy trousers, leather belt and cartridge-pouch, khaki shirt and a large, broad-brimmed hat sometimes adorned with a photograph of Kruger, a miniature replica of the *vierkleur* (the national flag) or, embroidered on cloth, a favourite motto such as 'For God, for country, for justice'.

On arriving at the mobilization centres the burghers formed themselves into commandos, which varied in number from about three hundred to three thousand men. In theory everyone was free to choose which commando to join, but in practice the inhabitants of the same region stayed together. The election of leaders was a formality, for their appointment had already been tacitly agreed in time of peace. The officers and N.C.O.s wore no distinguishing badges of rank; sometimes they were saluted by vaguely raising the hat, but the handshake was obligatory.[1] Discipline was unknown: no roll-call, no reveille, no lights-out. At first, these citizen-soldiers were entitled to ten days' leave every two months (apparently, their wives and mothers, in true Spartan style, used to send them back to the line before their leave expired).

It has been said that in battle every Boer was his own general. Indeed, he was his own general even before it began. At the councils of war summoned to decide on tactics, the opinion of a corporal counted for as much as that of the highest-ranking officer.[2] Once battle was joined, personal initiative played a predominant role. Outstanding marksmen—though allegedly less expert than their fathers[3]—the Boers had a remarkable talent for concealing themselves and taking deadly aim at their adversaries. They avoided hand-to-hand fighting and took a strong dislike to the British bayonet, a weapon they did not themselves possess. In surprise attacks they would leap off their horses (which were trained to

---

[1] So much so that British prisoners nicknamed their enemies 'the hand-shaking army'.

[2] See p. 208.

[3] This was explained by the gradual disappearance of big game.

stand still), discharge their rifles and then gallop off before the enemy had time to recover. The Transvaal ponies played an important part in the early Boer successes and the long resistance that followed. These precious beasts were accustomed to the climate, immune to the diseases which decimated other horses, and capable of doing fifty to sixty miles a day for several days on end. Their riders took care to give them as light a load as possible: one historian estimates their normal load (rider included) at two hundred and fifty pounds, whereas their British counterparts were supposed to carry about four hundred pounds.

The advantage of greater mobility which the Boers thus enjoyed over their foe was increased by their system of supplies, which were reduced to the minimum. 'For almost two months [at the beginning of operations] all the bread consumed by the army was prepared by the Boer women,' notes the observant correspondent of the *New York World.* Later, some commandos had a column of wagons following behind. Villebois-Mareuil[1] describes these 'massive wagons, covered with canvas, drawn by sixteen pairs of oxen', advancing slowly 'amid the cracking of whips and the howling cacophony of the natives'. It soon became general practice to live off the surrounding countryside, and even off the enemy. Deneys Reitz, son of the Transvaal Secretary of State and who, at the age of seventeen, had been one of the first to leave, recalls his comrades' joy when, after a victorious encounter, they took possession of 'mountains of luxurious food, camp stretchers and sleeping-bags'—a thrill which they were to experience time and time again. The blockade prevented the delivery of new weapons, and so the Boers made good this deficiency by taking their prisoners' weapons, including their cannon, and even their uniforms.

Bewildered by this constantly moving, invisible and deadly enemy, the British went into the early battles in fairly large numbers—'a disgraceful proportion to the casualty list', the young Winston Churchill indignantly observed on 10 November. Churchill held the Liberal Opposition responsible, but it would have been fairer to blame the British general staff. The troops sent out from Britain or India were not prepared for the type of war awaiting them. Without maps or any kind of intelligence service, they faced Boers who knew everything. 'I could not move a gun,' groaned General White, 'even if I did not give the order till midnight, but they knew it by daylight the next morning.' The Lee Mitford rifle was greatly inferior to the Mauser. More important still, tactics had not been adapted either to the terrain or to the enemy—the old methods had succeeded at Quebec and at Waterloo, and hitherto there had been no need to change them: infantry formation in dense masses, firing by command, attacking with bayonets; cavalry charges, but never in open order; and cannon lined up at regular intervals. Only one concession had been made to modern times—but a very important one when one thinks of the blue

[1] See p. 217.

greatcoats and red trousers of the French army in 1914: khaki uniforms had replaced the traditional red.

In spite of their differences, the armies had certain things in common. Bravery, first of all: on both sides men got themselves killed with admirable courage. It was tacitly agreed that this privilege should be reserved for the Whites. Both camps claimed that the Blacks were on their side, and each accused the other of using them. In fact, it appears that for some time the natives were employed only as servants, couriers, spies and transport drivers. By common agreement the neutrality of Basutoland was respected, which soon made this 'African Switzerland' the haunt of secret agents. By force of circumstance, the two sides were eventually obliged to adopt similar methods: anticipating the First World War, the armies started building blockhouses, underground shelters, fortified trenches protected by sandbags and barbed wire, and captive balloons served as look-outs.

Imagination was not one of the qualities of the Boer War generals. They remain fascinating figures, none the less, so great was the contrast between them, so perfectly did they personify their countries. In the Boer camp there were hardly any professionals. 'One had seriously studied warfare, only three had read military works.' The rest, mostly cattle-farmers and crop-growers, had known nothing but civilian life. They were not particularly young men, like the future marshals of France: in 1899 their ages ranged from twenty-nine to sixty-eight. Like their men, they cared little about badges of rank and uniforms. And yet, was it a fondness for protocol that induced one of them to appear on the battlefield in black frock-coat and top hat, to the amazement of the British? They were men of iron who knew neither fatigue nor discouragement; and, in the words of Villebois-Mareuil, all were endowed with 'a power of prayer in which there burned the faith of a people born for great hopes'.

Piet Joubert, the Boer commander-in-chief at the beginning of the war, was almost a septuagenarian. He has been accused of favouritism and his entourage nicknamed the 'royal family'. He was a peace-loving man who had reluctantly been drawn into violence: 'It would be barbarous to pursue and slaughter a Christian foe,' he was to say one day when he had the enemy at his mercy. He mistrusted anything modern; when a Russian nursing organization offered him an ambulance, he refused it: 'You see, my boy,' he said to one of his adjutants, 'we Boers don't hold with these new-fangled ideas. Our herbal remedies are good enough.' Pieter Cronje was also over sixty. His parents had left the Cape at the time of the Great Trek. His career had been both political and military, and he had achieved fame by forcing Jameson to surrender. Everybody was familiar with his severe face and flowing beard; above all, he was respected for his energy and feared for his truculence. By comparison with these two men, de la Rey (fifty-two) and de Wet (forty-five) were almost children—it was the war that was to bring them renown. De la Rey was 'dark with shaggy eyebrows, great aquiline nose, deeply lined face and a vast bushy beard just turning grey; he would have made a striking model for some prophet of the Old Testament'. But he did not look like a military man: '. . . kindly, grandfatherly eyes, less like a guerrilla leader I have never set eyes on,' notes an eye-witness. Yet historians of the war regard de la Rey as one of the few strategists among the Boers. De Wet was quite unlike him, except that in appearance he too invited comparison with an ancient world: 'It [his face] recalled one of those graven visages which one sees far up the Nile, hewn out of the very rocks.' At forty-five he was still full of life: 'his body seemed all muscle'. He had fought at Majuba, but on 11 October 1899 he was only in charge of a commando. His valour was quickly recognized: less than two months later he was made a general and thereafter he gradually became a legendary figure.

In this gallery of fame in which so many others could claim their niche, Botha and Smuts can hardly be omitted. Louis Botha was thirty-seven years of age. His family had settled in the Free State. He had started life as a sheep-farmer, then politics had drawn him. Moving to the Transvaal, he had represented the Republic in Swaziland. 'Tall, handsome, bright-eyed, dark-featured with moustache, a small beard, he looked more French than Dutch.' He had an air of 'mysterious charm' about him. A member of the *Volksraad*, he voted against the ultimatum; but, once the die was cast, he threw himself into the war with his customary ardour. Within three months he became commander-in-chief. He was a great soldier, but also a willing peacemaker. Jan Smuts, still a young man of twenty-nine, was of a quite different character: 'aloof, taciturn, a harsh and callous taskmaster, intolerant of failure and inefficiency, riding rough-shod over the feelings of others'. He was in charge of the Ministry of Justice when the war broke out; immediately he went to the front, where he soon made himself a reputation, but 'the lack of discipline of commandos infuriated him'.

Perhaps this was one of the reasons why he was later to get on so well with the British. In the eyes of the British generals the Boers did not 'play the game' and were not 'gentlemen'. This double reproach could not be applied to themselves, traditionalists and men of distinction ready to win victories and get themselves killed, provided that the rules of orthodoxy and propriety were observed. They, too, were zealous patriots—but how, measuring everything by the standard of Queen and Empire, could they possibly have understood these provincial republics that were daring to defy them?

Their careers almost invariably followed the same pattern. On leaving Eton and Sandhurst, they had become familiar with the exercise of command on the parade-grounds of Aldershot. The older men had taken part in the suppression of the Indian Mutiny and had gained experience of colonial wars in the expeditions to Afghanistan, Burma and the Sudan.

Many, such as French, Haig, Byng and Allenby, were to attain fame during the years 1914–18. By 1899 two had already achieved renown: Sir George White, who had been brought from India to take charge of Natal, and, in particular, Sir Redvers Buller, entrusted with overall command of operations. The aristocracy looked favourably on an officer whose mother was a Howard and a niece of the Duke of Norfolk. Buller's fondness for champagne and good living ('he only thinks of his cooks and the fleshpots', Rhodes protested angrily) was hardly likely to incur the disfavour of the army. Moreover, his corpulence and impassivity had a certain reassuring effect. Most important of all, 'bulldog Buller' was stubborn, a cardinal virtue in Victorian England. Churchill, who knew all about stubbornness, delivered this judgement: 'Perhaps his strongest characteristic was obstinately to pursue his plan, in spite of all advice, in spite, too, of his horror of bloodshed, until he himself is convinced that it is impracticable. . . . No modern general ever cared less for what the world might say.'

As soon as hostilities commenced, the Boers took the offensive in three directions.

A few commandos crossed the Orange and penetrated into the Cape Colony, joyfully annexing districts where they met with no resistance, but not daring to advance too far for fear of encountering superior forces. A two-pronged attack to the west, under Cronje, was of greater importance. On the day after the ultimatum a British armoured train fell into the invaders' hands, and a few days later Mafeking was encircled—Mafeking, from which the Jameson Raid had set out! Was it this disagreeable memory that led the Boers to attach such great significance to the capture of a town of little strategic value? Their superiority of numbers was overwhelming—eight thousand against a thousand. But, affirms a contemporary observer, 'when Cronje and the higher officers wanted to storm Mafeking, they were outvoted by the corporals and field cornets'. The siege thus began quietly, with bombardments at fixed times using 'Long Tom',[1] the pride of the Boer Republics—but never during meal-times or on Sundays. Baden-Powell, in command of the garrison and already well known for his successes in Rhodesia, delighted the British government by sending phlegmatic telegrams: 'Four hours of bombard-ment. Killed a hen. Wounded a dog and smashed a hotel window.'

Three hundred miles to the south, Kimberley was also besieged, if the word can be applied to such a vaguely defined settlement. The 'siege' was conducted in the same manner, although the town was defended only by four thousand men and about twenty cannon, which were supposed to cover a perimeter of ten miles. Besides, the prospect of such a splendid prize should have encouraged the besiegers. Rhodes, ignoring all advice, had considered it his duty to establish himself near 'his' mines as soon as

[1] A six-inch cannon built at Le Creusot.

the war had started. Naturally, he insisted on taking control of every-thing, strategy as well as administration, and made life impossible for the garrison commander, the unfortunate Colonel Kekewich, who had reached the end of his tether. Kekewich has been described as being 'in the unhappy position of a Lilliputian obliged to sit on the head of a Gulliver'; 'there was high comedy in the spectacle of the colossus and the colonel bound unwillingly together; the stiff-necked bufflement [sic] on one side, the squeaking rage on the other.' To Rhodes the problem was clearcut: 'If Kimberley falls everything is lost.' And so he continued to fulminate against the inactivity of the High Commissioner, who had still not sent a relief force to the diamond capital.

In fact the British high command had other things to worry about. The real struggle was taking place in Natal, which fourteen thousand Transvaal burghers and six thousand from the Free State had invaded immediately the ultimatum expired. 'There was not a man who did not believe we were heading straight for the coast,' one of them recalls. The odds were in their favour. Instead of waiting for them along the easily defended line of the Tugela, the British had rashly committed themselves in the far north of the colony in a salient of barely a hundred and fifty square miles which the two Boer Republics bordered to east and west. The early engagements did not go badly for the British troops, but they had little significance except to reveal yet again the deadly precision of the Boer marksmen. White, who was ill at ease in the face of such strange enemies, decided to regroup his forces round Ladysmith, a town commanding the route to Pieter-maritzburg and Durban, but which, surrounded by high hills, threatened to become a trap. Perhaps he realized his mistake immediately. At all events, two counter-attacks on 30 October, at Modderspruit and Nicholson's Nek, proved futile: without achieving anything the British sacrificed nearly eighteen hundred men, including twelve hundred prisoners, and immediately afterwards Ladysmith was besieged.

In this third siege the Boers made the same blunder as at Mafeking and Kimberley. If they had been bold enough to push on to Durban and capture the town in a surprise attack, the outcome of the war might well have been different, for the British would then have had to disembark the reinforce-ments from India at a much greater distance from the field of operations. But the Republicans believed in patience. 'The race horse is swifter than the ox, but the ox draws the heavier load. We shall see who wins in the end,' Kruger had said. Nevertheless, the younger Boers were growing impatient; these brilliant warriors so adept in guerrilla fighting were being condemned to the inactivity and routine of a siege! The fighting remained in a stalemate situation for several weeks. On 14 November a famous incident occurred. The twenty-five-year-old Winston Churchill, who had just arrived in South Africa as correspondent of the *Morning Post*, was having difficulty in keeping his journalist's profession and his military leanings apart, and found himself on an armoured train which was captured. He was astounded by the Boers' correctness of behaviour, but they showed no disposition to release him in spite of his protests. 'We don't catch the son of a lord every day', they politely replied. Eventually he managed to escape, thereby earning himself a triumphant return to England and, a few months later, election to Parliament.

The British dubbed the second week of December 1899 the 'Black Week'. Three defeats followed one after the other: on the 10th at Stormberg in the Cape Colony, on the 12th to the south of Kimberley at Magersfontein, where the relieving force impatiently awaited by Rhodes lost a thousand men and its commander; and, most serious of all, on the 15th at Colenso when Buller, at the head of twenty-three thousand men and forty-two cannon, attempted to relieve Ladysmith and had to fall back after six hours of fighting, leaving behind him on the battlefield eleven hundred men and ten pieces of ordnance, and giving his young adversary, Louis Botha,[1] his first taste of immortality. Five weeks later, on 24 January, another attack proved no more successful, this time at Spion Kop, some twenty miles south-west of Ladysmith: the British casualties were three hundred killed and thirteen hundred wounded, while the Boers had fifty dead and a hundred and twenty wounded.

During Black Week, Paul Cambon judged the situation with his customary lucidity. 'The British,' he wrote to the French Foreign Office on 11 December, 'will make themselves masters of the Orange Free State and the Transvaal; but, with an elusive and enterprising enemy impelled by national passions, the war will be long and will demand considerable sacrifices.' The disasters of December convinced public opinion in Britain, which now reacted with the admirable doggedness of which so many examples are to be found in its history. A small minority urged negotiation. W. T. Stead and *The Review of Reviews* took the initiative by forming a 'Stop the War Committee'; they even had the courage to publish a movingly passionate and sincere plea entitled *A Century of Wrong* which Francis Reitz, Secretary of State for the Transvaal, tried to circulate. But their efforts were futile. In the face of adversity the country braced itself, and the old Queen set an example. 'I will tell you one thing,' she had informed her entourage, 'I will have no depression in my house.' When she learned of the humiliation of Spion Kop, she showed no sign of emotion. 'The Queen is secretly distressed at the bad news, but outwardly as cheerful as ever', wrote one of her ladies-in-waiting.

By this time a series of measures had been taken. An army corps of more than forty thousand men was on its way. On 18 December the reserves had been called up. Even more important, the high command had passed into other hands. Lord Roberts had been appointed commander-in-chief and Lord Kitchener his chief of staff. The two men were quite

[1] Botha was finally appointed commander-in-chief of the Transvaal forces in March 1900.

different. Roberts had made his reputation in India and Afghanistan and had been made a field-marshal in 1895. When the war broke out he was sixty-seven, but he offered his services. He was thought to be too old, but a few months later the authorities changed their minds. According to his biographers he was a 'temperate, modest, simple' man. His son, also an officer, had just been killed in South Africa. The Queen received Lord Roberts before his departure. 'He knelt down and kissed my hand. I said how much I felt for him. He could only answer: "I cannot speak of *that* but I can of anything else."'

Kitchener was a more colourful character, 'a man of another planet, roundly detested in the army, but for the public a super-efficient hero'. Rewards and titles came naturally his way. When he recaptured Khartoum he was forty-eight years old; Parliament had granted him £30,000 and the Queen had raised him to the peerage. Nothing ever surprised him. On learning that he was second in command under Roberts, he simply telegraphed: 'Delighted.' Lord Curzon, whose colleague he was to be for two years in the War Cabinet of 1914, described him as 'aloof and alone, a molten mass of devouring energy and burning ambition'. He was quite without scruples when victory was at stake. He had shown a heavy hand with the Sudanese and was to prove no less tough with the Boers.

Roberts and Kitchener were a formidable team. When they left the Cape on 6 February 1900 to go to their headquarters, the period of British defeats was at an end.

20

The Boer War (II)

The disproportion of numbers was beginning to make itself felt. The Boers had been reinforced by a few hundred foreign volunteers—Dutch, Germans, Scandinavians, Irish and French. Among the latter Villebois-Mareuil, a former colonel in the Foreign Legion, had brought them the benefit of a military training acquired at the École de Guerre in Paris; above all, the crusader-like enthusiasm with which he had resolved to support their cause was symbolic of the sympathy that the Boer Republics had attracted from all directions. Yet the problem had not been solved. Thirty or forty thousand burghers remained the maximum that the commandos could muster on the two fronts in the Free State and Natal. Lord Roberts, on the other hand, had more than a hundred thousand soldiers at his disposal, most of them battle-hardened in colonial expeditions.

The British commander-in-chief's plan was simple and bold. Leaving the timid Buller to shout himself hoarse in his futile attempts to relieve Ladysmith, he decided to make the axis of his offensive the railway line from the Cape to Bloemfontein and Pretoria, thus aiming at the very heart of the enemy. This meant subjecting his troops to a four-hundred-mile march across the *veld* in the dry and scorching climate of the southern summer. On 11 February the main body of his army moved off: 25,000 infantry, 8,000 cavalry and mounted infantry, 100 cannon and thousands of wagons; a rearguard of 18,000 men protected the lines of communication.

For five months one British victory followed on another. On the 15th the daring French led his cavalry into Kimberley. Rhodes, snatching the limelight from his *bête noire*, the hapless Kekewich, received him in magnificent style. His instinct then got the better of him: 'Mr Rhodes's first concern had been to make his voice heard at a General Meeting of De Beers on 23 February,' observed the French consul-general in Cape Town. But the raising of the siege had more important consequences than the reopening of the diamond market. Cronje, who has been besieging the town with several thousand Boers, was afraid of being cut off from Bloemfontein. He therefore headed east up the valley of the Modder, but so slowly that, three days later, he found himself encircled on high ground overlooking the river at Paardeberg. An attempt to force his way out failed woefully, and eight days of blockade eventually proved too much for the Boers. On the 27th—why did he choose the anniversary of Majuba to capitulate?—Cronje hoisted the white flag. His surrender was not without greatness. 'He rode into the British camp on a decrepit horse, wearing a slouch hat, an old green overcoat and frieze trousers.' Roberts accorded him a chivalrous reception: 'I am glad to see you, Sir, you have made a gallant defence.' However, the vanquished were not accorded the honours of war; four thousand prisoners and their leader were dispatched to St Helena. Their fellow-Boers were horrified: 'It was as if the whole universe was toppling about in our ears,' wrote a young combatant. Even the indomitable de Wet was distressed: 'What pen could describe the stupor that gripped us! Every face showed desolation and discouragement.' In Britain the end was thought to be in sight. 'I trust this crushing blow may completely demoralize them,' remarked one of the Queen's ladies-in-waiting. Paul Cambon showed greater insight: 'Sensible persons [he was doubtless thinking of himself] consider that the capture of three or four thousand peasants, who have been surrounded for eight days by forty thousand regular troops, is not an exploit of which a great nation can be unduly proud.'

Four days later, however, the British gained another victory. Not wishing to leave all the laurels to his commander-in-chief, Buller finally succeeded in relieving Ladysmith on 1 March, after a hundred and eighteen days of siege. He then arranged a march-past, which the readily lyrical Winston Churchill compared with 'a procession of lions'. The Queen's entourage rejoiced: 'The bells are pealing, the Boers have melted away like snow in springtime.' These were dark days for the Boer Republics. The relief of Ladysmith meant that Thermopylae was threatened and the route to Pretoria clear. To the west the victors of Paardeberg were less than sixty miles from the capital of the Free State. The hitherto indomitable Boers were panic-stricken. Kruger saw them taking to their heels: 'Despair seemed depicted on his hard leaden features; threateningly he lifted his heavy stick against the fugitives whom no one seemed able to check; at last he ordered the detachment of Pretoria police to shoot everyone who attempted to pass; no one was in fact shot and the flight went on.'

The Republics resigned themselves to suggesting negotiation. 'As the British have recovered their prestige', wrote their two presidents, the time had come to talk. But all they proposed was a return to the *status quo*, and in any case the allusion to Britain's defeats was not likely to please their adversaries. Salisbury allowed eight days to pass and then replied haughtily that the annexation of the Orange Free State and the Transvaal was a preliminary condition of any peace. The chancelleries bustled with excitement: was a deal not possible? Each country encouraged the others to intervene while refraining from action itself. Only the United States dared to ask the Foreign Office if it would accept their good offices, but they were warned not to be too insistent.

The French ambassador met his Austro-Hungarian counterpart: 'He said to me: "Germany does not wish to propose mediation; the United States have seen theirs declined; there remain you and Russia; no one knows what you are going to do."

"Nothing", I simply replied,' wrote Paul Cambon, certain of not being disowned.[1]

Full of illusions as always, such was their ignorance of the international situation, the Boers decided to entrust three of their number with the task of pleading their cause before world opinion. On 17 April 'triumvirs' arrived in Switzerland, where they declared quite categorically that no Englishman would ever enter Pretoria. Then they went to seek comfort and advice in Holland; they were warmly received, but no attempt was made to conceal the futility of their mission. In order not to return empty-handed, they resolved to try their luck in the United States. A presidential election was due to take place in November. The Democrats, in opposition since 1892, tried to exploit their visit for political ends. The Republicans took refuge in caution: the Secretary of State, John Hay, received the delegates and even invited them to lunch.[2] Persons fond of historical comparisons recalled the mission of Benjamin Franklin, but the triumvirs had less success than their illustrious predecessor. A few months later, in September, they launched a final appeal for help in Paris.

When they drew up this text, which, like so many Boer documents, is of a touching nobility, they must have been grief-stricken by the news from South Africa.

The very day after Salisbury had notified the Republics of their sentence of death the British troops entered Bloemfontein. The Orange Free State was the first to find itself with a nomadic government. The Boer leaders, gathering a hundred miles to the north-east of the occupied capital, decided unanimously to continue the struggle. Rapidity of movement seemed to them, quite rightly, one of their best chances of success, and so they resolved to use no more wagons and to employ only mobile mounted commandos. Also, there would be no more women: wives were forbidden to follow their husbands as far as the line of fire, as many had done since the outbreak of hostilities. Driven by an energy that drew its strength not from desperation but from their conviction that they were defending a just cause, the Boers, after a period of despondency, regained confidence. Their enemies helped them by allowing them time to reorganize them-

[1] A note from the Foreign Minister, Delcassé, shows however that on 28 February 1900 the Council of Ministers considered the possibility of armed conflict with Britain.
[2] 'Lord Pauncefote [the British ambassador], who is showing indulgence,' writes Jules Cambon, then French ambassador to Washington, 'has excused himself, saying that he must make some concession to the electoral necessities of the present time.'

selves. Buller, true to form, was hanging on at Ladysmith. As for Roberts, the necessity of regrouping his forces and, in particular, an epidemic of enteritis which revealed the shortcomings of a mediocre medical service, compelled him to remain in Bloemfontein for six weeks. A series of skirmishes[1] in which the British did not always come off best induced sceptics to wonder if their opponents were really in as bad a way as was commonly claimed in the presence of the commander-in-chief.

The advance was resumed on 3 May. By their sheer weight of numbers —100,000 men, plus 50,000 in reserve and on the flanks—the British made it impossible for their enemies to engage in any pitched battles. A fortnight after the beginning of the offensive they received a heartening piece of news: a certain Colonel Plumer,[2] well known for the cut of his uniforms, his monocle and the gloves which he apparently always wore, had forced the Boers to raise the siege of Mafeking. A fit of mass hysteria erupted in Britain, and for a time a new word entered the vocabulary—'mafficking'. The streets of London were invaded by crowds shouting, singing and dancing. Baden-Powell, who had held the town for two hundred and fifteen days, became a 'hero among heroes'. The future architect of the Entente Cordiale was somewhat astonished. 'For three days,' wrote Paul Cambon, 'the inhabitants of the capital had only one thought and one occupation: to outdo one another in demonstrations of enthusiasm; they did so with a lack of taste, of moderation and of tact which has surprised even persons sceptical about the reputation for quietness and good behaviour attributed, often too readily, to the British crowds. Society men and women have surpassed the common people in bad manners.' Not until the Derby did the excitement subside.

One piece of good news followed on another. On 24 May, the Queen's birthday, 'the territories known as the Orange Free State' were annexed to the Crown. On the 31st the British army entered Johannesburg, which they found intact (the Boers had spread the rumour that they would demolish the mines, but they shrank from taking such a grave step). Four days later the capital of the Transvaal fell to them. 'For three hours,' wrote an enthusiastic Winston Churchill, 'the broad river of steel and khaki flowed unceasingly and the townsfolk gazed in awe and wonder at these majestic soldiers whose discipline neither perils or hardships had disturbed, whose relentless march no obstacles could prevent. With such pomp and the rolling of drums, the new order of things was ushered in.' On 1 September the South African Republic was in turn incorporated in Her Majesty's Dominions. To his title of High Commissioner, Milner added that of 'Governor of the Transvaal and Orange River Colony'. It would

---

[1] Villebois-Mareuil was killed in one of them. The British commander, who on this occasion had emerged victorious, made the gracious gesture of having a tomb erected at his own expense.

[2] He was to be promoted to field-marshal in 1919.

have been difficult to make a choice that would have rendered their new status as 'rebels' more intolerable to the Boers.

Kruger was determined not to fall into the hands of his victors. On 7 May he had addressed the *Volksraad* for the last time. 'I place myself in the hands of the Lord. Whatever He may have decided for me I shall kiss the rod with which He strikes me, for I too am guilty. Let each humble himself before the Lord. I have spoken.' Eight days before the fall of Pretoria the president said good-bye to his wife and set off for the mountainous regions of the north-east. The invaders found the coffers empty, for Smuts had had the presence of mind to have the Republic's gold holdings sent to the new seat of the government (hence the absurd legend of 'Kruger's treasure'). For four months the Boers fought a heroic but futile rearguard action. At the end of August an affecting decision had to be taken: Kruger, too old to take charge of the commandos, would leave for Europe on six months' 'leave', in the hope of obtaining assistance from the Powers; Schalk Burger would replace him temporarily as head of the Transvaal and, with Steyn, president of the Free State, would continue the struggle. The annexations were declared null and void.

Only one route remained open: Lourenço Marques. The Portuguese governor, highly embarrassed, offered Kruger a hospitality more like imprisonment. His guest was suspicious, telling one of his colleagues that this would be the first stage on his journey to St Helena. Yet his popularity was too great for the British to risk taking a step so contrary to human rights. Holland made the courteous gesture of placing a warship at the exile's disposal. The cruiser *Gelderland* raised anchor on 19 October. After two calls, at Djibouti and Suez, it arrived at Marseilles on 22 November. The authorities adopted an attitude of cautious reserve, but the crowd gave full expression to its feelings. 'An unforgettable spectacle', wrote *Le Petit Marseillais*. '. . . A popular reception was what this august old man needed, who today so wonderfully personifies patriotism at its most pure, fervent and heroic. . . . When one observes this old man of seventy-five, one has the impression of an old oak which tempests and storms may ravage but cannot destroy.'[1] Kruger left the following morning. At the station he found the same friendly atmosphere; the engine whistled, and the prefect breathed again—'Without incident', he telegraphed to his minister. His colleagues followed Kruger everywhere he went. At Tarascon the mayor introduced him to the town council, and a deputation of officers of the 11th dragoons, led by their colonel, was also present. Avignon, Valence, Mâcon and Chalon-sur-Saône organized an equally sympathetic welcome; at Lyons the prefect even dared to go to the station in a frock-coat. The president stayed the night at Dijon, which was partly illuminated and decorated with flags, and arrived in Paris on the 24th. At

---

[1] Document supplied by His Excellency Mr Willem Dirckse-van-Schalkwyk, formerly South African ambassador in France.

the Paris Exhibition the Transvaal pavilion and the reproduction of a Boer farm were attracting crowds of visitors, who were able to salute the portrait of Villebois-Mareuil, surrounded by crêpe, and the bust of Kruger. The walls of the capital were covered with stirring posters prepared by the Committee for Boer Independence: 'Let us all cry with a single voice: Long live Kruger! Long live the Boers! Long live the South African Republics!'

The official welcome was more reticent. Deeds and promises were replaced with gestures of courtesy. President Loubet sent Kruger a landau normally reserved for heads of state with an escort of cuirassiers; a little later he paid him a visit, observing the strictest protocol. The discussions were vague; Kruger was given to understand that France would favour arbitration by The Hague Tribunal. The Senate offered him 'the sincere expression of its respectful sympathy'. Nevertheless, there was a sigh of relief when he left for Germany. There he experienced the cruellest of disappointments. The Kaiser, impressed by a telegram from Queen Victoria, made a hunting party his excuse for not receiving him; cut to the quick, Kruger went no farther than Cologne, where his reception 'surpassed anything seen in France', according to the French ambassador in Berlin. Popular enthusiasm reached its climax in the Netherlands. At The Hague 'it took an hour to travel the short distance from the station to the Hôtel des Indes. The city was decorated with flags . . . the offices and shops closed.' The queen gave a quiet family dinner in his honour. Amsterdam displayed even greater fervour than the capital: 'Demonstrations of a kind never seen in living memory,' observed the French consul-general.

Suddenly it was all over. As 1900 drew to a close, a silence enveloped the exile, the helpless spectator of a tragedy in which he no longer had a part to play.[1]

At the same time that Holland was acclaiming Kruger, Britain, still feeling the effects of the Khaki Election of October in which the imperialists had won a crushing victory, was preparing to accord Roberts an apotheosis such as even Wellington had never known. A victim of *Veni, vidi, vici*, like Napoleon when he had thought that a few weeks would be enough to pacify Spain, the field-marshal had decided, after the annexation of the Republics, to hand over command to Kitchener. His arrival in London was arranged for 3 January 1901. 'The Prince of Wales will go to meet him, two divisions will be disposed along his route, the church bells will ring and the city will be decked out with flags.' At the last minute the programme was modified: 'The service of thanksgiving,' wrote Paul Cambon, 'has been replaced by a lunch with the Prince of Wales.' When

---

[1] Kruger stayed most of the time in Holland, spent the winter of 1902 at Menton and died at Clarens, on Lake Geneva, in 1904, at the age of seventy-nine. A Dutch warship took his body back to South Africa.

the great day came, 'the crowd was relatively small . . . and the cheering moderate.' What had happened?

The historian Rayne Kruger has given a perceptive analysis of the reasons for this disappointment. 'Roberts thought he was fighting first an army and then some rebels. But his opponents were neither: they were a nation.' Like the French in the Iberian peninsula after Napoleon's lightning campaign of 1808, the British were discovering that their military expertise was incapable of quelling a people determined to survive. All professional armies have experienced a similar mixture of bewilderment and rage whenever they have found themselves confronted by an enemy who would not abide by the rules of the game. In a hundred and fourteen days the victors had covered the four hundred miles separating the Orange river and Pretoria; in the course of their journey they had hustled several thousands of 'peasants' out of their positions and had sent them to die of boredom on the rock of St Helena; the Union Jack was flying over Bloemfontein and Pretoria; the so-called Republics were now Crown teritories—and yet here were the Boers, defeated, decimated and annexed, still looming up from all directions like statues of the Commendatore! De la Rey and Smuts in the western Transvaal, and Botha in the east, were playing on the nerves of their victors by carrying out a relentless succession of surprise attacks. In this game of blind-man's-buff in which the British, wearing the blindfolds, were unable to catch their adversaries, de Wet earned himself an unrivalled reputation, managing to be everywhere at once and yet never where he could be caught.[1] In December 1901 his furious pursuers suffered the crowning insult: two of his lieutenants, Kritzinger and Hertzog, crossed the Orange into the Cape Colony and there conducted a series of raids which took one of them as far as the Atlantic, less than a hundred miles from the capital. The news reached London at the very moment when the flags were being put out for the return of the conquering hero.

What was to be done? The eternal problem of reprisals now presented itself. In February 1900, even before his first successes, Roberts had hoped to coax the Boers with promises: no sanctions would be imposed on those who returned to their farms, cash payments would be made for all requisitions, and the soldiers would be forbidden to molest anyone. Was his proclamation known to the commandos? At all events, the plough did not replace the sword. When winter came the British general staff wondered if terror might not be a more effective reply to what is called 'the mosquito tactic'. Then, like so many other invaders in similar situations, the exasperated British adopted the doctrine of collective responsibility. The French consul-general in Cape Town explained the

---

[1] A saying attributed to the Prince of Wales was all the rage in the drawing-rooms of London. When a persistent mother finally succeeded in laying hands on an elusive son-in-law, the future Edward VII is supposed to have remarked: 'They ought to set her to catch de Wet.'

position very clearly. On 3 September 1900 he wrote: 'The unfortunate farmers who have submitted are not being protected. If a commando happens to pass by, they are forced to join it. . . . As for weapons and ammunition, they are buried in the ground.' On 29 October: 'The Boers are finding assistance and replenishments wherever they go, exchanging their tired horses for fresh mounts acclimatized to the country.' Threats were followed by action. In the event of an attack on a train the inhabitants of the neighbouring farms would be taken prisoner and their dwellings burnt down;[1] then it was decided that every farm where a rifle was fired would be mercilessly burnt, and any dwelling that sheltered a combatant would suffer a similar fate. Eventually the British resorted to both systematic and random destruction. The consul-general was sceptical: 'The farmer whose dwelling has been burnt down, his herds taken from him and his family reduced to begging has nothing more to lose and he will continue to fight, even if only to avenge himself for the injury done to him.' But the extremists were placing their hopes in radical solutions. 'For some time [29 October 1900] the Cape newspapers have been advocating the general internment of the entire male population of the two republics as the only means of achieving peace. . . . The women and children would remain in the charge of the British authorities, who would have to feed and house them.'

Lord Kitchener was growing impatient. He would have liked to be appointed to the vacant post of commander-in-chief in India. Moreover, his reputation was at stake. Were these South African peasants going to strip the crown of laurels which he had earned by his victories in the Sudan? He resolved to try new tactics.

The underlying principle of this policy was sound enough: to master the Boers it was essential to impede their mobility. The idea of chains of blockhouses was therefore put into practice. At irregular intervals, sometimes only a few hundred yards, circular forts were built and occupied by a garrison of several men—usually six or seven, thirty at the most. A roof and a double wall of galvanized iron protected them from bullets; the forts could easily have been demolished by artillery, but the Boers had none left. These miniature fortresses were surrounded by ditches and barbed wire. Intended originally to defend the railways, they gradually came to serve as spiders' webs which the Boers, it was thought, would not be able to penetrate. Flying columns composed mainly of mounted infantry were sent out to track down the commandos. Once again, however, the commandos proved elusive, and the irritation of the British grew day by day.

For one brief moment, in February 1901, peace seemed possible. Mrs Louis Botha acted as intermediary between Kitchener and her husband—

[1] The idea of placing hostages on the most exposed convoys was considered but never put into practice, owing to the storm of protest it provoked in Britain.

an incident typical of this strange war. The two men finally met at Middel-burg, in the Transvaal. The talks lasted three weeks. The atmosphere was friendly, but the positions of the negotiators proved to be far apart. One talked of annexation, the other of independence. Botha demanded a total amnesty for the 'rebels' of the Cape, but Kitchener's instructions forbade him to give ground. On 15 March Botha broke off the discussions. Kitchener, willing to continue the negotiations, expressed his displeasure: 'We are now carrying the war on to put two or three hundred Dutchmen in prison at the end of it,' he wrote to Milner. But the High Commissioner, who did not bear the burden of responsibility for operations, and who knew that he enjoyed the support of the Colonial Office, rejected any possibility of concessions. Lloyd George flew into a rage: 'There was a soldier who knew what was meant; he strove to make peace. There was another man who strolled among his orchids, six thousand miles away from the deadly bark of the rifles. He stopped Kitchener's peace.' It is highly unlikely that Chamberlain paid the slightest attention to this demagogic tirade; at all events, such invective did nothing to alter the government's resolve. A few days after the breakdown of the talks the French ambassador met a high-ranking Foreign Office official and asked him what he thought about it all: 'It is very annoying,' was the brief reply. It was 'very annoying' because the war was becoming increasingly expensive; because it would be necessary to send out reinforcements—which in fact was done; and because this accursed country of South Africa was building up a hatred of Britain the consequences of which were difficult to foresee. But compro-mise was unthinkable: Milner's elevation to the peerage, when he came to spend a few weeks in London in the spring, symbolized British determination.

The struggle would therefore be continued, using increasingly cruel methods. On 19 November 1900, for the first time, the correspondence of the French consul-general in Cape Town mentions 'camps where the women are cooped up in tents, guarded by sentries, without the most elementary comfort or care'. This was the beginning of a frightful episode. Two months earlier the British authorities had considered it advisable to protect from acts of vengeance the few Boers who had rallied to their cause: it was decided to assemble then in what were modestly called 'refugee camps'. Then, as has already been seen, reprisals had been intensified: farms destroyed, harvests burnt and cattle confiscated. This scorched-earth policy was reducing to famine hundreds of families whose menfolk were away fighting in the commados. An instinctive sense of their responsibility induced the military to provide these families with at least a minimum subsistence. They were herded into the so-called 'refugee camps', which became more and more numerous. Then the exponents of total war eventually began to wonder if the camps, originally presented as a humanitarian device, could not be used as a means of political pressure. The round-ups were systematically extended, but there was less method evident in the organization of the camps: thousands of women and children were interned with hardly any provision for their nourishment and care; epidemics brought countless deaths, especially among babies.

The tragic news eventually reached London. The committee of the 'South African Women and Children's Distress Fund' was stirred to action and sent Miss Emily Hobhouse to conduct an inquiry. Thirty-nine years of age and the daughter of a clergyman, Emily Hobhouse had six years earlier found her vocation in social work; in 1895 she had gone to the United States to help some British miners whose distress had touched her. From the outset of the war she had taken the side of the Boers and she could be seen at pacifist meetings, with her fair hair pushed back and an oval, regular face that would light up in a charming smile. She was one of those generous-hearted and iron-willed maiden ladies not uncommon in England. She stayed more than four months in South Africa. Her honesty led her to admit that, in certain camps, conditions were not as atrocious as had been claimed. But in others she encountered some dreadful sights. In Bloemfontein, on 28 January 1901, she found the heat inside the tents suffocating, flies everywhere and rain seeping through the canvas. She thought that the women were behaving admirably, seldom weeping and never complaining, concerned only with the suffering of their children who were lying in prostration and dying of starvation—they reminded her of faded flowers that had been thrown away. On 10 February, at Aliwal North, she found that there was no soap and had to listen to blithe comments about the dirty appearance of the inmates. At Springfield, on 4 March, she found the women weary of hearing the officers tell them that they were refugees enjoying the generous and benevolent protection of Britain. At Kimberley, on 12 March, she visited a dirty, foul-smelling camp with no nurses and where measles and whooping-cough were wreaking havoc. In despair, she came to the conclusion that those who possessed sufficient resources should be allowed to leave—had an entire nation, she wondered, ever been taken prisoner like this since Old Testament times?

Kitchener did not see the problem in the same light. To Lady Cranborne he wrote on 2 April 1901: 'The inmates are far better looked after in every way than they are in their own homes. The doctors' reports of the dirt and filth in which the Boer ladies from the veld revel are very unpleasant reading and I am considering whether some of the worst cases should not be tried for manslaughter.' Miss Hobhouse's report nevertheless made enough of an impression in Britain for an official inquiry to be entrusted to a Committee of Ladies presided over by Mrs Henry Fawcett, the wife of the economist and herself an active suffragette. The Liberal Opposition attacked the question with great passion. Campbell-Bannerman condemned these 'methods of barbarism', and Lloyd George predicted that 'a barrier of dead children's bodies will rise up between the British and the

Boer races in South Africa'. In the autumn of 1901 the administration of the camps was taken out of the army's hands. Milner accepted this new responsibility without enthusiasm: 'I could never have foreseen that the soldiers meant to sweep the whole population of the country higgledy-piggledy into a couple of dozen camps. A sad fiasco.' It is undeniable that, under a civil authority, the situation improved perceptibly. But not enough, alas. The archives of the French Foreign Office contain the following note, dating from early in 1902: '4 January. Political department. 'The "Sou des Boers" ["Boers' Pence"] Committee has been informed by its correspondents in southern Africa that it is now useless to send baby clothes. Infant mortality in the concentration camps has been such that these garments would remain unused.'

The total number of deaths varies according to the source used: 18,000 according to the British bluebook, 26,000 if one is to believe the Boers.

The war continued throughout 1901. It would make monotonous reading to retell the moving story of these encounters in which a weakened David still managed to strike a few blows at a Goliath stronger than ever. Kruger was following the struggle from Holland. He had not lost hope. When the Boers' representative in the United States paid him a visit, the president confided to him that, one night, God had commanded him to get up and open his Bible, and there he had read that God was with him. In South Africa itself the combatants were inspired by hope of a less mystical nature. The optimists reckoned that Britain would tire first; moreover, they were clinging to the illusion that the Powers would act on the report which their delegates in Europe had submitted to the court of arbitration at The Hague. London, however, was still not weakening, and only the Tsar—who two years earlier had posed as the champion of world peace[1]—showed any inclination to mediate, an idea he quickly abandoned in view of the attitude of the British government. From time to time a brilliant feat of arms would revive the Boers' spirits. In September 1901, Smuts carried out another dazzling raid: invading the Cape Colony yet again, his commandos advanced westward as far as the Atlantic and to the east found themselves near enough to the Indian Ocean to glimpse the lights of Port Elizabeth; one patrol even experienced the thrill of seeing Table Mountain in the distance. The Boers were not to be ousted from these conquered territories until the end of the war. Yet this had been a Pyrrhic victory, for both men and arms were dwindling. A report from de la Rey to Kruger sent on 10 December 1901 is revealing: '1. Our country is in ruin. . . . Only the walls of dwellings are left. . . . 2. All our cattle have vanished. . . . The animals have been massacred. . . . 3. The harvests have been destroyed and burnt. . . . 4. The women have been rounded up in camps. . . . My wife is wandering aimlessly with her six

[1] In the summer of 1899 Russia had taken the initiative in the calling of a Peace Conference at The Hague.

children. . . .[1] 5. There are now only two doctors in the Free State. 6. No clothing. . . .' In conclusion de la Rey wrote: 'Today we have nothing more to lose except our national existence, and to preserve this possession we are ready to give our blood to the very last man.'

Kitchener was adopting various tactics. In May he suggested that the possessions of all Boer combatants be confiscated, but London refused. That same month he granted Mrs Botha safe conduct to Europe, perhaps in the hope of influencing Kruger; her account of their meeting is recorded by Dr Leyds:

Kitchener: I know what the Boers think of me. They regard me as a butcher.

Mrs Botha: Yes, that's what they think.

Kitchener: They believe our plan is to exterminate them to the last man.

Mrs Botha: Yes.

Kitchener: In fact that is probably what we shall be forced to do.'

In the meantime, a solution of the kind adopted in Nova Scotia was germinating in the mind of the commander-in-chief. On 24 June, Kitchener wrote to the Colonial Office: 'The Boers are uncivilized Afrikander savages with a thin white veneer. . . . We have now got more than half the population, either as prisoners of war or in our refugee camps. I would advise that they should not be allowed to return. I think we should start a scheme for settling them elsewhere[2] and South Africa will be safe and there will be room for the British to colonize.' When his government failed to act on his advice, Kitchener resorted to a more selective threat: on 7 August he gave notice that all commando-leaders who had not laid down their arms by 15 September would be permanently banished. The only reply to this 'paper bombshell', as the Boers called it, was a proclamation by Botha announcing that at the same date all armed Britons would be outlawed and that the burghers would be authorized to shoot any such persons they might come across. On both sides these were merely empty threats. But Kitchener did strike a blow at the morale of his adversaries when he succeeded in recruiting a few hundred Boers, including two former generals, who, under the label of 'National Scouts', worked for him as scouts and spies. Furthermore, the commandos were disturbed by the fact that they were encountering armed natives with growing frequency. It was a far cry from the war of Whites and 'gentlemen' of 1899.

The Boers accomplished two final and glorious feats. On 7 March 1902, at Tweebosch in the western Transvaal, de la Rey took prisoner Lord Methuen, a personal friend of Edward VII. A month later, on 11 April, in the same region, the last soldiers of the Republics conducted what

[1] De la Rey's wife was arrested and interned.
[2] He had in mind the Fiji islands, the Dutch East Indies and, curiously enough, Madagascar.

Professor de Kock regards as the most heroic assault of the war. Perhaps their ranks included some of those ten- or eleven-year-old children whom their country's anguish had driven to take up rifles and some of whom, like their fathers, were deported to St Helena.

By this time negotiations were in progress. In January, prompted by the growing indignation of public opinion, Queen Wilhelmina had ventured to offer her services as mediator; the British government, anxious to bring matters to a speedy conclusion owing to the difficulty of postponing the coronation of Edward VII any longer,[1] had knitted its brows but had indicated that it would not be opposed to direct talks with the Boers. The latter did not decline the opportunity. In any case, differences of opinion were beginning to appear among them. The Transvaal government, installed in the east of the country among the wild animals, giraffes and antelopes, was not ruling out the idea of submission; the Free State government on the other hand, leading a mobile existence in the regions still free, was proving intractable. On 9 April, armed with the guarantees of safe conduct which the British wisely granted them, the delegates of the two states assembled at Klerksdorp, about a hundred and twenty miles south-west of Johannesburg. They came from all directions. Smuts, who had established himself not far from the Atlantic and had been obliged to travel four hundred miles to join them, described them thus: 'Rugged men clad in skins or sacking, their bodies covered with sores from lack of salt and food. . . . Their spirit was undaunted but they had reached the limits of physical resistance.' The delegates appointed a five-man commission and decided to ask Kitchener for an interview. Kitchener, alone, received them in Pretoria on 12 April. Milner joined the discussions on the 14th. The Boers began by demanding independence, but the British made a formal renunciation of any such claim a *sine qua non* condition of the continuation of the talks.

Using as their argument the popular sovereignty on which their system of government was based, the representatives of the Republics then declared that they could do nothing without consulting the people. Sixty men elected from the commandos, thirty for each state, gathered on 15 May at Vereeniging, a small mining town on the Vaal, to the south of the Rand. Two opposing points of view were put forward, each calling Providence to witness. Burger maintained: 'Perhaps it is God's will that the English nation should suppress us, in order that our pride may be subdued, and that we may become, through the fire of our troubles, purified.' De Wet, replying to those who argued that the silence of Europe justified their readiness to submit, insisted: 'If [there has been] no European intervention, it is the will of God. . . . Does it not show that He is minded to form us out of this war into a nation worthy of the name? Let us then bow to the will of the Almighty.'

After four days of impassioned debate, five plenipotentiaries left for

[1] Queen Victoria had died on 21 January 1901.

Pretoria: Botha, Smuts and de la Rey advocating peace, de Wet wanting to continue the war, and Hertzog wavering. On 19 May they made a counter-proposal: the Republics would renounce independence in the field of foreign affairs, but would retain autonomy in internal matters under the supervision of Britain and they would give up a part of their territory. Britain's representatives had no difficulty in exposing the inconsistency of these proposals. The Boers continued to fight every inch of the way. On 21 and 28 May two more sessions took place at which concrete details were discussed without any further mention of the fatal word 'independence'. On the 29th Kitchener and Milner demanded a final reply within forty-eight hours. A magnificent plea by Smuts in favour of peace won the support of the 'Assembly of the People', and on 31 May, at five o'clock in the morning, it was decided by fifty-four votes to six to accept the British conditions. This was the last business conducted by the last assembly of the Boer Republics. The session ended with a prayer. The final act, the agreement known as the Treaty of Vereeniging, took place in Pretoria that same day at eleven o'clock in the evening. Kitchener shook hands with his former adversaries, saying: 'We are good friends now.'

The British had taken great care not to give this document the form of a contract. Its title allowed of no ambiguity: 'Terms of surrender of Boer forces in the field'. By recognizing, however, that the signatories were 'acting as the government of the South African Republic and as the government of the Orange Free State', they conceded the Boers a status both evocative of the past and holding promise for the future. Though severe taken as a whole, certain clauses of the 'treaty' left grounds for hope—especially the article authorizing the teaching of Dutch in the former Republics and its use in courts of law; and, even more important, the clause promising that military occupation would be replaced 'at the earliest possible date by civil administration . . . leading up to self-government as soon as the circumstances permit'. At the same time, Britain undertook to pay £3 million in compensation for damages, not to impose any special land tax, not to confiscate property and not to institute any civil or criminal action 'except for certain acts contrary to laws of war' (which was hardly reassuring). These few concessions ill concealed the realities of the Boers' capitulation: the burghers must surrender their arms and ammunition,[1] cease all resistance, recognize their status as subjects of King Edward VII and swear an oath of loyalty to him before they would even be permitted to return home. 'It was all over. We were British colonists,' observed de Wet, whose hand must have trembled as he wrote these words.

By common agreement the solution of the native problem was

[1] They were, however, granted the right to keep a sporting gun on condition they obtained a licence.

postponed until calmer times. Article 8 stated: 'Question of granting franchise to natives not to be decided until introduction of self-government.'

Neither in London, Cape Town nor Johannesburg was the event celebrated by public rejoicing. People were more concerned to count the dead than to hoist flags. 449,000 British officers and soldiers had been involved: 256,000 regular troops, 109,000 volunteers, 31,000 recruits from the Dominions and 53,000 enlisted in South Africa itself. The casualties were estimated at roughly 100,000: 7,091 killed, 19,193 wounded and the rest stricken by disease. Some 90,000 Boers had taken up arms: 3,990 died in combat and 1,081 of disease; the number of wounded is not known; if to these figures are added the deaths in the concentration camps and among prisoners of war, the total Boer losses amount to over 34,000.

The British were taking possession of a country that had been decimated, devastated and humiliated. On 27 October 1902, five months after the conclusion of peace, Lord Salisbury told the French ambassador that it would take Britain thirty years to organize South Africa.

21

The Formation of the Union

The transformations which, within eight years, were to put the vanquished on an equal footing with their victors constitute one of the more astounding reversals of history. Their origin is to be found in the progress of liberal ideas in Britain, the determination of the Boers and the wisdom of a few men. Throughout this period the idea of a union made constant headway, at first slowly and hesitantly, but soon more swiftly and irresistibly.

Kitchener left South Africa shortly after Vereeniging.[1] Milner remained alone, the undisputed master of the country. He had not waited until the end of the conflict to set about the work of reconstruction. As soon as the Republics had been annexed, the British government had instructed him to adapt the administration of the former Free State to the new régime, but to reorganize completely that of the Transvaal. The Colonial Office mistrusted the South African Republic even more than the Free State. The High Commissioner appointed as his assistants a brilliant team of twenty or so young men, some of whom had only recently left university and the oldest of whom were not more than thirty years of age. This 'Kindergarten', as these budding statesmen soon came to be known, bore an astounding resemblance to the 'brains trust' which was to achieve fame in Roosevelt's New Deal: they showed the same enthusiasm for work, an enthusiasm that sometimes led to chaos, the same concern for the public weal and an inability to understand that this might not necessarily coincide with their own ideas, and the same wholehearted loyalty to their leader. They accomplished their task with zeal, efficiency and great administrative flair.

Nevertheless, what Milner had achieved before 1902 was nothing compared to what remained to be done when the cease-fire descended upon a devastated *veld*. The most recent research estimates the number of farms destroyed at 30,000, the population of the 'refugee camps' at 116,500 Boers and 100,000 Bantu, the *uitlanders* whom the war had deprived of

[1] According to his most recent biographer he took with him 'a great quantity of loot including some lifesize statues of Kruger and others which he planned to erect in a future park'. The statues are said to have been 'secretly restored to South Africa in 1909'.

their employment at 50,000, and prisoners of war at 31,000 (of whom 24,000 were sent to St Helena or Ceylon). Furthermore, the handshakes of the negotiators had not dispersed a miasma of hatred that was poisoning the atmosphere. On the very day on which the agreement was signed Botha and Burger had made a moving appeal to their fellow-country-men: 'Let us lay aside all feelings of bitterness and let us learn to forget and forgive'—noble words, but a reconciliation is always more difficult for the vanquished than for the victors. The Boer chiefs realized that their admonishments would carry more weight if they could reinforce them with evidence of goodwill, and so Botha, de la Rey and de Wet left for London in August. British 'fair play' did not fail to live up to its traditions. 'Their arrival has thrilled public opinion,' wrote the French ambassador. 'They have refused an invitation to the naval review, but this has in no way diminished their popularity. . . . Chamberlain has become gentle and gracious. . . . Invitations to the country are pouring in. . . . The King has received them.' This last gesture certainly impressed the visitors. 'I remember,' relates an eye-witness, 'the joyful pride and relief with which Botha told us of the reception by the king at Cowes: "He treated us as equals, he showed us over his yacht and introduced us to his lady." ' This revelation of society life was gratifying to such simple souls, but no con-cessions were forthcoming. When, a month later, the three envoys had the audacity to launch from Holland an 'Appeal to the Civilized World' —which brought them only a little over £125,000—the Colonial Office reminded them in no uncertain terms that, as subjects of His Majesty, they must address their complaints to London.

It would be unjust to accuse the British government of indifference. In November 1902 martial law was abolished and a civil administration replaced the military. In December the new colonies were visited by Chamberlain.[1] In Cape Town everything went perfectly. In Bloem-fontein, however, there was an incident between de Wet and the Secretary of State, and in Pretoria the Boers' enthusiasm was somewhat lacking in spontaneity, according to the reports of the French consul: 'It was at an order from Botha and de la Rey that the Boers stood up as he entered, and it was not until they were told: "Burghers, applaud!" that the acclama-tions were heard at the end of his speech. Such discipline in the presence of the victors had something menacing about it.' Chamberlain's journey had important consequences. The British government agreed to guarantee a loan of £35 million[2] to the Transvaal and Orange River Colony. An additional grant was allowed for the reconstruction of the devastated regions and the resettlement of their inhabitants: the figure of £3 million had been specified at Vereeniging, but £16½ million proved necessary and the victors provided this sum in full.

[1] He resigned in 1903 and was replaced by Lyttelton.
[2] The Paris market subscribed a considerable part of the loan.

A year after the end of the war, order had been substituted for chaos. But a twofold problem still existed. In the long term, what was to become of South Africa? In the immediate future, how were the interests of the Cape Colony, the Orange River Colony, the Transvaal and Natal to be reconciled?

Milner had his own ideas about the first question. To conceive of a South Africa not under British control was beyond the power of his imagination. Not that he despaired of the Boer: 'First beaten, then fairly treated, and then not too much worried on his own plans, in his own conservative habits, I think he will be peaceful enough.' It was, however, essential that the Boers should learn the language of their victors: 'Dutch should be only used to teach English and English to teach everything else.' Above all, they must resign themselves to becoming a minority. To anglicize the country by immigration was one of the High Commissioner's favourite schemes. He calculated the ideal proportions with rigorous precision: in industry and commerce, 45 per cent British and 15 per cent Boers; in agriculture, 15 per cent and 25 per cent. His idea of the perfect ratio was thus 60 British to 40 Boers. 'We not only want a majority of British but we want a fair margin, because of the large proportion of cranks that we British always generate and who take particular pleasure in going against their own people.' Professor Le May has harshly summed up Lord Milner's objectives as a British South Africa 'loyal with broken English and happy with a broken heart'.

Such large ambitions could not be realized in a few years. For the time being more urgent problems presented themselves. The South African territories might all be Crown Colonies, but they nevertheless had very different views about the levying of customs duties and the administration of the railways. The Cape and Natal, enjoying the monopoly of the coast-line, advocated high tariffs to meet the needs of their budgets. The point of view of the Transvaal and the Orange River Colony was quite different: situated far from the sea and, at least in the case of the Transvaal, having a pressing need of foreign products, they were anxious that the already considerable cost of transport should not be aggravated by high customs levies. The distribution of railway traffic was another bone of contention. The Rand (as the Witwatersrand region is commonly known) prided itself on being the land of the future, and the route by which its gold would be exported was a matter of great importance to each of the other three colonies. When, on the conclusion of the war, the experts once again found time to compile statistics, they observed that 63 per cent of the Transvaal's wealth was being transported by the Lourenço Marques line, 24 per cent by the Durban line and only 13 per cent by the Cape line. These figures had a certain irony about them: defeated on the battlefield, the Boers were emerging triumphant in the economic field— their old obsession, a direct route to the Indian Ocean, was in fact proving the most profitable solution. Two intercolonial conferences met in 1903 with the object of reconciling the interests of the four colonies. The first, held in March, was attended by Rhodesia and, as an observer, by the customs director of Portuguese Equatorial Africa: the creation of a customs union was decided and the principle of Imperial preference accepted. Two months later, an Intercolonial Council assumed responsibility for the railways, hitherto operated by private companies.

The labour problem provoked even fiercer emotions. It will be remembered that at the beginning of the war the majority of Bantu had left the Rand after the closing of the mines. Milner wanted to reopen the mines immediately after annexation. According to the French consul, he began by expelling all *uitlanders* not of British nationality. Although his decision was intended to create a monopoly for the benefit of his fellow-countrymen, they still needed a labour force at their disposal. The High Commissioner attempted a *modus vivendi* with the Portuguese, who undertook to send two to four thousand natives each month. However, such a small contribution did not solve the difficulty. From about £15½ million in 1899 the value of gold production had fallen to a little over £12½ million in 1903. A first solution, put forward by an engineer, Frederick Creswell, recommended the importation of White labourers; but, though impressive enough in theory, the idea was of no practical value—South Africa was attracting no more immigrants from Britain than it had in the previous century.[1]

It was therefore necessary to look in other directions. In November 1903 a commission, which apparently had a fondness for precision, declared that the mines needed 129,364 labourers. The Blacks were not flocking to the Rand, for they were being offered only 45 shillings a month instead of the 60 shillings of four years earlier. There remained the yellow races: Indians had been brought into Natal, and so why not Chinese into the Transvaal? Paul Cambon, who from London was keeping a close eye on developments in South Africa, summed up the problem shrewdly: 'Since the Black refuses to work and the White is too expensive, recourse must be had to the yellow man.' From 1904 onwards thousands of coolies were signed on at Tientsin and elsewhere. The Boers, who considered the Asian 'a dangerous monster' (according to the French consul-general in Pretoria), watched in horror as they began to arrive. At least the newcomers knew the meaning of hard work. 'The Dutch sulked but the mines prospered,' writes Professor de Kiewiet. Campbell-Bannerman, leader of the Liberal Opposition in Britain, exploded in anger, describing this measure as 'the end of the hope of making South Africa a white man's country' and accusing the Conservatives of having introduced 'a new element into the confusion already existing'. But was he really so dis-

---

[1] According to the historian Carrington, however, four thousand young people went out to South Africa to play a role similar to that of 'the king's daughters' in Canada (the women chosen by Louis XIV's representatives and sent out to Canada by Colbert, his Secretary of State, to find husbands there).

satisfied? His party had just found a wonderful platform for an election campaign known to be imminent.

As soon as the physical vestiges of war had been at least partially effaced, the vitality of the Boers asserted itself forcibly.

In 1904 the success of the 'Progressive Party' (that is to say, the British party) brought its leader, Dr Jameson, the office of Prime Minister of the Cape Colony. The failure of his raid and a few months in prison[1] had not exhausted the energies of this colourful character. In 1898 he had been seen again in Rhodesia. When war came, he had attempted to take part in the defence of Ladysmith, but his health had compelled him to seek a less adventurous destiny. Elected to Parliament, 'Dr Jim' had there acquired sufficient influence to appear the natural successor to Rhodes when the 'Colossus' died in 1902. Admittedly, his victory in 1904 was hardly a glorious one, for he had benefited from the emergency measures taken against the 'rebels'.[2] Finding themselves again confronted by the man who, eight years earlier, had tried to strike them a mortal blow might well have discouraged the Boers. But this apparently indestructible breed of men certainly did not feel itself doomed to extinction. A member of the Colonial Office staff is supposed to have said in 1901: 'The greatest enemies we have had to encounter are the "predicant" of the Dutch Reformed Church and the schoolmaster.' This was hitting the nail on the head. The protection which the Catholic Church gave the French Canadians in 1763 has often been likened to Noah's Ark. The same could be said of the Dutch Reformed Church in South Africa. Its pastors even went so far as to insist on public confession before admitting war-time 'collaborators'[3] to the communion-table. To the rest they issued incessant reminders of the 'divine mission' that had fallen to the Boer people. Most important of all, as had happened in Quebec, they made language an instrument of survival. English had become the only language spoken in the state schools; Dutch could be taught for only five hours per week and then only by special request. Private establishments were therefore opened with the help of Dutch funds, and soon there were two hundred under the control of parents' associations. In these schools the Afrikaans language was purified: a theologian, J. D. du Toit, otherwise known as Leopold Totius, a naturalist, Eugene Marais, and a poet, Jan Celliers, demonstrated that it was now capable of expressing the finer subtleties of thought. Traditions were thus perpetuated and, at the same time, the way was being paved for the future. The return of Kruger's ashes on 16 December 1904 was the occasion of an impressive demonstration of the moral solidarity of the Boers.

[1] See Chapter 16.
[2] Several thousand Afrikaners had been deprived of their civic rights. 'It is a simple and swift means of ensuring the imperialists a majority,' the French consul-general had commented in June 1902.
[3] The 'hands-uppers', as they were nicknamed, as opposed to the 'bitter-enders'.

Six months later Botha initiated their political regrouping. In founding *Het Volk*, 'The People'—a name evocative of the *Volksraad* of earlier days—he defined his intention thus: 'We have only one purpose, to stand with outstretched hands and ask the co-operation of the English people. . . . We are entering the future, the flag question is finished for ever.' To show that the Transvaal was no longer divided into *burghers* on the one hand and *uitlanders* on the other, the leader of *Het Volk* entered into an agreement with the 'Transvaal Responsible Government Association' which, composed of British residents, was also demanding self-government.

The circumstances were favourable. In March 1905, Lord Selborne replaced Milner. Married to Salisbury's daughter, Under Secretary for the Colonies at the beginning of the war and then First Lord of the Admiralty, Selborne was no less representative of imperialist trends than his predecessor. Unlike Milner, however, he was not in the habit of expressing his ideas in a dogmatic manner; even more important, he had the inestimable advantage of not having been involved directly in the tragedy of the war. Even during Milner's time things had begun to change. In 1901, Johannesburg and Pretoria had been granted municipal councils; two years later, so-called Legislative Councils had given the Transvaal and the Orange River Colony a modicum of participation in the administration of local affairs; but these institutions were so closely supervised by the High Commissioner that no Boer of repute had agreed to join them. In 1905 another step forward was taken when the Balfour government (Balfour had succeeded Salisbury in 1902) accepted the principle of elected assemblies. But this was too little, too late. *Het Volk* firmly opposed such a mockery of the parliamentary system. At this same time Britain was looking for change. In January 1906, after a campaign in which the Liberals had advocated both free trade and social reforms,[1] the general election gave them an overwhelming majority: 377 seats against 157 Unionists (Conservatives), 93 Irish Nationalists and 53 members of the nascent Labour Party.

It will be remembered that Campbell-Bannerman, the new Prime Minister, had protested against the 'methods of barbarism' of the concentration camps. A man of goodwill, he hoped for an honourable settlement of the South African problem. He appointed to the Colonial Office two specialists: Lord Elgin, former viceroy of India and subsequently chairman of a commission of inquiry into the conduct of the recent war, and Winston Churchill, whose conviction of British superiority disposed him to gestures of magnanimity towards less favoured peoples.

Events rapidly gathered momentum. One of the first actions of the new

[1] And in the course of which their spokesmen had virtuously talked of 'Chinese slavery' in the Rand.

government was to stop the importation of Chinese labourers. The Liberals were by no means unwilling to pose as the opponents of what would nowadays be called 'trusts'. Smuts, with his habitual shrewdness, saw the possibilities that such an attitude offered the Afrikaners. As soon as Campbell-Bannerman was installed in Downing Street, he left for London. He possessed a knack for the apt phrase; in his opinion, it was a question not of 'Boers against British' but of 'the liberties of the people as against the encroachment of money power'. The 'people' must be given the right to manage its own affairs—in other words, the Transvaal must be allowed to govern itself; then the Rand magnates would be brought to their senses, and the industrialists of Birmingham or Manchester would soon be. But, Smuts added, there must be no delay: 'There may be some danger in trusting the people too soon, but there may be much greater danger in trusting them too late.' Finally, a little flattery: 'I can conceive no nobler task for liberal statesmanship.'

Smuts later recounted how he persuaded Campbell-Bannerman, 'the Rock' as he called him. He had put his case in simple terms: did Campbell-Bannerman want the Boers as friends or as enemies? He could have them as his friends, and they had already proved the quality of their friendship. Smuts promised him the goodwill of both his colleagues and himself, if he wanted it. Alternatively, the British Prime Minister could choose to make the Boers his enemies and then, perhaps, to have another Ireland on his hands. The British, argued Smuts, believed in liberty, and so did the Boers. He had realized that he was dealing with a cautious Scotsman. Campbell-Bannerman said nothing, but when Smuts left he felt happy—his intuition told him that he had won. In 1913, Lloyd George told Lord Riddell, the proprietor of the *News of the World*, about the ministerial discussion that had followed Campbell-Bannerman's meeting with Smuts. When Riddell asked: 'This South African constitution, who was responsible, Campbell-Bannerman or Asquith?' Lloyd George replied: 'Oh! C.B.! He deserves all the credit. It was all done in a ten-minute speech at the Cabinet, the most dramatic and the most important ten-minute speech ever delivered in our time. He brushed aside all the checks and safe-guards devised by Asquith, Winston and Loreburn. . . .[1] It was the utterance of a plain, kindly, simple man. The speech moved one at least of the Cabinet to tears. . . . It captured General Botha by its magnanimity. If we had a war tomorrow, Botha and fifty thousand Boers would march by us side by side.'

In March 1906 the British cabinet, which had already decided to give way, nevertheless deemed it advisable to take shelter behind the screen of a commission of inquiry. This 'imperial patrol', to use Churchill's phrase, stayed in South Africa nine weeks, heard five hundred witnesses and received more than seventy deputations. It presented its report at the end of July. All that remained was to transform resolutions of principle into

[1] The Lord Chancellor. Loreburn had been pro-Boer during the war.

facts. On 6 December 1906—four years, six months and six days after Vereeniging—the Transvaal was endowed with a Parliament of two houses, elected on an exclusively White franchise and to which the government would be responsible. The French consul-general commented: 'The new constitution has been unanimously accepted by the Boer party. . . . The Boers are profoundly and quietly satisfied. Today (16 December), Dingaan's Day, the "Day of the Covenant",[1] the festival of the old Transvaal, crowds are making their way in silence to the cemeteries to pay their respects to the dead.' And from London, on 22 January 1907, Paul Cambon wrote to the French Foreign Office: 'It must be admitted that the British government is at this moment setting the world an astonishing example of tolerance and liberalism. . . . Events will prove if this confidence is not rash.' Smuts, for his part, was unreservedly optimistic: in his opinion Britain had made a wonderful gesture of trust and magnanimity.

In a poll which took place two and a half months later, *Het Volk* won thirty-seven constituencies out of sixty-nine. Botha became Prime Minister; Smuts, his *alter ego*, was appointed Colonial Secretary and then Minister of Education. Two of the six members of the cabinet belonged to the Responsible Government Association which, however, had obtained only six seats—clearly, the Afrikaners were determined not to appear any less generous than their former enemies.

On 5 June 1907 the Orange River Colony received a similar status. The Boers, who formed ninety per cent of the population, won the election easily. Abraham Fischer, who a year earlier had founded the *Orangia Unie* party, became Prime Minister, but everyone knew that General Hertzog would be the real head of the cabinet.

This reversal of fortune was certainly extraordinary, but it settled nothing. Placing the Transvaal and Orange River Colony on an equal footing with the other two territories did not put an end to the divergence of interests. Further discussions about the railways in 1905 and another customs conference in 1906 had produced only the most obviously fragile agreement. Lionel Curtis, a member of Milner's Kindergarten, realized the danger. A few weeks before the granting of parliamentary government, he made a speech that created a sensation: 'If nothing else were done, the former republics would soon drift into collision with the Cape Colony and Natal, and South Africa would be landed in another war. The only way to avoid this catastrophe is to unite all four colonies under one government.'

His chief, Selborne, was even more convinced and in January 1907 summed up his ideas in a Memorandum destined to become famous. 'Each colony is self-governing, but the people of South Africa are not

[1] See p. 95

self-governing because they have no South African government. . . . The High Commissioner is subject to the Secretary of State, subject himself to Parliament. . . . Thus, for the strictly internal affairs of South Africa, the ultimate authority is the Imperial Parliament at Westminster.' 'There are five[1] systems of law and five organizations for defence, the expense is at the maximum, the return at the minimum.' Three choices presented themselves: 'The makeshift régime of the High Commissioner, the jarring separation of the states of South Africa, the noble union of the states of South Africa.' To this latter objective Selborne gave his wholehearted support. In his view, history, ancient and modern, provided a guarantee of success. 'The fusion between the two races is merely a matter of time as it was with the Saxons and the Normans. . . . There is no reason why South Africa should not apply the remedy as quickly and effectively as it was applied in Canada.'[2]

At first the Afrikaners were sceptical. That experienced Cape politician, John Merriman, described the High Commissioner's reasonings as 'a windy effusion'. He saw a danger: 'I do not want to see a union hastily patched up so that the whole of South Africa may have one neck in order to fit the yoke easier on it.' He warned Steyn to beware of Selborne. Steyn was no more enthusiastic: to him the Memorandum seemed 'crude, full of rhetoric and bad history'. The Boers, however, found themselves in an ever weaker position to oppose union because of divisions among themselves. The Transvaal had no other objective, either in the long or in the short term, than the reconciliation and fusion of the two races under British control. In preparing for the future, the former Free State was more concerned to preserve the past. Steyn thought that his fellow-Boers beyond the Vaal were 'inclined to lay on the loyalty butter too thick'. Hertzog shocked the moderates when he proposed to enforce bilingualism in the Orange River Colony.

Botha's presence at a Colonial Conference in 1907 symbolized the conflict between these two trends. The Prime Minister had not been in power three months when he left for England. Perhaps less sure of himself than he pretended, he was given a welcome which inspired him with confidence and flattered his vanity. King Edward VII received him with his customary good grace. The former Boer commander-in-chief, wanting to make a gesture worthy of the sovereign of the Empire to which he was proud to belong, presented Edward VII with a 3,025-carat diamond, the largest that had ever been discovered, as a token of the loyalty and affection of the people of the Transvaal for the person of His Majesty and for his throne. The members of *Het Volk* did not disown these sentiments when the motion was put to the Assembly—but history has no record of their conversations in the lobbies. The friendship formed

[1] Including Southern Rhodesia, which belonged to the customs union.
[2] The Canadian Confederation had been formed in 1867. At the beginning of the twentieth century it seemed to have solved the problem of the 'two Canadas'.

in London between Botha and Jameson[1] was discussed with less reticence: it angered some, who regarded it almost as treachery, while others saw it as setting an example for a reconciliation which they considered essential.

The year 1908 proved decisive. In February the South African Party replaced the Progressive Party in the Cape. The victors were led by John Merriman who, though English by origin and language, felt 'a deep suspicion of British imperialism'. The new rulers of the Cape Colony, though utterly different from the leaders of the Transvaal and, in particular, those of the Orange River Colony, were none the less favourably disposed to the Afrikaner cause. The Afrikaners now controlled three of the four provinces, a good position from which to approach any discussions. An intercolonial conference which assembled in Pretoria in May and was then transferred to Cape Town, without the change of capital making the talks any more constructive, demonstrated the impossibility of perpetuating the *status quo*. In 1906, Natal had threatened to leave the customs union. A year later the Transvaal did likewise. But, if the Rand were not included, would not an economic community be meaningless? Merriman summed up the problem: 'We must unite or break.' Smuts, whose personality dominated the discussions, finally had a motion adopted urging the formation as soon as possible of a union of the four self-governing colonies under the British Crown.

The die was cast. On 12 October a National Convention assembled at Durban, the capital of Natal, a choice intended to appease the least enthusiastic of the colonies.[2]

Among the principal Afrikaner delegates Smuts deserves to be considered first, for he was at the same time actor, manager and producer. An enigmatic figure, he was to have many admirers and many detractors. His admirers discerned in him a statesman's vision, a mind which never lingered over details but viewed only the whole, and a historical culture which enabled him to put problems in their true perspective. His detractors dismissed him as a crafty politician (the epithet 'slim' was constantly being applied to him) with a gift for taking advantage of human weaknesses, in his utterances a great idealist but the most realistic of men when action was necessary. His role in the genesis of the Union was, however, a vital one. Botha and Smuts complemented each other perfectly, Smuts bringing his chief the benefit of 'an intellectual distinction and a capacity for sustained work' which the Prime Minister himself lacked, and Botha's common sense serving to confine within the limits of practical possibility

---

[1] Professor Spender offers a plausible explanation of this friendship, suggesting that Jameson was 'a natural hero worshipper' and that, when Rhodes died, he transferred his adulation to Botha.

[2] A portrait of Milner adorned the assembly hall. Professor Thompson says that at first it had been covered with a curtain of red serge; then 'someone had second thoughts and the curtain was removed'.

the day-dreams in which his colleague tended to indulge. Both knew what they wanted: a South Africa no longer divided into Boers and British, but united by a common loyalty to the Crown. How different was Hertzog! The delegate from the Orange River Colony was 'a shy man with scholarly tastes'. His knowledge of jurisprudence far surpassed that of either Botha or Smuts, but it had not prevented him from being a commando-leader, and it certainly had not mitigated the rigidity of his principles. One of his biographers relates that Field-Marshal Allenby, in speaking of Hertzog to a South African, is supposed to have said (twenty or so years after the Act of Union): 'You must have Hertzog done in bronze.'—'But Hertzog? Why not Smuts?'— 'No, by no means; Smuts is a romantic, let the painters paint him; Hertzog is a Roman, he must be done by the sculptors in bronze.' He was a man cast in a simple mould, insensible to praise and preferring criticism, clinging to his ideas and, when expressing them, not much concerned with fine distinctions. In his eyes the only 'good South Africans' were those whose only loyalty was to South Africa; the rest were merely imperialists, even foreign adventurers. To the fusion of the races advocated by Botha and Smuts, Hertzog opposed the notion of the 'two streams' which, flowing parallel one to the other, would each preserve its own special character. Needless to say, in his opinion the force of the Afrikaner stream would sooner or later ensure a position of pre-eminence for the descendants of the *voortrekkers*.

Side by side with these three dominant personalities were a host of others. For example, the chief justice of the Cape, de Villiers, chosen as president of the Convention and who controlled the debates with competence and firmness; Jan Hofmeyr, known as 'Onze Jan' and who, when he recalled the formation of the Afrikaner Bond,[1] must have reflected on how much had been achieved in thirty years; the ex-president of the Orange Free State, Marthinus Steyn, with his flowing white beard, respected by everyone, but whose health prevented him from taking an active role; de Wet and de la Rey, who had not shaken off the humiliation of their defeat; and, above all, John Merriman, the most experienced of all the delegates at the Convention, for he had been involved in political life since 1869—some of his fellow-countrymen called him a turncoat and a crank, for this Englishman, born in Somerset and who felt 'an almost romantic veneration for the British constitution', nevertheless put South Africa before Great Britain. Although twenty-nine years separated Smuts and Merriman, and although they held opposing views on a number of questions, the one more adventurous, the other more conservative, the two men maintained a close relationship and their correspondence provides invaluable information for historians of this period.

[1] The Afrikaner Bond, according to Professor Davenport, the first real political party in South Africa, had been founded in the Cape Colony in 1880. Jan Hofmeyr had later played a dominant role in the party.

The British delegation was not lacking in men of ability, but it could not claim the same diversity of origins as the Afrikaner contingent. Moreover, it was far from possessing the same political experience. Apart from Hull, a lawyer by profession, Sauer, who thought of himself as a radical philanthropist, and Jameson—who was bored by discussions of constitutional matters and who, according to Professor Thompson, was always 'longing to relax on the golf course or at the bridge table[1]—the British delegates were all businessmen, more accustomed to discussing balance-sheets than drafting laws. The two most influential had supported the Reform movement in the Transvaal and had been imprisoned after the Raid. One, Farrar, had been sentenced to death, reprieved and fined £25,000; he had then become president of the Chamber of Mines. The other, Fitzpatrick, had begun his career as a banker and had then entered the famous firm of Eckstein; also accused of high treason in 1896, he had been obliged to pay £2,000 to the Transvaal judiciary.[2] Natal was, admittedly, represented by its Prime Minister, Frederick Moor, and his predecessor, Charles Smythe, but in that colony it was a matter of pride not to worry about questions of principle and to attach importance only to personalities.

In all there were thirty delegates: twelve from the Cape, eight from the Transvaal, and five each from Natal and the Orange River Colony, plus three observers from Southern Rhodesia. In theory, government and opposition enjoyed equality of status: fifteen delegates for the parties in power in the Cape, the Transvaal and the Orange River Colony, eight for the parliamentary minorities of those three states, two for the 'Cape independents' and five for Natal. This arithmetical comparison, however, gives a misleading idea of the situation, for the last three groups displayed much less cohesion than the government representatives. But the delegates had one thing in common: a preference for concrete solutions and a horror of ideological argument. By their positive character their debates bore a much closer resemblance to those that had preceded the Canadian Confederation of 1867 than to the deliberations of the Founding Fathers of the United States or to those of the Constituent Assembly during the French Revolution.

The Convention met in three sessions: from 12 October to 5 November 1908 in Durban, from 23 November 1908 to 3 February 1909 in Cape Town, and from 3 to 11 May in Bloemfontein. It had no difficulty in agreeing on two principles. Like the British Constitution, the South African Constitution would not be of a rigid kind; in other words, it would be possible to amend it simply by passing a law. The federal idea,

---

[1] As regards the usefulness of bridge, it is worth noting that Botha also liked this game; was this one reason for their friendship?

[2] Fitzpatrick wrote several books, among them *Jack of the Bushveld* which he dedicated to his children and which, apparently, is something of a classic.

on the other hand, was rejected. De Villiers, who had returned from a visit to Canada, maintained that in that country federalism had prevented the fusion of the races and that its adoption would have the same effect with the British and the Boers. A unifying solution was agreed upon: a central government would dispose of maximum powers, and the functions of local authorities would be reduced to a minimum.

The choice of a capital was not an easy one. Durban was out of the question, and Bloemfontein's only claim to this honour was its central situation. It would therefore be a tussle between Pretoria and Cape Town. Pretoria based its claim on its association with the Great Trek and on the future awaiting the Rand; Cape Town conjured up the name of van Riebeeck, recalled its role as a half-way stage between the empires of West and East, and boasted of the splendour of its bay, the mildness of its climate and the beauty of its flowers. Since neither city was willing to give way, it was decided that they should both be given satisfaction: Pretoria would be the seat of the government, Cape Town the seat of the Parliament.[1] This judgement of Solomon has survived to the present day. Thousands of officials and documents are still transported from the Transvaal to Cape Town during parliamentary sessions. One can imagine the cost of such a system, with its duplication of premises and even of personnel. Yet these comings and goings between two such different cities probably make a greater contribution to national unity than one might think.

Deciding which would be the official language proved no easier. It seemed absurd to the British that Afrikaans should aspire to equality with the language of Shakespeare. But Hertzog won the argument by a passionate intervention which finally convinced even Jameson. He was defending Dutch, however, and not Afrikaans. The bilingual principle was clearly defined: 'Both the English and the Dutch shall be official languages and shall be treated on a footing of equality. All records of Parliament, all Bills, Acts and Notices of general public importance shall be in both languages.'

How people should express themselves and which cities should enjoy pre-eminence were both issues that gave rise to fierce controversy. The native problem, the repercussions of which were more far-reaching but less obvious, was discussed much more casually and, according to one historian, occupied only a few days of the Convention's four months of debate. Secretly, without actually saying so, everybody agreed that the native question should not be allowed to jeopardize the Union which it had been decided to create. According to the most recent census (1904), the population of the four colonies had risen to about 5,200,000. Out of this total there were 1,100,000 Whites; confronting them, about 100,000 Asians, 500,000 Coloureds and, the largest category of all, 3,500,000

[1] To placate the Orange River Colony, the Supreme Court was installed in Bloemfontein.

Blacks. The latter had hardly been heard of since the end of the Zulu Wars thirty years earlier. According to Professor de Kiewiet, the tribes were obeying the magistrates, paying their taxes and providing a reserve labour force. At all events, no uprising had occurred during the Boer War. At Vereeniging it had been decided to postpone the search for a solution. Yet to ignore the problem completely was distasteful. At the economic conference of 1903 it had been approached with caution. No one disputed that the natives must be strictly forbidden the consumption of alcoholic beverages. It was proposed to assign them territories of which they would be the sole owners and to develop 'reserves' where they would live in isolation from the Whites.

These were merely suggestions of principle, however, which had few practical consequences. The granting of self-government to the Transvaal and Orange River Colony had not altered the situation. The government in London now knew the Boers well and realized that they could not easily be coerced. In short, between Vereeniging and the Act of Union the native question made little progress. In 1906 a revolt broke out in Natal: thirty Europeans and three thousand Africans died, a proportion which says much for the effectiveness of its repression. Then Dinizulu, son of Cetewayo, grandson of Panda and grand-nephew of Chaka and Dingaan, was brought to trial. The British government intervened on his behalf and appointed as his counsel W. P. Schreiner, former Prime Minister of the Cape. Four years in prison and deportation to St Helena reminded the condemned man that the golden age of his ancestors was no more than a memory.

The Indian problem proved more complicated, demonstrating to the momentarily baffled Whites the power of passive resistance. A great many coolies, recruited for the sugar-plantations of Natal, had preferred to try their luck in the Transvaal, where they met with an unenthusiastic reception. Gandhi had an opportunity to observe the situation. At the beginning of his career as a barrister he had been invited to conduct a case in Pretoria. He arrived there in 1893, at the age of twenty-four. The shabbiness with which he was treated—he was told not to wear a turban, pushed off the pavements and forbidden to travel first-class—did not seem to worry him and certainly did not diminish his charitable instincts: during the war he ran a Red Cross organization and later, during an epidemic of plague, he opened a hospital in Johannesburg. Nevertheless, he felt that such gestures were unlikely to have any influence on the status of his fellow-countrymen, and so he resolved to make himself their champion. When the Transvaal recovered its autonomy, one of its government's first acts, in 1907, was to compel Asians to register and to have their finger-prints taken. This law was not being universally observed, at least not among the Indians, who agreed to abide by it only if they chose. When the authorities tried to enforce it, they refused and let themselves be taken off to prison, with Gandhi leading the way. Talks between Smuts and Gandhi took place in 1908, but appear to have resulted only in misunderstandings.

However irritating this conflict may have been, and whatever the uneasiness caused two years earlier by the Zulu revolt, neither event influenced the debates of the National Convention. There could be 'no greater illusion', observes Professor Mansergh, 'than to suppose that at this time English opinion—outside the Cape where the liberal tradition was cherished by Boers and British alike—was readily distinguishable from Boer opinion as regards natives.' Witness this memorandum sent by Selborne to Botha in January 1908: 'The black man is absolutely incapable of rivalling the white man. . . . No one can have any experience of the two races without feeling the intrinsic superiority of the white man.' This was not very different from the attitude of the old guard, of which de Wet made himself spokesman when the question came under discussion: 'Providence has drawn the line between blacks and whites and we must make that clear to the natives and not instil into their minds false notions of equality.' Botha was by nature less rigid in his views, but even he saw no other solution than to play for time: 'Our first duty is to bring about the union of the white races. After that it would be possible to deal with the native population.' Smuts thought along similar lines: 'On the question of native franchise, my mind is full of Cimmerian darkness and I incline very strongly to leaving over that matter to the Union Parliament.'

The members of the Convention concurred with this view. One must search long and hard among the hundred and fifty-two articles of the Act of Union to find the clauses concerning the 'non-Europeans'. In fact, there are only two: one providing for the maintenance of the *status quo*—in other words, no right to vote in the former Boer Republics and only a theoretical right in Natal;[1] the other guaranteeing that the more liberal legislation of the Cape could only be modified by a vote of two-thirds of the Parliament. This was a minimum concession to the Coloureds; on the other hand, they were denied access to the Union's legislative assemblies.

The deliberations of the National Convention were brought to a close on 11 May 1909. The Parliaments of the Transvaal and Orange River Colony unanimously approved the draft Act; in the Cape Parliament only two votes were cast against it. Natal proved more reticent: only 58 per cent of the electorate took part in a referendum, but three-quarters of the voters gave their consent.

It remained to obtain the royal assent. The High Commissioner and a deputation of delegates arrived in London at the end of June. They were received with the extravagant courtesy which Britain traditionally displays on such occasions. Botha was honoured with a personal invitation from the King. In the House of Lords the draft Act was adopted without

[1] In *An African Survey* written in 1938 Lord Hailey claims that only three natives had the franchise.

reservations. Representatives of the Bantu and the Coloureds, who had come to Britain in the hope of influencing opinion, were shown 'great courtesy, real sympathy and earnest attention', wrote W. P. Schreiner, who was acting as their mentor. But they achieved nothing in the way of results. The Commons rejected an amendment in their favour by 137 votes to 57. This was no time for ideology. The threat of war was becoming more acute in Europe; the Suez route was in danger of being cut off, and the British government did not want to upset South Africans who had at last been united under the Crown. Asquith closed the debate with an appeal which in no way compromised the terms of the Act, merely expressing the hope that 'South Africa, in the exercise of their undoubted and unfettered freedom, should find it possible, sooner or later, and sooner rather than later, to modify the provisions regarding the natives.' The draft Act was then passed as it stood.

Who was to be governor-general? The names of Winston Churchill, Wilfrid Laurier, Prime Minister of Canada, and de Villiers, chief justice of the Cape, were mentioned. The government's choice proved less dramatic, falling on 'the weak and insipid Herbert Gladstone', in the ungenerous words of Professor Pyrah. The lucky candidate admittedly had one thing in his favour: he was the son of a great man. But Edward VII was taken aback. 'The king said that if the Prime Minister cannot find a better Governor-General, he supposes he must approve of the appointment, but he thinks it is a very bad one.' Very few persons, however, disputed Gladstone's decision to entrust Botha with the task of forming the first government. Merriman refused to serve; he could not forgive the Prime Minister for 'his tortuous intrigues with Jameson and the cowardly silence he has kept in that matter'. Others did not share the same scruples or the same feelings of bitterness.[1] A cabinet of ten members, including seven Afrikaners, was swiftly formed. On 31 May 1910 the Union Parliament held its inaugural session.[2]

The enemies of ten years earlier now sat side by side. It is worth considering in a little detail the Act which had been designed to unite them.

The Union of South Africa comprised four provinces: the Cape of Good Hope, Natal, the Transvaal and the Orange Free State, which had its pre-war title restored. Provision was also made for the future incorporation of Southern Rhodesia and the three British protectorates of Bechuanaland, Basutoland and Swaziland.

At the head of the executive was a governor-general, appointed for five years by the Crown and representing the King. The real power

[1] There had been a possibility of Merriman becoming Prime Minister; but he was sixty-nine and Botha only forty-eight; his pessimism and bad temper also gave cause for apprehension.

[2] The ceremonies were reduced to a minimum owing to the death of the King twenty-five days earlier.

belonged to a cabinet presided over by a Prime Minister, the leader of the parliamentary majority and who was responsible to a Parliament which the governor-general had the power to convene, adjourn and dissolve. Parliament consisted of two houses. The Senate comprised 40 members, 8 appointed by the governor-general[1] and 8 chosen from each province by the Provincial Councils and by the province's representatives in the House of Assembly. This lower house numbered 121 members (51 for the Cape, 36 for the Transvaal, 17 for Natal and 17 for the Free State), elected by White male adults (except in the Cape, where in certain circumstances the Coloureds could vote). Some bold spirits had suggested that women be given the vote, but Merriman settled the matter by declaring that women were 'quite unfit' for this kind of responsibility.

Parliament voted the laws, but the governor-general had the right to withhold his assent or to submit the text for royal approval.

Judicial power was invested in a Supreme Court whose members were appointed for life and which was not empowered to interpret the Constitution.

In each province an Administrator represented the governor-general, presiding over an Executive Council of four members elected by the Provincial Council. The latter was chosen by the same electorate as the Assembly and comprised at least twenty-five members, or the same number as the province's representatives in the lower house. The powers of the provinces were strictly defined, being limited to the collection of direct taxes, the floating of loans, schools (but not higher education), agriculture, hospitals, public works, roads, weights and measures, and the regulation of hunting and fishing. All other matters came under the control of Parliament.

When the Canadian Confederation of 1867 came into force, Prime Minister Macdonald remarked that Canada had been created and that it remained only to create Canadians. If Botha knew of these words, he must have reflected on them when, forty-three years later, he assumed responsibility for the Union of South Africa.

[1] It was essential that they had a thorough knowledge of the needs and desires of the coloured races.

PART SIX

Towards Independence and the Republic
1910–61

List of Dates

1948		Electoral success of the Nationalists.
		Malan comes to power.
		Apartheid (separate ethnic development) replaces *Segregation* as policy.
		Law on mixed marriages.
1949		'Institution of S.A. Citizenship' and 'Law on mixed marriages'.
1950		Law on sexual relations between Europeans and 'non-Europeans'.
		Classification of the population into four population categories.
		Prohibition of Communism.
		Clashes between Zulu and Indians in Durban.
		Death of Smuts.
1951		First step towards granting self-government to Blacks (Bantu Authorities Act).
		Proposal to reform the status of the Coloureds.
1952		Campaign of passive resistance.
1953		Success of the Nationalists in the elections.
1954		Strijdom succeeds Malan.
1956		Final adoption of a new status for the Coloureds.
		Arrest of Luthuli.
		Tomlinson Report.
1958		Success of the Nationalists at the elections.
		Verwoerd, Prime Minister.
1959		Eight Black territorial units acknowledged in law (Promotion of Self-Government Act).
1960	20 January	Verwoerd announces a referendum on the question of a Republic.
	3 February	Macmillan's speech.
	21 March	Sharpeville.
	9 April	Attempted assassination of Verwoerd.
	5 October	A small majority vote for a Republic.
1961	15 March	South Africa withdraws from the commonwealth.
	31 May	The first president of the Republic assumes office.
	October	Another election victory for the Nationalists.

22

Growing Pains and the First World War

Optimism was in the fashion. It was pointed out that the former enemies (Boer and British) were both Protestant, but it was forgotten that the Dutch Reformed Church and the Anglican Church were as different from each other as they were from the Catholic Church. People deluded themselves that this apparent similarity of religion would be reinforced by the Germanic origins of the two nations, not anticipating that, four years later, this rather naïve racial theory would not prevent Germans and British from finding themselves in opposing camps.

The census of 1911 caused some alarm among British South Africans. Milner must have been disturbed to discover that its figures were far removed from his ideal proportion of three British to two Dutch.[1] The Boers already formed a majority, and the birth-rate indicated that their preponderance was likely to grow. Unless Union had been devised for their benefit, the fusion of the races would have to be accelerated. The British had no doubt that, in this amalgam of peoples, they would eventually gain the ascendancy. Was this what Botha himself secretly thought? Visiting England in 1911 for another Imperial conference, he recommended two decisions that were hardly of a nature to displease his hosts: the continuation of the annual subsidy of £85,000 which his government had undertaken to pay to the Admiralty and, in return, the financing by the British government of emigration to South Africa. He enjoyed his usual success in London. 'He was feasted at the Reform Club, dined at Norfolk House, given degrees by the great universities.'

He complained of having to wear 'an uncomfortable and stiff uniform'. But he was impressed rather then irritated by all this protocol. 'One must admit that they understand how to make this sort of thing beautiful, tasteful and brilliant, and so orderly too.'

All this was of no interest to his compatriots living in their rebuilt farms back in the *veld*. Many were wondering if their old commander-in-chief was still the same man. Lord Milner's philosophy had been that the Afrikaner 'should be slain like a plague-infested rat' and the majority of Boers

[1] See p. 229.

felt that Botha's flirtations with the British political bosses did very little to alleviate their plight under the new military rulers back home. They began to look for a new man more sympathetic to their grievances—and found that Hertzog was prepared to listen. War taught Hertzog to push aside material comforts and to concentrate on the development of moral power instead. He became firmly convinced that he had to teach his people the willpower to be themselves. Affairs of state suddenly became serious matters to him.

The language problem, among other issues, had already developed into a serious dispute. To Hertzog recognition and equal treatment of Dutch as one of the two official languages became the rallying point around which he could inspire his people to be themselves. He left no stone unturned to force the issue whenever possible. And gradually other political issues were raised by Hertzog who began to examine the future of the country with two white racial groups. Hertzog was of the opinion that Botha's over-conciliation with the British endangered the existence of the Afrikaans language and culture. His well-known 'two-stream' approach acknowledged the existence of an Afrikaans and English culture in South Africa and he argued that only if the Afrikaans culture's future was assured could the two White cultural groups be moulded into one nation.

Hertzog evolved the slogan 'South Africa first' and deplored the presence and influence in government of those who were not looked upon as true Afrikaners. And he made it clear that the term *Afrikaner* also included English-speakers, as long as their first loyalty was to South Africa. The argument came to a climax on 7 December 1912 at De Wildt when he outlined South African Nationalism. His speech created a furore among the English-speaking people of the country and prompted an English-speaking colleague in the Cabinet, Colonel Leuchars, to tender his resignation to Botha. Botha called a Cabinet meeting on 10 December and blamed Hertzog for Leuchars's resignation. Botha demanded to learn from Hertzog what steps he intended taking to set matters right and it was clear that he expected Hertzog to resign from the Cabinet. When Hertzog decided to remain in the Cabinet, Botha resigned as Prime Minister and, when requested to form a new Cabinet, left out Hertzog and Leuchars.

Although the relationship between Botha and Hertzog had cooled off considerably in the years between the Boer War and 1912, the final split between the two men did not occur until a year later, in November 1913, when Botha and Hertzog confronted each other at a party congress. Botha is described as 'strong, thickset, well-built, a frank, determined gaze, speaking simply, plainly, clearly'; and his opponent as 'thin, eager, nervous, fluent'. Hertzog nevertheless accused the Prime Minister of being a defeatist with no willpower to face up to his critics. At the November congress of the South African Party, the division between the Botha and

Hertzog followers was clearly drawn. Hertzog made it clear that he opposed the Prime Minister on various principles. Without actually admitting as much, they were putting forward two opposing interpretations of the Treaty of Vereeniging: in Botha's view the Boers had recognized the legitimacy of the Union Jack once and for all; Hertzog, on the other hand, regarded the agreement as no more than an armistice—simply a stage on the road to full and complete independence. Hertzog's viewpoint was shared by those still haunted by the memory of the war, among them De Wet. The elusive king of the commandos, openly supporting Hertzog, had indulged in a little rhetoric himself when a few months earlier he publicly declared: 'I would rather live with my own people on a dunghill than stay in the palaces of the British Empire.'

Following a vote of support for Botha at the congress (131 votes to 90), the fight within the party ended dramatically: Hertzog and his followers rose and walked out of the hall while De Wet turned round and bid those remaining in the hall a final 'adieu'.

A month later the two adversaries met again in Bloemfontein, at the unveiling of the touchingly simple memorial erected to the women who had died in the Boer War. They read the inscription: 'To our heroines and our dear children. Thy will be done.' But the emotions which stirred in their hearts were not powerful enough to lead to a reconciliation. In January 1914, Hertzog founded the Nationalist Party. In addition to antagonism between descendants of British and Dutch there was now discord among the Afrikaners themselves. These divisions were all the more unfortunate because no sooner had the Union been born than it found itself confronted by a variety of problems that admitted of no easy solution.

The census of 1911 confirmed that two out of three inhabitants of the Union were Blacks, a fact which could not possibly be ignored indefinitely, as it had been ignored for the past ten years. The 'non-Europeans', moreover, were displaying an unexpected vitality. In 1912 a group of them formed an African National Congress which boldly claimed political rights. At this same time the mining industry was attracting a growing number of Bantu into the urban centres. These Bantu flocked in mainly from tribal settlements in various parts of the country. These settlements were established by the Bantu when migratory tribes from the vicinity of the Great Lakes of Central Africa moved to the South at the end of the fifteenth century and crossed into South Africa in the course of the seventeenth century.

As various Bantu tribal settlements existed in and around the Boer Republics and the two British colonies, their future became one of the issues to be resolved after the Boer War. A Native Affairs Commission sat between 1903 and 1905 under the chairmanship of Sir Godfrey Lagden to prepare a report and recommendations as to the future of these settlements or reserves. Eventually in 1913 the Natives Land Act was passed by the Union Parliament. The Act defined and scheduled some 8·9 million hectares of land in the four provinces as permanent and inalienable Bantu territories. For the first time legal recognition was given to the areas which the various Bantu groups have historically occupied. The Natives Land Act, observes Professor Kruger, proclaimed for the first time the principle of territorial divisions between Blacks and Whites. The idea had been frequently advocated since the time of van Riebeeck, but had never been applied in such a systematic manner. Hitherto, both in the Cape and in Natal, the Blacks had been able to buy or lease land; even in the Transvaal they had enjoyed this right, though under the trusteeship of the state. Only the Free State had imposed a total prohibition on native ownership of land, and it was this system which was now applied to the Union as a whole. Although, as Professor de Kiewiet notes, these measures were implemented in a liberal manner, they proved disappointing in their results. The Blacks had only two alternatives: either to become agricultural wage-earners in White areas, or to seek refuge in their traditional tribal territories. Consequently, many found themselves forced to seek work in the mines, where their arrival aggravated the racial problem.

The Indians were also becoming restless. In 1913 an Immigration Act was passed which—although Smuts had omitted the word 'Asian' from the text so as not to hurt Gandhi's feelings—made immigration of Indians to South Africa impossible. The Act evoked violent protests and prompted Gandhi to demand the repeal of all Union laws which discriminated against Indians. He demanded that the Natal law which imposed a £3 tax on Indians; the law which prohibited Indians from entering the Free State; and all laws concerning land reform, liquor sales and immigration be repealed. He also demanded that marriages according to Indian custom should be recognized.

Although a law existed which precluded Indians from entering the Transvaal, Gandhi decided to add weight to his demands by organizing a march of more than 2000 Natal Indians into the Transvaal. As he fully knew, he would be arrested. The uproar that followed prompted Smuts to appoint a commission to examine the grievances of the Indians. Following the report of the commission, the Indian Relief Act was passed in 1914 which, inter alia, abolished the £3 tax on Natal's Indians. Smuts, according to Gandhi, realized that a remedy for this injustice must be found, but was in the unpleasant position of a snake that has caught a rat and can neither swallow it completely nor disgorge it. The two men resumed their talks. The realist and the mystic were poles apart, but they managed to reach a compromise. Smuts fondly hoped that this was a final settlement. Just before he left for India at the beginning of 1914, Gandhi dispelled any such illusion by insisting that only full citizenship would be acceptable. Nevertheless, Smuts must have breathed a sigh of relief: the saint had left the shores of South Africa—for ever, Smuts sincerely hoped.

These were minor difficulties compared to the problem of White labour. From the outset the specialization of jobs in the mines had confirmed the racial hierarchy: manual tasks were for the natives, the rest for the Europeans. Until the Boer War the Europeans had been mostly of British origin. After 1902, however, many Boer farmers, unable to earn a living from agriculture, had flocked to the Rand. They received miserable wages, but even so, when they compared them to the rates paid to the Blacks, they could consider themselves aristocrats. Gradually these 'poor Whites', as they were called (after their counterparts in the United States), organized themselves and strengthened the unions which were beginning to assert their influence. A first strike broke out in 1913. The employers, ill-prepared for such a situation, appealed to Botha and Smuts, who as generals turned politicians, were equally lacking in experience of such things. Shutting themselves up with the workers' leaders in a hotel in Johannesburg 'surrounded by a screaming, struggling mass of men, threatening to break through the police cordon', they signed an agreement which looked very much like a surrender.

Trouble erupted again at the beginning of 1914, in the more disturbing form of a general strike. This time the government was determined not to give in so easily. Smuts called in the army, the workers took fright and the movement collapsed. This was not the end of the matter: without further ceremony nine union leaders were deported and sent to England. The British government was not exactly pleased by the arrival of these victims of a blatant violation of *habeas corpus*. But what could be done? 'Mr Asquith must be telling himself how difficult it is to reconcile the exigencies of English democracy with those imposed by the government of a colonial Empire,' commented Paul Cambon.[1]

Smuts, whose personality was steadily overshadowing the weary and disillusioned Botha, showed apprehension at the outbreak of hostilities in Europe. 'I must admit the future is very dark if Germany wins, but . . . if Russia wins!' Botha and he had seen the conflict coming. In March 1906 the French consul-general in Pretoria had the good fortune to meet them on a train: 'They seemed to think,' he reported, 'that a Franco-German war is inevitable sooner or later. General Smuts openly professed a keen admiration for our country.'[2]

In 1914 they made up their minds to side with Britain: they were not the men to desert her at this dark hour and, although many Boers could not forget the past and would bitterly disapprove of their decision, Smuts was confident that Botha and he were only doing their duty. On the same day that Britain declared war, a telegram left Pretoria suggesting that the young South African army, which had been formed in 1912 and

---

[1] The deportees were repatriated a few months later.   [2] See Chapter 24.

comprised twenty-five thousand men, should assume sole responsibility for the defence of the country. The British cabinet welcomed the proposal, which would release much-needed troops for other purposes. In its reply it had a suggestion of its own to make: if the South African forces were willing and able to seize the radio stations in German South-West Africa, they would be doing a great service to the Empire. The South African leaders allowed themselves an appropriate interval for reflection and then, without consulting Parliament, gave their assent on condition that they received the co-operation of the British Navy.

Was the British government's proposal as much af a surprise to Botha and Smuts as has been claimed? Lord Riddell[1] wrote in his diary on 7 December 1911: 'I omitted to note that in the summer, when the German crisis was at its height,[2] General Botha cabled that in the event of war he was prepared to raise and lead an army to take possession of German East Africa.' Clearly, in a European conflict the government of the Union of South Africa had no desire to claim a neutrality which, in any case, its Imperial status precluded. On 15 August the Union Parliament approved the official position by 92 votes to 12. This expression of the *vox populi* aroused fierce controversy. The opponents of the official view were men of stature, among them General Beyers, who immediately resigned as commander-in-chief of the army, General Kemp, known for his role in the defeat of the Jameson Raid, Lieutenant-Colonel Maritz, commander of the frontier troops, and in particular the illustrious De Wet and De la Rey. Botha called his subordinates together: the atmosphere was icy, but he dared not demand their resignations. A conspiracy began to take shape, the precise objective of which has never been clearly explained by historians: was it to be simply a protest, or an insurrection in the hope of establishing a Republic? The situation was made all the more confused by some strange prophecies. A certain Van Rensburg, who had acquired a reputation as a visionary during the Boer War, had been announcing to anyone who would listen to him that the hour of independence had at last struck: the conflict between Britain and Germany would provide the opportunity, and De la Rey had been appointed as the instrument of Providence. The ageing hero (De la Rey was sixty-seven) was not in the habit of avoiding the limelight. However, an accident settled his fate. At a police barricade that had been set up along the road to apprehend the notorious Foster Gang he ordered his chauffeur to drive on. A policeman fired and a ricochet shot put an end to the days of the man who had come to be known as 'the lion of West Transvaal'.

With De la Rey gone, his accomplices engaged in a flurry of activity. Beyers and De Wet organized protest meetings against the Government's

[1] See p. 233.
[2] The entry of the *Panther* into the harbour of Agadir, in token of German pretensions in Morocco, had nearly unleashed a European war.

war policy. The Germans in South-West Africa apparently promised the rebels, once victory was theirs, a South African Republic that would include the Transvaal, the Free State, a part of Natal and of the Cape Province, the province of Mozambique and Rhodesia; until this mighty project could be realized, they undertook to supply arms to the rebels. De Wet, always a man of a passionate nature, meanwhile occupied a few towns. He then declared that he would leave for Pretoria, where he would pull down the British flag and proclaim independence. Everywhere commandos were re-formed: 7,123 men in the Free State, 2,298 in the Transvaal and 1,251 in the Cape.

Botha opposed them with a force three times as great (30,000 against about 11,000). Only about two-thirds were of Dutch descent, but the entire loyalist army spoke Afrikaans. The rebellion was swiftly put down. In February 1915, Kemp had surrendered, Maritz had fled to South-West Africa, Beyers had been drowned in the Vaal while trying to escape, and De Wet, whom no horseman had ever managed to catch, had fallen into the hands of a motorized column while on his way to join Maritz. The casualties of this pathetic venture were 190 dead and 350 wounded for the rebels, 132 dead and 242 wounded for the government forces. The victors showed generosity: only 281 rebels were brought to trial, although 5,000 had been taken prisoner. De Wet and Kemp were sentenced to imprisonment, but released the following year. Their comrades in arms suffered a similar fate, or merely had to pay a fine. Only one was found guilty of high treason and shot: Jopie Fourie, an officer in the regular army, who had joined the rebellion without taking the trouble to resign his commission or to remove his uniform, and who had been responsible for several deaths. As he walked before the firing-squad he recited from the Bible. With the victims of Slachter's Nek[1] and the other tragic heroes of Afrikaner legend, Fourie became a symbol of the piety, the spirit of sacrifice and the defiant attitude of his people.

These events had delayed the conquest of South-West Africa by six months. The operation, undertaken at the beginning of 1915, was tempting, but difficult none the less. The Germans, it will be recalled, had taken possession of the bay of Angra Pequena in 1883. Gradually penetrating inland, they had met mainly with rebuffs. In this vast and barren territory—over a thousand miles from north to south, four to five hundred miles from the coast to Bechuanaland—under a burning sun there lived a few nomad tribes of the purest Bantu race, the Hereros, a people of tall and noble stature who had destroyed or reduced to slavery some more primitive Hottentots. The Hereros' taste for independence cost the invaders dear. When they revolted in 1904, it took three years and 20,000 men of the German Imperial army to quell them. The methods employed were effective, it seems: 'Between 1904 and 1911 the Hereros melted from 90,000 to 12,000 under the bite of the German sun,' writes

[1] See p. 55.

Mr Paul Geniewski. The crushing of the revolt was a great relief to Berlin, especially in view of the fact that, about this same time, the hitherto unproductive colony had in its turn become a land of miracles: here, as at Kimberley, diamonds were discovered, then copper and also marble 'which surpasses in quantity all known marble deposits,' according to the French consul general in Bremen.

Taking possession of this territory therefore not only gave the Union an opportunity symbolically to affirm its loyalty, but also opened the door to new hope. The official documents estimate the German forces at 140 officers and 2,000 soldiers, augmented by a few hundred 'rebels' and 7,000 colonists, mostly of German origin and highly competent with a rifle. Botha had 40,000 men who, in four columns, converged on the capital, Windhoek. The campaign was brilliantly conducted, beginning in mid-April 1915 and ending in July. The victorious Botha, given a triumphant reception in Pretoria, unfolded his ideas about the future: 'It is now British South-West Africa and it must remain a province of the Union.' Smuts took a broader view: this had been 'the first achievement of a united South African nation in which both races have combined all their best and most virile characteristics.'

Not everyone viewed the situation in the same way. Merriman, for example, declared that he had never, in forty-six years of political life, observed 'such a feeling between British and Dutch, so bitter, so absolutely impossible'. Was he exaggerating? In September an attempt was made on Smuts's life; two months later he received an anonymous letter commemorating the anniversary of Joseph Fourie's 'murder' and wishing the 'murderer' a happy Christmas. But these were isolated incidents. The five-yearly general election took place quietly in October. The results were highly significant. The Nationalist Party, founded by Hertzog a little more than a year earlier, obtained 78,000 votes, only 16,000 less than the governing South African Party. The rest of the votes were divided among the Unionists (British), who polled 50,000, the Labour Party, with 24,000, and the Independents, with 10,500. Out of 130 seats Botha and Smuts now held only 54 and could therefore maintain a majority only by seeking the support of either the Nationalists or the Unionists. They regarded these with equal distaste: by choosing to combine with the Nationalists they would be in danger of being absorbed; by resigning themselves to an alliance with the Unionists they could expect to be called 'traitors' and 'Judas', as had happened during the election campaign.

Smuts, the brains behind the cabinet, thought these parliamentary games ridiculous compared to the opportunity which South Africa now had of establishing an international position for itself by playing its part in the war. To secure such a position, however, its troops would have to show themselves.

Two new fields of operations were selected. One was an obvious choice.

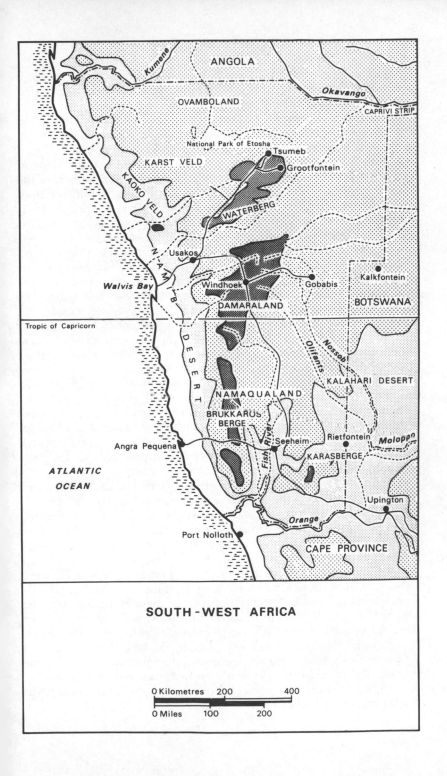

SOUTH - WEST AFRICA

| 0 Kilometres | 200 | 400 |
| 0 Miles | 100 | 200 |

Thirty or so years earlier Karl Peters, a businessman and something of a miniature Rhodes, had concluded with native chiefs a series of treaties that gave his company a mining monopoly in the territories adjacent to the Indian Ocean to the north of Mozambique. The Berlin government had granted him its protection and then decided to take control of the region. In 1895 the territory stretching between Lake Victoria and Lake Nyasa, and from the coast as far as the Belgian Congo, had become German East Africa. A glance at the map is enough to reveal the importance of the colony: as long as it existed the Cape to Cairo route would remain a dream. Immediately war broke out the British resolved to seize the territory. The undertaking seemed easy enough, for they would be confronted by fewer than 3,000 Europeans and about 12,000 natives. However, this handful of men was led by a soldier of uncommon intelligence and ability, General Von Lettow-Vorbeck, who routed the first assailants and then retired to the north-east of the colony, a region of mountains and bush at the foot of the snow-capped peak of the majestic Kilimanjaro. In 1916, Smuts was given the task of driving him out of his position. The force under his command was a polyglot army of 45,000 men—Indians, East and West Africans, Rhodesians, West Indians and British—whose confidence had been undermined by earlier failures. And what could be done about the mosquito and the tsetse-fly which, says Professor Kruger, caused more deaths than did firearms? The new commander-in-chief did his best, although it seems that his campaign had its critics as well as its admirers. When Smuts left his post at the end of the year, Von Lettow-Vorbeck was still proving elusive, and elusive he remained right to the end. Only the armistice induced him to lay down his arms, on 13 November 1918; according to the official history of the war, his army had been reduced to 155 Europeans and 1,168 askaris.

The South African troops found greater glory on the battlefields of France. In July 1915 the British government had accepted Botha's proposal to send a contingent of volunteers to Europe. The first soldiers, the equivalent of a brigade, embarked in the course of the following three months. No sooner had they arrived in England than they were re-embarked for Egypt, where they helped to repulse an attempted invasion by the Senussi on the western frontier. In April 1916 they were in Flanders. From then onwards they took part in most of the great battles: first the Somme, where Delville Wood still guards the memory of their exploits; then at Vimy and Ypres in 1917; and at Amiens when, in March 1918, the German onslaught temporarily broke through the British front. When they had arrived they had numbered 1,800; by this time only 500 were in a fit state to fight. A new brigade, restored to strength, was engaged in the battle of the Lys in May; in September it took part in the final offensive. On 11 November it had the honour of planting the Union Jack at the farthermost point reached by the British forces.

By this time Smuts had earned himself a personal reputation in the Allied war councils. Sent to London at the beginning of 1917 to represent his country at an Imperial Conference, he had not returned to South Africa. Whenever his thoughts turned to the past he must have said to himself how difficult it was to predict the future. His had indeed been an astonishing career! A commando-leader in 1901, a negotiator the following year of a 'treaty' that had seemed more like a surrender, the man who had brought peace to a country torn asunder and who was suspected by many of his compatriots—here he was, fifteen years later, being accepted by his old enemies as one of themselves! Not only was he one of the most active members of the Imperial Conference, not only did he belong to the War Cabinet in which the Dominions and India sat side by side with the British ministers, but—an unparalleled honour—he was invited in June 1917 to become one of the five members of the War Committee which in reality controlled British war policy. Lloyd George was chairman; Bonar Law, formerly leader of the Conservative Opposition, represented the Exchequer; Curzon, viceroy of India for six years and then Chancellor of the University of Oxford, was in charge of the aircraft development programme; and Milner, who twenty years earlier had played such an important part in the struggle with the Boers, was responsible for the overall conduct of the war.

The British treated Smuts with the deferential and vaguely condescending courtesy of which they are past masters. Bankers, bishops, industrialists and hostesses of political salons showered invitations on him, and honours of every kind were accorded to him: London, Plymouth, Cardiff, Manchester and Bristol gave him the freedom of the city; the Royal Geographical Society conferred on him the coveted title of 'Fellow'; the universities begged him to accept honorary degrees; and the King made him a Privy Councillor and a Companion of Honour. His old friend, Emily Hobhouse, still full of energy at the approach of her sixtieth year, was a little apprehensive: some years earlier she had predicted that the day would come when Smuts's name would appear in bold characters in *The Times*—that god-like institution which could humble one person and exalt another—and she had wanted to live long enough to see him Earl of Irene and Lord of Doornkloof.[1] And now he had virtually attained that exalted status, for, Miss Hobhouse observed, she knew that honours were heaped on those who followed the paths of imperialism. 'Still, I hope something of the old Oom Jannie[2] still remains, enough to enjoy association with the pacifist and anti-imperialist I am prouder than ever to be.'

Smuts hardly had time to indulge in the sort of reminiscences contained in this affectionately ironic letter, for he was being entrusted with a variety of tasks. Lloyd George was even to go so far as to describe him as

[1] Doornkloof was Smuts's farm, situated beside the village of Irene, near Pretoria.
[2] 'Uncle Jannie', the nickname by which Smuts was familiarly known.

the father of the Royal Air Force. In December 1917 he was sent to Switzerland to make contact with Count Mensdorf, the envoy of Czernin, the Austrian Foreign Minister. The talks proved no more fruitful than those between Prince Sixtus of Bourbon-Parma and the French government a few months earlier; but they inspired in Smuts the dream of an Austria that would become for Central Europe what the British Empire had become for the rest of the world.[1] Had a way of life so different from that he had known eventually impaired his judgement? One cannot help wondering after reading the letter which he sent to Lloyd George on 8 June 1918: 'Let the fighting command over the American army be entrusted to another commander [i.e. someone other than Pershing] . . . This is a very delicate matter. I do not think they have the man . . . It is doubtful whether they will be willing to accept an English or French commander . . . I am naturally most reluctant to bring forward my name, but I have unusual experience . . . I think if American *amour-propre* could be satisfied, I could in that capacity render very great service to our cause.' The Prime Minister was tactful enough not to act on this extravagant suggestion.

At all events, Smuts can hardly have been troubled by an inferiority complex when he arrived in Paris for the peace negotiations. Botha joined him there. The adulation with which the two men were surrounded was a measure of the reputation which their heroic resistance had earned the Boers. Their state of mind illustrates even more strikingly the extraordinary hold which the British Empire exercised over them. In their eyes, the Empire alone had won the war, and it alone could build peace. They paid little heed to France, except to wax indignant at the narrow-mindedness of its representatives and to obstruct its claims. Smuts attended the opening session of the Conference on 18 January 1919; his comments were hardly generous: 'What a farce that first meeting was. You should have heard the smug Poincaré roll out his periods about Justice!'

Smuts had one consolation: the proposed creation of a League of Nations, the draft project for which was to a large extent drawn up by himself. His idea of 'mandates' aroused Wilson's enthusiasm. The League of Nations, observed the American Secretary of State, Robert Lansing, was to acquire the mandated territories as the heir of the empire. Lansing remarked that this clever and attractive phrase of Smuts had caught the fancy of the president, as was evident from Wilson's frequent repetitions. But did Lansing share his leader's admiration? 'A product of the creative mind of General Smuts,' he commented, 'it was a novelty in international law which appealed strongly to those who preferred to adopt unusual and untried methods rather than to accept those that had been tested by

[1] His knowledge of European geography was a little hazy. H. W. Steed, then editor of *The Times*, saw Smuts on his return. Smuts asked him if Moravia was in Hungary or in Austria. Steed relates that he would have been less amazed if Smuts had asked him if the county of Northumberland was in England or Scotland.

experience.' The proposal certainly gave South Africa an opportunity for aggrandisement of a kind very similar to annexation. Article 22 of the Covenant was clear: 'There are territories, such as South-West Africa and certain of the Pacific islands, which, owing to the sparseness of their population, or their small size, or their geographical contiguity to the territory of the mandatory, and other circumstances, can be best administered under the laws of the mandatory as integral portions of its territory, subject to the safeguards above mentioned in the interest of the indigenous population.'

This was acceptable enough. But the rest of the proceedings dismayed Smuts, who would soothe his nerves by going for evening walks in the Bois de Boulogne. Botha, more philosophical, and whose health made exercise impossible, struggled as best he could with the Poles and the Ukrainians, on whose differences he had been appointed to arbitrate—on what grounds it is difficult to see. He had little sympathy with the Poles: in his opinion the Bolshevik danger was merely a bogy, and he did not think that any nation had the right to crush a smaller nation to gain a strategic advantage.

His colleague was no more favourably disposed to the claims of the new Ukrainian Republic. On 27 March, Lloyd George read to the Council of Four[1] a letter in which Smuts expressed strong misgivings about certain clauses of the draft treaty, in particular those concerning Danzig. Germany, Smuts predicted, would still remain a dominant part of continental Europe, and it would be folly to believe that the world could be rebuilt without its aid. This was a sound enough view, but it was presented in a manner so favourable to German aspirations that the 'Tiger' Clemenceau showed his claws: 'I am sure that General Smuts, who has shown his loyalty to England, is speaking not only as a friend of Germany, but I should like the French point of view also to be taken into account.'

Did this incident give the head of the British delegation the idea that it would be wise to separate the two antagonists for a time? The situation in Budapest, where Bela Kun and a group of communists had seized power, provided him with an opportunity. At first, it appears, the intention had been to entrust the Rumanian army, under Mangin's command, with the task of suppressing the revolt. Then it was decided to adopt a more cautious approach. On 29 March, Lloyd George informed his colleagues of his intentions: he would like to send someone like Smuts to Hungary, but he realized that Clemenceau did not much care for Smuts after the letter which had been read out. Clemenceau replied warily: 'I respect him, but I would prefer someone else.' Finally he gave way. Smuts left two days later, still very sure of himself. He would have liked the League of Nations Council to invite the Russians to meet him in Hungary, so that he could make recommendations that would lead to peace with Russia and complete the work of the Conference. The actual results of his visit were more

[1] Wilson, Lloyd George, Orlando and Clemenceau.

modest. The negotiator was accompanied, among others, by one of his staunchest admirers, Harold Nicolson. The young English diplomat thought that Bela Kun had a sullen, criminal look about him. Smuts insisted in receiving Kun on his train in Budapest station and nowhere else. A few days were enough to persuade Smuts of the futility of his discussions. A brief stay in Prague enabled him to spend a day conferring with Masaryk, no doubt expounding the extravagant projects to which he was so partial.

On returning to Paris his pessimism became more pronounced. Writing in his diary on 1 May, Harold Nicolson noted that Smuts deplored the influence which French 'shell-shock' seemed to be having on the peace; according to him, this was mere chauvinism and had spoilt the magnificent state of morale with which they had arrived in Paris. In his entry for 15 May, Nicolson records Smuts's belief that what had been done in Paris was much worse than the Congress of Vienna—the statesmen of 1815 at least knew what was at stake, but in Smuts's opinion the same could not be said for the men of Versailles. The presentation of the draft treaty to the German delegates filled him with sombre thoughts which he expressed in Shakespearean language: 'Behind the petty stage on which we pose and strut and play at making history, there looms the dark Figure which is quietly moving the pieces of world history.' Would he sign the final text? It was a terrible document, he informed his wife—not a treaty of peace but a treaty of war. Keynes listened to his confidences and did nothing to allay his misgivings. The two men would often spend the evening together after a good dinner, venting their spleen against the entire world and against the coming deluge. Eight days before the specified date he was determined to abstain. Then he changed his mind: after all, could he desert his Prime Minister? When, on 28 June 1919, in the Hall of Mirrors at Versailles, the head of protocol called on the delegates of the Union of South Africa, Smuts rose to his feet and did not refuse the pen offered to him.

23

The Nationalists in Power

Botha survived the peace treaty by only a few weeks. After a long illness he died on 25 August. Pretoria gave him a hero's funeral. The cortège was led by hundreds of cadets, each carrying a wreath; then a brigade of old commandos, followed by the dead man's friends and colleagues; behind the coffin walked Mrs Botha, the family and the members of the government. The procession followed a route over half a mile long, between a double line of soldiers with arms reversed.

The choice of a successor was an obvious one. Smuts became head of the government, reserving to himself the department of National Defence, for which he was excellently qualified, and that of Native Affairs, for which his experience had in no way prepared him. He did not feel wholly at ease; accustomed as he was to handling problems on a world scale, South Africa seemed small and its troubles trivial.

The elections of 1920 brought a further erosion of the government majority. Obviously, the birth of a new world was a matter of indifference to the electorate of the *veld*. Hertzog's Nationalist Party increased its representation from 26 seats to 44; even more impressive was the progress of the Labour Party which, under the impetus of Creswell's leadership, now found itself with 21 members instead of 4. By comparison with these two parties, neither of which had existed six years earlier, the traditional groupings cut a sorry figure: Botha's South African Party dropped from 54 to 41 members, and Smartt's Unionists from 40 to 25. Their defeat left them no choice but to unite, and so the weaker party agreed to merge with the stronger. Arithmetically, the amalgamation was shrewd; but, psychologically, it was unlikely to revive the prestige of a government that would be looking for support to English-speaking South Africans. Nevertheless, in 1921 Smuts decided on new elections, which this time brought him 79 members; Hertzog gained one seat, increasing his total to 45; Labour, still in its infancy, crumbled from 21 seats to 9.

This revised version of Vereeniging, this time under the control of Afrikaners, might have proved constructive if the next three years had been peaceful, which unfortunately they were not. In 1922 the country suffered the greatest jolt it had known since Union.

A few years of war had not halted the gradual transformation that was eventually to make South Africa a great industrial power. The formation of the Anglo-American Corporation of South Africa in 1917 by a man of genius, Ernest Oppenheimer, had been one of the most important stages in this process. Other firms had also invested capital at Kimberley and Johannesburg. Furthermore, in addition to diamonds and gold, the traditional sources of wealth, coal, copper and iron ore were offering by no means negligible possibilities, and their extraction required an increasingly large labour force. As long as profits could absorb the extra wages, stability had been more or less maintained. In 1920, however, the Western world was the victim of the first major economic crisis of the post-war years, a crisis that hit South Africa as well as Europe and America. Between February and December the price of gold fell from 130 shillings to 95 an ounce. A commission of inquiry reported that half the mines were operating at a loss. A study of the balance-sheets showed that economies were essential; however, never easy in practice, this was all the more difficult in a country where the economic and racial questions were so closely connected. Financially, the solution was obvious: since the Blacks were paid less for the same work (a pound a week instead of a pound a day), more natives and fewer Europeans would have to be employed.

In December 1921 the gold-mining companies announced that semi-skilled jobs would no longer be restricted to Whites; at the same time the coal industry made reductions in wages which the coal-miners refused to accept. Faced with the threat of Black competition, the workers of the Rand reacted with the same violence as those of Manchester and Lyons when their jobs were jeopardized by the introduction of machinery. On 1 January 1922 the coal-miners went on strike. On 10 January twenty thousand gold-mine workers came out on strike, reducing a hundred and eighty thousand Blacks to idleness. The movement quickly assumed the character of an insurrection, for the miners formed 'commandos' and drilled in military formation. This was a time when people thought they saw the shadow of Bolshevism looming up from all directions. Did the leaders of the revolt really envisage a régime of the Soviet type? At all events, they knew how to use language which would awaken nostalgic echoes. In February 1922 they adopted a resolution proposing the proclamation of a South African Republic and the formation of a provisional government; then, as in earlier days, they organized their troops in armed commandos, making their goal the preservation of white civilization and the removal of Smuts. Some preferred more immediate and limited gains to ambitious projects of this kind. Arson, looting and the murdering of Africans spread through a terrified Johannesburg cut off from the rest of the world. The Chamber of Mines did not make the situation any easier by telling the unions that it would not negotiate with people of their mental calibre. One of the more hot-headed ringleaders did not mince his words either: the rebels were determined to win the battle and, in the name of God, they would win it even if it meant razing the city to the ground.

This almost happened when, in the suburb of Fordsburg (where the headquarters of the strikers were established), torn-up paving stones, trees, broken doors, mattresses and furniture were used for barricades. On Friday 10 March Smuts proclaimed martial law. The following day Smuts arrived in Johannesburg to take personal command of the situation. According to Harold Nicolson, he was in an aggressive mood, his eyes like steel. That he assumed control of a military operation was not an exaggeration, for photographs show the infantry firing from trenches; the air force was also called in, dropping bombs[1] and machine-gunning the workers. Three days later it was all over. The gravity of the situation is indicated by the casualties: 153 dead and 534 wounded; 4,750 arrests were made, including 62 women and 4 children; 650 persons appeared before the courts, 18 were sentenced to death and 4 hanged. This was too good an opportunity for Hertzog to miss; in a turbulent debate in Parliament he declared that Smuts would go down in history as 'the man whose hands dripped with the blood of his own people'. The 'kaffir kings'[2] could breathe again: between 1920 and 1925 the average wage fell from £485 to £375; during these same five years gold production rose from 7,949,084 to 9,341,049 ounces.

A few half-hearted native uprisings also showed that the Prime Minister was not afraid of using strong-arm methods. In 1921, in the east of the Cape Province, a Bantu sect known as the Israelites had installed itself in a farm which it refused to leave. The police intervened and the death-toll was 103. A year later, immediately after the events on the Rand, a Hottentot tribe (the Bondelzwarts) took up arms in the former German South-West Africa. The air force was called in and the result was about a hundred deaths.

All this did not enhance Smuts's reputation. He needed a success to strengthen his position, but in 1922, undoubtedly a disastrous year for him, he suffered a major rebuff. He had made Southern Rhodesia's entry into the Union a personal objective. Like Rhodes, whom he sought to emulate, and Oppenheimer, whom he had inspired, he was obsessed by the idea of expansion northwards. The Opposition parties, however, saw things in a different light, for they were not anxious to find themselves responsible for governing an increased Black population. On the other hand, the Rhodesians mistrusted Afrikaner nationalism. When, in October 1922, they were asked in a referendum which they would prefer— inclusion in South Africa or self-government within the Empire—the 22,000 voters (women included) opted for the latter solution by a majority of over 3,800.

Hertzog and Creswell sensed that their time had come. The labour unrest and riots had drawn them together, and in 1923 they announced

---

[1] Many of them failed to explode. The South African air force had only just been formed and techniques had obviously not yet been perfected.

[2] See p. 184.

their alliance. The alliance was aimed at protecting the interests of the white workers. The Prime Minister decided to dissolve Parliament and bring forward the general election. Polling-day was fixed for 19 June 1924. The Nationalist Party increased its representation from 45 seats to 63, Labour from 9 to 18, the Independents obtained 1 and the South African Party lost 26. Smuts was not re-elected; according to his most recent biographer, this was for him a crushing defeat, both politically and personally. Smuts resigned and the Governor-General asked Hertzog to form a new cabinet.

Thus 19 June 1924 was an historic date: 'South Africa first', 'South Africa for the South Africans', had triumphed. Twenty-two years after their defeat, what use would the Afrikaners make of their victory?

The distribution of portfolios presented its problems. The Labour Party demanded a half-share of government posts, but Hertzog insisted on proportional representation and gave it two ministries out of a total of ten (of the 80 members of the coalition, 18 were Labour). The rest were allocated to the Nationalists. One of the leading Nationalists was Tielman Roos, a barrister who had achieved fame with two speeches: in 1915 he had defended De Wet after the collapse of the military rebellion, and in 1922 his eloquence had inflamed the workers in the Rand. He was a man of passionate temperament, 'clever, boisterous, and a biting tongue', says one historian; 'talkative and as excited as a cock sparrow', 'haphazard and unreliable', writes another. As Minister of Justice, Tielman Roos soon asserted his influence. Dr Malan was also a well-known figure, an austere personality whose sincerity no one questioned. He had started life as a pastor and missionary, then he had turned to journalism: when, in 1915, *Die Burger* became the mouthpiece of Nationalist ideas, he was invited to become its editor. Elected to Parliament, he won the esteem of the old guard by his rigid orthodoxy. In 1924 he seemed an obvious choice for Minister of the Interior.

Neither Roos nor Malan had any experience of public affairs. Neither had their colleagues, with the exception of the Prime Minister, who had played a prominent role in the Free State before Union and then, from 1910 to 1912, had spent two years working with Botha. 'A government of amateurs', whispered the losers in an attempt to console themselves. Smuts predicted that there would be fun and games in Parliament. Meanwhile, he decided to retire from the political battlefield. On his farm near Pretoria he discovered the illusory serenity which leisure briefly brings to men of action. But this quiet existence did not satisfy him for long. He had always been drawn to philosophy and in a few weeks he wrote his *Holism and Evolution*, in which he attempted to express his views of the future.[1] After reading the book Winston Churchill wrote to the author,

---

[1] 'Holism' is derived from a Greek word meaning 'whole'. Briefly, Smuts's thesis was that evolution is the result of a progression of 'wholes' which attain their perfection in the human personality. In his view, 'the whole is greater than its constituent parts'.

saying that he had 'peered into the book with awe'. Smuts was soon back among his old colleagues. The remarks about himself which he heard at parliamentary sessions were not all complimentary. Yet it seems that criticism, and even insults, merely strengthened his conviction of his own superiority. 'His forehead would grow scarlet and he would stare at the speaker with grey freezing eyes and with a steady, unwincing stare . . . his ability to sit still without moving a muscle for long periods became uncanny.'

The former Prime Minister was thoughtful nevertheless, and his meditations must have given him cause for irritation on more than one occasion.

This 'government of amateurs' certainly knew what it wanted. In fact, the new Cabinet proved to be confident and very able. Two ideas dominated Hertzog: at home, to preserve White pre-eminence; and abroad, to ensure the constitutional independence of the Union. From the outset luck was on his side. Between 1924 and 1929 South Africa, like the Western world, gradually emerged from the post-war economic crisis and enjoyed uninterrupted prosperity. In 1925 the gold standard was restored; in the years that followed, the discovery of diamond fields in the western Transvaal and in South-West Africa, the adoption of a policy of tariff protection, the mining of iron ore and the birth of a metallurgical industry[1] gave a rapid impetus to economic activity. The public finances, generally in deficit, benefited accordingly: from 1925 to 1929 the budget surpluses reached an annual average of more than £1 million.

Distributing wealth is even more difficult than creating it. The government was determined to reserve this extra 'manna' for the Whites, who still represented only a quarter of the population—attempts to encourage immigration had produced insignificant results.[2] As soon as the Nationalist-Labour 'Pact' assumed power, a Ministry of Labour was created, with very definite aims in mind, viz, the protection of the interests of white workers. The majority of these workers were English-speaking, a fact borne out by the election successes of Cresswell's Labour Party in the Witwatersrand. What is more, Cresswell himself was made Minister of Labour to ensure that their interests were safeguarded. To achieve this objective an ingenious theory was devised: 'civilized' labour was distinguished from 'non-civilized' labour. According to the official definition, 'civilized' labour was that capable of being performed by 'persons whose standard of living conforms to the standard of living generally recognized as tolerable from the usual European viewpoint'. The second category comprised those 'whose aim is restricted by the base requirements of the

---

[1] The creation of the state-controlled Iron and Steel Industrial Corporation (Iscor) met with opposition from the Senate. It was necessary to have recourse to the constitutional procedure of a joint session of the two houses to obtain parliamentary approval for the bill.

[2] About 25,000 new Europeans between 1911 and 1921.

necessities of life as understood amongst barbarous and undeveloped people.' Starting from these premises, the conclusion was obvious: decent remuneration for the Whites and miserable wages for the rest. This imbalance had existed for a long time, but the Pact Government considered it essential that the facts and the law should tally. An Act of 1926 laid down the principle of the Colour Bar: skilled and semi-skilled jobs would be open only to those possessing a 'certificate of efficiency', to which only Whites and Coloureds would be entitled. It would be a mistake to interpret this *lasciate ogni speranza* as a sign of hostility or even indifference towards the natives. After all, the Boers did not persecute or destroy the Bantu, as the Americans did the Indians. But, imbued as they were with the conviction that the divine will had predestined each race to a different role, it seemed to them only natural that they should abide by the intentions of Providence. About what might happen in the life hereafter they spoke less readily.

These Afrikaners were indeed astounding men, their relentless logic equalled perhaps only by that of the French Jacobins, pursuing their task untiringly until they attained the goal which they had set themselves! In 1925 they gave an astonishing example of their will-power. In that year Afrikaans, still a dialect two generations earlier, was admitted to the status of an official language on an equal footing with English; no sooner had they recovered from the effort of having to try to learn Dutch than English-speaking civil servants found themselves obliged to put their linguistic talents to the test yet again—a nerve-racking experience. Their pride, already hurt, suffered an even greater blow when it was decreed about this same time that His Majesty's subjects in South Africa would no longer be permitted to accept any titles which the Crown might choose to bestow on them.

The purpose of these decisions was obvious: by symbolical gestures the Hertzog government wished to loosen the bonds that still joined the Union to the Empire. Needless to say, there was great consternation among those South Africans who still looked on Britain as their native country. Not long afterwards, the flag question gave them further cause for resentment. Dr Malan set the ball rolling on 25 May 1926; in a speech that shattered the Union Jack loyalists, he announced that the time had come for South Africa to have its own national flag. But what flag? Fierce controversy erupted and a variety of proposals were put forward. The argument lasted two years; from time to time Natal, the stronghold of British traditions, threatened secession. In 1928 a compromise was reached: since the country had two capitals, it could have two flags. One, the national emblem, would be displayed on all occasions; in its colouring and design it would evoke the dual origins of South Africa: three horizontal bands of orange, white and blue, as had figured on the coat of arms of the House of Orange in van Riebeeck's time; in the centre, reproductions of the two flags of the South African Republic and the Free State, one with red, white and blue horizontal bands and a green vertical band, the other with alternating horizontal bands of orange and white and, in the top left corner, a red, white and blue canton; and finally, to complete this symphony of colours, a miniature Union Jack. The second flag would be that of the British Empire, the flag which Roberts had hoisted triumphantly at Bloemfontein and Pretoria in 1900; but it would fly only beside its successor, and then only in certain circumstances and in strictly defined places.

The new flag was introduced on 31 May 1928, on the occasion of the eighteenth anniversary of the Union. The criticisms which it provoked were purely academic. If South Africa had not yet obtained full legal independence, it was already autonomous in fact.

The process had begun shortly after the signing of the Treaty of Versailles. In 1922 an incident had tested the solidity of the Commonwealth: Mustapha Kemal's Turks—discreetly supported by France—had just hustled out of Asia Minor the Greeks whom Britain had rather recklessly installed there. A clash nearly occurred between the victorious Turks and a British garrison at Chanak, on the Dardanelles. Diplomacy averted a conflict, but in the meantime Britain had judged it advisable to consult its satellites about the possibility of their participation. Ottawa and Pretoria refused politely but firmly, arguing that they could do nothing without the approval of their Parliaments, and thereby depriving Westminster of its monopoly of decision making. Canada and the Union of South Africa, moreover, continued to pursue a common policy. Their similarity of views asserted itself at the Imperial Conference of 1923, when the British government had to accept that each country could henceforth negotiate and sign its own treaties, and it found an opportunity for concrete expression two years later, when the two leading Dominions, followed by the other members of the Commonwealth, refused to endorse the undertakings of the Treaty of Locarno.[1]

This was all well and good, but, in the eyes of such a legally-minded man as Hertzog, what went without saying was even better said. The Prime Minister therefore decided to attend another Imperial Conference in 1926. This was his third contact with Europe. As a young man he had spent four years at the University of Amsterdam, where he obtained his doctorate in law. After the First World War he crossed the Atlantic again, this time to Paris to ask that the republican independence of the Transvaal and Free State be restored. The journey cannot have left him with pleasant memories. The action of seamen of the Union Castle Line, the British shipping company which enjoyed a monopoly of transport between Europe and South Africa, forced Hertzog and his deputation to seek alternative arrangements. A less chauvinistic admiral offered them his

[1] This agreement, signed in 1925 by Britain, France, Belgium and Germany, was supposed to guarantee the frontiers laid down at Versailles, except for the more controversial boundaries in Eastern Europe.

hospitality on one of His Majesty's warships, but later withdrew his offer. The deputation eventually found themselves obliged to travel to France via New York. Their meetings with the Great Powers proved disappointing. They were courteously received, but the French government had other things to worry about than the liberty of the Afrikaners. Besides, the Union's official representatives seemed highly satisfied with the status they had accepted at Vereeniging. Lloyd George did not omit to stress this aspect of the problem to them and they finally departed with empty hands. The deputation was not despondent because they did not really expect that their demands would be met. The journey was more in the nature of a tactical move—it engendered support in South Africa for the party's political offensive.

When, seven years later, Hertzog landed in England, he felt less inclined to ask for favours than to lay down conditions. Shortly after coming to power he had affirmed his loyalty, but in enigmatic terms: 'I have not the slightest intention of recommending secession from the empire . . . I say here again that I am in favour of the British connection being maintained.' He was convinced, however, that the Union did have the *right* of secession and the *right*, should it so wish, to adopt a republican form of government. The precise form of the relationship which he envisaged was open to interpretation. In London the prestige of Mackenzie King, Prime Minister of Canada, and the ardour with which the young Irish Free State was asserting its claims, proved invaluable assets to Hertzog. He refused to be satisfied with vague approximations, and the terms of the Balfour Declaration had to be redrafted eight times before he would give it his approval. The final text was clear: the Dominions were recognized as autonomous communities, equal in law, in no way subordinate one to another, either in internal or in external matters, but, nevertheless, linked by allegiance to the same Crown and freely associated one with another as members of the British Commonwealth. There was only one reservation: for some time to come the British government would assume the bulk of responsibility in questions of foreign policy—a condition that revealed a great deal about the intention of the signatories.

In a moment of emotion worthy of Botha, Hertzog paid homage to the 'greatness' of Britain, declaring that 'the liberty of our country as a dominion within the British Commonwealth was all that the most ardent patriot could want'. But he lost no time in giving this 'liberty' as positive a form as possible. In 1927 a Ministry of External Affairs was created; two years later the Union opened its first legations in Washington, The Hague and Rome.[1] The Statute of Westminster, which the British Parliament approved in 1931, by 350 votes to 50, merely gave official sanction to a *de facto* situation. Henceforward, the Governor-General would be appointed only on the recommendation of the South African government and would become the personal representative of the King. A High Commissioner,

[1] The Paris legation was established in 1934.

an ambassador in fact if not in title, would maintain diplomatic relations between Pretoria and London, each the capital of a sovereign state.

Much had thus been achieved. Economically things were going well for the country; the Union's independent status had been formally recorded; the budget was balanced; and there was industrial peace.

The country was at this period less concerned with international prestige than with economic stability.

In the elections of 1929 the Labour Party had lost 10 of its 18 seats; but these losses had been compensated by the 15 constituencies gained by the Nationalists, and so Hertzog's majority had been increased by 5. Nevertheless, victory had been won in unpleasant circumstances. Smuts, haunted by the dreams of Cecil Rhodes, had committed the blunder of speaking of a 'greater South Africa,' which in his mind meant nothing other than the eventual inclusion of Rhodesia.[1] Roos and Hertzog himself seized the opportunity to raise the spectre of the 'Black Peril', accusing the leader of the South African Party of advocating a Kaffir state which would stretch from beyond the Limpopo as far as the Sudan and in which the Whites would be submerged. This demagogic interpretation of Smuts's intentions impressed the electors. Indeed, it showed how obsessed they were by the racial question, even if they preferred not to talk about it too much; above all, it revealed that the descendants of the *voortrekkers* were more eager for security than for adventure.

Consequently, South Africa was all the more severely shaken by the crisis that hit the country, like the rest of the Western world, after 1930. Three products which played an essential role in its economic life—gold, diamonds and wool—were particularly affected by the fall in prices which had started in 1929 and was still accelerating. Misfortunes never come singly, and during this same period a drought of unprecedented gravity ruined the country's livestock; 'the psychology of the desert is creeping over South Africa', remarked Smuts. When at last, in 1931, the queen of currencies, the pound sterling, went off the gold standard, he felt to be living a nightmare: 'the ark of the Covenant has gone', he groaned. The effect on his fellow-countrymen was no less profound, but derived from more down-to-earth considerations: would the Union be able to keep the gold standard now that Britain had abandoned it?

Hertzog made the issue a question of principle. By dissociating himself from British monetary policy, he believed that he had found an opportunity to assert the independence which he valued so highly. The Prime Minister did not know much about financial matters, which he entrusted to his Minister of Finance, Nicolaas Havenga, chosen as much for his technical abilities as for his personal loyalty (he had been seriously wounded in the Boer War, during which he had served as General Hertzog's secretary). The two men stuck to their position, however, and capital

[1] See p. 265.

poured out of South Africa. At the Imperial Economic Conference held at Ottawa in 1932, Havenga obtained substantial preferential treatment for the Union's goods, and Hertzog hoped that trading surpluses would mitigate the deficit on the balance of payments. Nothing of the sort happened, and so the expedient of exchange-control was adopted: mysteriously, money continued to desert a currency in which it no longer had confidence and to seek less hazardous channels. The result was more unemployment and more bankruptcies.

Hertzog was beginning to encounter growing opposition, also from within his own party. The Boers were fond of Latin quotations, and Caesar's *Tu quoque, fili!* must have come into Hertzog's mind when his former colleague, Tielman Roos, turned out to be the most treacherous of his adversaries. Ill-health had compelled the impetuous barrister to leave the government in 1929. He had been guaranteed a position as a judge, but studying legal documents and practising impartiality were not his strong points. When he felt that the crisis had become sufficiently grave he returned to the life of political intrigue for which he was infinitely better qualified, putting himself forward as the predestined saviour of the Union. He had no party behind him, but the financial policy of the 'two H's' was causing such great dissatisfaction that the Opposition was on the point of joining the small group of Nationalists whom the ex-judge had managed to gather round himself. Smuts thwarted the scheme, which did not appeal to him at all. But Roos was not discouraged. On 16 December 1932 he was to make a speech at a commemoration of the battle of Blood River.[1] Instead of talking about the past as expected, he launched into the political question. Announcing his resignation as a judge, he demanded the formation of a coalition government and an immediate devaluation. This dramatic appeal had a bombshell effect, resulting in a wave of speculation. On 27 December, Havenga was forced to announce that the Union was abandoning the gold standard.

The panic subsided and gradually a relative stability was restored. Nevertheless, if the economic crisis had apparently been overcome, it was only at the price of a political tension which seemed almost insoluble.

In the opinion of Roos the solution was simple: the formation of a non-party government of which he would be Prime Minister and in which Hertzog and Smuts would serve under him. But neither Hertzog nor Smuts could accept this as the answer. The Prime Minister had said on more than one occasion that, in the event of a devaluation, he would resign; but in fact he did nothing of the kind, afraid no doubt of betraying the Afrikaner cause. Yet he felt that his position had been weakened and realized that he would no longer be able to win an election alone. Smuts, for his part, had little desire to lend his prestige to his bitter political foe, but he himself faced disruption in his own ranks, particularly with his supporters in Natal, who were very strongly pro-British. The result was

[1] See pp. 96–7.

SOUTH AFRICA IN
1930

Union of
South Africa

+++++ Railways

☆ Diamonds

| 0 Kilometres | | 800 |
| 0 Miles | | 480 |

that Smuts indicated that he was ready to compromise. Perhaps, when the two men met, the fellow-feeling of their commando days induced them to seek a reconciliation. At all events, on 15 February 1933 a relieved South Africa learned of their decision to form a government together. The respective strengths of their two parties were reflected in the new ministry: Hertzog remained Prime Minister, while Smuts contented himself with the Ministry of Justice, a post which he had occupied under Kruger thirty-five years earlier, at the age of twenty-eight. 'And they call that justice', he wrote ironically to a friend.

Their agreement had been reached on the basis of seven points which bore a strange resemblance to the Nationalist programme. 'It was as if Gladstone had joined forces with Disraeli or General Booth was united with the Pope,' wrote a contemporary observer. The reaction of South Africans was one of astonishment and, in particular, of admiration for the humility that Smuts had displayed. Mrs Steyn, the widow of the deeply revered president of the Free State, wrote to him saying that she would never have believed it, even if an angel from heaven had prophesied it— she was astounded by his courage and self-sacrifice. The governor-general, Lord Clarendon, expressed the same sentiments in less emotional terms. He was particularly anxious to tell Smuts how much the country owed to him: he could have expected to win the forthcoming election, but he had renounced all personal advantage in the interests of the Union: his noble decision, insisted Clarendon, would enrich the pages of South African political history.

The electorate did not dispute this point of view. In May, 136 seats out of 150 went to the Hertzog-Smuts Coalition.[1] Yet a majority of this kind was soon seen to be somewhat artificial. The extremists cried treachery. In Natal, where some fanatics regarded even the Statute of Westminster as anti-British, the dark forebodings of Colonel Stallard, a nostalgic disciple of the Empire, awakened a favourable response, and seven intrepid die-hards founded the Dominion Party, disowning Smuts. Even more serious was the split in Hertzog's own party. Dr Malan, inflexible as ever, led the revolt. His faithful followers considered the Prime Minister a great man who had become the victim of an illusion. Determined to show their disapproval in no uncertain terms, they formed a new Nationalist Party, a title to which some ironically added the epithet 'purified'. As the saying went in France during the Third Republic, 'the two ends of the omelette were cut off', and so it was essential to ensure a solid centre. In December 1934, Hertzog and Smuts decided to fuse their parties under the title of the United South African National Party. Hertzog's favourite notion of the 'two streams' formed the basis of the new grouping. Its object, explained its founders, was to develop the sense of a national unity founded on the equality of the Afrikaans and English-speaking communities, in an

[1] Roos was by this time out of the running; disenchanted and deserted, he died two years later.

association where each would recognize and appreciate the cultural heritage which distinguished it from the other.

On these foundations men of goodwill could build, a goal which for several years South Africans believed to be attainable.

In his biography of Hertzog, Oswald Pirow, his colleague, describes those years as 'the happiest time South Africa has experienced since Union'. Perhaps he was biased, for, with Smuts and Havenga, he was one of the most influential members of the cabinet. It is nevertheless true that from 1933 to 1938, the return of prosperity created the illusion that political problems had been solved. New mineral deposits were worked, mines on the point of permanent closure were reopened, and people began making profits again, a habit they had lost. The benefit of these results was felt even by the least favoured section of the population, at least among the Europeans. The lot of the 'poor Whites', who in 1932 represented one-fifth of the population, gradually became tolerable. At the same time, the satisfactory state of the public finances enabled the government to undertake a few tentative programmes of social assistance. Subsidies and the control of agricultural prices alleviated the condition of those who had suffered most from the years of drought. The pensions of civil servants were improved, and a scheme for unemployment insurance gave the workers a feeling of security which they had never previously known. But it was in the field of communications and transport that official activity was most in evidence: the country was provided with the asphalt roads it needed so urgently, airlines were formed, and the ports of Cape Town and Durban were modernized. In 1937 the creation of the South African Broadcasting Corporation, under state control, confirmed the government's intention to protect the simultaneous development of the two cultures, British and Afrikaans.

With the return of prosperity and political calm, the moment seemed ripe to define relations between 'Europeans' and 'non-Europeans' by adopting a rather less negative formula than that of the Colour Bar law of 1926. The Indians were granted a few concessions of principle: the Union agreed to receive an Indian agent empowered to deal with matters concerning his compatriots; the Transvaal made a gesture of goodwill by accepting that, in certain clearly defined circumstances, Asians would at last be entitled to become landowners on its territory; most important of all, it was decided that India would encourage the immigrants to return home and that South Africa would supply them with the necessary resources—an undertaking which presented no threat to the public coffers, since hardly anyone sought to take advantage of the offer.

Although the Indian problem was not easy to solve, the questions it raised seemed minor by comparison with those posed by the Coloureds and, to an even greater degree, by the Blacks. The figures speak for themselves: in 1938 there were 2 million Whites, 219,000 Asians, 750,000

Coloureds, and 6½ million Blacks. It will be recalled that the last three categories were deprived of all civil rights in the Transvaal and the Free State; in the Cape Province, on the other hand, both the Coloureds and the Blacks could, on certain conditions, be included on the electoral rolls; the more hypocritical Natal, while ostensibly abiding by this same principle, made sure that it was never put into practice.

Hertzog made a clear distinction between Coloureds and Blacks, regarding the former as too close to the Whites not to enjoy the same political status. He thus hoped to extend to the Union as a whole the system practised in the Cape Province. It must be emphasized, however, that in his view this equality of rights could not be allowed to lead to true social equality; in other words, the Coloureds could vote, but a moral barrier would continue to separate them from the Whites. Smuts's ideas appear to have been very different, although he never expounded them with the precision of the more legally-minded Hertzog.

As far as the Blacks were concerned, the attitudes of the two men were very similar. In 1917, Smuts, South Africa's leading representative in Britain and a member of the War Cabinet, had an opportunity to explain his country's native policy in London: 'Instead of mixing Black and White in the old and haphazard way which, instead of uplifting the Black, degraded the White, we are now trying to lay down a policy of keeping them apart. . . . It may take a hundred years to work out, but in the end it may be the solution of the native problem.' Hertzog, in his turn, was in favour of segregation as a means of safeguarding races from becoming intermixed by crossbreeding and sparing the natives the fate of the continued existence of the white nation. Colonel Stallard, the pillar of out-and-out imperialism, declared that Hertzog must not imagine he had a monopoly of the segregation idea, thus showing how closely the views of English-speaking South Africans and Afrikaners coincided.

The general rule, then, was to be the separation of the races—total between Whites and Blacks, partial between Whites and Coloureds. Two years after coming to power Hertzog had introduced four draft bills based on these principles. Reduced to their essentials, they presented two contrary objectives: to extend to the Union as a whole the Coloured franchise practised in the Cape; and, on the other hand, to deprive the Blacks of the franchise which some of them enjoyed in that Province. The economic crisis and political changes had left the question in abeyance for ten years. Then, in 1936, two laws were finally passed which are worth considering in detail, since they represent an important stage on the road to *apartheid*.

The first, the Native Representation Act, concerned the franchise. The Blacks were still excluded, in law in both the Transvaal and the Free State, and in practice in Natal; in the Cape they retained their privilege, but no longer on the same electoral rolls as the Whites. Voting separately, they were entitled to elect to the Assembly three representatives, but only

Europeans. Hertzog found some ingenious arguments to justify the new system, explaining that 'the people in this country want the sword which has been hanging over their heads all these years to be removed'[1]—in other words, it was time to take measures to ensure that they would never find themselves in a minority, a typical example of the rigid reasoning which always induces Afrikaners to push their ideas to their extreme logical conclusion. The 'sword of Damocles' was certainly not about to fall in 1936: the obligation of presenting a certificate of elementary education and of providing proof of a minimum wage in order to be entitled to vote[2] guaranteed the Whites a 97 per cent majority. But Hertzog and his colleagues could never overcome their fondness for legal precision. Hertzog had explained their new status to the Blacks in an image worthy of Kruger:

'I hope you will agree that no injustice is done when different grazing is given to sheep from that given to cattle.'

Two other provisions gave the Blacks a few minimum guarantees. Electoral colleges, composed of delegates selected by the European authorities, together with tribal chiefs and members of local councils, would be permitted to choose three Whites to represent them in the Union Senate. Finally, a native Representative Council of twenty-two members—sixteen Blacks, twelve of them to be appointed by the electoral colleges and four by the government, plus six Europeans—would be empowered to submit requests both to the House of Assembly and to the Senate.

For the Coloureds nothing had changed. They retained their right to vote in the Cape Province, but Hertzog did not succeed in extending this privilege to the rest of the Union.[3]

The second law of 1936, the Native Lands Act, provided for 7,225,000 *morgen*[4] to be added to the 10,730,000 already designated as Black areas by the law of 1913.[5]

The value of these provisions depended entirely on the spirit in which they would be applied. A government in which Smuts and Hertzog were working together was certainly not likely to wish to transform this ostracism of the Black population into oppression. In time, the system might have been rendered less rigid. But, as had happened after 1910, a resurgence of Afrikaner nationalism and the imminence of an international crisis were to throw the political scene into confusion and push the Black problem into the background.

[1] The natives had been given the vote in 1875.
[2] Since 1931 these conditions had no longer applied to the Whites; in that year an extra 10,000 received the franchise and the percentage of Blacks had been reduced to about 3 per cent.
[3] Relatively, their position had been weakened since 1930, when 'European' women received the vote, but not Coloured women.
[4] About two acres.   [5] See p. 252.

The elections of 1938 reduced the government party's majority from 144 to 114. In itself this was by no means a fatal blow in an Assembly which consisted of only 150 seats. However, the success of the 'Purified' Nationalists—27 constituencies, after starting from scratch four years earlier—augured well for their future prospects. Malan and his followers had not spared Hertzog; if the Prime Minister had a good memory, he must have recognized echoes of his own speeches against Botha twenty-six years previously.

The centenary of the Great Trek provided the Opposition with an opportunity to stir up a wave of nationalism which revealed the deep feelings of the Afrikaners. Their sentiments had already found expression when, in spite of the indignant protests of English-speaking South Africans, it had been decreed that God Save the King would henceforth be played only on state occasions and would be replaced for everyday purposes by a national anthem in Afrikaans, Die Stem van Suid-Afrika ('The Voice of South Africa'). At the inauguration of a memorial to the voortrekkers near Pretoria, on 16 December 1938, a hundred years to the day since the victory of Blood River, memories and hopes mingled to give the ceremony an extraordinary resonance. To celebrate the occasion a symbolic trek was organized: from all directions old-fashioned ox-wagons converged on the place where the ceremony was being held—in this way the past was linked with the present, a past which included not only the desperate struggles against barbarous Blacks, but also the struggles against British imperialism. Along the route followed by the wagons festivities were organized. Periods costumes were worn, and the men had let their beards grow; in the evening, round the camps illuminated by bonfires, psalms and patriotic songs alternated. The people's enthusiasm became almost religious, sometimes hysterical, and women brought their babies to have them baptized in the shadow of the wagons. It seemed that the Afrikaners were all the heirs to the same principles and the same culture, separated from their English-speaking compatriots who had no roots in South Africa. Once again, the past, with its poignant memories, was exerting its influence on the political development of the country.

The organizers had decided that no politicians would take part in the ceremony in an official capacity. Hertzog did not attend, and Smuts appeared as an ordinary citizen. According to Professor Hancock, Malan here gained his greatest triumph. When one speaker dared to address the crowd in English, his voice was drowned by booing. In contrast, there was prolonged cheering when the 'rebel' of 1915, General Kemp, announced that the British headquarters of Roberts Heights, named after Lord Roberts, commander-in-chief during the Boer War, would be called Voortrekkerhoogte. Such passions could not be left unexploited. Whether sincere or prompted by self-interest, these outbursts of emotion led to the creation of two groups both of which breathed new life into the Nationalist Party: one wishing to devote itself to the economic 'revival' of the Afrikaners—which implied that they had been the victims of injustice; the other, more sentimental and bearing the symbolic name of 'Sentinel of the Ox-wagon' (Ossewabrandwag), seeking to perpetuate the ideal that had inspired the Great Trek.

But in the meantime echoes of the deteriorating international situation were beginning to be heard in South Africa. For the second time in less than thirty years the question could no longer be ignored: in the event of war, would the country align itself with Britain or would it follow a separate path?

The Union's desire for independence has asserted itself unceasingly. In 1935 its delegate in Geneva had voted for sanctions against Italy in connection with the Abyssinian affair. But, although this decision had received the approval of Smuts, there were those who opposed it and who would have preferred a policy of isolation. For a long time Smuts himself showed an extraordinary lack of awareness: he had deplored the Stresa agreement signed that same year by Britain, Italy and France in an attempt to curb German ambitions; he had expressed his satisfaction at the Anglo-German naval agreement, typical of the balancing game that Britain was hoping to play to each side of the Rhine; and even after the reoccupation of the Rhineland in 1936 he still believed in Hitler's good faith—in his opinion it was all the fault of the French, 'who had missed every opportunity since Versailles'.

At this time some of Hertzog's ideas were not so very different from his own. 'I maintain,' declared the Prime Minister in May 1937, 'that the peace of Europe can be and should be assured if Great Britain approached Germany in the same spirit of friendly collaboration in which she has always met France since 1919.' At the heart of the matter, however, was one fundamental point on which the two men were divided. Smuts considered that neither the Balfour Declaration nor the Statute of Westminster had severed the links which a common Crown maintained between Britain and South Africa; more concretely, South Africa had no right to dissociate its destiny from that of its mother-country in the event of a conflict. The apostle of 'South Africa first' saw things differently: in his eyes, the union of the two countries existed only in the person of the King, and the 'King of South Africa' might well make a decision different from that of the 'King of Great Britain'. He put forward this view clearly in May 1936: 'We shall not join in any war except where the interests of South Africa make such participation inevitable.' A few months later Hertzog put his idea into practice in a rather novel manner, at the time of the abdication of Edward VIII.

Pirow, then Minister of Defence, to whom Hertzog had delegated the drafting of legislation, relates how they had come to the conclusion that this was a unique opportunity to prove the divisibility of the Crown once and for all by giving South Africa a new king before the House of

Commons had accepted the abdication of the former king.[1] The British High Commissioner came to see Pirow in a state of great agitation. It seemed to him quite inconceivable that South Africa should take advantage of a quite fortuitous event to decide a burning question which every Imperial Conference had avoided. Pirow, greatly amused, assured him with all the necessary gravity that the situation would be even more extraordinary if there were a gap in the succession between the moment when it became effective in South Africa and the moment when the British Parliament recognized the abdication of Edward VIII and the accession of George VI. The High Commissioner left in a state of deep preoccupation. 'Thus,' writes Pirow, 'George VI was the King of South Africa before he was the sovereign of Great Britain.'

The Czechoslovakian crisis and the Munich agreement prompted Hertzog to reiterate his position. At a cabinet meeting on 28 September 1938 he read out a rather tortuously worded statement. That it signified in his own mind an intention of neutrality is hardly in doubt; neither is it improbable that Smuts interpreted it differently, limiting its possible application solely to the problems of Central and Eastern Europe. The discussion ended, it appears, on a misunderstanding. In the meantime, Oswald Pirow was entrusted with a fact-finding mission.

Pirow's knowledge of Europe was limited to what he had learned during his university studies in Germany (he was of German origin) and England. The impressions which he formed in the course of his official visit were both superficial and perceptive. He ignored France on the pretext of some menacing strikes taking place there. Salazar seemed to him to stand 'head and shoulders above the big men in Europe'. He observed 'remarkable similarities about Franco's views, those of Salazar and those of Hertzog'. He was attracted by Neville Chamberlain's obvious sincerity. When Queen Mary learned that the visitor from South Africa intended seeking an audience with Hitler, she commented: 'Well, tell him to stop his nonsense!' The British Prime Minister was more vague. Pirow was entrusted with a rather ill-defined mission of intervention on behalf of the Jews. On arriving in Germany he saw Goering and Ribbentrop. The latter did not appeal to him: 'Of all the ministers I met overseas, Ribbentrop impressed me least. He was closely followed by Eden and Ciano.' He was disappointed by Hitler, whom he had met briefly at the beginning of the Führer's career. 'In 1933, I talked to him in a simple farmhouse, his own; now we were surrounded by the luxury of a palace.[2] He had then made the impression of a simple peasant or worker, a militant, a mystic with a great grasp of international affairs. John the Baptist in jack-boots. Now he was a modern diplomat, very sure of himself and slightly arrogant.' The meeting, of course, led to nothing. In Rome, Pirow was

---

[1] In South African law, the royal decision was sufficient to make the abdication effective, without the ratification of Parliament.
[2] At Berchtesgaden.

no more successful. 'Most of my discussions were with Ciano, good-looking, vain and stupid.' Mussolini, who, Pirow was told, was at the time interested only in a new mistress, yawned when Pirow talked to him about the Jewish question. Yet the South African formed a high opinion of the man who had made a nation of what had been only a confused rabble.

Politicians are not in the habit of minimizing their importance. Yet Pirow must have been right when he claimed that his mission had a decisive influence on both Hertzog and Smuts, convincing them that war would break out in 1939, that Central Europe would be the starting-point of the conflagration, and that the conflict would not be due to German aggression against Great Britain and France. The two men drew different conclusions, however. Hertzog's determination to remain neutral was strengthened. Smuts, on the other hand, began his preparations to have the Union make a common front with the rest of the Commonwealth.

Both Smuts and Hertzog had referred to South Africa's neutrality during the days of fusion as something 'academic'. Members in the cabinet with strong British ties openly stated that South Africa could not remain neutral should Britain become involved in a war. Smuts supported them but told Platteland (rural) voters that only time would tell what attitude South Africa should adopt. Hertzog refused to get publicly involved.

South Africa's attitude soon became a burning issue during the crucial hours of September 1939. By sheer coincidence, Members of Parliament had been summoned to Cape Town for an urgent session of Parliament shortly before Hitler invaded Poland. Parliament had to meet to extend the life of the Senate for an extra few months. The cabinet met on 2 September to discuss the Nazi invasion and the divergence of opinion between Hertzog and Smuts came out into the open at this meeting. Hertzog pleaded for some qualified neutrality while Smuts opted for war. Seven ministers backed Smuts and six Hertzog. It was all over.

When Parliament met on 4 September for the formality to extend the life of the Senate, it came face to face with the crucial war issue. Hertzog proposed the adoption of a neutrality motion, while Smuts moved that the Union should sever its relations with Germany and not remain neutral in the conflict. After a bitter debate a vote was taken and 80 members of Parliament supported Smuts against the 67 who came out in support of Hertzog.

Hertzog might have won the argument if he had not given the impression that he was justifying Hitler's actions. Smuts was more skilful, and his view carried the day. One of the victors described the scene after the division: 'Hertzog looked like a damned man, shocked and sickly. Havenga, undoubtedly very upset, was trying to smile and Pirow had lost his jaunty air and was completely deflated.... Smuts's supporters were

wreathed in smiles, but there was no cheering. We did not rub it in.'
Hertzog tried to obtain a dissolution. The governor-general, Sir
Patrick Duncan,[1] who had no reason to grant his request, refused. On
5 September the Prime Minister resigned. That same day Smuts was
invited to succeed him. His first act was to hand the German minister his
papers.

[1] Appointed in 1937, Duncan was the first South African to occupy the post.

24

The Second World War

The war was the sole cause of Smuts's return to power. It was to bring him his moments of greatest glory, but it was also to reveal the insecurity of his position. Only three years after the end of the conflict the Nationalists were to gain a total victory. Though muffled by the noise of battle, the trend which had begun in 1910 had continued and become more marked. In discussing the period from 1939 to 1945 it seems necessary, therefore, to consider military events and these other developments separately. The former, despite their brilliance, exercised only a transient influence; but the latter, though less conspicuous, proved decisive. To try to combine these aspects chronologically would be to risk falsifying perspectives and allowing appearances to mask the realities.

South Africa was no better prepared in 1939 than in 1914. It had no navy; 6 modern aircraft and 63 old models; a standing army of 200 officers and 4,600 men, plus reserves amounting to 960 officers and 14,000 men; and a skeleton general staff co-ordinating these meagre forces. No plans had been made for manufacturing armaments. The war effort which the Union produced was thus all the more admirable. It is estimated that some 186,000 young men donned uniforms: 132,000 in the army, 45,000 in the air force and 9,000 in the navy; about 25,000 women were enrolled in the auxiliary services; and 120,000 'non-Europeans' were used behind the front lines. The government was wise enough never to contemplate conscription. Recruitment was entirely voluntary; an orange shoulder-badge distinguished those opting for service anywhere in Africa (at first, no one imagined that overseas postings would be envisaged). This citizens' army, which had emerged from nothing, obtained its equipment and armaments in South Africa itself. Under the impetus of a remarkable organizer, Hendrick (Hennie) van der Bijl, trained in American methods, industry adapted itself to its new tasks much more quickly than even the most optimistic would have dared to hope. By the end of the war South Africa was not only able to meet many of its military needs with its own resources, but was making an appreciable contribution to Allied war production.

  Anyone familiar with the sweetness and quiet beauty of springtime in the southern hemisphere will not need much imagination to understand how the majority of South Africans felt in September 1939. How remote, unreal and absurd the conflict must have seemed to them! In December an incident briefly ruffled their tranquillity. An aerial patrol spotted the German flag off the Cape; a warning shot was fired to indicate to the presumptuous captain that he should head for the nearest port; it was only a peaceful merchant ship, but the captain put his passengers into lifeboats and then scuttled the vessel. Although insignificant in itself, this encounter created an unprecedented feeling: would the war make itself felt even at the end of the world? The months passed and nothing happened. Then Italy's entry into the war gave events a new dimension: Mussolini's empire presented the Union with a battlefield, and Smuts was not the man to shirk the challenge. The first contingent of volunteers embarked for Kenya on 16 July 1940. The Prime Minister addressed them in soul-stirring language: 'We have fought for freedom in the past. We now go forth as crusaders, as children of the Cross to fight for freedom itself, the freedom of the human spirit, the free choice of the human individual to shape his own life according to the light that God has given him.'

When the Allied forces began the offensive against Abyssinia in December, two South African brigades took part. The troops found themselves advancing over barren ground of bush and shrub, or across deserts of sand and lava; the few existing paths were transformed into quagmires by tropical downpours, and in fine weather the soldiers marched along them in clouds of dust—and in temperatures sometimes above 120°F. The enemy offered only a feeble resistance, and on 6 April 1941, after travelling 1,700 miles, the victors entered Addis Ababa. Six weeks later the Duke of Aosta, commander-in-chief of the Italian forces, signed a general surrender. His adversaries courteously accorded him the honours of war.

Before the end of the year the South Africans were in Egypt. Some units were transported there by sea, while others took the land route—nearly three thousand miles under a burning sun. Raised to the strength of two divisions, they were attached to the Eighth Army, which had just been formed. Their arrival was greeted with enthusiasm, for the situation in North Africa was precarious. A seesaw contest between the British and the Germano-Italian forces had begun more than twelve months previously. The Italians had struck first. In September 1940, Graziani penetrated some fifty miles into Egypt. Then Wavell counter-attacked; in December 1940 he routed the invaders and pursued them to Benghazi, which he took two months later. Under the inspiration of Rommel the German reaction proved brutal; by April the victors of the previous year had been pushed back to their starting-point and the Egyptian frontier had again been crossed, though the port of Tobruk remained in the hands of an Australian garrison. The war of cut-and-thrust went on. In January 1942 the new British commander-in-chief, General Auchinleck, forced the Germans to abandon their conquests and to retreat once again as far as

El Agheila, on the border of Tripolitania. Tobruk was freed, but the 'Desert Fox' did not consider himself beaten. Three months later he seized the initiative again, and this time his onslaughts were shattering. General Koenig's French troops, placed to the south of the British disposition, halted him for six weeks at Bir Hakeim. But the German thrust seemed irresistible. Tobruk, encircled again, fell on 21 June, a sad day for South Africa: on this occasion the defence of the fortress had been entrusted to the 2nd South African Division, whose commander had no choice but to surrender; 25,000 men laid down their arms.

Their comrades were soon to avenge them. The men of the 1st Division helped to break the German advance on the fortified line of El Alamein. Then, under Montgomery, they launched an assault on 23 October 1942. It was no longer a question of advancing only to retreat again. On 13 November they entered Tobruk. They did not, however, have the satisfaction of being present at the final German surrender in Tunisia on 12 May 1943. After the losses they had suffered their meagre forces were in urgent need of reorganization. At the end of the year the South African units were repatriated and amalgamated in an armoured corps.

While the North African campaign was being fought, the Union government had decided to take part in an operation that presented fewer risks and also fewer opportunities for glory. On 12 February 1942 a member of the parliamentary majority, Leslie Blackwell, had spoken in the Assembly. He had just returned from a mission to Australia, and the fall of Singapore was expected at any moment. He imagined the Japanese fleet crossing the Indian Ocean to conquer a defenceless South Africa. What could stop them? Only Madagascar: 'The isle is entirely in the hands of the Vichy French and—as far as I know—there is no reason why they should not hand it to the Japs as they have done for Indochina.' The Opposition received the speech with jeering and insulting interruptions. Blackwell's words received a more favourable response from the Prime Minister. Like Churchill, Smuts now assumed that Marshal Pétain was resigned to giving up everything. The two leaders therefore resolved to take possession of the island, which otherwise, they believed, would shortly be handed over to the enemy. But there was the unfortunate precedent of Dakar, two years earlier. Consequently, for reasons of security, the Free French were not even informed. The operation was carried out swiftly. In the far north of the island Diego Suarez, impossible to defend, was seized by a British expeditionary force in May. Then, in September, the entire territory was occupied. This time a South African brigade made its contribution; when it encountered resistance from 135 French and natives, a bombardment was enough to convince them of the precariousness of their position.[1]

[1] On 14 December 1942 Madagascar was handed over to General de Gaulle's National Committee of Liberation. Diego Suarez remained a British base until the end of the war.

Nineteen forty-three brought an interlude in the activities of the Union troops. The Allied high command had decided to assign them to the Italian front, which had existed since the landings in Sicily in June. The decision presented a problem. Like Roosevelt, Smuts had solemnly promised that the 'boys', as he called the troops, would not be sent overseas as they had been thirty years earlier. Needless to say, the well-schooled Union Parliament saw no objection to releasing him from his promise. The South African forces landed at Taranto on 20 April 1944. They advanced up the peninsula in a series of fierce engagements, marched through Rome on the same day that the Allies were landing in Normandy, were the first to enter Florence and had reached the Po Valley by the time the armistice was signed. They were then entrusted with the task of occupying Lombardy and Piedmont.

753 South Africans died in Italy, 152 in East Africa and 2,104 in North Africa: in all, a little over 3,000 men had been lost in six years. Comparing this figure with the 34,000 victims of the Boer War, one is reminded of the cruelty of that conflict, which had lasted only three years.

From 1939 to 1945 Smuts continued to wield an influence which did not derive solely from his position. The power of his personality assured him a prestige which Churchill's support enabled him to exploit to the maximum. The understanding between the two men was exceptionally close. Anthony Eden, like so many others, was aware of this: 'The friendship of Churchill and Smuts always fascinated me. They were such contrasting personalities; the one with his neat philosophic mind, the other a man "so rammed with life" ... Yet the partnership was incomparable.'

There is abundant evidence of the closeness of their collaboration. As early as April 1940, even before South African troops went into action, General Wavell came to the Cape to establish contact with the Prime Minister. In the dark hours of July, Smuts made a broadcast to the British people. Churchill thanked him for what he considered to be a splendidly inspiring speech. He always kept Smuts fully informed; in June he even found the time to explain to him why he would not engage R.A.F. fighters in France. He made a point of seeking his advice: 'Please always give me your counsel, my old and valiant friend.' In the autumn of 1940 a meeting was arranged; Churchill could not leave the country himself, but sent his Foreign Secretary to Khartoum. The offensive against Abyssinia was decided. Eden observed that Smuts was warm in his appreciation of Winston.

On 1 January 1941 the South African Prime Minister made another broadcast to the people of Britain. He assured them that the world was coming to believe less and less in Hitler's victory and predicted that, sooner or later, America would come into the war; in any case, the year that had just begun would be 'the year of destiny'. In March he met Eden again, this time in Cairo, accompanied by Sir John Dill, Chief of the Imperial General Staff; in August he visited Auchinleck's headquarters; and in November he inspected his troops—the King had just bestowed on him the title of field-marshal, and a photograph shows him holding a baton, the emblem of a dignity flattering enough for a general, but a little unusual for a former commando-leader. Smuts was now discovering a world far removed from the *veld*: he had established a close relationship with the Greek royal family, who had taken temporary refuge in South Africa, and in particular with Princess Frederika,[1] who accepted his hospitality for two years and whom he converted to the 'holistic' philosophy,[2] according to Professor Hancock. Churchill maintained regular contact with him. On 16 May he wrote to Smuts: 'I am, as usual, in close sympathy and agreement with your military outlook.' And on 20 September he noted: 'As usual I kept Smuts informed.'

The year 1942 saw Field-Marshal Smuts asserting his authority. In May he again visited Auchinleck at his headquarters in the Libyan desert. On this occasion he was accompanied by his wife. 'Ouma', as she was known,[3] must have been quite a colourful person, if one is to judge by the descriptions of her British admirers. 'A quaint little dowdy figure, tied in a loose sort of black sack, with short curly grey hair, which looked as if it had not been brushed or combed for years . . . she was in the best sense direct and quick . . . Never anything else but two cotton frocks; the only innovation she consented to was to wear shoes in the house.' Mrs Smuts, it seems, was liked equally by notabilities, unaccustomed to this kind of simplicity, and by ordinary soldiers, whose hands she would shake and whom she called by their Christian names.

In the first week of August the Cairo Conference, at which the Alexander–Montgomery team was appointed, was dominated by Smuts even more than the previous conferences. Lord Tedder, Chief of the Air Staff, wrote: '. . . I thought him then, and still think him, incomparably the greatest man I have ever met, possessing Churchill's versatility and vision without his vices . . . he wore an aspect of wisdom and understanding. My wife . . . said after this meeting with Smuts: "There is something Christlike about that man." ' The future Viscount Alanbrooke commented: 'One of the biggest Nature's gentlemen I have ever seen, a wonderful grasp of all things coupled with the most exceptional charm.' Dr Moran, Churchill's doctor, observed: 'While they talked I kept asking myself what kind of a man is Smuts. Is he the Henry James of South Africa? Does he think of his fellow Boers as James came to think of the American scene as perhaps a little primitive? A South African here speaks of him as "remote"; even to his own people he is a stranger. No one really knows him. . . . It is as if he had been cut off from his kind. He lives to get things done. Anyone who steps in his path is ruthlessly pushed aside . . . social

[1] She was twenty-four and Smuts seventy-one.   [2] See p. 266.
[3] 'Ouma' meant 'Granny'. Smuts was called 'Oubaas', which meant 'Old Master'.

affairs in South Africa mean little to him: he is not interested in the slums of Johannesburg. Like Winston, he is sure that there is nothing in the world which he could not do as well as anyone. . . . I am fearful that his arrogance will trip him up.' Finally, the British Prime Minister, in the best Churchillian style, wrote: 'General Smuts was imperturbable. His mind moved majestically amid the vagaries of Fortune.'[1]

Churchill was on his way to Moscow, where he was to inform Stalin that Roosevelt and he had decided to occupy French North Africa. He invited Smuts to accompany him, but Smuts declined this flattering offer, as he was anxious to return to South Africa where elections were imminent.[2] He agreed, however, to spend five weeks in London, from 14 October to 19 November. In London, on 6 November, he listened to the bells ringing in celebration of the victory of El Alamein; after the landings at Algiers he heard Churchill proclaim that this was 'the end of the beginning'; a few days earlier, addressing the two Houses of Parliament gathered in joint assembly, he had himself announced that the defensive phase of the war was over and that the Allied offensive was the beginning of the 'final act'.

No man can resist the intoxication of power or the incense of flattery. By constantly playing the role of the oracle, Smuts finally came to regard himself as endowed with a gift of prophecy. As the end of the war approached, he became increasingly obsessed with his visions of the post-war world. In the autumn of 1943 he was in London again. 'He made himself so useful,' writes Professor Walker, 'that Churchill asked him to act as Prime Minister while he himself journeyed to Teheran.' Perhaps this suggestion, which he dismissed, strengthened his sense of omniscience, a quality which he had little difficulty in attributing to himself. In any case, he considered himself well qualified to sketch the broad outlines of the world of the future. In a first speech, on 19 October, he had confined himself to generalities. A second speech, delivered on 25 November and which he himself described as 'explosive', was more precise: the greatest war in history would be the prelude to the greatest peace. What would remain at the end of the conflict? The 'Russian colossus', whose shadow would extend over the Continent; across the Altantic, the United States; and between the two the United Kingdom, poor in material resources but rich in honour and prestige, supported by a Commonwealth whose bonds would have to be tightened. The world, Smuts believed, had need of the British system, of the mission which it fulfilled among men of goodwill, of the idea of solid government and human co-operation which it embodied, the symbol of liberty and happiness amid the perils confronting humanity.

It would thus be necessary to ensure that control of a new international

[1] Tobruk had fallen six weeks earlier.
[2] See later.

organization remained in the hands of this great trinity of powers. And the other nations? Germany and Japan would have been reduced to impotence. The little democracies of Western Europe would only have to ask for admission to the British Commonwealth. And France? Alas, 'France has gone and if ever she returns, it will be a hard and long upward pull for her to emerge again. . . . She has gone in our day and perhaps for many a day.' Three years earlier Smuts had murmured: 'If God would only send them a woman, another Joan of Arc, for her men have failed her.'

The South African Prime Minister's speech prompted a question in the Commons. In Churchill's absence, Attlee replied that it had been made in a private capacity and that it in no way constituted a declaration of policy by His Majesty's government. At all events, it had the effect of giving a rare unanimity to French opinion. In occupied France, Philippe Henriot protested against the speech of 'a certain Smuts, Boer by birth and English by profession', which he described in undiplomatic terms as 'the prattle of an incorrigible and megalomaniac soldier', the 'kick of a jibbing horse'. In Algiers less caustic language was used; but, through its spokesman Henri Bonnet, the future ambassador to the United States, the National Committee of Liberation let it be known that it was 'in violent disagreement' with the views of Smuts: 'By her own deeds France is proving that she is still a great power.'

Smuts returned to London in May 1944 to attend another Imperial Conference. He tried in vain to have the planned landing in Provence (which took place on 15 August) replaced by a more ambitious operation in the Balkans, in the direction of the Danube and the Save. Then, as was his habit, he philosophized. Montgomery relates that Smuts invited him to lunch. The conversation turned to the inter-war years: '. . . when it [the 1914–18 war] was over,' said Smuts, 'we were tired and we stood back, allowing France to take first place in Europe. The result was the present war. . . . France has failed dismally.' Three weeks later, on 4 June, the eve of D-Day, Smuts found himself in the presence of General de Gaulle, in Churchill's train near London. Not surprisingly, the atmosphere was 'tense', to quote Anthony Eden. The future president of the Fifth Republic noted: 'Also here is Field-Marshal Smuts, who seems rather ill at ease.' Was this really the case? The next day Smuts was to provide yet another example of his imperturbability. When Eisenhower decided, because of the bad weather, to postpone the departure of his Armada for a day, Ernest Bevin says that 'Churchill thundered, only Smuts was calm. . . . He spoke as the philosopher he was and he made us all feel a bit ashamed of ourselves'.

Another year was to pass before victory came. Smuts began to sink into pessimism, comparing the barrenness of his soul to the drought that desolated the *veld*. The shades of the past were slowly enveloping him. He had been one of the architects of the League of Nations, but now he was to play only a minor role in the formation of the United Nations. With Roosevelt gone and Churchill swept aside, the era of grand designs seemed to him to have come to an end. He found himself back in the old harness, pulling the old cart.

In six years, even though its attention had apparently been concentrated on the war, many political changes had taken place in the Union. The government formed by Smuts in 1939 certainly gave an impression of national unity. Led by a man whose authority no one disputed, it comprised Colonel Stallard[1] and his Natal diehards, the remnants of the Labour Party led by Walter Madeley, Jan Hofmeyr, spokesman of the Cape liberals and known as 'the genius',[2] and two legendary names from Boer folklore, Deneys Reitz and Colin Steyn, both the sons of presidents of the Orange Free State. In the face of such a powerful group, the Afrikaners carried little weight. Some heeded the call to arms; 'the parades and the prospects of adventures in the mysterious wilds of Africa proved irresistible', writes Professor Kruger; in this way they escaped the grip of political passions. For the rest, there were many questions to be answered. Should they forget wounds that were still fresh and try to strengthen the Union born thirty years earlier? Did not circumstances now provide an opportunity to revive the alluring dream of independence? By siding with the Empire, were they not betraying their ancestors? By adopting the opposite position, were they not in danger of associating themselves with trends that had no real roots in their country?

The choice would have been less difficult if the Nationalist Party had had an undisputed leader. The ageing Hertzog (he was seventy-three in 1939) now found his authority tottering. For several weeks after the declaration of war, Malan and he were reconciled; but the truce was not of a kind likely to last. Malan was posing as the champion of the future; against the hopes which he held out, Hertzog could offer only memories. In January 1940 Hertzog tabled a motion in favour of an immediate peace; he did not mince his words: 'South Africa's participation in the war is the greatest blunder and most fatal mistake ever made by a responsible government. . . . South Africa has been reduced to a hanger-on of Britain, to a vassal state.' Replying, Smuts went as far as to say that listening to him was like reading a chapter of *Mein Kampf*, a view which the Assembly endorsed by 82 votes to 59. Hertzog returned to the attack in August; this time he reproached Britain for not having considered the peace proposals put forward by Hitler after the defeat of France. In a violent debate Smuts called his former commando comrade a 'hands-upper'— forty years earlier this had been the worst insult one Boer could address

---

[1] See p. 274.
[2] The 'genius' had become a 'Rhodes Scholar' at the age of sixteen. His appearance attracted comment: 'He was a strange little man who should have been a parson not a politician', observed one writer. 'He always looked as if he had slept in his clothes.'

to another. The government's policy was then approved by the same majority as in January.

In the course of 1940 attempts were made to bring the followers of General Hertzog and Dr Malan together in a re-united National Party. Dr Malan and his followers placed great emphasis on the ideal of achieving a republican form of government for South Africa, moreover an independent republic divorced from the British Crown. Although Hertzog also favoured the republican ideal, he expressed a number of qualifications and reservations. The result was that the majority of delegates attending the inaugural meeting of the new National Party in the Free State rejected a draft constitution proposed by Hertzog. Hertzog regarded this as a vote of no-confidence; he retired from politics to his farm, where he died in 1942.

At this same time various trends of an extremely complex nature were helping to undermine Afrikaner unity. A small but determined minority was advocating direct action. Smuts had expected this; as soon as war broke out he had persuaded Parliament, in spite of violent opposition, to grant him special powers. It had been decided, in particular, that all firearms must be handed over to the government. To part with their rifles, the symbols of their independence, was a great sacrifice for the descendants of the *voortrekkers*, a sacrifice which many refused to make and to which the rest consented only with the utmost reluctance. Acts of sabotage were committed: telegraph lines were cut, electrical installations and post offices were blown up, and attempts were made to derail military convoys. These excesses were more sensational than damaging, and no one was killed. But they provided the government with an excuse for repression. Smuts did not resort to the extreme measures of 1922.[1] This time there was no open rebellion to justify death sentences. However, special courts were set up, and the 'traitors'—or so they were called— were interned in camps whose very existence was enough to bring unhappy memories to the survivors of the Boer War.

Two associations, while disowning these sporadic acts of terrorism, sought to exploit the uneasiness felt by so many Afrikaners. Pirow made himself the leader of the group which advocated the 'New Order', a symbolic and conveniently vague name. He proposed to apply the theories of Salazar to South Africa; but, either because he misunderstood them, or because he was only using them as a screen, he soon found himself closer to the ideas of Hitler than to those of the Portuguese dictator. The other movement, the *Ossewabrandwag*, had originally associated itself with strictly cultural aims; under its picturesque title, which meant 'Sentinel of the Ox-wagon', it had been founded in 1938[2] in memory of the Great Trek. After 1939 one of its leaders, Dr Hans van Rensburg, gave it a military orientation. It did not conceal its pro-German sentiments, and its members fervently hoped for a German victory.

[1] See pp. 264–5.   [2] See pp. 278–9.

As the war entered its fourth year the Afrikaners found themselves in an agonizing situation, torn asunder by divisive forces which showed every sign of becoming more marked. Some dreamed of an authoritarian republic like the Transvaal of old; others succumbed to an ill-digested form of National Socialism; a third group advocated the abolition of all parties; some clung to the memory of Hertzog; finally, there were those —the majority—who could see farther than the immediate situation and who realized that they would only be able to achieve their ideal within the framework of a parliamentary democracy. Smuts thus approached the elections of 1943 with a light heart. At the age of seventy-three, he was still in full possession of his faculties. 'The ice-blue of his remarkable eyes was as glacial, or remote, or contemptuous of emotion as ever. He stood very erect, slightly shrunken, but quite unbowed.'

The poll took place on 7 July. Once again, Smuts emerged victorious. With its allies in the Labour and Dominion parties, and being able to count on the support of the two Independents and the three members representing the natives, the government party numbered 110 seats in all. The Opposition had won only 43 constituencies, and the government majority had risen to 67, which was 54 more than the majority that had opted for entering the war.

A closer look at these figures, however, gave the Nationalists good reason for satisfaction. They had obtained 36 per cent of the total vote and won 2 seats. Even more important, their party was united again. Neither the *Ossewabrandwag* nor the 'New Order' had dared to put forward candidates, and those who had stood for the Afrikaner Party had all been defeated. 'Purified' or otherwise, the Nationalist Party was rid of its rivals. Fifty years earlier, the Afrikaners had rallied round Kruger; then had come Botha, Hertzog, and now Malan, a man of less wide-ranging abilities than his predecessors, but inspired none the less by the same relentless determination to which the Boers had owed their survival.

In 1944 a by-election provoked much comment: in a constituency represented by a member of the cabinet, the Opposition won an easy victory. Smuts admitted that his party had suffered a bad defeat, but his confidence remained unshaken. To all appearances he was right: when the war ended, he still dominated his adversaries; above all, he still enjoyed a prestige to which no other South African could lay claim. But the pedestal from which he looked down so scornfully was now made of clay.

25

Apartheid and Republic

It was during the fifteen years following the Second World War that South Africa assumed its present form. Consequently, in attempting to analyse this period, objectivity is of the utmost importance. There were two main developments during these years: the Afrikaners, finally establishing themselves in power, made it their policy to settle the racial question through the separate development of the white and non-white groups and, at the same time, entrenched finally the independence of the country by way of adopting a republican constitution.

The three years during which Smuts remained in power after the end of the war contributed little to his reputation. Perhaps, after a lifetime spanning three-quarters of a century, his faculties of statesmanship were becoming enfeebled. Perhaps, accustomed as he had been to handling international problems, he found domestic matters uninteresting. Whatever the reason, he proved incapable of finding any kind of solution to the problem which overshadowed all others. The statisticians were hardly reassuring: as early as 1921 they had predicted that, by 1970, the Union would comprise 3,650,000 Whites and 12 million Blacks. Smuts would merely raise his arms in the air without offering any suggestions: 'What can one do about it when (as Isie[1] says) the Lord himself made the mistake of creating colour?' If anyone happened to refer in his presence to the often agonizing consequences of the influx of Bantu into the industrial centres, his reaction was equally negative: 'You might as well try to sweep the ocean back with a broom!' His native policy was limited to the appointment of a commission of inquiry, the continued prohibition of strikes, and minimizing the role of the so-called Representative Council which, on its foundation in 1936, had seemed to offer some grounds for hope.[2]

The Indians did not allow Smuts to take refuge in this sort of passive attitude, and in 1946 he was obliged to undertake a general review of their situation. Their numbers had steadily increased to an estimated total of 228,000, and they had settled themselves in nearly every part of Natal where, though denied civil rights, they were free to start businesses and

[1] Mrs Smuts. [2] See p. 277.

buy land. In 1943, taking advantage of the war, the government had tried a temporary solution: rights already acquired would continue in existence for another two years, but no new settlers would be admitted. When this makeshift arrangement expired it was replaced by a compromise: the Asians would elect three White representatives to the House of Assembly, though on a separate electoral roll; they would have two representatives in the Senate (one elected, the other appointed); and they would have two seats on Natal's Provincial Council. To offset this political concession, their right to acquire estate would be subject to numerous conditions. This was giving with one hand and taking away with the other, and caused more antagonism than satisfaction. The Natal Conservatives, the Nationalists and a few members of the Labour Party, still jealous of the privileges of race, bitterly opposed the plan. The Indians, for their part, saw it as 'a diabolic attempt to strangulate the Indians economically and degrade them socially'. As a mark of its disapproval, India broke off trading relations with the Union.

Smuts's authority was too great for Parliament to reject his proposals. Nevertheless, his popularity was certainly not enhanced. At the end of the war he had been the victim of a double defection: Stallard's 'diehards', on the Right, the Dominion Party, and Madeley's Labour group, on the Left, left the government coalition. The government majority, however, remained undisputed; moreover, as in 1924, the Prime Minister found it difficult to conceive of the possibility of a personal defeat. Causes of discontent were not lacking. According to Professor Krüger, the Smuts administration now proved as incapable as it had been twenty years earlier. Only Hofmeyr was competent to exercise ministerial responsibility; but, since his liberal ideas had made him the *bête noire* of the Afrikaners, his intelligence was more of a liability than an asset to his party. The Nationalists had plenty of easy targets: the housing shortage, the slowness with which war industries were being reconverted, and the difficulties which the demobilized troops were having in finding work. Furthermore, the war had aroused currents of feeling which were slow to subside. Many Afrikaners were still wondering what advantage their country had derived from its participation. Had they not allowed themselves to be drawn into the most futile of ventures by the very people whom, forty years earlier, they had regarded as their deadly enemies? A semi-secret society, the *Broerderbond*—which was denounced, inevitably, by its opponents, as 'fascist'—fanned the flames of their rancour. For an even greater number of people, memories of this kind were accompanied by a feeling of uneasiness, even fear, at the Blacks' low but irresistible infiltration of every sector of economic life.

It was therefore in an atmosphere of considerable tension that the electors presented themselves, on 26 May 1948, for the five-yearly ballot prescribed by the constitution. The result confounded the prophets. The Nationalist Party gained 27 seats; the United Party lost 24 and Labour 3;

the 2 Independents and the 7 Conservatives from Natal were eliminated, and Havenga's Afrikaner Party returned with 9 seats. If this latter group were added to the 70 Nationalists, Malan now enjoyed a majority of 8 votes.[1] The defeated United Party could not believe its eyes. 'It seemed inconceivable that the pygmies in the Union would reject Smuts', wrote Senator Nicholls. 'Hofmeyr lost the election; nothing else. . . . The sole determining issue was the colour question, aided, of course, by the continued propaganda of the Broerderbond teachers and predicants. . . . The simple believed that their daughters might have to marry black men.' Smuts himself is said to have attributed his defeat to 'the poisonous fumes of apartheid'.

The word apartheid, destined to assume such a tremendous significance, was at this time almost unknown. The linguists have traced its first appearance to a newspaper article of March 1943; Malan used the term, it appears, in Parliament at the beginning of the following year; it is to be found again in a report of a commission of 1947; but, at the time when it was blamed for the United Party's defeat, it was still so rare that it did not feature in an Afrikaans dictionary published a year later. Apartheid means simply 'separateness'. It is a pity that South Africans did not stick to this unpretentious word, instead of adopting the grandiose term apartheid which has done their cause such great harm. Nowadays, having at last realized this, they speak only of 'separate development', a much more realistic and dynamic expression.

If the word apartheid was new, the idea which it was intended to express was not. The separation of Whites and Blacks was a goal which had been pursued at many stages of the country's history. At the very outset van Riebeeck had attempted something of the kind. Then Plettenberg thought he had found the ideal line of demarcation in the Fish river. The British governors simply carried on the tradition of their Dutch predecessors, and to retrace their numerous experiments would be merely to repeat much that has already been said. For a long time, moreover, military objectives took precedence over racial considerations. A century of Kaffir and Zulu wars left little room for peaceful solutions. The Boers were men of simple ideas: the master–servant hierarchy seemed to them to provide the only satisfactory solution, one to which they adhered with their customary rigidity, both in the Transvaal and in the Free State. The British South Africans proved more flexible—or perhaps one might say more hypocritical: they granted 'non-Europeans' the vote, but made this privilege subject to so many conditions that only a few thousand in the Cape Province, and practically no one in Natal, actually enjoyed the franchise.

The then British Government (the Liberal Party) simply transferred all responsibility for the political welfare of their former Black colonists to the White community of the new Union. The racial problem thus

[1] 79 against the United Party's 65 plus the 6 Labour members.

remained unsolved when the Union was formed. In 1913, admittedly, the first legislation was introduced to designate 'reserves' where the Blacks would become their own masters. But this timid attempt at a national native policy did little to help matters. The 1914–18 war then had a twofold effect on the situation: it postponed the application of a solution; and, at the same time, by precipitating industrialization and thus making Bantu labour indispensable, it made the coexistence of Blacks and Whites in the industrial centres a necessity. 'We have felt more and more that if we are to solve our native question it is useless to try to govern black and white in the same system, to subject them to the same institutions of government and legislation', said General Smuts at a speech in London on 22 May 1917. 'They are different not only in colour but in minds and in political capacity, and their political institutions should be different, while always proceeding on the basis of self-government. One very important Commission had, I believe, Sir Godfrey Lagden as chairman, and as a result of that and other Commissions we have now legislation before the Parliament of the Union in which an attempt is made to put into shape these ideas I am talking of, and to create all over South Africa, wherever there are any considerable native communities, independent self-governing institutions for them.

'Instead of mixing up black and white in the old haphazard way, which instead of lifting up the black, degraded the white, we are now trying to lay down a policy of keeping them apart as much as possible in our institutions. In land ownership, settlement and forms of government we are trying to keep them apart, and in that way laying down in outline a general policy which it may take a hundred years to work out, but which in the end may be the solution of our native problem. Thus in South Africa you will have in the long run large areas cultivated by blacks and governed by blacks, where they will look after themselves in all their forms of living and development, while in the rest of the country you will have white communities, which will govern themselves separately according to the accepted European principles. The natives will, of course, be free to go and to work in the white areas, but as far as possible the administration of white and black areas will be separated, and such that each will be satisfied and developed according to its own proper lines. This is the attempt which we are making now in South Africa to solve the juxtaposition of white and black in the same country, and although the principles underlying our legislation could not be considered in any way axiomatic, I am sure that we are groping towards the right lines, which may in the end tend to be the solution of the most difficult problem confronting us.' This was later described as one of Smuts's most notable—and prophetic—speeches on South Africa's racial problem.

It was not until nearly twenty years later, in 1936, that Hertzog succeeded in obtaining approval for the programme of legislation described in an earlier chapter. Then, as in 1914, international events diverted

South Africa's attention. Smuts was content to philosophize. If 1948 is a date of unique significance in South African history, this is because in that year, for better or for worse, an approach to the racial problem was made which was founded on one fundamental principle, a principle which the Afrikaners, with their rather terrifying logic, then proceeded to push to its limits.

For the first time since 1910 the South African cabinet was not presided over by a general. For the first time, also, all its members were of Boer descent and, although bilingual, conducted their deliberations solely in Afrikaans. The Prime Minister, Malan, serious of personality and with a highly developed sense of purpose, was not a man to compromise. He knew what he wanted and proved it.

Three months had not passed since the general election when an argument began in Parliament. The commission appointed by Smuts had delivered its report at the beginning of the year. Its conclusions were cautious: it did not condemn segregation, but at the same time did not see this as a solution; it deplored the influx of Blacks into the urban centres without indicating how this movement should be halted; and it pointed to the overpopulation of the reserves without recommending either their abolition or their extension. Nevertheless, the leader of the United Party regarded the documents as the most thorough inquiry ever made into the problem; and he accused his victors of having used the word *apartheid* like a secret weapon, without defining its meaning. His criticisms induced the Prime Minister to explain his position more clearly on 16 August in a speech which deserves attention, for the ideas expressed in it have remained the Nationalists' charter to this day.

First, the Bantu. According to Malan, the Nationalists' policy was not, as had often been claimed, a policy of repression. He said that justice could exist on both sides of the line of demarcation; in the Black areas it was proposed to develop institutions that would allow the Blacks to enjoy a broad measure of autonomy and preserve their national character. On the other hand, they would need a permit to reside in the European zones. Why should this be considered unjust? The Whites, after all, would be subject to a similar status in the Black territories. Finally—a point of fundamental importance—the Blacks would no longer be represented in Parliament.[1] As for the Coloureds, they would retain the vote, but on a separate electoral roll. The 'Indians' (the word, though not actually used, was understood) were considered unassimilable and consequently were to lose even the limited privileges they had been granted in 1946.

The point of view of the Opposition, though it sought to appear different, was very similar to that of the government. Smuts himself

[1] In 1936 it had been decided that, of the 153 members of the Assembly, three (Whites) would represent the Cape Blacks.

said: 'Equal rights never has been our policy.... Our policy has been European paramountcy.... We never had any truck with equal rights. ... We have always stood and we stand for social and residential separation . . . and for the avoidance of all racial mixtures.' The United Party, maintained Smuts, recognized a *de facto* situation: in South Africa there existed not only differences of colour, but also differences of race. The reserves should be developed, made as pleasant as possible and provided with all the necessary amenities. But it should be recognized that 60 per cent of the blacks were living among the White population: they were an integral element of the European zones, and there must be no question of their being expelled. All that could be done was to improve their living conditions. 'We have to go in for what has been called the satellite village, the parallel township—not *apartheid* in that sense but side by side in our urban areas, in our industrial areas, you will have Blacks and Whites not far from each other, both playing their part in the economic activities and forming the economic structure of this country.'

When Malan inquired if this was not just another kind of *apartheid*, Smuts admitted that all the parties had much in common on this subject, a comment that brought laughter from his opponents. Realizing the weakness of his position, he devoted the rest of his speech to the arguments for maintaining the few civil rights already accorded to the Blacks and Coloureds. He saw no reason to go back on what had been done; on the contrary, it should be improved upon gradually. This was the great task awaiting South Africa's rulers. Perhaps they would not succeed—in that case it would be they who would suffer. Every effort must be made to create an atmosphere of mutual understanding and to avoid bitterness.

The argument continued for two months without either side modifying its position. Obviously, Smuts and the United Party were hoping that a pragmatic approach would eventually produce a solution for a problem the gravity of which they did not deny, but which they dared not face squarely. The mood of the Nationalists was quite different. Convinced that they were the interpreters of the divine will, dogmatic to the marrow, logical to the last degree, dispensing generosity and justice in the most high-handed and arbitrary manner, they were swept along by a relentless will-power, impelled by a whirlwind of burning passions. They were to spend the next ten years constructing the legislative framework within which they could put their theories into practice.

In 1948 a first decision was taken which, though in itself of minor importance, was an example of what later came to be called 'petty *apartheid*', an expression coined by the critics of the government. Hitherto, the Cape Peninsula had been the only part of the Union where Whites and non-Whites travelled in the same railway carriages. This exception was now abolished. More ominously, the Indians were deprived of the vote. In 1949 the devaluation of the currency improved the financial situation;

the death of Smuts, two years after that of Hofmeyr, left the Opposition even weaker; the arrival in Parliament of six representatives from South-West Africa strengthened Malan's position; and the prohibition of mixed marriages was extended to unions between Europeans and Coloureds. In 1950 developments gathered momentum. Sexual relations between Whites and non-Whites became punishable under criminal law. Then three measures of far-reaching significance were passed. The first provided for the classification of the entire population into four groups: Whites, Coloureds, Blacks and Asians; everyone would be given a document indicating to which category he or she belonged. The second law, the Group Areas Act, decreed that each category would be assigned its own residential areas, with compulsory transfers of population if necessary. The third law prohibited Communism, of which it gave a definition both precise and elastic: 'Communism as the doctrine of Marxist socialism as expounded by Lenin or Trotsky, the Comintern or the Cominfern, or, still more broadly, as any related form of that doctrine expounded or advocated in the Union for the promotion of the fundamental principles of that doctrine'. As a result, the Communist Party was dissolved[1] and 'suspect' publications were suppressed. The implementation of all these measures was entrusted to a new Minister for Bantu Affairs, Dr Verwoerd, known for the orthodoxy of his opinions. At the same time, a Nationalist of a similar complexion, Ernst Jansen, became Governor-General. Finally, Professor F. R. Tomlinson was placed in charge of a new inquiry into the development of the Black Homelands.

In 1951 a law on the administration of the Black Homelands decreed that Bantu councils could be organized, under government supervision, on a local, regional and territorial basis. Its purpose was declared to be twofold: to restore the authority of the tribal chiefs, and gradually to lead the Black population groups to self-government.

The status of the Coloureds, a question which had been shelved for the past three years, was raised again. According to the constitution of 1909, however, it could be modified only by a two-thirds majority of the Assembly and the Senate in joint session. The issue provoked strong feelings. In the Cape Province a petition drawn up on behalf of the Coloureds gathered 100,000 signatures. Ex-servicemen and women organized a protest group which held demonstration marches with burning torches and thus became known as the 'Torch Commando'; they submitted hostile resolutions to Parliament, but to no avail. The government argued that, since the Statute of Westminster, Parliament had been sovereign; consequently, it claimed, the terms of the Act of Union could not be invoked against it. A Bill was introduced by the Minister of the Interior, Dr T. E. Dönges, whereby the Coloureds would only be allowed to vote on separate electoral rolls: four Whites chosen by

[1] A Communist who had been elected to the Assembly in the Cape in 1948 was expelled.

them would represent them in the Assembly; and a Senator, also White and appointed by the governor-general, would be their spokesman in the Upper House. As a first step towards self-government, a Council of eleven members—eight elected in the Cape, and three appointed in the Transvaal, Natal and the Free State—was to be endowed with certain consultative powers under the chairmanship of a Commissioner for Coloured Affairs. Then events took a dramatic turn: the Supreme Court, displaying the independence that has always characterized South African justice, quashed the law.

Malan, though momentarily disconcerted, was not discouraged. In 1952 an extraordinary procedure was adopted: the two houses of Parliament, sitting as a High Court, were empowered to annul the decisions of the Supreme Court by a majority vote: so that they could be applied to the Court's recent judgement, these provisions were made retroactive. The Supreme Court, refusing to give way, declared the government's action to be unconstitutional, and the government was compelled to accept its verdict.

In 1953 another general election took place. The Nationalists reaffirmed their programme, putting themselves forward as the champions of the territorial and political separation of the Blacks, the separation of Whites and non-Whites, generally and in residential districts in particular, and also, as far as possible, in the industrial centres. They won a crushing victory: including the 9 representatives of the former Afrikaner Party, they had previously numbered 79; they now returned with 94 seats. The United Party was reduced to 57 and Labour to 5. The Opposition, moreover, was disintegrating. Within a year three different splinter groups had been formed: on the Left, two members joined the Liberal Party which, under the inspiration of the distinguished writer Alan Paton, was daring to demand equality of political rights; on the Right, the Union Federal Party, founded by Senator Nicholls, adopted federalism as its platform; and, a little later, seven of Smuts's faithful disciples, who had little confidence in his successor, J. G. N. Strauss, called themselves Conservatives and professed their willingness to support the government.

All this did not, however, give Malan the two-thirds majority he needed, a fact of which he was reminded during the winter of 1953: three times he presented his Bill to a joint session of the two houses of Parliament, and on each occasion he was defeated. He consoled himself by legislating on labour disputes; a conciliation procedure was adopted, but Black trade unions were not recognized. Most important of all, he placed the education of Blacks under the control of the Union government, which meant the end of the majority of missionary schools.

Dr Verwoerd, then Minister of Bantu Development, stated that this was in line with developments in White education which once was clerical education and gradually was freed from the church; this was a universal trend. The Government felt that it would not be possible to establish a national education policy linked to the general development programme for the Bantu peoples. The result of the Act was that the control and administration at the local level passed to the representatives of the Black communities, and in fact thousands of Black parents and local leaders subsequently becoming directly involved in education for the first time.

Finally, various forms of 'petty *apartheid*' were introduced: separate entrances were provided in railway stations and post offices, Whites and non-Whites were forbidden to sit on the same benches in public gardens or on adjacent seats on public transport, special hospitals and even beaches were set aside for non-Whites, all in an attempt to impose the principle of racial separation.

The Blacks congregated round Johannesburg in settlements which represented the shanty-town at its worst. The government decided to undertake a massive urban renewal project in respect of the shanty-towns. In what the South Africans claim to be one of the largest housing projects in the Southern Hemisphere, more than 300,000 houses for Blacks were built in urban-industrial areas in the period 1952–1972. Although the houses were rather modest, they at least offered decent accommodation. Schools, recreation centres, shopping centres, churches, community halls, clinics and post offices were provided. All persons over the age of sixteen had to be able at all times to produce an identity book and proof of their work contract.

Malan, who was over eighty, decided to retire. His natural successor appeared to be Havenga, the longest-serving of his ministers, but the Right wing of the Nationalist Party preferred one of his colleagues, the 'lion of Waterberg', Johannes Strijdom, who enjoyed great popularity with the militants. Strijdom was a man of the earth, simple and uncompromising, a powerful personality and an eloquent orator, utterly devoted to the republican ideal. One historian decribes him as 'brisk, stocky, easily moved to wrath and given to hitting back hard, but patently sincere and honest . . . a great inner source of strength like his friend Verwoerd, a devout *Dopper*,[1] married to the daughter of a parson, utterly convinced of the 'divine mission' of the Afrikaners.

The new Prime Minister was certainly not an opportunist. Hitherto, *apartheid* had been presented as a necessity, and also as a means by which to lead the Blacks to a higher level of civilization. Strijdom insisted on White hegemony from the outset. His first speech was revealing, for he was not afraid to speak his mind: 'Call it paramountcy, *baaskap*[2] or what you will, it is still domination . . . the only way the Whites can maintain domination is by withholding the vote from the Blacks. . . . To suggest that the white man can maintain leadership purely on the grounds of his greater competency is unrealistic. . . . We are not hostile [here again, he

---

[1] The strictest of the Calvinist sects.

[2] 'Supremacy of the Master'—a term which, with *apartheid*, has done the greatest damage to South Africa's reputation.

meant what he said].... Separation is in the interest of both.' In the opinion of Professor Kruger, Strijdom's intentions were pure, but his choice of tactics unwise.

In 1955 the government announced its intention of establishing industrial centres near the borders of the Black Homelands in the hope of dissuading the Blacks from moving to the White areas. Even more important, it now seemed determined to settle the question of the Coloureds once and for all. Two Bills were introduced: the first raised the number of judges in the Court of Appeal from 6 to 11; the second envisaged a Senate of 89 members instead of 48. The judiciary and the legislature, thus prudently reinforced, would obviously prove more tractable. The Opposition accused the government of acting in an arbitrary manner; but it was reminded that there was no other way out of the impasse for which it was held responsible, and the two Bills were passed.

Nineteen fifty-six was a year of intense legislative activity. In February—after eight years of argument—the political status of the Coloureds was fixed along the lines envisaged by Malan. Henceforth, 45,000 Coloureds would be able to vote only for their own representatives, on a separate roll. A month later the Tomlinson Commission delivered its report of 4,000 pages, 17 volumes and 63 maps. It recommended that the areas historically settled and occupied by the Black tribes be consolidated as much as possible, resulting in some seven Black Homelands, coinciding with the major Black ethnic groups.[1] Here, it suggested, 60 per cent of the native population would be located; it recognized, however, that by the end of the twentieth century the number of Bantu living outside the Homelands would still be higher than the total White population; the Commission also forecast that it would be necessary to spend over a £100 million on developing the Homelands. A series of laws was then passed: one reaffirmed the principle that certain skilled jobs should be reserved for the Whites; a second gave the Governor-General powers over all Blacks, even in the Cape Province where they had enjoyed a special status; a third provided for the expulsion to the Homelands of any Bantu considered a threat to peace and order; a fourth curbed the Blacks' rights of property-ownership; and a fifth tightened control of the private schools. In October, finally, the enlarged Supreme Court recognized the constitutionality of the law defining the political status of the Coloureds.

Nineteen fifty-seven saw a pause, even a slight setback, in the progress of Nationalist policy. When the government proposed to prohibit Blacks from taking part in religious services without the approval of the local authorities, the churches, led by the Catholics and Anglicans, protested

[1] The total area would have been equivalent to 45 per cent of the Union's territory; the report envisaged the inclusion in the 'homelands' of Bechuanaland, Basutoland and Swaziland, which were still under British control. See pp. 326–7.

violently; even certain leaders in the Dutch Reformed Church entertained misgivings. Verwoerd produced a compromise: the prohibition of mixed religious services would be at the discretion of the government, which meant that it would be the exception rather than the rule.

The five-year period was approaching its end, and in April 1958 a general election was held. The Nationalists enjoyed yet another triumph, increasing their number from 94 to 103; Labour lost its 5 seats, and the United Party was reduced from 57 to 53, in spite of the qualities of its new leader, Sir de Villiers Graaff, who was himself defeated in his constituency near Cape Town. None of the three Liberal candidates was elected.

Shortly afterwards, confident that youth was on its side, the government lowered the voting age from twenty-one to eighteen.

Strijdom, who had been in poor health, died on 24 August. Three candidates began manœuvring for the succession, and Verwoerd won on the second ballot.

It is time to pause to consider this man, the most hated and most admired figure of modern South Africa. Hendrik Frensch Verwoerd was born in Amsterdam in 1901. He was two years old when his parents emigrated to the Cape. He completed his studies at the university of Stellenbosch, one of the political hotbeds of Afrikaner nationalism. Then he travelled, to Germany, Holland and the United States. On his return he taught psychology and sociology. Then he was attracted to journalism, and in 1937 he became editor of the *Transvaal*, the official organ of the Transvaal Nationalist Party. During the war he sided against the British and the Jews. In 1948 his orthodoxy was rewarded with a seat in the Senate.

Verwoerd was one of those Dutchmen who are born to defy nature and destiny. He was a giant in stature, over six feet tall and heavy in proportion, weighing fourteen stone. With a rosy complexion, fair hair which was easily dishevelled and blue eyes whose expression could suddenly harden, courteous in his manners but not given to making concessions, quiet by nature and yet capable of fits of anger, imperturbable except sometimes when contradicted, indefatigably hard-working— 'he could outwork half a dozen normal strong healthy men,' complained his secretary—he was, above all, a staunch optimist endowed with a will that was all the less inclined to give way because it was nurtured by an unswerving faith.

It is worth referring to a few of his speeches, for they are revealing. On 16 December 1958 (he had just become Prime Minister): Verwoerd declared: 'Perhaps it was meant for us to have been planted here at the southern point of Africa within the crisis area, so that from this resistance group might emanate the victory whereby all that has been built since the days of Christ may be maintained for the good of all mankind.' In a speech on 9 April 1960,[1] he proclaimed his deep faith in the South African

[1] The day on which an attempt was made on his life. See p. 307.

people and his conviction that all the intelligence and courage they had inherited would help them to build a greater South Africa in the next fifty years. In another speech, on 31 May 1960, he uttered a warning that if, in times of danger, South Africans allowed themselves to pursue a selfish course in order to preserve material advantages, if they were not ready, like their ancestors, to sacrifice all for freedom, then they would lose everything. What they needed above all was the will to resist. Mutual understanding between Afrikaners and English-speaking South Africans was therefore essential: South Africa must be not only a union of provinces, but a union of hearts.

To what purpose? In order to survive, but also to ensure the peaceful and orderly development of the other racial groups. There were only two alternatives: either a multi-racial society in which, sooner or later, the force of numbers would submerge the Whites; or a separation of the races which would permit their coexistence—in other words, to each his own domain, the Blacks in their 'homelands' where the Whites' interests would be subordinate, the Whites in the rest of the country where the Blacks would still come to work, but in a temporary capacity. And later? 1978 was, for some unknown reason, the date by which Verwoerd thought that the flow of Blacks back into the Homelands would be sufficiently advanced for at least a relative equilibrium to have been established. Then, he announced on 19 March 1961, he could foresee a South African commonwealth in which Blacks and Whites would co-operate in separate and independent states, a policy of good neighbourliness founded on two principles: political independence and economic interdependence —the same system which Europe was in the process of attempting. And eventually, who knows, perhaps even a golden age? On 16 October 1952 Verwoerd had made a speech in which he promised that if, by the year 2052, South Africans had remained faithful to the spirit of their ancestors, the future of their country would have been assured. By then the Blacks would have attained a high degree of civilization and would remember, with gratitude, what the Europeans had done for them.

One should not smile at such a vision. To deny Verwoerd's idealism would be completely to misunderstand his personality; to distort his ideas, as has been done, to the point of comparing him to Hitler reduces the man to a caricature. Human nature is not such a simple thing. Stubborn, tough, single-minded and convinced that he was an instrument of Providence, Verwoerd had a ruthless quality about him. According to the *Natal Witness*, his principles were frightening and even his virtues dangerous. This doctrinarian revealed an extraordinary capacity for action. He was in a sense like the Crusaders of old, ready to commit all manner of deeds to propagate their faith.

Nineteen fifty-nine brought a further series of measures. The reserves were grouped into eight units, each under a commissioner-general— White, of course—who would be responsible for guiding them towards self-government. The reasoning was simple: from the moment that the Blacks began to exercise their own political rights within these territories, there was no longer any reason why they should enjoy such rights elsewhere; consequently, the three seats allocated to them in the Assembly since 1936 were abolished. At the same time, the plan to promote frontier industries on the borders of the Homelands, near enough for Bantu labourers to be able to commute between the Homelands and the factories, was finally put into action. A corporation, the Bantu Development Corporation, was formed to encourage investment, particularly in the Transkei. Finally, to complete the programme, universities for 'non-Europeans' were created: two for the Blacks, one for the Coloureds and one for the Indians. The government explained its motives: it wished to give non-Whites an opportunity to develop themselves, to be what they were, and not to be cut off from their national roots.

Nineteen-sixty was the year of the referendum, which will be discussed later; it was also the year of violent upheavals. In ten years the broad lines of the policy of separate development had thus been fixed; what followed were merely variations in the manner of its implementation. Under Verwoerd the rather defensive attitude to race relations, as reflected in Malan and Strijdom's policy of *apartheid*, was replaced with a more dynamic positive approach—the government began to talk in terms of separate development of the races. The new approach catered for the national aspirations of the Black groups while at the same time safeguarding the future of the Whites. An attempt will be made in another chapter[1] to deliver a judgement on this unique approach. In the preceding pages it has been the author's intention to confine himself to facts, with as little comment as possible. Yet the picture would be incomplete without some mention of the resistance which such rigorous decisions, applied so swiftly, could not fail to provoke.

First, it must be observed that the number of Whites who took part in anti-government demonstrations was tiny. Such incidents, moreover, remained sporadic, except in 1952 and 1960 when an attempt was made to extend their scope and give them a revolutionary character.

In 1949 violence erupted in Durban, serving as a reminder to those inclined to forget that the racial question was not simply a matter of Whites against 'the others': the Zulu clashed with the Indians, and the police had to intervene. The Zulu casualties were 83 dead and about 1,100 wounded, while the Indians had 53 dead and 768 wounded.

The following year the Blacks in the Rand held a protest march which resulted in a dozen or so casualties. An attempted general strike collapsed in 1951, but in a series of clashes eighteen Blacks lost their lives. This time the African National Congress[2] tried an ultimatum (the worst possible attitude to adopt with the Afrikaners), demanding the repeal of six

---

[1] See Chapter 27.   [2] See p. 251.

discriminatory laws which, it claimed, were an insult to the African people; otherwise it would urge the Blacks to take further action. Malan, not surprisingly, refused to give way. Then, in 1952, there began a campaign of passive resistance which lasted four months; the natives went about without passes, used railway carriages reserved for Whites, ignored the curfew, displayed banners bearing the colours of African independence (black, yellow and green) and deliberately had themselves arrested—after a few weeks there were 8,000 under arrest. This exercise in non-violence was followed by riots. There were disturbances at Kimberley, Port Elizabeth and East London. In this last-named town the worst instincts of savagery were suddenly reawakened when a Catholic nun, whose life had been devoted to caring for the Blacks, was burnt alive in her car; her body was then mutilated and her flesh is said to have been eaten by her executioners.

During the next four years the government strengthened its police force, increased penalties and obtained authority from Parliament to declare martial law should it judge it necessary. The large mass of Blacks remained passive, but a majority of agitators tried to exploit the situation. In 1955 a 'Congress of the People', attended by some three thousand delegates from various organizations, adopted a 'Freedom Charter'.

The Nationalists' concern with Communist activities was shown when in 1956 the Soviet consulate was closed down. On the internal scene, 56 people were arrested at the end of 1956 on charges of high treason. A few White women organized a form of silent protest: they could be seen standing in front of the Parliament or ministry buildings, wearing a black sash as a sign of mourning (they later became known as the Black Sash movement). In particular the arrest of the new president of the African National Congress, Albert Luthuli, created a stir, for Luthuli was a convinced Christian and a self-proclaimed apostle of non-violence (though his admirers have somewhat exaggerated his stature).[1] He stayed in prison for nine months, as did four-fifths of the suspects; the others were released in 1961.

For about eighteen months relative calm prevailed; then, in 1959, new outbreaks of violence occurred. There were riots in Pretoria, near Durban, at Pietermaritzburg, near Cape Town, and also at Windhoek in South-West Africa; 18 Blacks were killed and 154 wounded. Luthuli was placed under house-arrest in Natal. Following the classic pattern, he was now overshadowed by the extremists who, under the leadership of Robert Sobukwe, founded the Pan African Congress, which made no attempt to conceal its revolutionary objectives.

If Verwoerd and his colleagues had not been men of great determination, they would doubtless not have been capable of resisting the buffetings to which they were subjected during the tragic year of 1960.

[1] 'This man in any sane country should have been Prime Minister or perhaps Minister of Education,' wrote one admiring lady.

On 24 January 1960, nine policemen were murdered at Cato Manor, near Durban. On 21 March the most famous drama of that year took place. As far as it is possible to reconstruct them from the tangle of contradictory accounts, the facts appear to have been as follows: Sobukwe had asked his followers to go to the police stations and hand in their identity books as an act of protest. At Sharpeville, in the Transvaal, the Blacks carried out these instructions *en masse*. How many and in what frame of mind they were is difficult to establish: according to some eye-witnesses there were 3,000 to 4,000 in a good humour and unarmed; according to the official report they numbered 15,000 to 20,000 and were carrying arms. The police claimed that two shots came from the crowd. The security forces comprised a mere 75 men. It seems to have been proved that no order to fire was given. However—perhaps in panic, prompted by the memory of the murders at Durban—the police did open fire with rifles, and the crowd surged back in terror. The firing must have continued for some time, for it was found that most of the casualties had been hit in the back. In all there were 69 dead and 80 wounded. A commission of inquiry, which was appointed immediately, was probably too far from the truth when it condemned the organizers of the demonstration for irresponsibility but, at the same time, declared that the behaviour of the crowd did not justify opening fire.

The Sharpeville affair assumed international dimensions. The State U.S. Department published, rather hastily, a strongly-worded official communiqué. The United Nations Security Council passed, by nine votes to nil (with two abstentions—Britain and France), a resolution declaring that the events in Sharpeville had endangered world peace. Nehru likened the Nationalists to the Nazis. The Prime Minister of New Zealand proposed a minute's silence. In Norway, flags flew at half-mast. The Canadian and British Parliaments moved motions of disapproval. To complete the picture, Luthuli was later awarded the Nobel Peace Prize.

Calm was not restored without some difficulty. On 21 March, the day of the Sharpeville incident, there was a demonstration of Blacks at Langa, near Cape Town, resulting in 2 dead and 49 wounded. On the 25th all meetings were prohibited. On the 28th Blacks began burning their identity books, and martial law was proclaimed in eighty districts. On the 30th, 30,000 Blacks marched quietly through the streets of Cape Town and Langa, where they lived, was encircled by the army; a hundred or so arrests were made. On 1 April, 3 Blacks were killed in Durban. On 9 April a man of unbalanced mind, whose action had nothing to do with racial problems, tried to assassinate the Prime Minister.[1] Finally, on 31 August, the state of emergency was lifted, and life resumed its normal course.

For well over a decade and a half—until a series of violent riots occurred in many non-white townships in 1976—South Africa experienced no upheaval of a similar magnitude to that of Sharpeville.

[1] Verwoerd's activities were interrupted for only a few weeks.

After the defeat of 1870, Gambetta's dictum concerning Alsace–
Lorraine was often quoted in France: 'One must always think about it,
but never speak of it.' This was largely the attitude of the Nationalists
with regard to a Republic when they came to power in 1948. Clearly,
the time was not yet ripe to broach the subject. To refer to it openly
would have aroused strong feelings among those South Africans still
loyal to the Crown; but to forget all about it would have offended the
majority of Afrikaners, who were inclined to regard total sovereignty as
the symbol of their final freedom.

Within thirteen years this goal had been attained, by that same relentless
will which was applied to the implementation of *apartheid*.

Although still a member of the Commonwealth, South Africa was
determined nevertheless to remain the master of its foreign policy. The
South African air force contributed to the Berlin airlift of 1948; it also
played a part, at the request of the UN, though rather more reluctantly,
in the Korean War; on the other hand, the Union hastened to proclaim
its neutrality at the same time as the Anglo-French intervention at Suez
in 1956. Its determination to have complete control over its national
defences was also made clear at this same period by the transfer to the
South African navy of the strategic naval base of Simonstown, near the
Cape, which, like Gibraltar, Malta and Singapore, had been the pride of
the British navy.

The Afrikaners like to have things cut and dried. Few relics of the past
irritated them so much as their dual status as citizens of the Union and
subjects of the British monarch. Strijdom had expressed their feelings
well: 'As long as we have the position that one section of the population
stands with both feet on African soil while the other section unfortunately
gives its loyalty and love not to South Africa but to Great Britain . . . so
long as we shall fail to have unity here.' Less than a year after the fall of
Smuts this dual status was abolished. In 1949 a South African citizenship
exclusive of all other allegiances was created. The only privilege left to
bearers of British passports was the right to become naturalized a year
earlier than other foreigners. With similar haste the government freed
itself from the last remaining constitutional links with Britain: in 1950 the
Crown lost its right to refer a decision of the South African government
to the Privy Council; and in 1953 it was unequivocally established that,
if the titles of Queen of Great Britain and Queen of South Africa
continued to be borne by the British monarch, there no longer existed
between them the slightest legal correlation.

One consequence of this last measure was that the existence side by side
of two flags and two anthems became a mere fiction.[1] In 1957 the Union
Jack disappeared and 'God Save the Queen' finally made way for 'Die
Stem van Suid-Afrika'—a symbolic step of the utmost importance which

[1] See pp. 268–9 and 278.

was followed by countless other small gestures, sometimes unimportant in themselves but none the less significant. When, for example, the traditional toast to the sovereign was drunk, the members of the government, as they rose, would forget to take their glasses in their hands. Their wives were equally forgetful: gradually they stopped curtsying to the Crown's representative. On one occasion, the Prime Minister made his excuses for not being able to be present at a banquet in honour of the royal birthday; on another occasion, the South African High Commissioner in London refused to attend the laying of a plaque commemorating the victims of the war. Even in their manner of dress the Afrikaners took the opportunity to express their sentiments. The army adopted a uniform different from that of the British troops; the Governor-General preferred a tailcoat to the British ceremonial dress, and at his receptions some of the women guests appeared in traditional costumes, The accession to the throne of a young and charming queen did little to bring warmth to official functions, which government ministers tried to avoid. When they did attend they would utter hardly more than two English words—'The Queen!'—as the toast was proposed, in an icy atmosphere, at the end of the dinner; the rest of the time they would speak only in Afrikaans.

Such behaviour would have been affected, if not misplaced, had it not been founded in popular feelings. In 1949 the inauguration of a monument to the *voortrekkers* was attended by 200,000 people; Smuts appealed for a reconciliation, but was feebly applauded; a speaker who addressed the crowd in English was received in silence. Every Day of the Covenant (16 December 1838) the atmosphere was always the same: the thousands of participants, some of them in national costume, spoke only in Afrikaans. In 1954 further proof was given of the power still exercised by the past. For a long time it had been proposed to move a statue of Kruger into the centre of Pretoria, to a site worthy of it. The town council, ill-disposed towards the Nationalists, had opposed the idea, but under pressure from the government it was forced to give way—such was the enthusiasm of Afrikaners for their glorious heroes.

Verwoerd crossed the Rubicon on 20 January 1960. On that day, to the great surprise of the Opposition which had not expected anything of the kind, he announced his intention of holding a referendum to decide whether South Africa should become a Republic. He took care to point out that he did not intend that South Africa should leave the Commonwealth. Then he added that he was not making the issue a question of confidence: 'I do not even want the question of confidence or no confidence to be linked with it. The Government is in power and will remain in power.'

His announcement created a great stir. It found all the more favourable a response when, a fortnight later on 3 February, Mr Macmillan, who was on a private visit, addressed the two houses of the Union Parliament in a speech that angered many. He had not informed his hosts of the text of his speech, which Verwoerd's secretary described as 'ten pages of silken, smooth-tongued and calculated insult, of cautiously phrased, remorseless condemnation of the country whose guest he was'. When one reads the British Prime Minister's words today, at an interval of fifteen years, such indignation rings a little melodramatic. What must have stung his audience was Macmillan's preaching tone. It was not in very good taste to pose as a redresser of wrongs. One phrase in particular was to become famous: 'The wind of change is blowing through this continent.' Macmillan was telling his audience that national feeling was a fact and should be accepted as such.

'Verwoerd did not move. . . . His face was inscrutable.' Listening to Macmillan speak of 'wind', his thoughts must have turned to the storms which he was having to face and which were to culminate six weeks later in Sharpeville. But he made no direct reference to these events. He said that South Africa's policies were not at variance with the new direction in Africa. The tendency for nations to become independent did not only mean being just to the Black man of Africa but also being just to the White man of Africa. He added that it was South Africa's policy to provide the Black population groups with the fullest rights and opportunities in those areas which their forefathers had settled; equally, South Africa believed that the White man was entitled to possess the same rights and opportunities in the areas he had settled. His reply was courteous, with a touch of irony. 'May you find in Great Britain fewer problems to deal with than we unfortunately have to meet!'

This incident, coupled with the racial problem, swelled the ranks of those in favour of a Republic. The government obviously thought that the battle was already won, for without the slightest compunction it had van Riebeeck's effigy substituted for that of Queen Elizabeth on the medals struck to commemorate the fiftieth anniversary of the Union (31 May 1960). It was not mistaken. The referendum took place on 5 October. South-West Africa was allowed to take part. It was an indication of the extraordinary interest shown in the issue that 90·73 per cent of the electorate turned out to vote: 850,458, or 52·85 per cent, voted 'yes'; 775,878, or 47·49 per cent said 'no'. The Republic obtained the largest majority in the Free State; it only just won in the Cape Province and was rejected by more than three to one in Natal.[1]

[1] Territories	Yes	No
Free State	110,171	33,438
Transvaal	406,632	325,041
Cape Province	271,418	269,784
Natal	42,299	135,598
South-West Africa	19,938	12,017

Two days later Verwoerd delivered a message to the people, congratulating them on the peaceful manner in which the ballot had taken place; he invited Afrikaners and English-speaking South Africans to unite around the national ideal and, above all, he urged them to stop thinking of the past: an epoch had come to an end and now the hand of the future was beckoning to them; by looking back they could certainly find inspiration, but they could not stand still. Verwoerd insisted that South Africa sought only friends and did not want enemies; it desired happiness and progress for all, White and Black, but this could be achieved only by the methods appropriate to South Africa. The anniversary of the birth of Kruger, on 10 October, provided the Prime Minister with the opportunity for a speech which, by improvisation, was at times raised to the level of eloquence. Once again he appealed for mutual understanding and trust: South Africans must be not only the creators of a unified nation, but the servants of the civilization and the religion from which they had issued and which they represented in this country, the anchor to which Christianity could cling; difficult times lay ahead, but there was no reason to be afraid; and when, on occasion, the Whites felt themselves encircled by a vast Black Africa, they must remember how few in number were the *voortrekkers* when they, too, were similarly encircled.

The Republic was proclaimed in Pretoria, in the shadow of Kruger's statue, on 10 May 1961. The constitution of 1909 remained in force with only one modification: the replacement of the governor-general by a state president, elected by the two houses of Parliament for seven years. The first holder of this office, Mr C. R. Swart (who had been governor-general for the past year), took up his post on 31 May 1961—fifty-one years after the foundation of the Union and fifty-nine years after Vereeniging.

South Africa was now fully independent; it was to retain no formal connections, not even with the old British Empire. As he had promised, Verwoerd had left for London in March with the intention of asking that the Republic be allowed to remain in the Commonwealth. The reception he received was very different from the ovations to which he was accustomed. The press displayed its hostility in cartoon. At the airport and at the Dorchester Hotel, where he was to stay, demonstrators were waiting for him with banners condemning South Africa and the colour bar and bearing inscriptions such as 'Go home, Verwoerd!', 'Remember Sharpeville, murderer!' and 'Read your Bible!' A procession of several hundred persons was organized. The Prime Ministers' Conference assembled on 8 March, four days after the arrival of the South African delegate. The 'Black Sash' movement,[1] including in its ranks Mrs Barbara Castle, later a member of the Wilson government, took up its position in front of Lancaster House where the conference was being held. India, Pakistan, Ceylon, Ghana and Nigeria, which had all become republics, had been

[1] See p. 306.

admitted into the Commonwealth unconditionally. This was not the case with the former Union of South Africa. Macmillan, acutely embarrassed, made repeated attempts at conciliation, with the support of Australia and New Zealand. Nevertheless the Afro-Asian group—somewhat strangely supported by Mr Diefenbaker, Prime Minister of Canada (where the Indians were not recognized as citizens)—proved immovable: either no more *apartheid*, or go away! The Ghanaian and Nigerian leaders were particularly eager to offer advice on good behaviour. The discussions went on for fifteen hours during a week in which the tension never slackened. On 15 March, finally realizing the futility of the situation, Verwoerd withdrew his request to remain in the Commonwealth. He emphasized that relations between the United Kingdom and the Republic would not be affected by this decision. An enthusiastic crowd of fifty to sixty thousand gave him an ecstatic welcome when he descended from the aeroplane at Johannesburg.

In October 1961 the South African Prime Minister called an early general election. The Nationalist Party gained another two seats, increasing its number to 105; the United Party was reduced from 57 to 53; the Progressive Party won its first seat, as did a phantom group called the National Union Party; and on their separate roll the Coloureds elected the four representatives to which they were entitled.

PART SEVEN

South Africa in Recent Years
1961-76

List of Dates

1962	Riot at Paarl.
	The U.N. adopts sanctions.
1963	Rivonia conspiracy.
	Self-government for the Transkei.
1964	Dr H. Muller, Minister for Foreign Affairs.
1966	General election.
	The International Court of Justice dismisses the action brought by Ethiopia and Liberia.
	Assassination of Verwoerd.
	Mr J. Vorster, Prime Minister.
1967	Professor Barnard's first heart transplant.
	Diplomatic relations established between Malawi and South Africa.
1968	Mr J. Fouché, President of the Republic.
	Partial self-government for Ovamboland and Tswanaland.
1969	The Coloured Representative Council assumes its functions.
	Partial self-government for the Southern Sotho.
	The U.N. calls on South Africa to evacuate South-West Africa.
1970	General election.
1970-1	Preliminary discussions with the other African states.
1972	President Fouché pays an official visit to Malawi.
	Dr Waldheim, Secretary-General of the United Nations, visits South-West Africa.
1973	Creation of a Consultative Council in South-West Africa.
	Tenth anniversary of the self-government of the Transkei.
	Six homelands out of eight attain self-government.
	Appointment of a commission to study the status of the Coloureds.
1974	General election.
	Portugal withdraws from its African possessions.
	Contacts renewed between South Africa and the African states.
	Mr Kaunda, president of Zambia, describes a speech by Mr Vorster as 'the voice of reason'.
	Talks on the future status of Rhodesia.

1975	Civil war in Angola.
1976	Bophuthatswana officially asks for independence.
	Soweto and other townships' disturbances.
	First meeting of cabinet council including representatives of Coloured and Indian communities.
	South-West Africa independence fixed for 1978.
	Prime Minister Vorster meets Dr Kissinger in Zürich.
	Dr Kissinger visits South Africa.
	Independence of Transkei.
	Opening of the Geneva Conference on Rhodesia.

26

Years of Tranquillity

During the next ten years or so the future of South Africa seemed to be assuming a final shape. Beyond its frontiers there lay no apparent perils, while at home it enjoyed a political continuity to which a few minor disturbances hardly posed a serious threat—all this against a background of impressive economic growth.

In retracing a past which, though so recent, can already be seen to be very different from the present, it is necessary first to consider how the Republic's neighbours evolved.

South-West Africa, over four times the area of Great Britain and with a thousand miles of coastline, was for a long time known as 'the ageless land', an ideal description of this vast territory with its mysterious past. The Namib desert, sixty miles across, with not a blade of grass or a trace of life, but only sand and yellow stones, separates the mountainous plateaux of the interior and the Atlantic seaboard. To the east another, even more enormous desert, the Kalahari, isolates the plateaux from Botswana. To the north lies a zone of plains where four-fifths of the population are concentrated; this is the only region where an occasional fall of rain solves the water problem which dominates local life. 'The story of South-West Africa's progress is in great part the story of success in the endless search for water,' writes one specialist. In the most desolate areas it sometimes does not rain for several years. It has been calculated that an ordinary dam loses 98 per cent of its water in three years of drought. Modern technology has devised some ingenious solutions, but has only partially succeeded in taking the place of nature, which is here so lacking in generosity that only three rivers flow permanently: to the south the Orange, to the north the Kunene, and to the east the Nosob. Now and again a miracle occurs. 'At dawn a wind blows from the north. The sky darkens, rent by lightning, and the water streams down. The rivers become full and pour in torrents over the deserts. . . . The seeds begin to germinate. . . . The flowers open, and their heavy scent hovers above the plateau. . . . The grass grows so tall on the roads that it becomes entangled in the radiators of cars. . . . But in a day or two the river-beds are dry again.' In this strange land, under a burning sun, 'one finds dunes that "sing", lizards with semi-transparent bodies that "swim" with their webbed feet in the shifting sands, rock-paintings of distant times, and prehistoric plants that have somehow managed to survive. As they make their way across the endless plains of the far north, the tribes still take their bearings from the stars and, when they have been to work in the south, the men bring back stones, just stones, to show to their wives and children, for such things are quite unknown out in the sands where they usually live.'

On this barren soil, near a farm with a name that would provide a useful test of memory—Otjaenemaparero—the prints of three toes of a dinosaur have been discovered. Certain wall-paintings, similar in inspiration to those of Egypt or Crete, seem to point to the existence of a human species that must have become extinct. The Bushmen and Hottentots can boast of being the oldest aborigines. These wretched tribes were persecuted by all invaders and reduced to roaming the Kalahari desert in search of sustenance. About three hundred years ago began the great migrations of the Bantu, a race whose military prowess has already been described and who, though they had no difficulty in taking possession of the territory, found it much less easy to divide it among themselves. Finally the Whites arrived—soldiers, farmers and missionaries, at first Germans, then South Africans.

According to the most recent official census (1970) the population of South-West Africa has risen to more than 762,000, including some 90,000 Whites. The Coloureds number only a little over 40,000. The large majority consists of Blacks, grouped in tribes of unequal size which are divided by greater differences than are the nations of Europe. By far the most numerous tribe, the Ovambo (353,000), lives in the north, a people of peaceful temperament, content with the pastoral existence which a soil suitable for stockraising enables them to lead. Under a system of universal suffrage their sheer weight of numbers would ensure them a position of predominance. But it is difficult to imagine the other natives, especially the Nama (about 32,000) and the Herero (over 50,000), bowing to their supremacy: the Nama because their Asiatic blood inclines them to consider themselves superior to any Black, the Herero because they are by nature reluctant to submit to any laws other than their own. The Herero are a nomad people, aristocratic, tall in stature, well-built and of noble bearing, their womenfolk carrying themselves with a haughty pride. It will be recalled how fiercely they resisted the German conquerors,[1] and today the South Africans in their turn are having to face up to the fact of their existence. They are a fanatical and uncompromising minority, transformed by favour of the United Nations into a mouthpiece of progress and liberty.

If the Second World War had not erupted, the problem of South-West Africa would no doubt have presented itself differently. As early as 1925

[1] See p. 255.

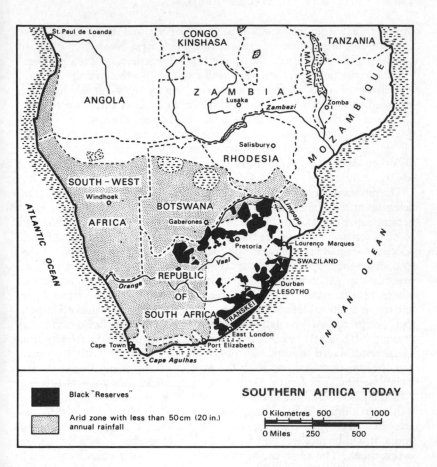

St. Paul de Loanda

CONGO
KINSHASA

TANZANIA

ANGOLA

ZAMBIA

Lusaka

Zambezi

Zomba

MALAWI

MOZAMBIQUE

SOUTH–WEST

Windhoek

BOTSWANA

Gaberones

Salisbury

RHODESIA

Limpopo

AFRICA

Pretoria

Lourenço Marques

SWAZILAND

ATLANTIC OCEAN

Vaal

REPUBLIC

Orange

OF

SOUTH AFRICA

TRANSKEI

Durban
LESOTHO

INDIAN OCEAN

East London

Cape Town

Port Elizabeth

Cape Agulhas

Black "Reserves"

Arid zone with less than 50cm (20 in.)
annual rainfall

SOUTHERN AFRICA TODAY

0 Kilometres   500   1000

0 Miles   250   500

the territory, administered by a governor assisted by a consultative Council, had been given a partly elected Legislative Assembly (white, of course); at the same time, the Union Parliament had assumed responsibility for the only question that really mattered—the natives. Pretoria was thus gradually transforming into sovereignty what initially had been intended to be no more than a mandate. In Geneva there were feeble murmurs of disapproval; in 1935 the authorities there even avoided taking any firm position on an express demand for incorporation made by the recently created Legislative Assembly. In the opinion of one historian, diplomatic discussions with a view to annexation were well advanced by 1939.

The upheavals of the next few years transformed the situation. The delegates at the United Nations, fresh from the new schools of thought, became intoxicated with words. In 1946 Smuts decided that the time had come to renew his request for the territory's incorporation into the Union. South Africa had been playing the fashionable game: the right of peoples to manage their own affairs was considered sacred, and it had made one practical application of this principle in the deserts of South-West Africa, where 242,000 natives had taken the opportunity to make their views known in a referendum: 208,850 had voted in favour of incorporation and 33,250 against (the latter included 27,950 Herero, who were still proving intractable); 57,000 nomads had taken no part in the referendum. These results failed to impress Smuts's audience; in reality, the argument was already concerned less with the problem of mandates than with the racial question. The South African delegate found his own words being turned against him. 'We declare our faith in basic human rights,' he had written in a draft of the United Nations Charter. Mrs Pandit, the Indian delegate, asked him what he was doing about it in his own country (India, it will be recalled, had found itself at loggerheads with the Union at this time).[1] The affair ended in compromise: by 37 votes to nil, with 9 abstentions, the General Assembly refused incorporation, but did not insist on the transfer to the United Nations of the rights previously exercised by the League. In 1947 and 1948 South Africa, for its part, continued to send reports on its administration of a mandate the validity of which it was disputing.

The Afrikaners do not like hybrid solutions. No sooner had Malan come to power than he decided to stop sending these reports. In New York voices were raised in protest. Then began a series of manœuvres and counter-manœuvres, discussions, arguments and votes, which would seem amusing if they had not been concerned with a matter of such gravity.

In 1949 the United Nations heard the testimony of two witnesses: a missionary, the Reverend Michael Scott, and a Herero student. Scott, having spent three weeks in South-West Africa, had acquired the reputation of an expert and had made himself the spokesman of the Herero's

[1] See pp. 293–4.

desire to be recognized as faithful disciples of Jean-Jacques Rousseau. The General Assembly had no wish to disappoint him and expressed its misgivings about the Union's racial policy; then, either because it was less sure of its case than it pretended, or because it wanted support, it sought the opinion of the International Court of Justice. The Court, after weighing the arguments for and against, came up with a judgement that was by no means clear: it recognized that South Africa was under no legal obligation to place its former mandate under the trusteeship of the United Nations, but maintained that it was bound nevertheless to furnish annual reports.

This judgement was delivered in 1950. Malan, preoccupied with the implementation of *apartheid*, ignored it. In dismay the United Nations in New York decided to form an *ad hoc* committee to make a close study of the question. For some time, however, the Korean War dominated the international scene. In 1952 the Reverend Scott reappeared; once again the General Assembly expressed its indignation and condemnation. This time South Africa recalled its principal delegate and withdrew from UNESCO, then from the Food and Agriculture Organization (FAO) and eventually (1963) from the International Labour Organization (ILO). The battle of the initials escalated: the ECA, the WHO and the ITU[1] refused to allow South African representatives to attend their meetings. This mattered little to the Nationalists, whose success at the elections of 1953 made them even more determined. In 1954 they made the final gesture: the administration of native affairs was transferred from Windhoek, the local capital, to Pretoria, which was tantamount to giving the territory the same status as the other provinces of the Union.

In New York, resolution followed resolution.[2] The Black states, weary of international impotence, then took matters into their own hands. Assembling at Addis Ababa in 1960, they resolved to submit the whole question to the International Court of Justice. Ethiopia and Liberia, the only two African members of the League of Nations at the time of its dissolution, were given the task of instituting the action. In 1961 the UN General Assembly, galvanized by this intiative, upheld by 90 votes to 1 (Portugal) and 4 abstentions (including France) the inalienable right of the peoples of South-West Africa to independence and national sovereignty. Then it sent a Filipino, Dr Carpio, and a Mexican, Dr de Alva, to Pretoria. The story of their mission is indeed a strange one. After a tour of ten days the envoys published an unexpected communiqué in which they went as far as to say that the situation in South-West Africa in no way constituted a threat to peace, and that they had found no indication of genocide nor any evidence of political prisoners. In New York there was great excitement. An inquiry was ordered at which

---

[1] Economic Commission for Africa, World Health Organization and International Telecommunications Union.
[2] Professor Cadoux has counted 73 resolutions passed between 1946 and 1966.

Dr Carpio said that he had been the victim of a plot: he had been forced into giving his signature while ill, and it was claimed, though without proof, that he had been drugged.

This comic episode did not halt proceedings. In 1962, by eight votes to seven, the Court declared itself competent to judge the issue. South Africa, which had been pleading inadmissibility, now affirmed its readiness to argue its case in full. The plaintiffs were represented by an American attorney assisted by another American and a Liberian. The defence team, composed of jurists, advocates and diplomats, all South Africans, accomplished a remarkable feat. Ethiopia and Liberia were accusing the Republic of oppressing and exploiting the peoples of South-West Africa. [1] After three years, however, they were forced to drop this first allegation, for which they substituted another, based on the practice of *apartheid*: in their opinion the policy of separate development was a 'flagrant violation' of the law of non-discrimination as established by the international community; South Africa had betrayed the 'sacred trust' conferred upon it by the mandate of 1919.

The Court announced its decision on 8 July 1966. It made no judgement on the main issue, but confined itself to ruling that the plaintiffs could not be considered 'to have established any legal right or interest appertaining to them in the subject-matter of their claims'; consequently, their case was dismissed. The voting had been equally divided: six in favour of the defendants (Australia, Poland, Greece, United Kingdom, Italy and France) and six against (Nationalist China, Russia, Japan, the United States, Mexico and Senegal); the casting vote of the Australian judge, the president of the Court, decided the verdict. The reaction was one of total stupefaction. Only recently the symbol of justice, the Court became overnight the image of iniquity. The United Nations refused to accept its ruling, and on 27 October, by an overwhelming majority, the General Assembly decided that the mandate was no longer valid and then proceeded to set up another committee, whose task would be to study how the United Nations could gain effective control of the territory in question, in UN circles henceforth known as Namibia.

Until 1974 no further headway was made. Informal contacts between the General Secretariat of the United Nations and South Africa did not bring much progress; neither did terrorist operations directed from Zambia. Pretoria, undaunted, stuck to the argument that 'separate development' was applicable in South-West Africa as elsewhere in the Union. In 1973 two tribes, the Ovambo and the Kavanga, were organized as 'homelands' and given a Legislative Council elected on a limited franchise. [2]

[1] In particular by the presence of large armed forces. Mr Marshall, an American historian and a specialist in military matters who agreed to give evidence, maintained that South-West Africa was less militarized than any other territory of similar size.

[2] It is interesting to note that, in the first case, 1,300 electors out of 50,000 took part in the ballot, while in the second case the proportion of voters was as high as 66 per cent.

Angola, adjoining South-West Africa over a distance of some seven hundred miles, was still held by Portugal.

This enormous territory, roughly six times the size of Britain, has had a varied history. The Portuguese landed there in 1482, ten years before the discovery of America. For nearly four hundred years they never thought to explore the interior. It was not until 1836 that the first colonists arrived, but from this time onwards immigration was continuous, reinforced towards the end of the nineteenth century by some South African trekkers who decided to settle there.

Before the Portuguese departure, Angola had a very small population, about five million, divided into four and a half million Blacks, 400,000 Whites and 100,000 mulattoes. It is an underdeveloped country (personal income is one-sixth that in South Africa), a land of woods and savannahs whose main resources for a long time remained timber, a few cereals, fishing and sugar-cane. Deposits of diamonds, iron ore, copper, zinc, phosphates and petroleum, possibly in large quantities, now point to a slow transformation of the economy which is already evident in the development of the capital, Luanda, which has a population of half a million. The importance of Angola lies, however, less in its possibilities for the future as in its geographical situation. Bordered to the north and north-east by Congo-Brazzaville and Zaire, and to the east by Zambia, the territory was, like Rhodesia and Mozambique, an outpost of southern Africa.

The racial policies of the two neighbours were totally different, at least in theory. The Portuguese have never glorified either *baaskap*[1] or *apartheid* In fact, the question did not arise for them in the same way as for the Boers; until about a hundred years ago their contacts with the natives hardly extended beyond the coastal region. As soon as he came to power, Salazar, who had a fondness for political philosophy, attempted to justify by doctrine what was a *de facto* situation. There was much talk of *dignidad*, of a 'Pan-Lusitanian community, united by the spiritual links peculiar to Portuguese culture', the 'concept of identity', 'human brotherhood,' 'equality before the law deriving from the equality of merit, which is characteristic of progressive societies'—all epitomized by the incessantly repeated formula: 'One state, one race, one faith, one civilization.'

The Portuguese were more pragmatic than the Afrikaners. Although they discarded the hated word 'colony' and replaced it with 'province', in the hope of giving their overseas territories the same status as the mother-country, differences nevertheless existed between their 'provinces' in Europe and those in Africa. Until 1961 these differences were reflected in a hierarchy of status which in practice resulted in a discrimination condemned in principle. Two categories of inhabitant were recognized: on the one hand, the mass of the 'natives' (a 'native' was 'a person of the Negro race who has not sufficiently evolved to be governed by the same laws as a Portuguese citizen' and who therefore remained subject to

[1] See p. 301.

tribal customs); and on the other, a minority of Whites, mulattoes and *assimilados*. This latter term was defined with precision: to be an *assimilado* a person had to be over eighteen, speak Portuguese, be earning enough for his family, be of good character, and to have performed his military service. These conditions must have been highly restrictive, since it is estimated that in 1952 only about thirty thousand Blacks were regarded as fulfilling them.

Was it the slowness of this 'assimilation' that in 1961 induced Salazar to take a decision in the Roman manner? Like Caracalla extending citizenship to the inhabitants of the Empire in 212, he decided that differences should no longer be allowed to exist among those subject to Portuguese sovereignty. Whites, mulattoes, Blacks and those of yellow race, in Africa and Asia as well as in Portugal itself, would enjoy equal rights. The principle of a multi-racial society was thus recognized. But, since universal suffrage was far from occupying in Salazar's mind the place it holds in democratic thinking, the risk of Black supremacy was slight. In fact, the governors of the Portuguese colonies remained the puppets of Lisbon, and, though they were now assisted by a consultative assembly where the races were intermingled, the mass of the natives had little chance of determining their own destinies. Professor Spence seems to have summed up the situation well when he writes: 'The policies of Portugal and South Africa differ in principle, if not in their practical implication from the non-white point of view.'

That the two countries were viewed with equal disfavour by the African states is evident from the constant tension that existed along the frontiers of the Portuguese 'provinces'. To the east the situation was the same as in the west and the problems identical. Mozambique is only three-fifths the size of Angola, but is more densely populated (eight million, including 300,000 Whites and mulattoes). The land is fertile and undercultivated (according to the latest statistics, the average income is half that in Angola). Cotton, tea, coffee and rice are grown, while sugarcane and coconut plantations are particularly flourishing. Gold and coal have long been the chief resources of the subsoil, but explorations for petroleum are also producing good results. Mozambique's contiguity with South Africa, Swaziland and Rhodesia guaranteed it peace to the south and west. Tanzania and Zambia, on the other hand, proved unreliable neighbours; along the frontier their guerrillas, trained in Dar-es-Salaam, maintained a constant threat to security, and consequently, as in Angola, Portugal was forced to keep a large number of troops there.

Rhodesia, bordering to the east on Mozambique, to the south on South Africa and Botswana, linked with South-West Africa by the narrow band of land commonly known as the 'Caprivi Strip'[1] and bounded to the

[1] This corridor, extending horizontally to the centre of the continent, was acquired in 1890 by Germany, which hoped thereby to link the South-West to its colony of Tanganyika on the Indian Ocean. Caprivi was the German chancellor at the time.

north by Zambia, seemed rather more secure. Its 250,000 Whites did not appear to be afraid of the 4,200,000 Blacks.

It will be recalled that in 1922[1] a referendum had rejected incorporation into the Union. Perhaps this was a missed opportunity for both countries. Whatever the case may be, the former territory of Cecil Rhodes's British South Africa Company became a Crown Colony with a system of representative government. The British here practised the same policy as in Natal: in theory everyone, Blacks as well as Whites, received the vote, but in practice only 453 Africans had their names on the electoral rolls in 1951. It was not a question of *apartheid*. The coming to power of the Nationalists had merely deepened the mistrust with which the colonists in Salisbury regarded South Africa, and they were therefore tempted to look for stability to the north rather than to the south. In 1952, at the instigation of the British government, Southern Rhodesia joined with Nyasaland and Northern Rhodesia to form the Central African Federation, with a Parliament composed of thirty-six Whites and nine Blacks, the latter elected on the basis of three per territory. This experiment delighted the optimists. The future Prime Minister of the new state described it as the 'eighth dominion'; no less enthusiastically, a member of the Churchill government saw it as 'a great new bastion of British power'.

Alas, ten years later the 'bastion' had crumbled. This association with the Whites held little appeal for the Blacks who, seeing Black states emerging all around them, began to ask themselves why they too should not be entitled to independence. This they were granted in 1964. A change of status seemed to call for a change of name, and so Northern Rhodesia became Zambia and Nyasaland Malawi. As will be seen later, their presidents, Kenneth Kaunda and Hastings Banda, were to give their respective countries a very different political orientation.

What was Southern Rhodesia to do? With tiny Gambia, it remained one of the only two Crown Colonies left in Africa. It now entered into a dialogue with Britain which could only lead to an impasse. London bolstered its shaky authority with a slogan, NIBMAR ('No independence before majority rule'),[2] which it considered an essential condition for an agreement. Salisbury was determined not to accept this formula, except in a future so distant as to be meaningless. It therefore retaliated with another slogan, UDI ('Unilateral Declaration of Independence'), proclaiming the independence of the country on 11 November 1965, regardless of the Crown. The subsequent course of events is well known. The Wilson government, supported by the United Nations, resorted to the invariably unsatisfactory tactic of economic sanctions, too weak to be effective, but sufficiently annoying to create discontent. A series of meetings brought no result, except to reveal the determination of the Rhodesian

[1] See p. 265.
[2] The principle already adopted by the other two former members of the Federation.

326 A HISTORY OF SOUTH AFRICA

Prime Minister, Ian Smith. At the end of 1969 all pretence was finally abandoned when the effective independence of Rhodesia was confirmed by a referendum.

South Africa and Rhodesia were at least agreed on the need for friendly relations with the new Black states which were their neighbours or formed enclaves within their territories.

Bechuanaland, Basutoland and Swaziland, it will be recalled, were under British control at the time of Union. Bechuanaland had come under British administration in 1895, to satisfy Rhodes's desire for a route lying outside the frontiers of the Transvaal and which would thus guarantee communication between the Cape and the north of the continent. At this date the Union Jack had been flying over Basutoland for twenty-seven years. Swaziland, for its part, had been the object of bitter argument; providing access to the Indian Ocean, its strategic value was considerable. After falling into the Transvaal's sphere of influence around 1875, it had recovered its independence a few years later. It became a protectorate of the Transvaal in 1894, but naturally changed its 'protector' after the Boer War.

From 1910 the three territories were administered jointly by the British High Commissioner in South Africa. The Act of Union had envisaged their incorporation. Botha raised the question, unsuccessfully, in 1913 and again at the Peace Conference. Hertzog, between the wars, had no greater luck. In 1943 Smuts reminded Britain of the services rendered by South African troops, but the argument fell on deaf ears. In 1948 an incident provided Malan with an opportunity to intervene even more vigorously: a native chief of Bechuanaland, Seretse Khama, married an Englishwoman, and in Pretoria this was seen as an indirect assault on *apartheid*, which the South African government was just beginning to put into practice. When Malan raised the matter before Parliament, London considered it advisable to make a gesture by forbidding the young couple to return to Bechuanaland for five years. On the main issue, however, South Africa obtained no relaxation of Britain's attitude. Sometimes it was told that the time was not 'ripe', sometimes that the local inhabitants would have to be consulted and that it would be impossible to organize a genuine referendum. In 1956, forty-three years after Botha, Strijdom made yet another fruitless approach.

On this issue, as on many others, his successor, Verwoerd, showed that he saw further than the immediate present. It seemed to him that it would be in his country's interests to prove itself able to maintain good relations with Black states, rather than to enlarge its area and, in so doing, increase the natives' numerical preponderance. He was thus endorsing in advance the independence of the three territories. Britain hesitated, for little had been done to prepare the 'protected' countries for sovereignty. On 30 September 1966, however, Bechuanaland—renamed Botswana, under the presidency of Seretse Khama—became independent. On 4 October it was the turn of Basutoland, henceforth Lesotho, which preserved a monarchic form under King Moshoeshoe II, but entrusted the real power to Chief Jonathan. Swaziland, which kept its old name, was given similar status on 6 September 1968.

The two kingdoms and the republic, which are in a customs and monetary union with South Africa,[1] are very different from one another, but all derive the greater or a substantial part of their revenues from the wages earned by their numerous nationals employed in the industrial centres of the Transvaal (South Africa).

Botswana is the giant, occupying some 300,000 square miles, partly desert to the south and west. On the high plateaux lies some good stock-raising land, but crop-growing is almost non-existent (according to Professor Cadoux, only 5 per cent of the total area is cultivated). As everywhere in southern Africa, the subsoil seems to promise riches for the future. The statistics indicate that 4,000 Whites, 3,500 Coloureds, 400 Asians and 568,000 Blacks inhabit this unprivileged land. From Pretoria the Republic of South Africa pays close attention to what happens there, for the strategic position of Botswana, as a crossroads between South-West Africa, Zambia and Rhodesia, is a matter of no little importance to both friends and enemies.

Of the former protectorates Lesotho has, by virtue of its history and geography, the strongest national identity. The shadow of the great Moshesh, who brought its people together and built them into a nation, still protects it from disintegration. It is isolated from the rest of the world by high mountains (over 10,000 feet in the Drakensberg) and deep valleys over which a mist often hovers. The soil is poor and subject to erosion by violent rains. The construction of dams and hydro-electric installations has made it possible, however, to expect a development of stockraising and crop-growing. The only possible mineral resource would appear to be diamonds. A population of 976,000, including several thousand Whites and Coloureds, inhabits this alluring and mysterious land whose area is less than 10,000 square miles.

Swaziland is even smaller—barely 7,000 square miles—but more densely populated, with 385,000 Blacks and 10,000 Whites. Some excellent pasture-land, sugar-cane and maize plantations, and especially the existence of gold, coal, iron ore, asbestos and manganese, give the country a standard of living 50 per cent higher than that of Lesotho.

Even before these three territories became independent, their existence posed the problem of South Africa's relations with the rest of the continent.

In this respect the policy of Pretoria has changed rapidly over the past twenty years. The beginnings of decolonization took the Nationalists by

[1] South Africa pays them a quota of the custom duties—something which, under British rule, the Cape and Natal never conceded to the Boer Republics.

surprise. Malan dreamed of an African NATO in which the European powers would join with South Africa to check the progress of Communism. But meetings in Dakar and Nairobi achieved nothing, except to prove that Britain and France, reluctant enough to fight to preserve their own empires, were even less inclined to do so if it was a question of defending another's possessions. In 1955 Strijdom had the sense to see that this policy was leading nowhere.[1] He started talking of 'coexistence' and 'technical cooperation', but they were seen as a Machiavellian ploy, and the African states replied by ostracizing the Republic.

Practical necessities often succeed in triumphing over conflicts of ideas. Under Verwoerd, South Africa began to show a much greater flexibility in its relations with the new Black nations. Mr Vorster followed this example and went even further. In May 1967, shortly after coming to power, he made his position known, declaring that it was not his intention to build Rome in a day, but, slowly and systematically, for the benefit of all, to establish relations with South Africa's neighbours and also further north where, he maintained, healthier ideas prevailed. This policy would naturally be based on mutual respect, equal sovereignty and non-intervention in the internal affairs of each state. Vorster justified his attitude with some basic ideas the soundness of which would be difficult to dispute. It was in the Republic's interests, he argued, to be surrounded by stable and contented neighbours; and South Africa could do much for their development, for it was in a better position than any other to supply them with goods, capital and technicians. Thus, by trading contacts, Black and White states would get to know one another; in this way they would discover that they were all Africans and had an equal right to a place on the continent. History had, moreover, assigned South Africa a special role—a concept which Mr Vorster explained, in November 1968, in true Afrikaner tradition. South Africans, he declared, would not shirk their destiny: they faced a challenge, and it was inconceivable that they should fail in their mission. Africa had been good to them, and it was their duty to give back to the continent a part of what they had received.

In Hastings Banda, the colourful president of Malawi, Mr Vorster found a man perfectly capable of understanding the implications of what he was saying. Born in 1905 near the valley of the Zambezi, Hastings Banda received a technical education in the old missionary school of Lovedale in the eastern Cape Province. His first employment was as a workman in the gold-mines, but he had higher ambitions. He went to the United States, studied medicine at Nashville and then practised in England. In 1958 he was back in his own country. He is a man of imposing personality and, when Nyasaland became independent, he had no difficulty in having himself elected as its Prime Minister. Dr Banda's views are exactly the opposite of those held by some of his Black colleagues, whose overriding purpose is to strangle South Africa by boycott. His aim, on the other hand, is to influence its doctrines by frequent contacts. His colleagues would readily have recourse to violence if they had the means at their disposal, but Dr Banda places greater faith in the weapon of persuasion. He does not mince his words: in his eyes the resolutions of the United Nations are merely empty threats which will not cause the walls of *apartheid* to crumble; this goal, he believes, can be achieved only by patience and regular exchanges of views. He has taken his reasoning to its logical conclusion. Trading exchanges are not, in his opinion, enough. He once prophesied that there would be those who would howl and gnash their teeth like hyenas, and there was indeed a great uproar when, in 1967, he decided to establish diplomatic relations with the country cursed by his fellow-Blacks. A representative of the South African government received his envoys in Cape Town at the legendary Mount Nelson Hotel, that bastion of Victorian Britain. At first they talked in private apartments, then they appeared in the hotel's crowded dining-room; an eye-witness tells how a stupefied silence greeted their entrance, and how the buzz of conversation then resumed as if nothing had happened.

No other Black leader went quite as far as Dr Banda. But contacts continued to multiply: with countries in French-speaking Africa such as the Ivory Coast, Gabon and (for a while) Madagascar, with Mauritius (where trade links are still strong) and even with that arch-enemy of South Africa, Ghana, during the brief Premiership of Dr Kofi Busia. Then, perhaps because the South Africans had missed their opportunity, perhaps because the Black leaders, smitten with scruples, had decided it would be wise to go no further, it suddenly seemed that hardly anything remained of this fragile scaffolding. In reality, the foundations were still intact and the work of building on them was to continue.[1]

The internal evolution of South Africa has furnished abundant proof of this instinct for continuity.

In 1966 Verwoerd was assassinated by a Greek whom the courts pronounced mentally unbalanced. It might be expected that the sudden disappearance of a man who had become the symbol of *apartheid* would have been followed by a period of instability, but this was not so: a week was enough for Mr Johannes Vorster to be appointed his successor.[2] The electorate had, moreover, shown this same desire for stability six months earlier when the Nationalist Party, already victorious at the elections of 1953, 1958 and 1961, had won 126 constituencies out of 166. Even more important was the fact that a great many English-speaking South Africans had voted for it. Admittedly, the Nationalists lost 9 seats in 1970,[3] but

[1] See p. 342.
[2] Mr Vorster had been interned during the war for his hostility to South African participation. He became Minister of Justice in 1961. He was fifty-one.
[3] In 1969 Dr Albert Hertzog, son of the famous general, defected and founded a breakaway Nationalist Party which advocated the unconditional hegemony of the Afrikaners and even proposed to confine English to the status of a 'second language'. He failed to get any of his candidates elected.

they regained 6 of these in 1974. Their hold is even stronger at local level: in the Provincial Councils they occupy 142 seats out of 179 (160 out of 187 if one includes those in South-West Africa).

Thus, between 1961 and 1976, when the black township riots and disturbances occurred, there were no political upheavals, nor any serious social disturbances; in 15 years there had been only one attempt at insurrection and only one conspiracy of any significance.

In 1962, in the little town of Paarl, near Cape Town, it seemed briefly that the experience of Sharpeville was about to be repeated. A riot broke out during the night of 21 November, shop-windows were smashed, petrol-pumps set on fire, two Whites murdered and three seriously wounded; the intervention of the police resulted in the deaths of six Blacks and more than three hundred arrests. Perhaps this incident persuaded the leaders of the revolutionary movements that they would get nowhere without concerted action, for they then hatched a plot to seize the country by a military operation in which commandos would be landed at strategic points; an organization called 'Spear of the Nation' would supply the shock-troops.The conspirators' meeting-place was an apparently highly respectable farm near Rivonia, one of the residential suburbs of Johannesburg. The police became suspicious, and luck was on their side: in a raid on 11 July 1963 they were able to seize documents containing damning evidence, and three Whites, two Indians and six Blacks were arrested. Four managed to escape in mysterious circumstances; one was acquitted, another sentenced to life imprisonment and the rest were given less severe sentences.

This planned campaign of subversion had been preceded by isolated acts of sabotage at the instigation of the 'Pogo', an extremist group that claimed membership of the Pan African Congress, dissolved in 1961.[1] Since then, until the dramatic and fateful township riots of 1976, peace had been disturbed only by sporadic agitation on the part of extreme Left-wing students. In 1967 the funeral of Luthuli passed without incident; in this same year the government felt able to release Robert Sobukwe[2] from prison, restricting him to the district of Kimberley where he is practising as a lawyer.

Such a state of affairs raises a number of questions, to which opponents and supporters of the government offer conflicting answers. The critics maintain that 'peace' reigns in South Africa in the same way that it reigned in Warsaw, and it is true that security laws leave nothing to chance. The South African government, on the other hand, claim that drastic measures are necessary to counteract threats and acts of terrorism and subversion. A law passed in 1963 and amended in 1965 authorizes the government to hold a 'witness' (the word was rather loosely interpreted) in preventive detention for 170 days, which applies to all races. The authorities can also restrict the movements and activities of indi-

[1] See pp. 306–7.   [2] See p. 306.

viduals through measures such as so-called 'house arrest' or 'banning'.[1] There is no recourse to a court of law in respect of the application of this severe penalty, which applies to both Whites and Blacks and which is generally imposed for periods of five years, with the possibility of renewal. The 'banned' person is obliged to stay at his home, except when presenting himself to the police once a week; he may be forbidden any visits, even by his lawyer if the latter is also a 'banned' person.

It has been all the easier for propaganda to label South Africa a 'police state' because, in most cases, the government considers it unnecessary to indicate the reasons for its decisions. Moreover, it can hardly be denied that the South African police is not composed of choir-boys. Yet what impartial observer could honestly maintain that the country lies under a cloud of oppression? The author is not qualified to assess the quality of the secret services, said to be excellent and omnipresent. Certainly it would be hard to be more 'secret'. Of a visible police force there was until recently hardly a trace, either in the Black townships or in the White residential districts: the occasional patrol-car, a few traffic policemen as the offices close, helmeted motor-cyclists as can be seen in any part of the world, and that is all. To represent the Republic of South Africa as a concentration camp with the 'non-Europeans' enclosed behind barbed wire is as far from the truth as the idyllic picture painted by some South Africans for the benefit of foreigners.

The prevailing atmosphere of calm can, perhaps, be explained by reasons more complex than simple images of Paradise or Hell. It is important not to underestimate the prestige that still, to some extent, attaches to the 'White Man', who is seen as capable of doing much good (and also much evil). Furthermore, the optimists are certainly not wrong when they point out that the standard of living enjoyed by the Blacks is higher in South Africa than in the rest of Black Africa, and that the Indians of Natal are more fortunate than their fellow-Indians of the Ganges. Wealth is transmitted by osmosis. Does not the extraordinary expansion of post-war years explain, at least partly, why they had been such astonishingly peaceful years?

South Africa's mineral riches are fabulous: a diamond and platinum production the value of which is unequalled anywhere; 75 per cent of the gold of the non-Communist world; 90 per cent of Africa's coal; second place in the economic honours list for manganese, antimony, chromium, lithium, uranium and zircon; third place for asbestos and titanium; fifth place for nickel; and in the first ten for cadmium, beryl, bismuth and magnesium. There is only one important gap: as yet South Africa produces no petroleum.

Such a superabundance of the raw materials essential to the modern economy was bound to lead to a rapid growth of production. A few

[1] The word can give rise to misunderstanding, as it does not mean banishment (only foreigners are deported).

figures will suffice: from 1950 to 1960 the gross national product increased at an annual rate of 5·2 per cent and from 1960 to 1970 it exceeded 6 per cent.

The policy of 'separate development', facilitated by this regular increase of wealth, directed by a strong and stable government, hated by some and idealized by others, has been pursued slowly but surely during the past decade.

27

Towards a New South Africa

It is now time to outline the situation prevailing today. The events of 1974 only serve to heighten the contrast between the uncertainty which seems to shroud South Africa's future and its present all-round vitality. Until 1974, protected to the north by the Portuguese colonies and Rhodesia, and in other directions by the sea, the Republic felt secure, as if enclosed within a fortress. Now, however, it finds itself facing the march of Black nationalism at close range.

No one in Pretoria imagined that Portugal would hold on to its empire indefinitely, but few persons anticipated that it would abandon that empire so suddenly. Independence has unfortunately not brought peace or stability to either Angola or Mozambique and the future of these states is open to speculation.

The division of the Blacks in Angola into factions unwilling to become reconciled had unexpected consequences. The factions had recourse to arms, compelling some African neighbours to intervene. The Soviet Union seized the opportunity of establishing itself in Southern Africa through the medium of Cuban soldiers. The South African and moderate African States generally had reasons to expect counter-measures from the U.S.A. But the American Congress, in a presidential election year, prevented the Administration from acting against Russian imperialism. The M.P.L.A., which was the most leftist-inclined faction in Angola, with the help of Cuban troops and of Russian armaments, took control of the country, notwithstanding resistance of unforeseeable duration and consequences on the part of tribal and political factions. Moreover, the bulk of the Whites fled to Portugal, South Africa, Brazil and other countries.

In Mozambique, Frelimo is showing moderation in its attitude towards South Africa and has good reason to continue to do so, for the fate of the new nation depends to a large extent on South Africa: those of the country's population who work in South African factories contribute a substantial part of Mozambique's revenues; without South African trade Maputo[1] would find itself under sentence of death. It is hardly necessary to add that the pessimists scorn these arguments. According to them, passion will prevail over reason; and, in any case, the Chinese and the

[1] The former Lourenço Marques.

Russians, equally determined to demolish South Africa, will make it their task to create a permanent state of insecurity along its frontiers.

Everyone seems to hold a different view of the situation and to change that view from one day to the next. Divergences of opinion are much less marked when it comes to Rhodesia. A look at the map shows that Beira and Maputo are Rhodesia's closest outlets on the Indian Ocean—by no means a new problem, for already in Kruger's time the Transvaal and the Orange Free State were obsessed by the search for access to the sea. Now that the frontier with Mozambique is closed, where can Rhodesian exports be sent? Admittedly, there is a railway line southwards (the first stage of the Cape to Cairo route of which Cecil Rhodes dreamed), but it passes through Botswana, whose goodwill cannot be taken for granted. Another line has just been completed, passing directly through the Transvaal and therefore not in danger of being cut off. But, even in the most favourable circumstances, Rhodesian goods would have to be transported to Durban, or even to the Cape, and the South African ports are so congested that it is common to see fifteen, twenty or even thirty ships anchored out to sea because they cannot find room to dock. From this point of view, an important improvement will result from the completion of Richards Bay, a new deep-sea harbour between Durban and the Mozambique border, inaugurated by Mr Vorster in January 1976, and destined to become larger than Durban, Africa's largest port, before the end of the century.

The problem of Rhodesia is not only economic. South African feelings towards that country are complex. On the one hand, South Africans have a strict policy of non-intervention in the domestic affairs of other countries and have adhered to this policy despite provocation at times from neighbouring states' leaders. On the other hand, however, their own domestic policy, which they claim to be 'liberal' in that it pursues the goal of self-determination for each of the Republic's divergent ethnic groups, prevent them from giving public endorsement to the Rhodesian policy which they see as ostentatiously flaunting White supremacy. The South African dilemma has been complicated by the fact that, with the independence of aggressive neighbours in Angola and Mozambique, the old concept of Rhodesia being a 'buffer state' is no longer valid. In short, no one is prepared to die for Salisbury. The cynics jump to the conclusion that 'Rhodesia is finished'. More subtle minds give it a chance of survival, but in a form hardly likely to please its present government: a Black state like Lesotho, Swaziland and Botswana, where the rights of the White minority would be safeguarded. In recent times, South Africa has withdrawn the police force that at one stage undertook counter-insurgency operations against terrorists based in Black states.

The South African Foreign Minister also reacted favourably to the call by the American Secretary of State, Dr Kissinger, in August 1976 for a transition in Rhodesia to a government based on majority rule and minority rights. The Foreign Minister stated that nobody could expect South Africa to withhold its support from the efforts by Dr Kissinger simply because majority rule was the point of departure—after all, the Minister pointed out, the majority principle had been inherent in Rhodesian constititutional philosophy. The Minister hoped that a peaceful settlement of the Rhodesian issue would be based on adequate guarantees for the rights and interests of the White minority.

The door is thus open to compromise. The same can be said for the former German South-West Africa,[1] despite the prodigious mineral wealth which its land appears to contain. The Afrikaners, recalling their struggles against the British, like to boast of having been the first anti-colonialists in Africa. Although their position in this former mandate of the League of Nations for a long time unconsciously offended the logic of which they are so proud, they are now actively supporting a policy of self-determination for South-West Africa, as evidenced by the constitutional conference which started its deliberations in September 1975. Blacks and Whites are represented at this conference. Prime Minister Vorster has pledged to accept any constitution produced by the people of South-West Africa—and has said that all options are open to them in deciding on their constitution. In August 1976 the conference stated that their deliberations were making such good progress that 31 December 1978 could be accepted as a likely date for full independence for the territory.

Putting aside hypotheses and concentrating on probabilities, it seems that, in the not too distant future, on all its northern frontiers, the Republic of South Africa runs the risk of facing unfriendly neighbours—a situation which its rulers contemplate with the fortitude of their ancestors, but which only adds to the already long list of their problems.

The basic difficulty is this: how to make 4,200,000 Whites, 2,300,000 Coloureds, 700,000 Indians and various Black groups totalling more than 17 million live together amicably? To complicate matters, each of these demographic terms must first be defined, for in none of these four groups is there sufficient unity to ensure its coherence.

Since the Whites claim responsibility for the country, they will be considered first. Of the Whites 64 per cent, it is estimated, regard Afrikaans as their mother tongue and 36 per cent English. The English-speaking population, the majority of whom have long since buried their British heritage and regard themselves as 100 per cent South African, play only a modest role in the political and civilian administration of the country. Not that their position as a minority embarrasses them: they are used to it, and, moreover, it is compensated by their still dominant influence in business. A minority of English-speakers are to be found in the strongly anti-government camp on the left wing of South African politics.

For the Afrikaners things are quite different. Since the beginning of the

[1] Known now as Namibia in U.N. circles.

century they have enjoyed such an astonishing run of success that for them the past is a source of confidence rather than regret. Today they rule the country, occupy four-fifths of the important posts in the army and the civil service, and are gradually penetrating the world of business. Sure of themselves, full of vitality and bent on surmounting the obstacles with which the path of their future is scattered, they look on the Republic as their country, their only country—they cannot remember or even conceive of any other. Naturally, they do not all think along identical lines. Some, described as *Verkramptes* (ultra-conservative), generally oppose change; the rest, described as *Verligtes* (enlightened), and who form the majority, believe in evolutionary change. On one point, however, all are agreed: if their existence is threatened, they will die fighting like their ancestors at the beginning of the century. In this they have the support of the large majority of English-speakers with national unity against external aggression highly developed.

Finally, among the descendants of Dutch, French, Germans and British there has emerged a nucleus of more recent immigrants who, for the most part, speak English in preference to Afrikaans. Jews are particularly numerous; in fact, after New York and Tel Aviv, Johannesburg has the largest Jewish community in the world.

The Whites, then, may number four million, but among these four million many differences obviously exist. There is, however, much cohesion on crucial national issues.

Differences are more pronounced among Blacks. In their case, it is not just a question of two groups whose intermixture is dictated by necessity, culture, their European origin, a common religion[1] and a similar life-style. The ethnologists distinguish four main categories of Bantu:[2] the Nguni, the Sotho, the Bavenda and the Shangaan-Tsonga. This classification gives only an imperfect idea of the fragmentary nature of the Bantu population, which comprises at least eight different nations. The two largest, the Xhosa (3,930,000) and the Zulu (4,026,000), both enjoy numerical equality with the Whites. The rest are divided into numerous tribes varying in size from over a million and a half to less than 200,000. The existence of clans and tribes within these groups accentuates a centrifugal tendency which the use of at least seven languages or dialects is hardly calculated to remedy. Already separated by ancestral traditions and feuds, the Blacks are also divided by the wide variety of their living conditions.[3]

A handful have attained wealth, and the liberal professions have enabled

[1] The Dutch Reformed Church is by far the largest Protestant denomination. The proportion of Catholics is only 6 per cent.

[2] The 'Bantu' or Blacks prefer to be called 'Africans'. The Afrikaners are in no position to deny them the name, as their own has an identical meaning.

[3] It is estimated that seven million live in the homelands, that seven to eight million work in the industrial centres, and that about three and a half million are employed in rural areas, mostly on farms.

a somewhat larger number to achieve an acceptable standard of living. For the latter the concept of 'negritude' has assumed its full significance. But it is a concept foreign to the vast majority which still lives a relatively primitive existence.[1] The gap between them and their more fortunate brethren is, as in all countries of Africa, infinitely wider than that between Whites of different standards of living.

Unity, not yet absolute among the Europeans and barely evident among the Blacks, is not very much stronger among the Coloureds. The 'Coloured' or half-caste population is of mixed and diverse ethnic origin. They have a mixture of brown, black and white blood in their veins; these are the descendants of Khoisan tribes (mainly Hottentots), slaves from West Africa and the East Indies, as well as Europeans. The Coloured people also includes a small subcultural group, known as the Cape Malays—a mixture of Malays, Arabs, Indians, Sinhalese, Chinese and Malagasy. While 90 per cent of all Coloureds are members of some Christian church, the Cape Malays (some 7 per cent) are Moslems. Geography has helped the Coloureds towards an awareness of their solidarity: some 87 per cent live in the Cape Province and in its capital they represent nearly half of the population. Over the centuries language, religion and custom have forged increasingly close bonds between themselves and the Whites. Yet there still exists an indefinable difference which even a skin of different colour does not explain.

The Indians, 83 per cent of whom live in Natal, have outwardly more pronounced characteristics. Moreover, their economic status, at least among the upper classes, is closer to that of the Whites; the luxurious villas in which some of them live in the Indian quarter of Durban stand witness to the feat they have accomplished since their ancestors arrived in South Africa, a little over a hundred years ago, as impecunious immigrants. Nevertheless, they are the first to admit that, under the common description of 'Indian', they are divided by profound differences of caste, religion and custom.

In brief, then, there are some twenty-five million South Africans, but they have little in common except their frontiers. Where is that common fund of memories and hopes—which is the foundation of all national aspirations—to be found among people whose view of the past is motivated largely by resentment and for whom the future seems to hold only the prospect of division? How are they to be united by the bond of patriotism? Alternatively: what system of co-existence can be worked out to accommodate all these groups?

A few years ago the question hardly arose, but today the problem is a

---

[1] The huts in which many Zulus live cannot be much different from those of Chaka's time.

real one and the risk of an explosion[1] confronts a country whose evolution is accelerating daily.

One solution immediately suggests itself: South Africa will be compelled to yield to external pressures. But one cannot help being sceptical about such an eventuality. It is perfectly true that 'the country of *apartheid*' —to use the language of those who pose as the spokesmen of the 'universal conscience'—does not wish to leave the United Nations; even a limited contact with the rest of the world seems preferable to total isolation. South Africa does not, however, rule out this possibility and does not consider itself incapable of meeting the challenge. Its government is well aware of the strength which, whatever may happen, it will continue to derive from its economic resources. Furthermore, without an unlikely intervention by the Great Powers, it knows that no other country in Africa is capable of standing up to its military might. Finally, it is hardly necessary to add that the Afrikaners are inclined to confuse liberty with intransigence. Who knows if, by trying to compel them to change their ways, one will not merely make them even more rigid?

What, then, is the reason for this new atmosphere, obvious to anyone who can see below the surface? Why this ferment of suggestions, plans and theories? Why all this discussion and argument, which prove that, in this so-called 'police state', freedom of expression has not disappeared? One can attempt to interpret this effervescence of ideas with the aid of a few indisputable facts, and, better still, by analysing the psychological transformation that has taken place among the men in power.

A first point: the population of South Africa is now twenty-five million and, according to all the statisticians, it will double during the next twenty-five years. Even more important, by the year 2000 the racial imbalance will have become more marked: by then, it is predicted, there will be over thirty-five million Blacks, six million Whites, six million Coloureds and possibly two million Indians. The birth-rate is estimated at 43 per thousand for the Blacks, 36 for the Coloureds, 33 for the Indians and only 23 for the Whites, a difference which is not compensated for by a small annual influx of immigrants (40,000 arrivals[2] and 10,000 departures every year). During this same period, continue the prophets, industrialization will have made such progress that production will have tripled and the average standard of living will have reached, and perhaps even overtaken, that of the Europe of today. According to a statement by the former Minister of Finance, Dr Diederichs, the country can look forward to an 'unprecedented boom'. Dr Diederichs' optimism is based on two observations; first, South Africa is certain to benefit from the rise in the

[1] As shown by the violent disturbances which took place in Soweto and other areas in 1976.

[2] Present developments may increase the number of immigrants. But will the 'new South Africans', from the former Portuguese colonies and Rhodesia, help to strengthen national unity? And who will benefit by their arrival—the Afrikaners or the English-speaking South Africans?

price of raw materials; and second, it holds a unique trump card—a vast reserve of Black labour from which it will be able to recruit as many skilled workmen as it will need to increase its productivity.[1] Exaggerated or not, these figures and prognostications reveal a tendency. The South Africa of the end of the century will bear little resemblance to the country of today. The South Africa of 1976 is already vastly different from that of twenty years ago, when the doctrines on which the present structure has been built were first conceived and put into practice. Until about 1968–9 the Afrikaners gave little thought to the eroding power of time. Now, however, ideas are moving forward, sometimes visibly, but most often beneath the surface. The country's rulers must have been influenced, albeit unconsciously, by the experience of their ancestors. A nation does not win its independence by three centuries of sweat and blood without knowing that at certain times rigidity, however instinctive, must make way for flexibility if circumstances so dictate. The present government has understood this necessity: these men, by nature direct and blunt, are now proving remarkable tacticians; their logic is being reinforced by pragmatism, their ultra-conservatism is making way for a greater adaptability; they are now tackling problems not with the aid of doctrines alone but in the light of new realities and new circumstances.

It is interesting to note that so-called 'petty apartheid' is disappearing remarkably fast. There are still separate entrances for 'Europeans' and 'non-Europeans' at railway stations, although inside they mingle with each other; post offices, cinemas and bathing beaches still practise segregation, but in the streets, in shops, in lifts and in many hotels and restaurants everybody mixes. Africans, Asians and Coloureds are making it clear that they find these pinprick tactics increasingly intolerable. It would not be surprising if, at some time in the near future, their protestations were to meet with success.

What is happening in so many different fields would appear to justify this prediction. In the foreground of this gradual transformation—allowing for the place it occupies in local life—one must put sport: in the two 'bastions' of segregated sport, rugby and cricket, multi-racial teams are playing on the international level. At the same time, economic expansion is undermining legal prohibitions. The laws remain, but are no longer applied. For example, the Whites can no longer claim a monopoly of those jobs formerly reserved for them and for which they cannot now provide enough qualified personnel; strikes by Blacks do occur;[2] and the unrecognized trade unions negotiate with the employers without the

[1] Hence the importance of professional training. At present there are forty-three technical schools for Blacks. 'African education has made phenomenal strides in the past decade', observes the South Africa Foundation.

[2] Sixty thousand Blacks stopped work at Durban in 1973; for the first time the police did not intervene. The strikers obtained nearly everything they were demanding.

government interfering.[1] Another development, perhaps less rapid but of more far-reaching significance, is also evident. The appalling gap between the earning of Whites and those of the rest is being reduced—perhaps too slowly, as the Opposition maintains, but at least it seems to be steadily narrowing and in some cases wages have reached parity.[2] Many people say that, especially at the highest level, equal pay will be common practice in a few years' time, a development the importance of which should not be overestimated: if treated on an equal footing financially, the élite of each of the four racial groups will inevitably feel a certain solidarity, and in this way contacts will multiply.

Much is already being done. The South Africa Foundation, as well as other similar organizations, now includes Blacks, Indians and Coloureds among its trustees. It will be recalled that, at a recent meeting of the United Nations, the official South African delegation was accompanied by a representative of each of the other three population groups. The responsibility for representing South Africa abroad is no longer restricted to Whites, and Black diplomats are working on an equal basis in South African embassies abroad. Opportunities for contact are becoming increasingly common in South Africa itself. Whites and Blacks, Whites and Coloureds, Whites and Indians are meeting more often at professional gatherings and receptions. Their places of residence remain separate, but by working in the same buildings they are able to mix more and more.

It is quite true that, as yet, there has been no abandoning of principles: political power in the White areas of the Republic remains the monopoly of the four million Whites. A humiliating situation for the Blacks who live in these areas, and no doubt even more humiliating for the two minorities, the Coloureds, who not long ago enjoyed a position of relative equality with the Whites, and the Indians proud of their ancient civilization. What can be done to change this state of affairs? The Progressive Reform Party,[3] which has 13 of the Assembly's 171 seats, claims to have

[1] The most revealing example is, perhaps, a very picturesque Black lady who controls—apparently with a rod of iron—an organization of over thirty thousand female workers in the clothing industry. She successfully negotiates collective agreements without possessing any official status.

[2] Between September 1970 and April 1973 wages appear to have increased in the following proportions: 38·3 per cent for the Coloureds, 29·8 per cent for male Blacks; 20·9 per cent for Indians and 17·3 per cent for the Whites. Another statistic indicates that, in the twelve months ending August 1973, the wages of Blacks rose twice as quickly as those of Whites. A similar trend for the wage gap to be narrowed has been discernible in the years since those statistics became known. It is also noted that during the period 1968 to 1975 the South African government's Central Bantu Labour Board succeeded in obtaining, amongst other improvements, wages increases of R280 million for 837,000 Black workers.

[3] The Progressive Party, which broke away from the United Party in 1959, at first had only one representative in Parliament, Mrs Suzman. In 1974 it succeeded in winning an additional six seats at the expense of the United Party, and in 1975, with the co-operation of a further dissident group from the United Party, the new Progressive Reform Party was formed.

discovered a panacea. It insists that South Africa is one country and envisages its future in the form of a federation of geographical units whose citizens would all enjoy equal status. For a time there would be a restricted franchise based on a minimum educational and income qualification,[1] and eventually universal suffrage would ensure the triumph of democracy. A constitution defining the rights of everyone and a Supreme Court responsible for ensuring that those rights are respected would protect the minorities. A curious mixture of high-ranking capitalists,[2] former United Party members, Left-wing intellectuals and a younger element avid for novelty, the Progressive Reform Party has about it an extraordinary air of unreality.

The United Party, an infinitely more moderate Opposition group, formed in 1938 and until 1948 dignified by the personality of Smuts, has the advantage of its experience of political skirmishing. Moreover, it has 35 representatives,[3] many of them men of ability. If it was not torn by factions, which are drawn in turn to Right or Left, it would have some chance of making its voice heard. Its doctrine is not lacking in subtlety. It, too, advocates a federation, but one composed of ethnic units, which means that it does not reject the principle of separate development. It hopes, however, to mitigate the drawbacks of segregation, at first by gradually introducing universal suffrage within each group, then by entrusting local authorities with as many powers as possible. At the top of the structure there would be an Assembly representative of all; but population would not be the only criterion that would be taken into account in the allocation of its members; each constituency would have a number of representatives that would vary according to the contribution it made to society. Since the 'contribution' of the Whites would obviously be greater than that of the rest, they would thus preserve in practice a supremacy[4] which they would have renounced in law.

The National Party, fortified by its majority of more than two-thirds (123 out of a total of 171 members) and its twenty-eight years of power,[5] pays scant attention to such schemes. It is led by a man of the first rank, whose deep convictions, sincerity and goodwill are obvious. Flanked by the ultra-conservatives who are hostile to change and the

[1] The system proposed is a complicated one. Persons who have reached 'standard 8' (approximately third-form standard in Britain), earn a minimum monthly salary and possess a minimum capital, would elect 90 per cent of the Assembly; the remaining 10 per cent would be chosen by persons able to read and write and earning a certain minimum wage. Since the proportion of illiterate Blacks is estimated at 30 per cent, is this not just another example of discrimination?

[2] It is well known that the sympathies of the Anglo-American Corporation lie with the Progressives.

[3] But its strength (110 members of Parliament at the time of its formation) has steadily dwindled.

[4] The United Party prefers to use the word 'leadership'.

[5] In 1974, the National Party gained its seventh electoral victory, which has almost restored it to its highest-ever level of 1955.

extremists who want immediate upheaval, Mr Vorster has chosen the path of practical accommodation, adapting the principles of yesterday to the realities of tomorrow, a path along which he is advancing step by step and with rare skill.

In foreign policy, a closer understanding between South Africa and the other African states is his constant objective. At one time this 'outward policy', as it was called, seemed doomed.[1] Later it was revived, the fruit of much patience and skilful negotiation on the part of the Afrikaners. In October 1974, Mr Vorster made a speech, the significance of which even the hullabaloo raised by the United Nations could not conceal. In his view, the African continent is at a crossroads: either it will take the road leading to escalation of violence, and in the ensuing confrontation South Africa will not necessarily be the loser, for its means of defence are 'not inconsiderable';[2] or it will take the road of negotiation and closer understanding, with the rights of all respected. One reaction to the speech was quite unexpected. To everyone's surprise it came from Zambia, whose president, Mr Kaunda, declared on two successive days that he had just heard 'the voice of reason'—an appraisement that can hardly have been reassuring for Rhodesia, but which said a great deal about the secret talks that Pretoria was engaged in conducting. It was not unreasonable to think that this success would be followed by others and in fact, since making that speech, Mr Vorster has made a number of visits to various Black states, including the Ivory Coast and Liberia. Black Africa is in dire straits, and the hand being offered her by South Africa is obviously a tempting one.

In his attempts to normalize relations with Black Africa, Mr Vorster, with the aid of President Kaunda of Zambia, created the climate in which White and Black Rhodesians could meet in the historic bridge conference in August 1975 to discuss the future of Rhodesia. The Geneva Conference which opened at the end of October 1976 will seal the fate of Rhodesia. It should be noted that the Prime Minister, Mr Ian Smith, has accepted the principle of the transfer of power to the Blacks within two years. Much depends on the declared recognition by certain Black Heads of State, as well as by Dr Kissinger, that the Whites of South Africa are accepted as part of Africa and are not regarded as colonists.

These diplomatic successes of Mr Vorster suffered a setback as a result of the Angolan civil war, in which South Africa became implicated because of the presence of Cuban soldiers armed with sophisticated Soviet weapons. However, despite the condemnation which South Africa received for this involvement, many countries in Africa came to the realization that South Africa was firmly committed to opposing Communist subversion in Southern Africa. It was also clear that Dr Kissinger's desire to meet Mr Vorster was prompted to a large degree by America's concern to prevent Communist penetration in Southern Africa. The historic Vorster-Kissinger meeting in 1976 was likely to have far-reaching effects on events in Southern Africa.

At the Franco-African conference held in Paris in May 1976, the President of the French Republic, Mr Giscard d'Estaing, emphasized that African problems should be left to the Africans to solve without interference from outside. South Africa's efforts on the diplomatic front have not been confined to Africa. Mr Vorster is endeavouring, with some success, to establish friendly relations with a number of medium-sized countries around the world, Paraguay and Israel, which he visited officially, Iran and some others.

The West has long recognized that South Africa commands a strategic position on the economic life-line between East and West, and that should South Africa fall to one of the two Communist giants, the shipping lanes to Europe round the Cape would be seriously endangered. Britain's withdrawal from the naval base at Simonstown has therefore created a vacuum which could easily be filled by one of the other major Western powers, were it not for the fear of offending the African states by seeming to support the 'land of apartheid'. The importance of the Cape sea-route has been greatly emphasized since a Communist presence has been established on both the East and West coasts of Africa.

Everything, however, depends on South Africa's internal evolution. The Afrikaners seem as determined as ever not to deviate from their history of a 'separate development' that will lead to what they call a 'multi-national' country. Here one point must be made. The people who have invented this idea and are attempting to put it into practice deserve neither irony nor hatred. To portray them as the champions of racialism is a calumny. If the word is understood in the sense which it has acquired from certain monstrous political creeds, there is no such thing as 'racialism' in South Africa. Many Whites count Coloureds and Blacks among their best friends. How many examples can one quote of the sort of hideous explosions of violence that in some parts of the world have ended in lynchings? The Afrikaners, considering themselves to have been entrusted with a divine mission, endowed with an unswerving will, conscientious and relentless, are the victims of their own sincerity and simplicity; and so, in an experiment which they are attempting in all good faith, they are often thought to possess a Machiavellian intention of which they are quite incapable. One must try to understand precisely what sort of future they have in mind for the three population groups collectively described in administrative terminology as 'non-Whites'.

First, the Blacks. The idea of recognizing the existence of the historical homelands of the various Black groups is over half a century old. Botha was the first to put it into practice, in 1913. In 1936 Hertzog decided to add 7,225,000 morgen to the 10,700,000 specified in 1913. But the White owners of the land had to be willing to relinquish it, and the process of purchase or expropriation was a slow one. Today the programme is almost complete. These Black homelands represent 13 per cent of the total area of South Africa, a figure often quoted and contrasted with the proportion of Blacks to Whites. It is generally forgotten, however, that 70 per cent of the country is desert or semi-desert; the zones assigned to the Africans represent over 40 per cent of South Africa's arable land and comprise the most fertile areas.[1]

The implementation of this programme has encountered numerous obstacles. One problem is that of fragmentation. Except in the Transkei, the territories do not form a bloc, and consequently an attempt has had to be made to join together parcels of land of varying dimensions in order to make them into territorial units. Much progress has already been made: there were as many as 264 separate pieces of land in 1950, 167 in 1969 and only 82 in 1974. When the present stage of consolidation is complete, there will be no more than 30 to 40, and in Kwazulu—the most difficult case— no more than 10. In any case, it is argued, does not history offer examples of a sovereign territory not forming one contiguous unit?[2] But this is not the only problem. The Bantu are traditionally cattle-breeders rather than crop-growers. If the land is to be used for cultivation rather than for pasturage, they will have to be educated in a whole new way of life. And there is another difficulty: how can agriculture be prevented from remaining almost their sole activity and thus slowing down the gradual assimilation of their population into a Western type of civilization? How can a large part of the country avoid being excluded from the process of industrialization on which South Africa's wealth is based? An important step has recently been made in this direction: foreign firms who wish to establish branches in the 'homelands' are now allowed to negotiate directly with the appropriate local authorities. There seems to be no reason why they should not avail themselves of the opportunity. The subsoil has hardly been explored, and it is quite possible that it contains mineral riches. Labour, moreover, is plentiful and cheaper than elsewhere; all jobs are open to the native population, who eventually, with an appropriate professional training, will doubtless be able to fill them.

All these developments are, in the thinking of the South African government, stages along the road that will bring the homelands to independence. Today the homelands are nine in number: Qwaqwa, Bophuthatswana, Ciskei, Gazankulu, Kwazulu, Lebowa, Swazi, Transkei and Venda; six

[1] The case of the Transkei is significant. A visitor cannot but admire the order and tranquillity that prevail in this land of magnificent horizons, but he is surprised to observe that the land is hardly ever cultivated. It is the opinion of one expert that, if a million French peasants were settled here, in two years there would be enough to feed the whole of South Africa.

[2] Chief Buthulesi, the leader of the Zulu and a lover of rhetoric, boasts of being the *vox populi* and also of being descended on the female side from the Zulu heroes of earlier days. It would be interesting to know if he would also take pride in being compared with the Emperor Charles V . . . .

of them have their own Parliament, cabinet and Prime Minister, who is responsible to Parliament; two others have a legislative assembly and an executive council.

The Transkei, which became independent in October 1976, is by far the most advanced. The legislative power is exercised by an Assembly of 150 representatives (75 tribal chiefs who are members by right and 75 elected by universal suffrage). The cabinet comprises the Prime Minister and a maximum of 14 other members. The Transkei enjoys all attributes of sovereignty: it has its own flag, national anthem and citizenship, educational system, police force and the nucleus of an army. Xhosa, spoken by its four million citizens, is recognized as the official language.

By all accepted international standards such as those relating to geographical size, population, fixed boundaries, the existence of a proper independent government, the Transkei has every right to claim membership of the United Nations. With the birth of the independent Republic of Transkei, a decisive stage was reached in the creation of a horseshoe of fully sovereign Black states and of that South African community which is the distant dream of the champions of 'separate development'. This process is continuing as is evidenced by the fact that Bophuthatswana has also directed a request for independence to the South African government.

The optimists forecast that, by the end of the century, twenty million Blacks could find a livelihood in the homelands. What about the rest? It is estimated that some three and a half million still work on White farms scattered throughout the country; they pose no real problems. The same cannot, however, be said for the millions who make up the labour force in the industrial centres and whose numbers are increasing every year. If agriculture had remained the main economic activity, 'separate development' would not have raised the same problems. Regrouping the majority of Blacks in the territories where their household gods await them would have presented no insuperable difficulties. At all events, there would have existed no fundamental contradiction of the segregation principle. Today, however, every new factory that opens and every machine that turns are temptations which the Africans cannot easily resist. They are being drawn by the prospect of less wretched conditions and the attractions of a completely new life. They are arriving from all directions: the number of labourers who have secretly crossed the frontier from neighbouring countries to seek work in 'the country of *apartheid*' is estimated to be at least 500,000, and possibly a million. The Whites welcome this labour force because their factories could not function without it. And so, at the same time as theory is seeking to separate the races, necessity is conspiring to bring them together.

Officially, the Blacks in the urban centres[1] are supposed to remain

---

[1] The Black settlements, known as 'townships', that have been built side by side with the White towns are sometimes enormous: Soweto, near Johannesburg, already has more than a million inhabitants.

members of their tribe of origin: in this way, it is explained, they will continue to exercise their political rights by taking part in the ballots provided in their 'homeland'—not by postal vote, but by going to the polling stations organized at their places of residence.[1] The government's opponents claim that this is all a fiction: some of these Black families, they maintain, have been Westernized, or, rather, Americanized, and a distant 'homeland' no longer means anything to them. But the argument goes on, with the authorities insisting that this is a mistaken view: these Blacks may have been 'detribalized', but they have certainly not been 'denationalized'; just as their ancestors were Xhosa and Zulu, so they and their children are Xhosa and Zulu—the fact that they seize every opportunity to return to their homeland is proof enough.[2] If this is so, comes the retort, those Black workers who have recently arrived should be sent home and the rest should be given the vote—a suggestion that is hardly likely to be heeded. What, then, is to be done? The townships already have a sort of town council elected by the Blacks. Many people say that the government must go further: why should the township not be made into another kind of 'homeland' by extending its boundaries, granting its inhabitants full property-owning rights (at present they may purchase their houses but not the land itself) and even allowing them to establish industrial enterprises there? The idea is all rather vague. In reality, no one has yet found a final solution to the problem.

The question of the Coloureds is also a complex one. A powerful current of opinion is emerging which favours a closer link-up with the White community, even integration. But objections arise immediately. If a concession of this sort is offered to the Coloureds, why not to the Indians? Neither group has 'homelands' like the Blacks. History—and various regroupings resulting from *apartheid*—have determined where they live: the Coloureds around the Cape, the Indians in the vicinity of Durban. Four million Whites, two and a half million Coloureds and seven hundred thousand Indians would, it is argued, constitute a grouping whose weight would balance that of the Black townships. That may be so, but is there not reason to fear that a bloc of 'non-Blacks' would simply be substituted for the present bloc of 'non-Whites'?

In 1969 the Coloureds lost the right to be represented in Parliament by four Whites. In return, they were granted a Representative Council of sixty members (twenty nominated and forty elected). This institution, destined to become entirely elective at the next election, already exercises wide powers in the fields of education, social welfare and general planning. A speech made by Mr Vorster on 8 November 1974 envisaged the possibility of a considerable extension of its powers. The Prime

[1] It is estimated that 1,501,000 Africans in six homelands took part in the most recent elections; nearly a third—475,932 to be precise—voted in the townships.

[2] One reason why they return is to be with their lawful wives. The extent of this traffic is confirmed by the exceptionally high profits made by the petrol and service stations opened in the townships.

Minister also proposed that the Council's executive committee be transformed into a cabinet co-ordinating the activities of ministerial departments.

The Indians, like the Coloureds, have a Representative Council (thirty members, half of them elected) which enables them to manage their own affairs. This is shortly to become an all-elected body. But between the Indians and the other races an important distinction exists: the Whites are in power and intend to stay there; the Blacks are moving towards independence in their 'homelands'; and the Coloureds are convinced that in the near future they will obtain some form of integration; but the ultimate political future of the Asians, who differ so profoundly from the rest of the population, is uncertain.

A further important step in the political evolution of the Coloureds and Indians is that they are to have representation on a number of national advisory bodies such as the Prime Minister's Economic Advisory Council, the Defence Council, the Industrial Council and so on.

The most far-reaching development in the constitutional arrangement between Whites, Coloureds and Indians was the proposal by Mr Vorster that representatives from the White Parliament and the Coloured and Indian Councils should meet from time to time as a Cabinet Council to deal with matters of concern common to the three groups. The first meeting of this new institution was held in September 1976. The time is past when Whites made laws without consulting with their Coloured and Indian fellow-countrymen.

How is one to form conclusions in the face of a situation that is evolving so rapidly? The important thing is to emphasize the fundamental transformation that is taking place in South Africa, and to stop confusing two quite distinct ideas. It is true that discrimination based on colour is odious, especially when it assumes its meaner aspects. But it is no less true that the separate existence of the races, with equality of rights respected, involves no offence against justice—in fact is this not the very basis of the idea of nationhood? It is along this path that the South African authorities are at present moving: discrimination is disappearing, separateness remains. A new South Africa is emerging.

Epilogue

Inevitably the question is asked: what will happen tomorrow? But the function of history is not to forecast the future; rather, it is to enable one to evaluate an immensely complex present.

First, it must be remembered that South African policy is not the product of an abstraction: it is explained—one might even say rendered necessary—by five centuries of history. It offers a solution which, compared with others put forward, at least has the merit of taking a realistic view of the present and an imaginative view of the future. It is, nevertheless, a makeshift policy. In other words, it is acceptable only as a temporary, not as a permanent solution. Time is against the Republic. If South Africa wishes to achieve success in the bold course it has taken, it must realize the need for rapid changes. Yet this evolution will not be accomplished without sacrifices—financial sacrifices (setting the future Black states on their way is only feasible at heavy cost); moral sacrifices (to safeguard their basic position the Whites will have to be prepared to renounce some of their privileges); and territorial sacrifices (the Coloured and Indian communities, like the majority of the homelands, seem viable only if given more space).

There is a great deal at stake, but the gamble is worth taking. If historians are not entitled to make prophecies, they are not forbidden to make wishes. Dare the author express the hope that the Western world will eventually acknowledge the close bond that exists between it and South Africa; that, without refraining from criticism, it will be able to temper its judgements with objectivity; and, above all, that it will show some understanding and indulgence towards a country that is having to face a complex problem which exists nowhere else in the world?

1 November 1976

Money, Weights and Measures

Since 1961 the monetary unit has been the *rand*, divided into 100 *cents*.

It is estimated that, to compare present-day prices with those of the period of the Great Trek (*c.* 1834), the latter should be multiplied by five. (Information kindly provided by Professor M. L. Truu of the School for Business Leadership, University of South Africa.)

The Republic of South Africa has adopted the metric system.

Bibliography

GENERAL BIBLIOGRAPHY

I History of South Africa

Cambridge History of the British Empire (vol. VIII, *South Africa*). London, 2nd edn, 1963.
Cory, Sir G.: *The Rise of South Africa*. 5 vols, Cape Town, 1964.
Joos, L. C. D.: *Histoire de l'Afrique du Sud*. Paris, 1965.
Keppel-Jones, A.: *South Africa: A Short History*. London, 1966.
Kiewiet, C. W. de: *A History of South Africa. Social and Economic*. Oxford, 1966.
Marquard, L.: *The Story of South Africa*. London, 1956.
Muller, C. F. J., ed.: *Five Hundred Years. A History of South Africa*. Pretoria, 1969.
Theal, G. McCall: *History of South Africa*. 10 vols, London, 1919–27.
Walker, E. A.: *A History of South Africa*. London, 1928.

II History of the British Empire
Carrington, C. E.: *The British Overseas, Exploits of a Nation of Shopkeepers*. Cambridge, 1950.
Williamson, J. A.: *A Short History of British Expansion*. 2 vols, London, 1947.

III History of Africa
Cornevin, R. and M.: *Histoire de l'Afrique*. Paris, 1964.
Ganiage, J., Deschamps, H., Guitard, O.: *L'Afrique au XXe siècle*. Paris, 1966. Guitard, O.: *L'Afrique orientale et australe*.

IV Economic History
Arndt, E. D. H.: *Currency and Banking Development in South Africa (1627–1927)*. Cape Town, 1928.
Kock, M. H. de: *Selected Subjects of the Economic History of South Africa*. Johannesburg, 1924.

V Documents
Bell, K. N. and Morrell, W. D.: *Select Documents on British Colonial Policy (1830–1860)*. Oxford, 1928.
Eybers, G. W.: *Select Constitutional Documents of South African History (1795–1910)*. London, 1918.

VI Bibliography
Muller, C. F. J., van Jaarsveld, F. A.,Wyck, T.: *A Select Bibliography of South African History*. Pretoria, 1966.

BIBLIOGRAPHY BY CHAPTERS

Prologue

General works listed above and, on geography:
Isnard, H.: *Géographie de l'Afrique tropicale et australe*. Paris, 1964.
Vidal de Lablache, P. and Gallois, L.: *Géographie universelle*, vol. XII, Fernand Maurette, Paris, 1938.

On palaeontology:
Note by M. Jean Piveteau, member of the Institut and professor of the Faculty of Sciences, Paris.

1 The beginnings of the Cape Colony

General works listed above and, on the Portuguese:
Axelson, E.: *Portuguese in South Africa (1600–1700)*. Johannesburg, 1960 (*Journal of African History*. May 1961, pp. 55–63).
Randles, W. G. L.: *L'Image du Sud-Est africain dans la littérature européenne au XVIe siècle*. Lisbon, 1960.

On the Cape as port of call in the early days:
Raven-Hart, R.: *Before Van Riebeeck*. Cape Town. 1967.

On the Dutch:
Boxer, C. R.: *The Dutch Seaborne Empire (1600–1800)*. London, 1966.
Déhérain, H.: *Le Cap de Bonne-Espérance au XVIIe siècle*. Paris, 1909.
Leibbrandt, H. C. V., ed.: *Précis of the Archives of the Cape of Good Hope: Van Riebeeck's Journal*, Cape Town, 1897.

On the Bushmen and the Hottentots:
Schapera, I.: *The Khoisan People of South Africa. Bushmen and Hottentots*. London, 1965.

2 The arrival of the French Huguenots

General works and:
Allier, J.: 'A la mémoire des huguenots français émigrés en Afrique du Sud', *Bulletin de la Société de l'Histoire du Protestantisme français*, 1st quarter, 1967.
Botha, C. G.: *The French Refugees at the Cape*. Cape Town, 1919.
Bulletin de la Société de l'Histoire du Protestantisme français, vols XVI, XXXI, XLVIII.

Déhérain, H.: *op. cit.*, 1909.
Huguenot Society of South Africa. Bulletin no. 5, 1967.
Leibbrandt, H. C. V.: *Rambles through the Archives of the Cape (1688–1700).* Cape Town, 1887.
Nathan, M.: *The Huguenots in South Africa.* Johannesburg, 1939.
Réveillaud, E.: 'Les Huguenots réfugiés au sud de l'Afrique', *Foi et Vie*, 1 and 15 March, 1 and 16 April, 1 May 1900.
Wciss, C.: *Histoire des réfugiés protestants*, vol. II. Paris, 1853.

3 Clashes with the Bantu and internal difficulties

General works and, on the 'trekboers':
Déhérain, H.: *op. cit.*

On the Bantu:
Brunschwig, H.: *L'Avènement de l'Afrique noire du XIXe siècle à nos jours*, Paris, 1963.
Fagan, B. M.: *Southern Africa during the Iron Age.* London, 1965.
Kirkman, J. S.: *Men and Monuments of the East African Coast.* London, 1964.
Randles, W. G. L.: *'Matériaux pour une histoire du Sud-Est africain jusqu'au XVIIIe siècle'*, Annales, no. 5, September–October 1963.
Schapera, I., ed.: *The Bantu-speaking Tribes of Southern Africa.* London, 1962.
Soga, J. H.: *The Ama-Xosa: Life and Customs.* London, 1931.

On the events of 1795:
Marais, J. S.: *The Cape Coloured People (1652–1937).* Johannesburg, 1957.

4 South Africa at the beginning of the nineteenth century

General works and, on Suffren's landing:
Lacour-Gayet, G.: *La Marine militaire sous le règne de Louis XVI.* Paris 1905.

On life at the Cape and in the Colony:
Barnard, Lady A.: *South Africa a Century Ago.* London, 1901.
Barras, Victomte P. de: *Mémoires*, vol. I. Paris, 1895.
Barrow, J.: *Travels into the Interior of Southern Africa*, 2 vols. London, 1806.
Bernardin de Saint-Pierre, J. H.: *Voyage à l'Isle de France*, 2 vols. Amsterdam, 1773.
Bougainville, L. A. de: *Voyage round the World*, 2 vols. Eng. trans. London. 1772.
Boxer, C. R.: *op. cit.*, 1966.
Colvin, I. D.: *The Cape of Adventure.* London, 1912.
Déhérain, H.: *L'Expansion des Boers au XIXe siècle.* Paris, 1905.
Lichtenstein, M. H.: *Travels in South Africa (1803–1806)*, 2 vols. London, 1812.
Weiss, C.: *op. cit.*, 1853.

5 Reform and tentative experiment

General works and, on the missionaries:
Agar-Hamilton, J. A. I.: *The Native Policy of the Voortrekkers (1836–1858)*, ch. VI. Cape Town, 1928.
Campbell, Rev. J.: *Travels in South Africa*. London, 1815.
Groves, C. P.: *The Planting of Christianity in Africa*, vol. I. London, 1948.
Marais, J. S.: *op. cit.*, 1957.
Philip, Rev. J.: *Researches in South Africa*. London, 1828.

On relations with the Bantu:
Déhérain, H.: *op. cit.*, 1905.
Macmillan, W. M.: *Bantu, Boer and Briton: the Making of the South African Native Problem*. Oxford, 1963.

On the 1820 settlers:
Edwards, I. E.: *The 1820 Settlers in South Africa*. London, 1934.
Hockly, H. E.: *The Story of British Settlers of 1820 in South Africa*. Cape Town, 1949.

On Somerset:
Millar, A. K.: *Plantagenet in South Africa. Lord Charles Somerset*. Cape Town, 1965.

6 Black potentates

General works and:
Becker, P.: *Path of Blood*. London, 1962.
Casalis, E.: *Les Basoutos*. Paris, 1860.
Ritter, E. A.: *Shaka Zulu*. London, 1965.
Soga, J. H.: *op. cit.*, 1931.

7 Difficult coexistence

General works and:
Brookes, E. H.: *The History of Native Policy in South Africa from 1830 to the Present Day*. Cape Town, 1924.
Galbraith, J. S.: *Reluctant Empire. British Policy on the South African Frontier (1834–1854)*. Los Angeles, 1963.
Macmillan, W. M.: *op. cit.*, 1963.
Marais, J. S.: *op. cit.*, 1957.

8 The Great Trek

General works and:
Becker, P.: *Rule of Fear: the Life and Times of Dingaan*. London, 1964.
Brookes, E. H. and Webb, C. de B.: *A History of Natal*. Pietermaritzburg, 1965.

Cloete, H.: *The History of the Great Boer Trek and the Origin of the South African Republics*. London, 1900.
Déhérain, H.: *op. cit.*, 1905.
Delegorgue, A.: *Voyage dans l'Afrique australe (1838–1844)*, 2 vols. Paris, 1852.
Nathan, M.: *The Voortrekkers of South Africa*. London, 1937.
Omer-Cooper, J. D.: *The Zulu Aftermath*. London, 1966.
van Jaarsveld, F. A.: *The Afrikaners' Interpretation of South African History*. Johannesburg, 1962.
Walker, E. A.: *The Great Trek*. London, 1938.

9 Years of expectation and confusion

See preceding chapters and:
Smith, H. G. W.: *The Autobiography of Lieutenant-General Sir Henry Smith*, 2 vols. London, 1901.
Voigt, J. C.: *Fifty Years of the Republic in South Africa, 1795–1845*, 2 vols. London, 1899.

10 Economic and constitutional transformations

General works and:
Keane, A. H.: *The Boer States*. London, 1900.
Neame, L. E.: *The History of Apartheid: the Story of the Colour Bar in South Africa*. London, 1962.
Smith, H. G. W.: *op. cit.*, 1901.

11 The beginnings of the Boer Republics

General works and:
Macmillan, W. M.: *op. cit.*, 1963.
Nathan, M.: *op. cit.*, 1937.
Omer-Cooper, J. D.: *op. cit.*, 1966.

On the Free State and the Transvaal:
Fisher, W. E. G.: *The Transvaal and the Boers*. London, 1900.
Kok, K. J. de: *Empires of the Veld*. Durban, 1904.
Nixon, J.: *The Complete Story of the Transvaal from the Great Trek to the Convention of London*. London, 1885.
Uys, C. J.: *In the Era of Shepstone*. Lovedale, 1933.

On British policy:
Kiewiet, C. W. de: *British Colonial Policy and the South African Republics*. London, 1929.

12 The discovery of diamonds

General works and, on British policy:
Kiewiet, C. W. de: *op. cit.*, 1929.

On the diamond mines:
Chilvers, H. A.: *The Story of the De Beers.* London, 1939.
Churchill, Lord R.: *Men, Mines, and Animals.* London, 1892.
Gregory, T.: *Ernest Oppenheimer and the Economic Development of Southern Africa.* Cape Town, 1962.
Leroy-Beaulieu, P.: *Les Nouvelles Sociétés anglo-saxonnes. Australie, Nouvelle-Zélande, Afrique du Sud.* Paris, 1897.
Rosenthal, E.: *River of Diamonds.* Cape Town, no date.

13 Annexation and liberation of the Transvaal

General works and, on the Transvaal:
Fisher, W. E. G.: *op. cit.,* 1900.
Fitzpatrick, Sir P.: *The Transvaal from within.* London, 1899.
Kiewiet, C. W. de: *The Imperial Factor in South Africa.* Cambridge, 1937.
Nixon, J.: *op. cit.,* 1885.
Uys, C. J.: *op. cit.,* 1933.

On the Zulu:
Binns, C. T.: *The Last Zulu King: The Life and Death of Cetshwayo.* London, 1963.
Morris, D.: *The Washing of the Spears. The Rise and Fall of the Zulu Nation.* London, 1967.

On Afrikaner nationalism:
van Jaarsveld, F. A.: *The Awakening of Afrikaner Nationalism (1868–1881).* Cape Town, 1961.

On the Prince Imperial:
Binns, C. T.: *op. cit.,* 1963.
Decaux, A.: *Le Prince impérial.* Paris, 1964.
Morris, D.: *op. cit.,* 1967.
Roberts, B.: *Ladies in the Veld.* London, 1965.

14 The discovery of gold

General works and:
Cartwright, A. P.: *The Corner House.* Johannesburg, 1965.
Chilvers, H.: *Out of the Crucible.* London, 1929.
Churchill, Lord R.: *op. cit.,* 1892.
Lewinsohn, R.: *Barnato, roi de l'or.* Paris, 1937.
Marais, J. S.: *The Fall of Kruger's Republic.* Oxford, 1962.
Neame, L. E.: *City built on Gold.* No date or place of publication given.

15 Rhodes and Kruger

General works and:
Marais, J. S.: *op. cit.,* 1962.
van Jaarsveld, F. A.: *Lectures at the University of South Africa (1881–1895).* Pretoria, no date. (Supplied by the author.)

On Hofmeyr:
Davenport, T. R. H.: *The Afrikaner Bond. The History of a South African Political Party (1880–1911)*. London, 1966.

On Jameson:
Colvin, I.: *The Life of Jameson*, 2 vols. London, 1922.

On Kruger:
Nathan, M.: *Paul Kruger*. Durban, 1941.

On Rhodes:
Gross, F.: *Rhodes of Africa*. London, 1956.
Lockhart, J. G. and Woodehouse, C. M.: *Cecil Rhodes*. London, 1963.
Millin, S. G.: *Cecil Rhodes*. London, 1952.
'Vindex': *Cecil Rhodes. His Political Life and Speeches (1881–1900)*. London, 1900.

16 The Jameson Raid

See preceding chapter and:
A.A.E. (Archives of the French Ministry of Foreign Affairs): *Transvaal-Orange*, N.S. 5 (unpublished).
Headlam, C., ed.: *The Milner Papers*, vol. I. London, 1931.
Hobson, J. A.: *The War in South Africa, its Causes and Effects*. London, 1900.
Maurois, A.: 'La Vie de Cecil Rhodes', Paris, *Les Œuvres libres*, July 1953.
Rhoodie, D.: *Conspirators in Conflict. A Study of the Johannesburg Reform Committee and its Role in the Conspiracy against the South African Republic*. Tafelberg, 1967.
Twain, M.: *More Tramps Abroad*. London, 1898.
Vulliamy, C. E.: *Outlanders; a Study of Imperial Expansion in South Africa (1877–1902)*. London, 1938.
Wrench, J. E.: *Alfred Lord Milner; the Man of No Illusions*. London, 1958.

17 On the brink of catastrophe

General works and:
A.A.E.: *Transvaal-Orange*, N.S. 4, 6–10 (unpublished).
Headlam, C., ed.: *op. cit.*, 1931.
Hobson, J. A.: *op. cit.*, 1900.
Marais, J. S.: *op. cit.*, 1962.
van Jaarsveld, F. A.: *Lectures at the University of South Africa*. (Supplied by the author.)
Vulliamy, C. E.: *op. cit.*, 1938.
Wrench, J. E.: *op. cit.*, 1958.

18 South Africa at the end of the nineteenth century

General works and:
Bigelow, P.: *White Man's Africa*. London and New York, 1900.
Bryce, Lord: *Impressions of South Africa*. London, 1897.
Churchill, Lord R.: *op. cit.*, 1892.
Gindre, H.: *En Afrique australe et à Madagascar*. Paris, 1897.
Hobson, J. A.: *op. cit.*, 1900.
Leroy-Beaulieu, P.: *Les Nouvelles Sociétés anglo-saxonnes. Australie, Nouvelle-Zélande, Afrique du Sud*, vols I and II. Paris, 1897 and 1901.
Little, J. S.: *South Africa*, 2 vols. Cape Town, 1884.
Little, Rev. W. J. Knox: *Sketches and Studies in South Africa*. London, 1899.
Manheimer, E.: *Le Nouveau Monde sud-africain*. Paris, 1896.
Markham, V. R.: *South Africa, Past and Present*. London, 1900.
Neame, L. E.: *op. cit.*, 1962.
Noble, J.: *Handbook of the Cape and South Africa*. London, 1893.
Twain, M.: *op. cit.*, 1898.
Younghusband, F.: *South Africa of Today*. London, 1898.

19 The Boer War (I)

General works and:
A.A.E.: *Transvaal-Orange*, N.S. 10, 12, 13 (unpublished).
Amery, L. S., ed.: *The Times History of the War in South Africa*, 7 vols. London, 1899–1902. Vol. II, chs I and II.
Bülow, Prince von: *Mémoires*, vol. I (1897–1902). Paris, 1930.
Churchill, W.: *From London to Ladysmith*. London, 1900.
Comtes, P.: *Cent ans de luttes. Les héros boers*. Paris, 1901.
Crafford, F. S.: *Jan Smuts*. Cape Town, 1946.
Hillegas, H. C.: *With the Boer Forces*. London, 1900.
Holt, E.: *The Boer War*. London, 1958.
Kruger, R.: *Good-bye, Dolly Gray*. London, 1961.
Le May, G. H. L.: *British Supremacy in South Africa (1899–1907)*. Oxford, 1965.
Leroy-Beaulieu, P.: *op. cit.*, 1901.
Mallet, M.: *Life with Queen Victoria. Letters from the Court*. London, 1968.
Niessel, A.: *Enseignements à tirer au point de vue de la tactique générale de la guerre d'Afrique du Sud*. Paris, 1902.
Reitz, D.: *Commando: a Boer Journal of the Boer War*. London, 1950.
Reitz, F. W.: *A Century of Wrong*. London, 1900.
Spender, H.: *General Botha*. London, 1916.
Wet, Gen. C. R. de: *Three Years' War*. London, 1902.

20 The Boer War (II)

See preceding chapter and:
A.A.E.: *Transvaal-Orange*, N.S. 4, 13–19, 21–27 (unpublished).

Churchill, W. S.: *Ian Hamilton's March*. London, 1900.
Comité pour l'indépendance des Boers: *Rapports officiels du général J. H. De la Rey et du général J. C. Smuts, et autres documents*. Paris, no date.
Guillen, P.: 'Les Accords coloniaux franco-anglais de 1904 et la naissance de l'Entente cordiale', *Revue d'histoire diplomatique*, October–December 1968.
Hobhouse, Miss E.: *La Guerre dans l'Afrique du Sud. Les camps de concentration*. Paris, no date (published by the Comité pour l'indépendance des Boers).
Magnus, P.: *Kitchener: portrait of an imperialist*. London, 1958.
Nathan, M.: *op. cit.*, 1941.

21 The formation of the Union

General works and:
A.A.E.: *Transvaal-Orange*, N.S. 3, 23, 27 (unpublished).
Brand, R. H.: *The Union of South Africa*. Oxford, 1909.
Le May, B. H. L.: *op. cit.*, 1965.
Mansergh, N.: *South Africa (1906–1961): the Price of Magnanimity*. London, 1962.
Newton, A. P.: *Select Documents relating to the Unification of South Africa*, 2 vols. New York, 1924.
Pyrah, G. B.: *Imperial Policy and South Africa (1902–1910)*. Oxford, 1955.
Riddell, Lord: *More Pages from my Diary*. London, 1934.
Thompson, L. M.: *The Unification of South Africa (1902–1910)*. Oxford, 1960.
van Jaarsveld, F. A.: *Lectures on the History of South Africa (1902–1910) at the University of South Africa*. (Supplied by the author.)

On Botha:
Magnus, P.: *King Edward the Seventh*. London, 1964.
Spender, H.: *op. cit.*, 1916.

On Gandhi:
Andrews, C. F., ed.: *Mahatma Gandhi, his Own Story*. London, 1930.
Rolland, R.: *Mahatma Gandhi*. Paris, 1926.

On Hertzog:
Pirow, O.: *General J. B. M. Hertzog*. Cape Town, 1957.

On the 'Kindergarten':
Curtis, L.: *With Milner in South Africa*. Oxford, 1951.

On Smuts:
Hancock, W. K.: *General Smuts. I. The Sanguine Years (1870–1919)*. Cambridge, 1962.

22 Growing pains and the First World War

General works and:
A.A.E.: *Sud-africain allemand*, N.S. 2, and *Transvaal-Orange*, N.S. 1 and 3 (unpublished).

On general policy:
Hancock, W. K.: *op. cit.*, I; and II, *The Fields of Force (1919–1950)*. Cambridge, 1968.
Krüger, D. W.: *The Age of the Generals*. Dagbreek Books Store, 1958.
Neame, L. E.: *General Hertzog*. London, 1930.
Pirow, O.: *op. cit.*, 1957.
Spender, H.: *op. cit.*, 1916.

On native policy:
Neame, L. E.: *op. cit.*, 1962.

On the Indians:
Andrews, C. F., ed.: *op. cit.*, 1930.

On German South-West Africa:
Giniewski, P.: 'Le nazisme avant la lettre: la solution finale du problème Herero au sud-ouest africain', *Revue française d'études politiques africaines*, March 1968.

On the 1914 rebellion:
Davenport, R. R. H.: 'The South African Rebellion (1914)', *English Historical Review*, 1963.
O'Connor, J. K.: *The Afrikander Rebellion. South Africa To-day*. London, 1915.

On the First World War:
Buchan, J.: *History of the South African Forces in France*. London, 1920.
Riddell, Lord: *op. cit.*, 1934.
Union of South Africa. Official History: *Union of South Africa and the Great War*. Pretoria, 1924.

On the Treaty of Versailles:
Lansing, R.: *The Peace Negotiations*, London, 1921; *The Big Four and Others at the Peace Conference*. London, 1922.
Mantoux, P.: *Les Délibérations du Conseil des Quatre (24 mars–28 juin 1919)*, 2 vols. Paris, 1955.
Nicolson, H.: *Peacemaking*. London, 1919.
Steed, H. W.: *Through Thirty Years*. London, 1924.

23 The Nationalists in power

General work and:
Armstrong, H. C.: *Grey Steel*. London, 1946.

Barlow, A. G.: *Almost in Confidence*. Cape Town, 1952.
Blackwell, L.: *Farewell to Parliament*. Pietermaritzburg, 1946.
Hancock, W. K.: *op. cit.*, 1968.
Herd, N.: *1922: The Revolt on the Rand*. Johannesburg, 1961.
Krüger, D. W.: *South African Parties and Politics (1910–1960)*. Cape Town, 1960; *op. cit.*, 1958.
Long, B. K.: *In Smuts's Camp*. London, 1945.
Neame, L. E.: *White Man's Africa*. Cape Town, 1952; *op. cit.*, 1930; *op. cit.*, 1962.
Nicholls, G. H.: *South Africa in my Time*. London, 1961.
Pirow, O.: *op. cit.*, 1957.
Walker, I. D. and Weinbren, B.: *2,000 Casualties: a History of the Trade Unions and the Labour Movement in the Union of South Africa*. Johannesburg, 1961.

24 The Second World War

General works and:
Barlow, A. G.: *op. cit.*, 1952.
Blackwell, L.: *op. cit.*, 1946.
Hancock, W. K.: *op. cit.*, 1968.
Krüger, D. W.: *op. cit.*, 1958.
Nicholls, G. H.: *op. cit.*, 1961.
Pirow, O.: *op. cit.*, 1957.

On military operations:
Klein, H., ed.: *Springbok Record*. Johannesburg, 1946.

On Smuts:
Churchill, W. S.: *The Second World War*, 6 vols. London, 1948–54.
Eden, A.: *The Eden Memoirs. The Reckoning*. London, 1965.
Gaulle, C. de: *War Memoirs*, vol. III, Eng. trans. London, 1960.
Henriot, P.: Radio broadcast on 12 December 1943.
Koesing's Contemporary Archives (1940–1946).
Montgomery of Alamein: *Memoirs*, London, 1958.
Moran, Lord: *Winston Churchill. The Struggle for Survival (1940–1965)*. London, 1966.
Tedder, Lord: *With Prejudice. War Memoirs*. London, 1966.

25 Apartheid and Republic

General works and:
Barnard, F.: *Thirteen Years in the Shadow of Dr. H. F. Verwoerd*. Johannesburg, 1967.
Benson, M.: *Chief Albert Lutuli of South Africa*. London, 1963.
Brookes, E. H.: *Apartheid, a Documentary Study of Modern South Africa*. London, 1968.

Cadoux, C.: *L'Afrique du Sud.* Paris, 1966.
Calvocoressi, P.: *South Africa and World Opinion.* Oxford, 1961.
Carter, G. M.: *The Politics of Inequality: South Africa since 1948.* London, 1958.
Huddleston, Rev. T.: *Naught for Your Comfort.* London, 1956.
Krüger, D. W.: *The Making of a Nation: a History of the Union of South Africa (1910–1961).* Johannesburg and London, 1969; *op. cit.,* 1960.
Neame, L. E.: *op. cit.,* 1962.
Nicholls, G. H.: *op. cit.,* 1961.
Pelzer, A. N.: *Verwoerd Speaks.* Johannesburg, 1966.

26 Years of tranquillity

General works, review articles, official reports and:
Cadoux, C.: *op. cit.,* 1966.
Calvocoressi, P.: *op. cit.,* 1961.
Carter, G. M., ed.: *Five African States. Responses to Diversity.* London, 1964.
Cope, J.: *South Africa.* London, 1965.
Duffy, J.: *Portuguese Africa.* Harvard, 1959.
Hailey, W. M.: *The Republic of South Africa and the High Commission Territories.* London, 1963.
Halpern, J.: *South Africa's Hostages: Basutoland, Bechuanaland and Swaziland.* London, 1965.
Harrigan, A.: *Red Star over Africa.* Johannesburg, 1964.
Krüger, D. W.: *op. cit.,* 1969.
Legum, C. and M.: *South Africa: Crisis for the West.* London, 1964.
Marquard, L.: *The Peoples and Policies of South Africa.* London, 1969.
Molnar, T.: *Africa, a Political Travelogue,* New York, 1965.
Munger, E. S.: *Afrikaner and African Nationalism.* Oxford, 1967.
Rhoodie, E.: *South West: the Last Frontier in Africa.* Pretoria, 1967.
Spence, J. E.: *Republic under Pressure: a Study of South African foreign policy.* London, 1965.
Steward, A.: *La Mission sacrée,* French trans. Johannesburg, 1963.

27 Towards a new South Africa

General works, review articles, official reports and:
Brookes, E. H.: *op. cit.,* 1968.
Cadoux, C.: *op. cit.,* 1966.
Carter, G. M.: *op. cit.,* 1958.
Cloete, S.: *South Africa. The Land, its People and its Achievements.* Johannesburg, 1969.
Cope, J.: *op. cit.,* 1965.
de Guingand, Sir F.: *African Assignment.* London, 1953.

Drury, A.: 'A Very Strange Society'. A Journey to the Heart of South Africa. New York, 1967.

Francos, A.: L'Afrique des Afrikaners. Paris, 1966.

Giniewski, P.: Une autre Afrique du Sud. Paris, 1962.

Hahlo, H. R. and Kahn, E.: The Union of South Africa. The Development of its Laws and Constitution. Cape Town, 1960.

Harrigan, A.: op. cit., 1964.

Holloway, J. E.: Apartheid. Johannesburg, 1964.

Horrell, M.: Action, Reaction and Counteraction. A Companion Booklet to the Legislation of Race Relations. Johannesburg, 1963.

Huddleston, Rev. T.: op. cit., 1958.

Lesourd, J. A.: La République d'Afrique du Sud. Paris, 1963.

Molnar, T.: L'Afrique du Sud. Paris, 1966.

Munger, E. S.: op. cit., 1967.

Rhoodie, N. J.: Apartheid and Racial Partnership in South Africa, ch. XII. Pretoria, 1969.

Siegfried, A.: Notes de voyage. Paris, 1949.

Spence, J. E.: op. cit., 1965.

Villiers, H. H. W. de: Rivonia Operation Mayibuye. Johannesburg, 1964.

Among the encyclopaedias consulted in the writing of this book:
Rosenthal, E.: Encyclopaedia of Southern Africa. London, 1967.

Glossary

Afrikaans: Language of Dutch origin which, with English, became one of South Africa's two official languages.

Afrikaner: Name applied to South Africans of Dutch descent and also to those of German or French stock. The term finally replaced that of 'Boer' at the beginning of the twentieth century. It represents an idea of nationhood, 'Afrikanerdom'.

Amapakati: Council of ministers of the native kings.

Apartheid: Literally, 'separateness'. The term is no longer used in South Africa and had been replaced by 'separate development'.

Assegai: Native spear.

Baaskap: Supremacy of the master.

Banning: House arrest.

Bantu: This term, which means 'men', originally referred to a group of languages used by certain Negro tribes; eventually it came to be applied to the Black tribes of southern Africa as a whole. In 1974 the South African government decided to abandon the use of the term 'Bantu' to designate the Black population.

Boer: The word originally meant 'farmer', 'peasant'. It is still used in this sense in Dutch.

Broederbond: 'Association of brothers'. Political organization.

Burgher: Person with rights of citizenship, as in medieval towns.

Cape-Dutch: Architectural term.

Coloured: In South Africa this term is applied only to the half-breed population, never to the Blacks or to the Asians.

Dopper: A member of one of the strictest Calvinist sects.

Dutch: Term used at the end of the nineteenth century to refer to the Afrikaners of the Cape Colony.

Emigrants: Name adopted by the Boers at the time of the Great Trek.

European: The word is used to refer to the Whites of South Africa, whatever their origins. The term 'non-European' is applied to the Blacks, the Coloureds and the Asians alike.

Free burgher: See *Burgher*.

Griqua: Race of mixed origins, Europeans and Hottentot.

Group Areas Act: Act allocating land to the different races, in accordance with the principles of 'separate development'.

Hands-upper: Term of contempt used by the Boers to refer to those who collaborated with the British during the Boer War.

Heemraden: Title of certain officials in the Cape Colony who, up to 1828, served on councils which managed local affairs under the authority of the *landdrost*.

Het Volk: 'The People'. Political party formed in the Transvaal after the Boer War.

Hindu: Although the term was in common use until recently, 'Indian' has been used in preference throughout this book.

Impis: Zulu regiments.

Israelites: Bantu religious sect formed in 1921.

Kaffir: The term is now used only in a derogatory sense and is considered insulting by Blacks.

Kopje: Flat-topped, cone-shaped hillock on the *veld*.

Kraal: Native village.

Laager: Ox-wagons arranged in a circle or a square and with thorn-bushes placed between each wagon. The *laager* was used as a fortress by the *voortrekkers*.

Landdrost: District administrator. The title, abolished in 1828, was revived in 1957 and applied to a magistrate.

Lobola: Promise made by a Bantu to provide his future father-in-law with a certain number of cattle. Nowadays the *lobola* is sometimes paid in money.

Maatskappy: Community of *voortrekkers*.

Mafficking: Word which came into use in England to describe the almost hysterical rejoicings on the relief of Mafeking during the Boer War.

Mfecane: Bantu term for the wars of extermination between Blacks during the nineteenth century.

Nagmaal: Mass gathering of Boers for Holy Communion.

National Scouts: Pejorative term for the handful of Boers who sided with the British during the Boer War.

N.I.B.M.A.R.: 'No independence before majority rule', the principle proclaimed by the British government in its relations with Rhodesia.

Ossewabrandwag: Literally, 'Sentinel of the Ox-wagon', an organization formed to perpetuate the memory of the Boer War.

Pogo: Black revolutionary association.

Raad: See *Volksraad*.

Rand: Abbreviation of *Witwatersrand*. Now used for the South African monetary unit.

Stem van Suid-Afrika, Die: 'The Voice of South Africa', the national anthem.

Taal: 'Language'. The word is sometimes used in a derogatory sense to refer to the dialect from which *Afrikaans* is derived.

Trek: Journey by ox-wagon.

Trekboers: The semi-nomad Boers, as distinct from the *veeboers*, the cattle-farmers.

Trekkers: See *trekboers.*

U.D.I.: Unilateral Declaration of Independence proclaimed by Rhodesia.

Uitlander: Name given by the Boers to foreign immigrants in the Transvaal after the discovery of gold.

Veld: High plateaux of South Africa.

Verkrampte: Name given today to ultra-conservative South Africans who oppose all change.

Verligte: Name given to those South Africans in favour of change.

Vierkleur: Flags of the South African Republic (Transvaal) and the Orange Free State before the Boer War.

Volksraad: 'Assembly of the People'.

Voortrekkers: Literally, the 'trekkers in front', i.e., the pioneers.

Index

Index

© *Cassell & Co. Ltd. 1977*

Marquard, L. (quoted), 113
Masaryk, Thomas, 262
Mashonaland, 166
Matabele, 65–6, 91–2, 165–6
Mauritius, 329
Maurois, André (quoted), 176
Maynier, H. C. D., 31
Merriman, John X., 183, 235, 237, 242, 256
Methuen, Lord, 223
Milner, Alfred, Lord, 181–2, 187, 198, 236n, 249, 259; attitude to Cape Afrikaners, 181–2, 249; aim to acquire Transvaal, 182, 183–6; 'helots' dispatch, 185; and Boer War, 202, 215, 220, 222, 225; and reconstruction, 227, 229, 230, 232
minerals, 133–40, 153–9, 197, 264, 331
missionaries, 49–50, 66, 70, 73n, 101, 126–7, 165
'Missionaries' Road', 120, 137
Mntatisi (Queen of the Mantati), 65
Mocke, Jan, 105
Modderspruit, 209
Moffat, Robert, 165; quoted, 51, 66
Mombasa, 10
Monomotapa, 10, 13, 153
Montgomery, Viscount, 285, 289
Moore, Frederick, 238
Moran, Lord, 287
Moravian Brethren, 49–50
Moshesh, 66, 105, 106, 108, 109, 122–3, 126–7, 194, 327
Mozambique, 10, 11, 13, 324, 333
Msilikazi (Matabele chief), 65–6
Mussolini, Benito, 281

Nama tribe, 318
Namibia (former German South-West Africa), 322, 335n
Napier, Sir George, 75, 97, 100, 101, 102, 103, 114
Napoleon, 56, 57n
Natal: Boers' trek to, 81–94; arrival at, 94–8; British evacuation, 97; Republic of, 98, 99; administration of, 99–100; Volksraad, 100, 103; union with Transvaal, 100; annexed by Britain, 102–4; Indians in, 112, 117, 230, 252, 293–4, 337; banking, 113;

low population density, 113; constitution, 116, 193–4; Supreme Court, 116n; and natives' exclusion from electorate, 117, 193, 276, 295; annexation of Basutoland, 127; and federation idea, 142; and Zulu War, 146–8; annexation of Zululand, 148n, 166; area, 193; mineral wealth, 198; and Boer War, 202, 209; customs union, 229, 236; and National Convention, 238, 241; native revolt in, 240; voting on Republic, 310
Nathan, M. (quoted), 120
National Convention (1908–9), 236–41
National Union, 171
National Union Party, 312
Nationalist Party: founded (1914), 251; success in 1915 election, 256; increased representation, 263, 266; 1924 success, 266; policy of White pre-eminence and constitutional independence, 267–71; 1929 election, 271; opposition to Hertzog, 272, 274; 1933 coalition with South African Party, 274; split in, 274; becomes United South African National Party, 274
Nationalist Party (new), 341; formed (1933), 274; 1938 elections, 278; 1943 elections, 292; 1948 victory, 294–5; apartheid policy, 297–303; 1953 victory, 300, 321; 1958 victory, 303; progress to republic, 308–12; 1961 victory, 312; increasing hold, 329–30, 341n
Native Affairs Commission, 251
Native Lands Act (1936), 277
Native Representation Act (1936), 276–7
natives. See Bantu; Blacks
Natives Land Act (1913), 252
Negroes, 39
Neptune (convict ship), 115
'New Order' group, 291, 292
Nguni, 336
Nicholls, Senator, 295, 300
Nicholson's Nek, 209
Nicolson, Harold, 262, 265
Noailles, Marquis de, 180